Social Solutions to Poverty

Great Barrington Books

Bringing the old and new together
in the spirit of W. E. B. Du Bois

∾ An imprint edited by Charles Lemert ∾

Titles Available

Keeping Good Time: Reflections on Knowledge, Power, and People
by Avery F. Gordon (2004)

Going Down for Air: A Memoir in Search of a Subject
by Derek Sayer (2004)

The Souls of Black Folk,
100th Anniversary Edition
by W. E. B. Du Bois, with commentaries by Manning Marable, Charles Lemert,
and Cheryl Townsend Gilkes (2004)

Sociology After the Crisis, Updated Edition
by Charles Lemert (2004)

Subject to Ourselves
by Anthony Elliot (2004)

The Protestant Ethic Turns 100:
Essays on the Centenary of the Weber Thesis
edited by William H. Swatos, Jr., and Lutz Kaelber (2005)

Postmodernism Is Not What You Think
by Charles Lemert (2005)

Discourses on Liberation: An Anatomy of Critical Theory
by Kyung-Man Kim (2005)

Seeing Sociologically: The Routine Grounds of Social Action
by Harold Garfinkel, edited and introduced by Anne Warfield Rawls (2005)

The Souls of W. E. B. Du Bois
by Alford A. Young, Jr., Manning Marable, Elizabeth Higginbotham, Charles
Lemert, and Jerry G. Watts (2006)

Radical Nomad: C. Wright Mills and His Times
by Tom Hayden with Contemporary Reflections by Stanley Aronowitz, Richard
Flacks, and Charles Lemert (2006)

Critique for What? Cultural Studies, American Studies, Left Studies
by Joel Pfister (2006)

Everyday Life and the State
by Peter Bratsis (2006)

Social Solutions to Poverty: America's Struggle to Build a Just Society
edited with contributions by Scott J. Myers-Lipton

Forthcoming
Thinking the Unthinkable:
An Introduction to Social Theories
by Charles Lemert

Social Solutions to Poverty

America's Struggle to Build a Just Society

edited with contributions by Scott J. Myers-Lipton
foreword by Charles Lemert

Paradigm Publishers

Boulder • London

This book is dedicated to the people who lived,
and sometimes died, struggling to end poverty.

Copyright © 2006 by Scott J. Myers-Lipton

Published in the United States by Paradigm Publishers, 3360 Mitchell Lane, Suite E, Boulder,
Colorado 80301 USA.

Paradigm Publishers is the trade name of Birkenkamp & Company, LLC,
Dean Birkenkamp, President and Publisher.

Library of Congress Cataloging-in-Publication Data

Myers-Lipton, Scott J.
    Social solutions to poverty : America's struggle to build a just society / Scott J. Myers-Lipton.
        p. cm.
    Includes index.
    ISBN-13: 978-1-59451-210-0 (hc : alk. paper)
    ISBN-10: 1-59451-210-8 (hc : alk. paper)
    ISBN-13: 978-1-59451-211-7 (pb : alk. paper)
    ISBN-10: 1-59451-211-6 (pb : alk. paper)
1. Poverty—United States—History.   2. Social justice—United States—History.   3. Social
reformers—United States—History.   4. Social movements—United States.   5. Economic
assistance, Domestic—United States—History.   I. Title.
    HC110.P6M94 2006
    362.5'52—dc22

                                                                                    2006012368

Printed and bound in the United States of America on acid-free paper that meets the standards
of the American National Standard for Permanence of Paper for Printed Library Materials.

Designed and Typeset by Straight Creek Bookmakers.

10 09 08 07 06   1 2 3 4 5

Contents

Foreword: The Poor, Always with Us

"You have the poor with you always." No line on the subject is more abused. In point of fact, the poor have always been with us. Their presence, however, contradicts one of the more fundamental principles of the civilization that too often misreads this ancient saying as justification for resignation before the fact. The source of the words meant something quite different.

"You have the poor with you always." The words were first and most memorably uttered at the near mid-point of the ancient Greco-Roman civilizations from which modern liberalism drew its inspiration and many of its moral and legal ideas. From Cleisthenes of Athens, who around 510 BCE laid the political foundations for the Golden Age of Greece, and Augustine of Hippo, who interpreted the fall of Rome in 410 CE, the principles of fairness and equality certainly suffered an uneven history. But, without ancient Greece's institutions of democratic politics and their codification in Roman law, it would be hard to imagine how the eighteenth century Enlightenment could have defined the varieties of modern liberal theories of individual rights and social responsibilities. Yet, as any schoolchild will tell you, the long Greco-Roman millennium was punctuated by war, decline and revival, slavery, and human miseries of all the normal kinds.

The saying in question appeared at one of the more tumultuous moments in that long, uneven history—early in the Age of Augustus Caesar, when the Republic was restored to put an end to corruption and decline in the first century of Roman rule. Even then, those living outside the protection of Roman civilization enjoyed a kind of benign neglect, if not the more robust benefits of citizenship. In *The City of God,* Augustine of Hippo masterfully teaches the lessons to be drawn from the Sack of Rome by the Goths in 410. Among the poignant passages in the book are those where Augustine praises the Roman City of Man for its relative generosity to those it conquered and, by implication, those who would conquer them (a virtue he attributes to the influence of the City of God).

As it happens the much-abused line in question was uttered under a circumstance in which the speaker was about to suffer at the hands of Rome's benign neglect of the unreasonableness of local practices. The speaker was, of course, Jesus of Nazareth as he rebuked his followers with an eye to his pending execution by local authorities. The abuse of the saying is that it leaves off the fuller meaning Jesus lent it. "For you have the poor with you always, and whensoever you will you may do them good: but me you have not always." To the pious witnessing this long ago scene, the saying made little sense. Jesus was in fact rebuking those who were honoring the poor by anointing them with oil, when they should have been anointing him.

In our ever more corrupt and pious day, the point of the saying may be still more obscure. We forget, however, that self-righteousness spills not just from religious tongues but from loose tongues of all kinds—and none more glib than the liberal pieties of the modern age. Modern liberal cultures have proclaimed the good of human progress, yet suffered little to bring it about. In time—and no time more shameful than ours early in the 2000s—these liberals of the left and right have unctuously given up on the poor. If the poor are always with us amid the obscene wealth of the privileged it is because the modern idea of human fairness has been all but abandoned everywhere but on the tip of pious tongues.

Why travel back so far to introduce this wonderful book on the history of poverty in America? For one, because no other modern nation has been as proud of its alleged republican virtues as they came down from the Roman era. For another, because astonishingly none has so ignored the intent of the very religious ideas to which it professes evangelical devotion.

Jesus was not dismissing the poor of this world in favor of personal adoration of another. On the contrary, he was saying, in effect, the only way you can honestly serve the poor is by fixing your first attentions on the wide worlds to which all human things are bound. This was the point Augustine of Hippo understood well—the City of Man owes what sense of justice it may attain not to the virtue of individuals but to its own reluctant acquiescence to the political realities at hand. Hence, the terrible contradiction of the democratic polities that came down from Cleisthenes. Only the state can put an end to poverty. Yet the state has little reason to indulge itself in pursuit of economic justice.

This was the point made, closer to our time, by Reinhold Niebuhr during the Great Depression of the 1930s. In *Moral Man and Immoral Society,* Niebuhr drew from Augustine the distinction that influenced Martin Luther King, Jr., and many others. The state governs out of self-interest. The individual is moral for reasons of his or her interior disposition. Poverty is among those evils of this world that cannot be allayed by the charitable acts of well-intended individuals. It requires no less than the resources of the social whole. Poverty is the consequence thus of a failure of the collective will to, in a word, share its wealth.

Why indeed would the better-off sacrifice their advantages in such a considerable degree as would be needed to heal the sick, feed the hungry, and house the homeless? Whatever may be the calculable degree of that sacrifice, what remains true is that there is little in modernity's culture of individualism to encourage this kind of massive collective sacrifice.

Yet there are times when it happens. Those are times, of course, of grave threat to the social whole—whether local, national, or global. Leaving aside the faith elements in the Jesus story, the truth is that he appeared in just such a time—when Rome was at risk of losing its hold. No one living then in Mesopotamia could have failed to understand that, as for centuries before that time and still today, the region was one of near constant instability as empires rose and fell. Before Greece and Rome, there were the Persians, Babylonians, Macedonians, Sumerians, even the brief Davidic period in Judah. They had grown up on tales of the rise and fall of empires and powers. As mighty as Rome was, those outside its higher circles of culture and power could read the signs of what would come. The restoration of the republic held the whole together for nearly half a millennium more, but there was nothing in those long centuries to compare to the ideal of peace that had held the imagination since the best days of Athens.

When the cities of man die, then the privileged are in the same boat as the poor. *All* must look elsewhere for guidance and sustenance. And, as Durkheim once taught, in such times the poor have the upper hand—being accustomed to looking elsewhere for what morsels can be scrounged. The poor have always been with us because we, if there is a we, have not looked beyond our present comforts to the global, even extraterrestrial, realities where, amid the far stars, we see just how miniscule our time is against the history of all things known and unknown.

"The poor are always with you" is, thus, not a joke nor a throwaway line but a lesson of the human condition. The poor with us are ourselves; and we —whatever we may endure—will never return to the sacrificial work required until we recognize this most basic of the facts of life.

Scott J. Myers-Lipton's *Social Solutions to Poverty: America's Struggle to Build a Just Society* comes just at the right time in history—and just *in* time if the lesson of the poor is to be taken to heart. It is addressed, to be sure, to the history of that one republic, America, that thinks of itself as ever more generous than was

Rome. One that just the same still today uses little of its power to restructure the global political economy in ways that will ameliorate the suffering of the larger half of the world's population who bear the brunt of poverty and its sequelae.

This wonderful book permits the reader to overhear, as if she were present, the historical debates on the solutions to poverty. One may be alarmed to encounter in the earliest of days, when the continent was just being settled by Europeans the same sort of naïve ignorance of the poverty of the human condition. One may be shocked anew to read of the terrible violence that was part of the struggle for justice—from the genocide of native peoples to slavery and Haymarket to today's dispiriting homelessness and pandemic of hunger. But, also, one will be challenged, if not always thrilled, by the evidence that since the earliest of American times there were bold experiments by those who took seriously the dangers of their human situation to propose solutions—from Thomas Paine's agrarian justice through the Freedmen's Bureau and the Settlement House movement to the War on Poverty and the fair trade movement.

Social Solutions to Poverty: America's Struggle to Build a Just Society is one of those rare books that should be bought, read, kept, and used again and again. It is not only an unsettling story of poverty and the attempts to relieve it, but a reference work that teachers, students, and serious thinkers of whatever station will want to keep close at hand. I have never met its author, and know nothing of his personal beliefs. But still I say, with some confidence, that this is a book composed by a person who understands very well the poverty of the city of man—by a man, that is, who can help others learn the honest truth of our failures without giving up the prospect of change.

Charles Lemert

Preface

When Hurricane Katrina blew through the Gulf Coast states in late August of 2005, it exposed to the nation and world that the United States of America has a secret that for the most part has been kept hidden from mainstream society. The secret is this: although the United States is the wealthiest country in the world, it is also the leader in poverty when compared with other industrialized nations. Today, 37 million people, or almost 13 percent of the U.S. population, live in poverty.

Yet, poverty has not just plagued this generation, but rather has been a defining issue in the United States, from its founding right up to today. Unquestionably, the United States has paid, and continues to pay, a price for its high rates of poverty, as it damages the individual citizen and the larger society. Social science research demonstrates that poor people have higher rates of infant mortality, childhood lead poisoning, crime, and divorce as well as lower test scores in school and life expectancy.

Poverty is a description of want of the basic needs of life, as well as a set of relationships operating in a social structure. Thus, poor people have difficulty providing themselves with food, shelter, health care, and education. The poor also are at the bottom of the American social hierarchy, so they have difficulty in obtaining power and status.

I wrote this book out of a desire to end this want as well as to alter the set of social relationships currently operating in the United States. In my academic training, I was amazed by the contradiction that the United States was the richest country in the world but also the leader in the industrialized world in poverty rates. My interest in poverty solutions intensified after studying the civil rights movement, which had defeated the legal foundations of segregation and racial discrimination, but left many leaders in the movement feeling as if the changes were only at the surface level since poverty was still pervasive in communities of color. The final motivation was the reaction of my students to the high poverty rate in the United States. By mid-semester of my courses, students understood that poverty was a major problem, but they were frustrated that social science seemed to focus on the problem rather than the solution. I wanted to respond to this frustration, and perhaps in some small way move the field of social science closer to a solution-based approach.

The idea of this book is to follow one theme—the social solution to poverty—from Thomas Paine's "agrarian justice" to Josiah Quincy's proposal for the construction of poorhouses; from the Freedmen's Bureau to Sitting Bull's demand for money and supplies; from Coxey's army of the unemployed to Jane Addams's Hull House; from the Civil Works Administration to Dr. Martin Luther King, Jr.'s call for an Economic Bill of Rights; and from William Julius Wilson's universal program of reform to George Bush's "armies of compassion." Although the book follows one theme, I recognize that the poor are not a homogeneous group. Some of the categories of the poor include:

- children (35 percent of all Americans in poverty, or 13 million, are kids, making the United States first in child poverty in the industrialized world)
- seniors (10 percent, or 4 million seniors, live in poverty)
- working poor (66 percent of all poor people work for some portion of the year)
- whites (9 percent, or 16.9 million whites, live in poverty)
- blacks and Latinos (9 million for each group, but with poverty rates more than twice that of whites)
- female-headed households (4 million, or 28 percent of all households with no husband present, live in poverty)
- people living in suburban and rural settings (9 percent of the poor live in the suburbs, 14 percent in rural areas, and 14 percent in urban inner-city cores)
- the severely poor (12.2 million, or 39 percent of the poor, are at or below one-half the poverty line)

This book attempts to address this level of diversity and complexity by focusing on poverty solutions that speak to such issues as social security, welfare, wages, labor conditions, education, hunger, racism, health care, deindustrialization, the feminization of poverty, suburbanization, homelessness, and wealth inequality.

The book is organized into chapters, with each chapter containing three parts. The first section introduces a discussion of the social context and a general overview of the solutions from a certain era in U.S. history. The goal of this first section is to provide a general understanding of the context in which the various solutions arose. The second section contains five to ten original documents (speeches, articles, and proposals) that highlight various grassroots and elite plans. Note that some proposals are mentioned in the social context section, but not included in the document section, since it was impossible to include all of them due to page constraints. The third section raises discussion of the outcomes of each proposal. Here is where the reader will learn what happened with the various plans.

Every effort has been made to ensure the accuracy of the documents and data in this book. Possible errors brought to the attention of the publisher and author will be researched, and if verified, will be corrected in future editions.

I would like to thank the Dr. Martin Luther King Jr. Library in San Jose, which was the ideal place to conduct this research; Jean Shiota, who was indispensable in the scanning of documents; and my partner Diane, for making the space in our lives to complete this book.

Scott J. Myers-Lipton

Painting of a Huron (Wyandot) couple from the 1700s

Chapter 1

Native American Contributions to Egalitarianism

Prologue: Social Context and Overview of Solutions

Americans from the United States are rightfully proud of the opening lines of the Declaration of Independence, which assert that all people are created equal. However, this American belief in equity, which would inspire social reformers and social justice advocates in the United States and around the world, is not grounded solely in European philosophy. Rather, a strong argument can be made that the American notion of egalitarianism entered modern social thought as a result of European and Euro-American thinkers being challenged by the equality of Native American society, and as a result, a new way of thinking emerged.

The fact is that European cultures did not have a deep commitment to equality or freedom at the time of the American Revolution, as European societies were highly stratified by social class. Thomas Jefferson, the author of the Declaration of Independence, believed that Europe was divided into two classes, the rich and the poor, and that under the pretense of governing, the former took advantage of the latter, as wolves prey on sheep. The historian Henry Steele Commager added that "everywhere Europe was ruled by the wellborn, the rich, the privileged, by those who held their places by divine favor, inheritance, prescription or purchase."[1]

The European belief that the wealthy were superior to the poor is revealed when one examines who was allowed to participate in political affairs. In late eighteenth-century England, only 1 in 20 men could vote, and in Scotland, only 3,000 men could vote. Furthermore, egalitarian democracy, with its belief that since all were created equal then all should be allowed to participate in political affairs, did not develop in the other European colonies, whether it was in New Spain under the Spanish (the direct descendants of Roman language, custom, and religion), Haiti under the French, South Africa under the British, or Indonesia under the Dutch.[2]

To appreciate the great intellectual debt owed to Native Americans, it is necessary to look at what European and Euro-American intellectuals were writing at that time. After examining the record, the consistent theme is that Native Americans lived with a level of equality and freedom greater than that in European society. This theme can be seen in the writings of Europeans soon after contact was made in the sixteenth and seventeenth centuries, in the writings of Euro-Americans around the time of the American Revolution, and in the testimonies of Native Americans.

In one of the earliest descriptions to reach Europe, Michel de Montaigne, the French essayist, described what the first Europeans saw when they made contact with Brazilian indigenous society. Montaigne reported in 1575 that "Indian" society lacked poverty, riches, or inheritance, and that it was wrong to label this culture as savage or barbarian. Montaigne's essay, as well as other initial post-contact commentaries that stressed egalitarianism, had a profound impact on European ideas about equity and what type of society was possible. For example, William Shakespeare used the words of Montaigne in *The Tempest.* In act 2, scene 1, the honest and aging counselor, Gonzalo, speaks about the ideal commonwealth; to describe it, Shakespeare used Montaigne's description of Native America almost verbatim. Furthermore, Thomas More, the English politician, humanist scholar, and Catholic saint, wrote *Utopia* after reading the letters of Amerigo Vespucci. More's *Utopia,* which described an earthly paradise where one has equality without money, was partly based on Vespucci's description of

American Indians' egalitarianism. More's book was seen as a direct challenge to European society to deal with its poverty and inequity.[3]

Over a century later, in 1703, Louis Lahontan reported details of a conversation he had with Adario, a Huron (Wyandot) male, where the latter described how American Indians lived in egalitarian relationships. According to Lahontan's account, Adario was stunned by the high level of European poverty and repulsed by the inequality between rich and poor. Adario described Huron society as devoid of this type of inequality and argued that this would not be allowed among the Hurons. Some question the veracity of Lahontan's account of the dialogue; others claim that although it may not have been recorded verbatim, it does contain significant truths about Native American life. Once again, these ideas had a strong effect on European society, as Lahontan became an international celebrity after his popular writings were adapted and made into a successful play in Paris in 1721. In fact, the theme of Native American life offering more equity and liberty was so popular in Europe that others copied it and produced additional plays, operas, farces, and burlesques on this same topic.[4]

In the period of the American Revolution, Europeans and Euro-Americans continued to be impressed with the level of equality in Native American society. St. John de Crèvecoeur described the American Indian way of life as superior to that of Europeans living in America, since indigenous people lived "with more ease, decency, and peace." James Adair, who wrote *The History of the American Indians* in 1775, stated that in every Indian nation a person "breathes nothing but liberty" and lives with "an equality of condition, manners, and privilege." Benjamin Franklin noted that this high degree of equity and freedom was the reason that many whites decided to go and live in Native American communities; at the same time, Franklin knew of no case where an Indian had chosen to live in white society. Franklin believed that Native Americans were disgusted by "civil society," since it required "The Care and Labour of providing for Artificial and fashionable Wants, the sight of so many Rich wallowing in superfluous plenty, whereby so many are kept poor and distress'd for Want." The absence of human suffering due to poverty in native communities can also be seen in the reflections of Buffalo Bird Woman, a Hidatsa born around 1839 in North Dakota, who told an interviewer that in the old times, "we had plenty to eat and wear then, abundance of meat and fur robes and tanned skins."[5]

To achieve an egalitarian society required creative strategies. Some tribes dealt with economic inequality by redistributing their resources. For example, Lieutenant Governor Cadwallder Colden of New York observed that within the Iroquois Confederation, the most important men gave away the presents or rewards they received as part of treaties or war, and thus had fewer material goods than the common person. In addition, Colden discussed how the Five

Nations did not believe in the superiority of one person over another, and how they had an absolute understanding of liberty. This lack of interest in attaining wealth over others was also noted by John Hunter, who observed in the early 1800s that the chiefs and other important people of the Plains tribes "render themselves popular by their disinterestedness and poverty." The Plains Indians, in a similar way to the Iroquois, liberally distributed the property they had acquired. Hunter explained that the Plains Indian leaders "pride themselves in being estimated the poorest men in the community."[6]

Many Native American communities also ensured a high level of economic equality by holding their land in common. Communal ownership of property ensured that all shared in the resources of society and that suffering due to lack of basic necessities was minimized. This focus on communal ownership of property led to a preoccupation with group relationships and generally a lack of central authority, which led to a high degree of freedom. Clearly, communal ownership of property was diametrically opposed to the European perspective, with its belief in private property, which has tended to fixate on commerce, competition, and the ultimate act of domination, war.[7]

It is true that not all of the more than 500 Native American tribes in the Western Hemisphere valued equity and liberty. For example, the Tlingit in the Pacific Northwest, the Natchez of the lower Mississippi Valley, and the Aztecs in Mesoamerica possessed stratified social class systems. At the same time, it is possible to say that the new European consciousness gained from Native Americans about the possibility of living in a society that was both equal and free allowed for a counterpoint to the "Old World." Europeans and Euro-Americans had the opportunity to appraise theoretical ideas from the Enlightenment, like Locke's notion of "liberty, equality, and property" and Rousseau's "social contract," in light of what they observed in Native American societies. As Bruce Johansen states, "They [the transplanted Europeans] found in existing native politics the values that the seminal European documents of the time celebrated in theoretical abstraction—life, liberty, happiness, and government by consensus, under natural rights, with relative equality of property." What came out of this appraisal and reassessment led to the creation of a new philosophy of government based on equality and liberty. This may have given impetus to the American Revolution as it provided the founders of the country a living example of people who governed themselves with freedom and equality, living in a society not ruled by a monarch, but by the people.[8]

The effect of Native Americans on early America is evident in the work of Thomas Paine. Paine, the great intellectual and activist of the American and

French Revolutions, was a keen student of Indian life. After observing that Native American life was a "continual holiday" in comparison with that of poor people in Europe, Paine was inspired to develop a poverty reduction plan. In Paine's 1797 book, *Agrarian Justice,* he argued that "civilized" people should create a social order that was as equal and free as that of Native Americans. Paine called for the creation of a social insurance plan for the elderly and a onetime payment to men and women when they turned twenty-one years of age so as to ensure a good start in life. The money would come from a national fund to be financed by a 10 percent assessment on all land at the time of death of the owner. Paine felt this assessment was justifiable since before cultivation, all land was common property of the human race, and therefore, every landowner owed rent to society. Paine's plan of "natural inheritance" attempted to give meaning to the words in the Declaration of Independence that all are created equal and born with an inalienable right to pursue happiness, which for Jefferson included economic security.[9]

Ironically, Paine and Jefferson as well as other prominent Americans argued that Native American political and economic development was less advanced than their own. Most Europeans and Euro-Americans claimed that Native Americans were living in a "natural" or "primitive" state, and thus were at a lower level of development. At best, some claimed that Native Americans were "noble savages" since they believed that Indian culture had many positive qualities, but it was still supposedly "uncivilized." Ironically, the Native Americans who had inspired this new thinking about equity, with the belief in freedom from autocratic rulers and the privileged elite, were labeled primitive and uncivilized. Once they were deemed inferior, it was easy for white Americans to justify removing them from their land.

The European colonists began the process of taking Indian land as the two groups competed for resources such as places to plant, fish, and hunt. After the United States won its independence from Britain in the Revolutionary War, the process of moving Native Americans off the land continued. In 1783, the Continental Congress declared that Native Americans were a defeated enemy, as many of them had fought on the side of the British, thus forfeiting all rights granted under earlier territorial treaties. Congress announced a plan to move Native Americans to Canada or to areas beyond the Mississippi River. Many Indians actively resisted this decree, and their defiance came in forms ranging from petitions to the U.S. government to military action. One of these petitions was sent by a group of Wabash Indians in the summer of 1793 to the new U.S. government. In the petition, the Wabash came up with a "win-win" solution to the U.S. government's plan to take the land, which was to give the money they were offering for the Wabash land instead to the poverty-stricken U.S. settlers. The Wabash argued that this would solve both the problem of losing their land to competition and the problem of poverty in the United States.[10]

In summary, when the Europeans arrived in the Western Hemisphere in 1492, there were approximately 75 million people on the two continents. In what is now the continental United States, it is estimated that there were 2 to 5 million people, in Alaska and Canada there were 2 million people, and in Mexico there were 7 million people. The holocaust that would follow over the next 400 years would devastate the Indian population. Most U.S. citizens have only a vague understanding of this holocaust. They have even less knowledge of the contributions that indigenous ideas have had on American and European social and political thought. I hope the readings in this chapter will contribute to a more accurate understanding of how the modern idea of democracy arose from the interaction of our founders with Native Americans.[11]

On Cannibals (1575)

Michel de Montaigne

Montaigne's essay was one of the first to be read by Europeans about Indians in the Americas.

When King Pyrrhus invaded Italy, after he had surveyed the army that the Romans had sent out against him, drawn up in battle array, "I know not," he said, "what barbarians these are" (for the Greeks so called all foreign nations), "but the disposition of this army that I see is in no wise barbarian." The Greeks said the same of the army that Flaminius led into their country; and Philip, when he saw from a little hill the order and arrangement of the Roman camp in his kingdom under Publius Sulpicius Galba. Thus we see how we should beware of adhering to common opinions, and that we must weigh them by the test of reason, not by common report.

I had with me for a long time a man who had lived ten or twelve years in that other world which has been discovered in our time in the region where Villegaignon made land, and which he christened Antarctic France. This discovery of a boundless country seems to be worth consideration....

This man that I had was a simple, plain fellow, which is a nature likely to give true testimony; for intelligent persons notice more things and scrutinise them more carefully; but they comment on them; and to make their interpretation of value and win belief for it, they can not refrain from altering the facts a little. They never represent things to you just as they are: they shape them and disguise them according to the aspect which they have seen them bear; and to win faith in their judgement and incline you to trust it, they readily help out the matter on one side, lengthen it, and amplify it. It needs a man either very truthful or so ignorant that he has no material wherewith to construct and give verisimilitude to false conceptions, and one who is wedded to nothing. My man was such a one; and, besides, he on divers occasions brought to me several sailors and traders whom he had known on his travels. So I am content with this information, without enquiring what the cosmographers say about it....

Now, to return to what I was talking of, I think that there is nothing barbaric or uncivilised in that nation, according to what I have been told, except that every one calls "barbarism" whatever he is not accustomed to. As, indeed, it seems that we have no other criterion of truth and of what is reasonable than the example and type of the opinions and customs of the country to which we belong: therein [to us] always is the perfect religion, the perfect political system, the perfect and achieved usage in all things. They are wild men just as we call those fruits wild which Nature has produced unaided and in her usual course; whereas, in truth, it is those that we have altered by our skill and removed from the common kind which we ought rather to call wild. In the former the real and most useful and natural virtues are alive and vigorous—we have vitiated them in the latter, adapting them to the gratification of our corrupt taste; and yet nevertheless the special savour and delicacy of divers uncultivated fruits of those regions seems excellent even to our taste in comparison with our own. It is not reasonable that art should gain the preëminence over our great and puissant mother Nature. We have so overloaded the beauty and richness of her works by our contrivances that we have altogether smothered her. Still, truly, whenever she shines forth unveiled, she wonderfully shames our vain and trivial undertakings.

> The ivy grows best when wild,
> and the arbutus springs most beautifully in some lovely cave;
> birds sing most sweetly without teaching.
>
> [Propertius]

All our efforts can not so much as reproduce the nest of the tiniest birdling, its contexture, its beauty, and its usefulness; nay, nor the web of the little spider. All things, said Plato, are produced either by nature, or by chance, or by art;

the greatest and most beautiful by one or other of the first two, the least and most imperfect by the last.

These nations seem to me, then, wild in this sense, that they have received in very slight degree the external forms of human intelligence, and are still very near to their primitive simplicity. The laws of nature still govern them, very little corrupted by ours; even in such pureness that it sometimes grieves me that the knowledge of this did not come earlier, in the days when there were men who would have known better than we how to judge it. I am sorry that Lycurgus and Plato had not this knowledge; for it seems to me that what we see in intercourse with those nations surpasses not only all the paintings wherewith poetry has embellished the golden age, and all its conceptions in representing a happy condition of mankind, but also the idea and aspiration, even, of philosophy. They could not conceive so pure and simple an artlessness as we by experience know it to be; nor could they believe that human society could be carried on with so little artificiality and human unitedness. It is a nation, I will say to Plato, in which there is no sort of traffic, no acquaintance with letters, no knowledge of numbers, no title of magistrate or of political eminence, no custom of service, of wealth, or of poverty, no contracts, no successions, no dividings of property, no occupations except leisurely ones, no respect for any kinship save in common, no clothing, no agriculture, no metals, no use of wine or grain. The very words that signify falsehood, treachery, dissimulation, avarice, envy, slander, forgiveness, are unheard of. How far from such perfection would he find the Republic he imagined:

> Men recently from the hands of the gods.
>
> [Seneca]

> These are the first laws that nature gave.
>
> [Virgil]

For the rest, they live in a country with a most agreeable and pleasant climate; consequently, according to what my witnesses have told me, it is a rare thing to see a sick man there; and they have assured me that any one palsied, or blear-eyed, or toothless, or bent with old age is never to be seen. These people are settled on the sea-shore, and are shut in, landward, by a chain of high mountains, leaving a strip a hundred leagues or thereabouts in width. They have a great abundance of fish and meats, which bear no resemblance to ours, and they eat them without other elaboration than cooking. The first man who rode a horse there, although he had been with them on several other voyages, so terrified them in that guise that they shot him to death with arrows before they could recognise him.

Their buildings are very long and can hold two or three hundred souls; they are built of the bark of large trees, fastened to the earth at one end and resting against and supporting one another at the ridge-pole, after the fashion of some of our barns, the roofing whereof falls to the ground and serves for side and end walls. They have wood so hard that, they cut with it and make swords of it, and gridirons for cooking their meat. Their beds are a cotton web, hung from the roof like those in our ships, each person having his own, for the women lie apart from their husbands. They rise with the sun and eat immediately after rising, for the whole day's need; for they have no other meal than this. They do not drink then, as Suidas says of certain Oriental nations who drank when not eating; they drink many times during the day, and a great deal. Their beverage is made of some root, and is of the colour of our light wines; they drink it only luke-warm. This beverage will keep only two or three days; it is rather sharp in taste, not at all intoxicating, good for the stomach, and laxative for those who are not accustomed to it; it is a very pleasant drink for those wonted to it. Instead of bread they use a certain substance like preserved coriander. I have tasted it; its flavour is sweetish and rather insipid. The whole day is passed in dancing. The young men go hunting wild animals with bows. A part of the women employ themselves meanwhile in warming their drink, which is their chief duty. Some one of the old men, in the morning, before they begin to eat, counsels the whole collected household, walking from end to end of the building and repeating the same phrase many times, until he has completed the turn (for the buildings are fully a hundred paces in length). He enjoins upon them only two things—valour against the enemy and friendship for their wives. And they never fail, by way of response, to note the obligation that it is their wives who keep their drink warm and well-seasoned for them. There can be seen in many places, and, among others, in my house, the fashion of their beds, of their twisted ropes, of their wooden swords and the wooden armlets with which they protect their wrists in battle, and of the long staves, open at one end, by the sound of which they mark time in their dancing. They are clean-shaven, and they shave much more closely than we do, with no other razor than one of wood or stone....

Three of this people—not knowing how dear the knowledge of the corruption of this country will some day cost their peace of mind and their happiness, and that from this intercourse will be born their ruin, which conjecture may be already in process of confirmation; most miserable in having allowed themselves to be tricked by the desire for things unknown, and in having left the sweetness of their own skies, to come to gaze at ours—were at Rouen at the time that the late King Charles the Ninth was there. The king talked with them a long while; they were shown our modes of life, our magnificence, and the outward appearance of a beautiful city. Thereafter some one asked them what they thought of all this, and wished to learn from them what had seemed to them most worthy of admiration. They mentioned in reply three things, of which I have forgotten the third, and am very sorry for it; but I remember two. They said that, in the first place, they thought it very strange that so many tall, bearded men, strong and well armed, who were about the king (they probably referred to the Swiss of the Guard), should humble themselves to obey a child, and that they did not rather choose some one of themselves to command them. Secondly (they have a fashion of speech of calling men halves of one another), they had perceived that there were among us some men gorged to the full with all sorts of possessions, and that their other halves were beggars at their doors, gaunt with hunger and destitution; and they thought it strange that these poverty-stricken halves could suffer such injustice, and that they did not take the others by the throat or set fire to their houses. I talked with one of them a very long while; but I had an interpreter who followed me so badly, and who was so hindered by his stupidity from grasping my ideas, that I could not have any pleasure in it. When I asked what advantage he derived from his superior position among his people (for he was a captain and our seamen called him king), he said that it was the privilege of marching at their head in war. By how many men he was followed. He indicated a certain extent of ground, as if to signify that it was by as many men as that space would hold—perhaps four or five thousand. Whether, when there was no war, all his authority was at an end. He said that he still retained the right, when he visited the villages that were in his dependence, to have paths made for him through the thickets of their forests, by which he could travel easily.

All this does not seem too much amiss; but then, they do not wear breeches!

Curious Dialogues (1703)

Louis Armand de Lom d'Arce Lahontan

Lahontan's account of his dialogue with Adario, a Huron man he befriended, although perhaps not recorded verbatim, reflects important differences between European and Native American life.

Lahontan. Well, my Friend; thou hast heard what the Jesuit had to say; he has set matters in a clear light, and made 'em much plainer than I could do. You see plainly there's a great difference between his Arguments and mine. We Soldiers of Fortune have only a superficial knowledge of our Religion, tho' indeed we ought to know it better; but the Jesuits have Study'd it to that degree, that they never fail of converting and convincing the most obstinate Infidels in the Universe.

Adario. To be free with thee, my dear Brother, I could scarce understand one tittle of what he meant, and I am much mistaken if he understands it himself. He has repeated the very same Arguments a hundred times in my Hutt; and you might have observ'd, that yesterday I answer'd above twenty times, that I had heard his Arguments before upon several occasions. But, what I take to be most ridiculous, he teases me every minute to get me to interpret his Arguments, word for word, to my Countrymen; upon the Plea that a Man of my Sense may find out in his own Language, more significant terms, and render the meaning of his Words more Intelligible, than a Jesuit who is not throughly Master of the *Huron* Language. You heard me tell him, that he might Baptise as many Children as he pleas'd, tho' at the content our selves in denying all manner of Dependance, excepting that upon the Great Spirit, as being born free and joint Brethren, who are all equally Masters: Whereas you are all Slaves to one Man. We do not put in any such Answer to you, as if the *French* depended upon us; and the reason of our silence upon that Head is, that we have no mind to Quarrel. But, pray tell me, what Authority or Right is the pretended Superiority of your great Captain grounded upon? Did we ever sell our selves to that great Captain? Were we ever in *France* to look after you? 'Tis you that came hither to find out us. Who gave you all the Countries that you now inhabit, by what Right do you possess 'em? They always belong'd to the *Algonkins* before. In earnest, my dear Brother, I'm sorry for thee from the bottom of my Soul. Take my advice, and turn *Huron;* for I see plainly a vast difference between thy Condition and mine. I am Master of my own Body, I have the absolute disposal of my self, I do what I please, I am the first and the last of my Nation, I fear no Man, and I depend only upon the Great Spirit: Whereas thy Body, as well as thy Soul, are doom'd to a dependance upon thy great Captain; thy Vice-Roy disposes of thee; thou hast not the liberty of doing what thou hast a mind to; thou'rt affraid of Robbers, false Witnesses, Assassins, etc. and thou dependest upon an infinity of Persons whose Places have rais'd 'em above thee. Is it true, or not? Are these things either improbable or invisible? Ah! my dear Brother, thou seest plainly that I am in the right of it; and yet thou choosest rather to be a *French* Slave than a free *Huron*. What a fine Spark does a *Frenchman* make with his fine Laws, who taking himself to be mighty Wife is assuredly a great Fool; for as much as he continues in Slavery and a state of Dependence, while the very Brutes enjoy that adorable Liberty, and like us fear nothing but Foreign Enemies....

Long live the *Hurons;* who without Laws, without Prisons, and without Torture, pass their Life in a State of Sweetness and Tranquility, and enjoy a pitch of

Felicity to which the *French* are utter Strangers. We live quietly under the Laws of Instinct and innocent Conduct, which wise Nature has imprinted upon our Minds from our Cradles. We are all of one Mind; our Wills, Opinions and Sentiments observe an exact Conformity; and thus we spend our Lives with such a perfect good understanding, that no Disputes or Suits can take place amongst us. But how unhappy are you in being expos'd to the lash of Laws, which your ignorant, unjust, and vicious judges break in their private Actions, as well as in the Administration of their Offices? These are your just and equitable judges; who have no regard to Right; who make their Interest the Standard of their Conduct, in the way of their Office; who have nothing in view but the Inriching of themselves; who are not accessible by any but the Demon of Silver; who never administer Justice, but thro' a Principle of Avarice or Passion; who give Countenance to Crimes, and set aside Justice and Honesty, in order to give a full range to Cheating, Quarrelling, and the carrying on of tedious Law Suits, to the abuse and violation of Oaths, and to an infinity of other Disorders. This is the practice of these doughty Assertors of the fine Laws of the *French* Nation....

But if no body had given me any such Information, I am not so dull Pated as not to see with my own Eyes, the Injustice of your Laws and your judges. I'll tell thee one thing my dear Brother; I was a going one day from *Paris* to *Versailles,* and about half way, I met a Boor that was going to be Whipt for having taken Partridges and Hares with Traps. Between *Rochel* and *Paris,* I saw another that was Condemn'd to the Gally's for having a little Bag of Salt about him. These poor Men were punish'd by your unjust Laws, for endeavouring to get Sustenance to their Families; at a time when a Million of Women were got with Child in the absence of their Husbands, when the Physicians Murder'd three fourths of the People, and the Gamesters reduc'd their Families to a Starving Condition, by losing all they had in the World; and all this with Impunity. If things go at this rate, where are your just and reasonable Laws; where are those judges that have a Soul to be Sav'd as well as you and I? After this, you'll be ready to Brand the *Hurons* for Beast. In earnest, we should have a fine time of it if we offer'd to punish one of our Brethren for killing a Hare or a Partridge; and a glorious fight 'twould be, to see our Wives inlarge the number of our Children, while we are ingag'd in Warlike Expeditions against our Enemies; to see Physicians Poison our Families, and Gamesters lose the Beaver Skins they've got in Hunting. In *France,* these things are look'd upon as trifles, which do not fall within the Verge of their fine Laws. Doubtless, they must needs be very blind, that are acquainted with us, and yet do not imitate our Example....

I would gladly embrace any opportunity of working my self into that Belief before I die, for I have a natural affection for the *French;* but I am very apprehensive that I shall not meet with that Consolation. Upon this foot, your judges ought to begin first to observe the Laws, that their example may influence others; they ought to discontinue their Oppression of Widows, Orphans, and poor Creatures; to give dispatch to the Suits of Persons that come an hundred Leagues off for a Hearing; and in a word, to form such judgments of Causes as the Great Spirit shall do. I can never entertain a good thought of your Laws, till they lessen the Taxes and Duties that poor People are constrain'd to pay, at a time when the Rich of all Stations pay nothing in proportion to their Estates; till you put a stop to the course of Drunkenness that spreads thro' our Villages, by prohibiting the *Coureurs de Bois* to import Brandy among us. Then indeed I shall hope that you'll compleat your Reformation by degrees, that a levelling of Estates may gradually creep in among you; and that at last you'll abhor that thing call'd Interest, which occasions all the Mischief that *Europe* groans under. When you arrive at that pitch, you'll have neither *Meum* nor *Tuum* to disturb you, but live as happily as the *Hurons*....

Thou'rt mistaken, my dear Brother, in all thou hast said; for I have not form'd to my self any false Idea of your Religion, or of your Laws. The Example of all the *French* in General, will ever oblige me to look upon all their Actions as unworthy of a Man. So that my Idea's are just; the prepossession you talk of is well grounded; and I am ready to make out all my advances. We talk'd of Religion and Laws, and I did not impart to you above a quarter of what I had to say upon that Head. You insist chiefly upon our way of living, which you take to be Blame-worthy. The *French* in general take us for Beasts; the Jesuits Brand us for impious, foolish and ignorant Vagabonds. And to be even with you, we have the same thoughts of you; but with this difference, that *we* pity you without offering invectives. Pray hear me, my dear Brother, I speak calmly and without passion. The more I reflect upon the lives of the *Europeans,* the less Wisdom and Happiness I find among 'em. These six years I have bent my thoughts upon the State of the *Europeans:* But I can't light on any thing in their Actions that is not beneath a Man; and truly I think 'tis impossible it should be otherwise, so long as you stick to the measures of *Meum* and *Tuum*. I affirm that what you call Silver is the Devil of Devils; the Tyrant of the *French;* the Source of all Evil; the Bane of Souls, and the Slaughter-House of living Persons. To pretend to live in the Mony Country, and at the same time to save one's Soul, is as great an inconsistency as for a Man to go to the bottom of a Lake to preserve his Life. This Mony is the Father of Luxury, Lasciviousness, Intrigues, Tricks, Lying, Treachery, Falseness, and in a word, of all the mischief in the World. The Father sells his Children, Husbands expose their Wives to Sale, Wives betray their Husbands, Brethren kill one another, Friends are false, and all this proceeds from Mony. Consider this, and then tell me if we are not in the right of it, in refusing to finger, or so much as to look upon that cursed Metal....

You fob me off very prettily, truly, when you bring in your Gentlemen, your Merchants and your Priests. If you were Strangers to *Meum* and *Tuum*, those distinctions of Men would be sunk; a levelling equality would then take place among you as it now do's among the *Hurons*. For the first thirty years indeed, after the banishing of Interest, you would see a strange Desolation; those who are only qualify'd to eat, drink, sleep and divert themselves, would languish and die; but their Posterity would be fit for our way of living. I have set forth again and again, the qualities that make a Man inwardly such as he ought to be; particularly, Wisdom, Reason, Equity, etc. which are courted by the *Hurons*. I have made it appear that the Notion of separate Interests knocks all these Qualities in the Head, and that a Man sway'd by Interest can't be a Man of Reason....

If I had not been particularly inform'd of the State of *France*, and let into the knowledge of all the Circumstances of that People, by my Voyage to *Paris*; I might have been Blinded by the outward appearances of Felicity that you set forth: But I know that your Prince, your Duke, your Marshal, and your Prelate are far from being happy upon the Comparison with the *Hurons*, who know no other happiness than that of Liberty and Tranquility of Mind: For your great Lords hate one another in their Hearts; they forfeit their Sleep, and neglect even Eating and Drinking, in making their Court to the King, and undermining their Enemies; they offer such Violence to Nature in dissembling, disguising and bearing things, that the Torture of their Soul leaves all Expression far behind it. Is all this nothing in your way? Do you think it such a trifling matter to have fifty Serpents in your Bosom? Had not they better throw their Coaches, their Palaces and their Finery, into the River, than to spend their life time in a continued Series of Martyrdom? Were I in their place, I'd rather choose to be a *Huron* with a Naked Body and a Serene Mind. The Body is the Apartment in which the Soul is lodg'd; and what signifies it, for the Case call'd the Body, to be set off with Gold Trappings, or spread out in a Coach, or planted before a Sumptuous Table, while the Soul Galls and Tortures it? The great Lords, that you call Happy, lie expos'd to Disgrace from the King, to the detraction of a thousand sorts of Persons, to the loss of their Places, to the Contempt of their Fellow Courtiers; and in a word, their soft Life is thwarted by Ambition, Pride, Presumption and Envy. They are Slaves to their Passions, and to their King, who is the only *French* Man that can be call'd Happy, with respect to that adorable Liberty which he alone enjoys. There's a thousand of us in one Village, and you see that we love one another like Brethren; that whatever any one has is at his Neighbour's Service; that our Generals and Presidents of the Council have not more Power than any other *Huron;* that Detraction and Quarreling were never heard of among us; and in fine, that every one is his own Master, and do's what he pleases, without being accountable to another, or censur'd by his Neighbour. This, my dear Brother, is the difference between us and your Princes, Dukes, etc. And if those great Men are so Unhappy, by consequence, those of inferiour Stations must have a greater share of Trouble and perplexing Cares....

At that rate you prefer Slavery to Liberty. But 'tis no Surprisal to me, after what I have heard you maintain: Tho after all, if you happen'd to enter into your own Breast, and to throw off your prepossession with regard to the Customs and Humours of the *French* Nation; I cannot see that the Objections you've now Started, are of such Moment as to keep you from falling into our way of living. What a mighty difficulty you meet with in bringing your self to approve of our old Men's Counsel, and our young Men's Projects! Are not you equally gravell'd, when the Jesuits and your Superiours make impertinent demands? Why would not you choose to live upon the Broth of all sorts of good and substantial Meat? Our Partridges, Turkeys, Hares, Ducks, and Roe-Bucks; do not they eat well when they're Roasted or Boil'd? What signifies your Pepper, your Salt, and a thousand other Spices, unless it be to murder your Health? Try our way of living but one fort-night, and then you'll long for no such doings. What harm can you fear from the Painting of your Face with Colours? You dawb your Hair with Powder and Essence, and even your Cloaths are sprinkled with the same: Nay, I have seen *French* Men that had Mustaches like Cats, cover'd o'er with Wax. As for the Mapple-Water, 'tis sweet, healthy, well-tasted, and friendly to the Stomach: And I've seen you drink of it oftner than once or twice: Whereas Wine and Brandy destroy the natural Heat, pall the Stomach, inflame the Blood, Intoxicate, and create a thousand Disorders. And pray what harm would it do ye, to go Naked in warm Weather? Besides, we are not so stark Naked, but that we are cover'd behind and before. 'Tis better to go Naked, than to toil under an everlasting Sweat, and under a load of Cloaths heap'd up one above another. Where's the uneasyness of Eating, Singing, and Dancing in good Company? Had not you better do so than sit at Table moping by your self, or in the Company of those that you never saw or knew before? All the hardship then, that you can complain of, lies in conversing with an unciviliz'd People, and being robb'd of the Pageantry of Compliments. This you take to be a sad Affliction, tho' at the bottom 'tis far from being such. Tell me, prithee; do's not Civility consist in Decency and an affable Carriage? And what is Decency? Is it not an everlasting Rack, and a tyresome Affectation display'd in Words, Cloaths and Countenance? And why would you Court a Quality that gives you so much trouble? As for Affability; I presume it lyes in giving People to know our readyness to serve 'em, by Caresses and other outward Marks; As when you say every turn, Sir, *I'm your humble Servant, you may dispose of me as you please*. Now, let's but consider to what purpose all these Words are spoke; for what end must we lie upon all occasions, and speak otherwise than we think? Had not you better speak after this fashion; *Ho! art thou there, thou'rt welcome, for I honour thee?* Is not it an ugly show, to bend one's Body half a score times, to lower one's hand to the ground, and to say every moment, *I ask your Pardon?* Be it known to thee, my dear Brother, that this Submission alone would be enough to unhinge me quite, as to your way of living. You've asserted that a *Huron* may easily turn *French;* but believe me, he'll meet with other difficulties in the way of his Conversion than those you speak of. For supposing I were to turn *French* out of hand, I must begin with a complyance to Christianity, which is a Point that you and I talk'd enough of three days ago. In order to the same end, I must get my self Shav'd every three days, for in all appearance I should no sooner profess Gallicism, than I should become rough and hairy like a Beast; And this inconvenience shocks me extreamly: Sure 'tis much better to be Beardless and Hairless; and I'm equally sure you never saw a rough Savage. How d'ye think it would agree with me to spend two hours in Dressing or Shifting my self, to put on a Blue Sute and Red Stockins, with a Black Hat and a White Feather, besides colour'd Ribbands? Such Rigging would make me look upon my self as a Fool. How could I condescend to Sing in the Streets, to Dance before a Looking-Glass, to toss my Wigg sometimes before and sometimes behind me? I could not stoop so as to make my Honours, and fall down before a parcel of Sawcy Fools, that are intitled to no other Merit than that of their Birth and Fortune. D'ye think that I could see the Indigent languish and pine away, without giving 'em all I had? How could I wear a Sword without attacking a Company of Profligate Men who throw into the Gallys an infinity of poor Strangers, that never injur'd any Body, and are carried, in a woful Condition, out of their Native Country, to Curse in the midst of their Chains, their Fathers and Mothers, their Birth, and even the Great Spirit. Thus 'tis that the *Iroquese* languish, who were sent to *France* some two years ago. Can you imagine that I would speak ill of my Friends, caress my Enemies, contemn the Miserable, honour the Wicked, and enter into Dealings with 'em; that I would triumph o'er my Neighbour's Misfortunes, and praise a naughty Man; that I would act the part of the Envious, the Traitours, the Flatterers, the Inconstant, the Liars, the Proud, the Avaricious, the Selfish, the Taletellers, and all your double Minded Folks? D'ye think it possible for me to be so indiscreet as to boast at once of what I have done, and what I have not done; to be so mean as to crawl like an Adder at the feet of a Lord, that orders his Servants to deny him; and to take a Refusal tamely? No, my dear Brother, no; I can't brook the Character of a *French* Man; I had rather continue what I am than pass my Life in these Chains. Is it possible that our Liberty do's not Charm you? Can you live an easier life than what you may have in our way? ... Did ever a *Huron* refuse another, either the whole or part of what he had catch'd at Hunting or Fishing? Do not we make dividends of our Beaver-Skins, in order to supply those who have not enough to purchase such Commodities as they have occasion for? Do not we observe the same Method in the distribution of our Corn, to such as have not sufficent [*sic*] Crops upon their Fields for the maintenance of their Families?... This is a quite different way of living, from that of the *Europeans,* who would Sue their nearest Relations for an Ox or a Horse. If the *European* Father asks Mony of his Son, or the Son of the Father, he replys he has none. If of two *French* Men who have liv'd twenty years together, and eat and drink at one Table every day; if of these two *French* Men, I say, one should ask the other for Mony, the answer is, there's none to be had. If a poor Wretch that goes naked in the Streets, and is ready to dye with Hunger and Hardships: does but ask a rich Man for a Farthing, his answer is, *'Tis not for him.* Now since all this is true, how can you have the presumption to claim a free access to the Country of the Great Spirit? Sure, there's not a Man upon Earth that does not know, that Evil is contrary to Nature, and that he was not Created to do Mischief. What hopes then can a Christian have at his Death, that never did a good Action in his Life time. He either must believe that the Soul dies with the Body (tho' there's none of you that owns that Opinion) or else supposing the Immortality of the Soul, and supposing your Tenents of Hell, and of the Sins that waft Sinners to that Region, to be just and true, your Souls will have a hot time of it.

Distresses of a Frontier Man (1783)

J. Hector St. John de Crèvecoeur

As the American Revolution approached, Crèvecoeur decided to leave his house and farm in the American colonies. He was torn between his British citizenship and his new identity as an American. As Crèvecoeur was a man of peace, and a father concerned with his family's safety, he took them to live with an Indian community. He deliberately omits names and places here to protect his family's location.

... Do you, my friend, perceive the path I have found out? It is that which leads to the tenants of the great _____ village of _____, where, far removed from the accursed neighbourhood of Europeans, its inhabitants live with more ease, decency, and peace, than you imagine: where, though governed by no laws, yet find, in uncontaminated simple manners all that laws can afford. Their system is sufficiently compleat to answer all the primary wants of man, and to constitute him a social being, such as he ought to be in the great forest of nature. There it is that I have resolved at any rate to transport myself and family: an eccentric thought, you may say, thus to cut asunder all former connections, and to form new ones with a people whom nature has stamped with such different characteristics! But as the happiness of my family is the only object of my wishes, I care very little where we be, or where we go, provided that we are safe, and all united together. Our new calamities being shared equally by all, will become lighter; our mutual affection for each other, will in this great transmutation become the strongest link of our new society, will afford us every joy we can receive on a foreign soil, and preserve us in unity, as the gravity and coherency of matter prevents the world from dissolution....

Yes, I will chearfully embrace that resource, it is an holy inspiration: by night and by day, it presents itself to my mind: I have carefully revolved the scheme; I have considered in all its future effects and tendencies, the new mode of living we must pursue, without salt, without spices, without linen and with little other cloathing; the art of hunting, we must acquire, the new manners we must adopt, the new language we must speak; the dangers attending the education of my children we must endure. These changes may appear more terrific at a distance perhaps than when grown familiar by practice: what is it to us, whether we eat well made pastry, or pounded àlagrichés; well roasted beef, or smoked venison; cabbages, or squashes? Whether we wear neat homespun, or good beaver; whether we sleep on featherbeds, or on bear-skins? The difference is not worth attending to. The difficulty of the language, fear of some great intoxication among the Indians; finally, the apprehension lest my younger children should be caught by that singular charm, so dangerous at their tender years; are the only considerations that startle me. By what power does it come to pass, that children who have been adopted when young among these people, can never be prevailed on to re-adopt European manners? Many an anxious parent I have seen last war, who at the return of the peace, went to the Indian villages where they knew their children had been carried in captivity; when to their inexpressible sorrow, they found them so perfectly Indianized, that many knew them no longer, and those whose more advanced ages permitted them to recollect their fathers and mothers, absolutely refused to follow them, and ran to their adopted parents for protection against the effusions of love their unhappy real parents lavished on them! Incredible as this may appear, I have heard it asserted in a thousand instances, among persons of credit. In the village of _____, where I purpose to go, there lived, about fifteen years ago, an Englishman and a Swede, whose history would appear moving, had I time to relate it. They were grown to the age of men when they were taken; they happily escaped the great punishment of war captives, and were obliged to marry the *Squaws* who had saved their lives by adoption. By the force of habit, they became at last thoroughly naturalised to this wild course of life. While I was there, their friends sent them a considerable sum of money to ransom themselves with. The Indians, their old masters, gave them their choice, and without requiring any consideration, told them, that they had been long as free as themselves. They chose to remain; and the reasons they gave me would greatly surprise you: the most perfect freedom, the ease of living, the absence of those cares and corroding solicitudes which so often prevail with us; the peculiar goodness of the soil they cultivated, for they did not trust altogether to hunting; all these, and many more motives, which I have forgot, made them prefer that life, of which we entertain such dreadful opinions. It cannot be therefore, so bad as we generally conceive it to be; there must be in their social bond something singularly captivating, and far superior to any thing to be boasted of among us for thousands of Europeans are Indians, and we have no examples of even one of those Aborigines having from choice become Europeans! There must be something more congenial to our native dispositions, than the fictitious society in which we live; or else why should children, and even grown persons, become in a short time so invincibly attached to it? There must be something very bewitching in their manners, something very indelible and marked by the very hands of nature. For, take a young Indian lad, give him the best education you possibly can, load him with your bounty, with presents, nay with riches; yet he will secretly long for his native woods, which you would imagine he must have long since forgot; and on the first opportunity he can possibly find, you will see him voluntarily leave behind him all you have given him, and return with inexpressible joy to lie on the mats of his fathers. Mr._____, some years ago, received from a good old Indian, who died in his house, a young lad, of nine years of age, his grandson. He kindly educated him with his children, and bestowed on him the same care and attention in respect to the memory of his venerable grandfather, who was a worthy man. He intended to give him a genteel trade, but in the spring season when all the family went to the woods to make their maple sugar, he suddenly disappeared; and it was not until seventeen months after, that his benefactor heard he had reached the village of Bald Eagle, where he still dwelt. Let us say what we will of them, of their inferior organs, of their want of bread, etc. they are as stout and well made as the Europeans. Without temples, without priests, without kings, and without laws, they are in many instances superior to us; and the proofs of what I advance, are, that they live without care, sleep without inquietude, take life as it comes, bearing all its asperities with unparalleled patience, and die without any kind of apprehension for what they have done, or for what they expect to meet with hereafter.... In my youth I traded with the_____, under the conduct of my uncle, and always traded justly and equitably; some of them remember it to this day. Happily their village is far removed from the dangerous neighbourhood of the whites; I sent a man, last spring to it, who understands the woods extremely well, and who speaks their language; he is just returned, after several weeks absence, and has brought me, as I had flattered myself, a string of thirty purple wampum, as a token that their honest chief will spare us half of his wigwham until we have time to erect one. He has sent me word that they have land in plenty, of which they are not so covetous as the whites; that we may plant for ourselves, and that in the mean time he will procure for us some corn and some meat; that fish is plenty in the waters of _____, and that the village to which he had laid open my proposals, have no objection to our becoming dwellers with them....

Agrarian Justice (1797)

Thomas Paine

Paine's article provides the first plan for a U.S. old-age pension.

Preface

The following little piece was written in the winter of 1795 and 96; and, as I had not determined whether to publish it during the present war, or to wait till the commencement of a peace, it has lain by me, without addition, from the time it was written.

What has determined me to publish it now is, a Sermon, preached by Watson, Bishop of Landaff. Some of my readers will recollect, that this Bishop wrote a book, entitled "An Apology for the Bible," in answer to my "Second Part of the Age of Reason." I procured a copy of his book, and he may depend upon hearing from me on that subject.

At the end of the Bishop's book is a list of the works he has written, among which is the Sermon alluded to; it is entitled "The Wisdom and Goodness of

God in having made both rich and poor; with an Appendix containing Reflections on the present State of England and France."

The error contained in the title of this Sermon, determined me to publish my *Agrarian Justice*. It is wrong to say that God made *Rich* and *Poor*; he made only *Male* and *Female*; and he gave them the earth for their inheritance.

Instead of preaching to encourage one part of mankind in insolence it would be better that the Priests employed their time to render the condition of man less miserable than it is. Practical Religion consists in doing good; and the only way of serving God is, that of endeavouring to make his creation happy. All preaching that has not this for its object is nonsense and hypocrisy.

[Considerable pains have been taken to procure a perfect copy of this pamphlet, but it does not appear that any such thing was ever printed in England. The publisher is therefore reluctantly compelled to insert the asterisks as in the former edition.]

Agrarian Justice

To preserve the benefits of what is called civilized life, and to remedy, at the same time, the evils it has produced, ought to be considered as one of the first objects of reformed legislation.

Whether that state that is proudly, perhaps erroneously, called civilization, has most promoted or most injured the general happiness of man, is a question that may be strongly contested. On one side the spectator is dazzled by splendid appearances; on the other he is shocked by extremes of wretchedness; both of which he has created. The most affluent and the most miserable of the human race are to be found in the countries that are called civilized.

To understand what the state of society ought to be, it is necessary to have some idea of the natural and primitive state of man; such as it is at this day among the Indians of North America. There is not, in that state, any of those spectacles of human misery which poverty and want present to our eyes in all the towns and streets in Europe. Poverty, therefore, is a thing created by that which is called civilized life. It exists not in the natural state. On the other hand, the natural state is without those advantages which flow from Agriculture, Arts, Sciences, and Manufactures.

The life of an Indian is a continual holiday, compared with the poor of Europe; and on the other hand, it appears to be abject when compared to the rich. Civilization, therefore, or that which is so called, has operated two ways, to make one part of society more affluent, and the other part more wretched than would have been the lot of either in a natural state.

It is always possible to go from the natural to the civilized state, but it is never possible to go from the civilized to the natural state. The reason is, that man, in a natural state, subsisting by hunting, requires ten times the quantity of land to range over to procure himself sustenance, than would support him in a civilized state, where the earth is cultivated. When, therefore, a country becomes populous by the additional aids of cultivation, arts, and science, there is a necessity of preserving things in that state; without it, there cannot be sustenance for more, perhaps, than a tenth part of its inhabitants. The thing, therefore, now to be done is, to remedy the evils, and preserve the benefits that have arisen to society, by passing from the natural to that which is called the civilized state.

Taking then the matter upon this ground, the first principle of civilization ought to have been, and ought still to be, that the condition of every person born into the world, after a state of civilization commences, ought not to be worse than if he had been born before that period. But the fact is, that the condition of millions, in every country in Europe, is far worse than if they had been born before civilization began, or had been born among the Indians of North America of the present day. I will show how this fact has happened.

It is a position not to be controverted, that the earth, in its natural uncultivated state, was, and ever would have continued to be, the COMMON PROPERTY OF THE HUMAN RACE. In that state every man would have been born to property. He would have been a joint life-proprietor with the rest in the property of the soil, and in all its natural productions, vegetable and animal.

But the earth in its natural state, as before said, is capable of supporting but a small number of inhabitants compared with what it is capable of doing in a cultivated state. And as it is impossible to separate the improvement made by cultivation, from the earth itself, upon which that improvement is made, the idea of landed property arose from that inseparable connection; but it is nevertheless true, that it is the value of the improvement only, and not the earth itself, that is individual property. Every proprietor, therefore, of cultivated land, owes to the community a *ground-rent,* for I know no better term to express the idea by, for the land which he holds; and it is from this ground-rent that the fund proposed in this plan is to issue.

It is deducible, as well from the nature of the thing, as from all the histories transmitted to us, that the idea of landed property commenced with cultivation, and that there was no such thing as landed property before that time. It could not exist in the first state of man, that of hunters; it did not exist in the second state, that of shepherds: neither Abraham, Isaac, Jacob, or Job, so far as the history of the Bible may be credited in probable things, were owners of land. Their property consisted, as is always enumerated, in flocks and herds, and they travelled with them from place to place. The frequent contentions at that time about the use of a well in the dry country of Arabia, where those people lived, show also there was no landed property. It was not admitted that land could be located as property.

There could be no such things as landed property originally. Man did not make the earth, and, though he had a natural right to *occupy* it, he had no right to *locate* as *his property* in perpetuity any part of it; neither did the Creator of the earth open a land-office, from whence the first title-deeds should issue. From whence then arose the idea of landed property? I answer as before, that when cultivation began, the idea of landed property began with it; from the impossibility of separating the improvement made by cultivation from the earth itself upon which that improvement was made. The value of the improvement so far exceeded the value of the natural earth, at that time, as to absorb it; till, in the end, the common right of all became confounded into the cultivated right of the individual. But they are nevertheless distinct species of rights, and will continue to be so as long as the world endures.

It is only by tracing things to their origin, that we can gain rightful ideas of them; and it is by gaining such ideas that we discover the boundary that divides right from wrong, and which teaches every man to know his own. I have entitled this tract *Agrarian Justice,* to distinguish it from *Agrarian Law.* Nothing could be more unjust than Agrarian Law in a country improved by cultivation; for though every man, as an inhabitant of the earth, is a joint proprietor of it in its natural state, it does not follow that he is a joint proprietor of cultivated earth. The additional value made by cultivation, after the system was admitted, became the property of those who did it, or who inherited it from them, or who purchased it. It had originally an owner. Whilst, therefore, I advocate the right, and interest myself in the hard case of all those who have been thrown out of their natural inheritance by the introduction of the system of landed property, I equally defend the right of the possessor to the part which is his.

Cultivation is, at least, one of the greatest natural improvements ever made by human invention. It has given to created earth a ten-fold value. But the landed monopoly, that began with it, has produced the greatest evil. It has dispossessed more than half the inhabitants of every nation of their natural inheritance, without providing for them, as ought to have been done, an indemnification for that loss; and has thereby created a species of poverty and wretchedness that did not exist before.

In advocating the case of the persons thus dispossessed, it is a right and not a charity that I am pleading for. But it is that kind of right which, being neglected at first, could not be brought forward afterwards, till heaven had opened the way by a revolution in the system of government. Let us then do honour to revolutions by justice, and give currency to their principles by blessings.

Having thus, in a few words, opened the merits of the case, I proceed to the plan I have to propose, which is,

To create a National Fund, out of which there shall be paid to every person, when arrived at the age of twenty-one years, the sum of Fifteen Pounds sterling, as a compensation in part for the loss of his or her natural inheritance by the introduction of the system of landed property; and also the sum of Ten Pounds per annum, during life, to every person now living of the age of fifty years, and to all others as they shall arrive at that age.

Means by Which the Fund Is to Be Created

I have already established the principle, namely, that the earth, in its natural uncultivated state, was, and ever would have continued to be, the COMMON PROPERTY OF THE HUMAN RACE—that in that state every person would have been born to property—and that the system of landed property, by its inseparable connection with cultivation, and with what is called civilized life, has absorbed the property of all those whom it dispossessed, without providing, as ought to have been done, an indemnification for that loss.

The fault, however, is not in the present possessors. No complaint is intended, or ought to be alleged against them, unless they adopt the crime by opposing justice. The fault is in the system, and it has stolen imperceptibly upon the world, aided afterwards by the Agrarian law of the sword. But the fault can be made to reform itself by successive generations, without diminishing or deranging the property of any of the present possessors, and yet the operation of the fund can commence, and be in full activity the first year of its establishment, or soon after, as I shall show.

It is proposed that the payments, as already stated, be made to every person, rich or poor. It is best to make it so, to prevent invidious distinctions. It is also right it should be so, because it is in lieu of the natural inheritance, which, as a right, belongs to every man, over and above the property he may have created or inherited from those who did. Such persons as do not choose to receive it, can throw it into the common fund.

Taking it then for granted, that no person ought to be in a worse condition when born under what is called a state of civilization, than he would have been, had he been born in a state of nature, and that civilization ought to have made, and ought still to make, provision for that purpose, it can only be done by subtracting from property a portion equal in value to the natural inheritance it has absorbed....

I shall conclude with some observations.

It is not charity but a right—not bounty but justice, that I am pleading for. The present state of what is called civilization is * * *. It is the reverse of what it ought to be, and * * *. The contrast of affluence and wretchedness continually meeting and offending the eye, is like dead and living bodies chained together. Though I care as little about riches as any man, I am a friend to riches, because they are capable of good. I care not how affluent some may be, provided that none be miserable in consequence of it. But it is impossible to enjoy affluence with the felicity it is capable of being enjoyed, whilst so much misery is mingled in the scene. The sight of the misery, and the unpleasant sensations it suggests, which though they may be suffocated cannot be extinguished, are a greater drawback upon the felicity of affluence than the proposed ten per cent. upon property is worth. He that would not give the one to get rid of the other, has no charity, even for himself.

There are in every country some magnificent charities established by individuals. It is, however, but little that any individual can do when the whole extent of the misery to be relieved is considered. He may satisfy his conscience, but not his heart. He may give all that he has, and that all will relieve but little. It is only by organising civilization upon such principles as to act like a system of pullies, that the whole weight of misery can be removed.

The plan here proposed will reach the whole. It will immediately relieve and take out of view three classes of wretchedness: the blind, the lame, and the aged poor. It will furnish the rising generation with means to prevent their becoming poor; and it will do this, without deranging or interfering with any national measures.

To show that this will be the case, it is sufficient to observe, that the operation and effect of the plan will, in all cases, be the same, as if every individual was voluntarily to make his will, and dispose of his property, in the manner here proposed.

But it is justice, and not charity, that is the principle of the plan. In all great cases it is necessary to have a principle more universally active than charity; and with respect to justice, it ought not to be left to the choice of detached individuals, whether they will do justice or not. Considering, then, the plan on the ground of justice, it ought to be the act of the whole, growing spontaneously out of the principles of the revolution, and the reputation of it to be national, and not individual.

A plan upon this principle would benefit the revolution by the energy that springs from the consciousness of justice. It would multiply also the national resources; for property, like vegetation, increases by off-sets. When a young couple begin the world, the difference is exceedingly great, whether they begin with nothing or with fifteen pounds apiece. With this aid they could buy a cow, and implements to cultivate a few acres of land; and instead of becoming burthens upon society, which is always the case, where children are produced faster than they can be fed, they would be put in the way of becoming useful and profitable citizens. The national domains also would sell the better, if pecuniary aids were provided to cultivate them in small lots.

It is the practice of what has unjustly obtained the name of civilization (and the practice merits not to be called either charity or policy) to make some provision for persons becoming poor and wretched, only at the time they become so. Would it not, even as a matter of economy, be far better to devise means to prevent their becoming poor? This can best be done by making every person, when arrived at the age of twenty-one years, an inheritor of something to begin with. The rugged face of society, checquered with the extremes of affluence and of want, proves that some extraordinary violence has been committed upon it, and calls on justice for redress. The great mass of the poor, in all countries, are become an hereditary race, and it is next to impossible for them to get out of that state of themselves. It ought also to be observed, that this mass increases in all the countries that are called civilized. More persons fall annually into it, than get out of it....

The state of civilization that has prevailed throughout Europe, is as unjust in its principle, as it is horrid in its effects; and it is the consciousness of this, and the apprehension that such a state cannot continue when once investigation begins in any country, that makes the possessors dread every idea of a revolution. It is the *hazard*, and not the principles of a revolution, that retards their progress. This being the case, it is necessary, as well for the protection of property, as for the sake of justice and humanity, to form a system, that whilst it preserves one part of society from wretchedness, shall secure the other from depredation.

The superstitious awe, the enslaving reverence, that formerly surrounded affluence, is passing away in all countries, and leaving the possessor of property to the convulsion of accidents. When wealth and splendour, instead of fascinating the multitude, excite emotions of disgust; when, instead of drawing forth admiration, it is beheld as an insult upon wretchedness; when the ostentatious appearance it makes serves to call the right of it in question, the case of property becomes critical, and it is only in a system of justice that the possessor can contemplate security.

To remove the danger, it is necessary to remove the antipathies, and this can only be done by making property productive of a national blessing, extending to every individual. When the riches of one man above another shall increase the national fund in the same proportion; when it shall be seen that the prosperity of that fund depends on the prosperity of individuals; when the more riches a man acquires, the better it shall be for the general mass; it is then that antipathies will cease, and property be placed on the permanent basis of natural interest and protection.

I have no property in France to become subject to the plan I propose. What I have, which is not much, is in the United States of America. But I will pay one hundred pounds sterling towards this fund in France, the instant it shall be established; and I will pay the same sum in England, whenever a similar establishment shall take place in that country.

A revolution in the state of civilization is the necessary companion of revolutions in the system of government. If a revolution in any country be from bad to good, or from good to bad, the state of what is called civilization in that country, must be made conformable thereto, to give that revolution effect. Despotic Government supports itself by abject civilization, in which debasement of the human mind, and wretchedness in the mass of the people, are the chief criterions. Such Governments consider man merely as an animal; that the exercise of intellectual faculty is not his privilege; *that he has nothing to do with the laws, but to obey them;* and they politically depend more upon breaking the spirit of the people by poverty, than they fear enraging it by desperation.

It is a revolution in the state of civilization, that will give perfection to the revolution of France. Already the conviction that Government by representation, is the true system of Government, is spreading itself fast in the world. The reasonableness of it can be seen by all. The justness of it makes itself felt even by its opposers. But when a system of civilization, growing out of that system of government, shall be so organized, that not a man or woman born in the Republic, but shall inherit some means of beginning the world, and see before them the certainty of escaping the miseries, that under other Governments accompany old age, the revolution of France will have an advocate and an ally in the heart of all nations.

An army of principles will penetrate where an army of soldiers cannot—It will succeed where diplomatic management would fail—It is neither the Rhine, the Channel, nor the Ocean, that can arrest its progress—It will march on the horizon of the world, and it will conquer.

Message from the Western Indians to the Commissioners of the United States (1793)

The General Council of Indians at Miami Rapids

The Wabash, or Western, tribes (Miami, Potawatomi, Mascouten, Piankashaw, Kickapoo, and Illinois) were Algonquian-speaking people who lived in what was then called the Northwest Territory, and what is now Ohio, Michigan, Indiana, Wisconsin, and Illinois. On August 13, 1793, the Wabash Indians met in General Council at the foot of the Miami Rapids and wrote this letter to the commissioners appointed by President George Washington.

... BROTHERS;—Money, to us, is of no value, & to most of us unknown, and as no consideration whatever can induce us to sell the lands on which we get sustenance for our women and children; we hope we may be allowed to point out a mode by which your settlers may be easily removed, and peace thereby obtained.

BROTHERS;—We know that these settlers are poor, or they would never have ventured to live in a country which has been in continual trouble ever since they crossed the Ohio; divide therefore this large sum of money which you have offered to us, among these people, give to each also a portion of what you say you would give to us annually over and above this very large sum of money, and we are persuaded they would most readily accept it in lieu of the lands you sold to them, if you add also the great sums you must expend in raising and paying Armies, with a view to force us to yield you our Country, you will certainly have more than sufficient for the purposes of repaying these settlers for all their labour and improvements.

BROTHERS;—You have talked to us about concessions. It appears strange that you should expect any from us, who have only been defending our just Rights against your invasion; We want Peace; Restore to us our Country and we shall be Enemies no longer.

BROTHERS;—You make one concession to us, by offering us your money, and another by having agreed to do us justice, after having long and injuriously withheld it. We mean in the acknowledgement you have now made, that the King of England never did, nor never had a right, to give you our Country, by the Treaty of peace, and you want to make this act of Common Justice, a great part of your concessions, and seem to expect that because you have at last acknowledged our independence, we should for such a favor surrender to you our Country.

BROTHERS;—You have also talked a great deal about pre-emption and your exclusive right to purchase Indian lands, as ceded to you by the King at the Treaty of peace.

BROTHERS;—We never made any agreement with the King, nor with any other Nation that we would give to either the exclusive right of purchasing our lands. And we declare to you that we consider ourselves free to make any bargain or cession of lands, whenever & to whomsoever we please, if the white people as you say, made a treaty that none of them but the King should purchase of us, and that he has given that right to the U. States [sic], it is an affair which concerns you & him & not us. We have never parted with such a power.

BROTHERS;—At our general council held at the Glaize last Fall, we agreed to meet Commissioners from the U. States [sic], for the purpose of restoring Peace, provided they consented to acknowledge and confirm our boundary line to be the Ohio; and we determined not to meet you until you gave us satisfaction on that point; that is the reason we have never met.

We desire you to consider Brothers, that our only demand, is the peaceable possession of a small part of our once great Country. Look back and view the lands from whence we have been driven to this spot, we can retreat no further, because the country behind hardly affords food for its present inhabitants. And we have therefore resolved, to leave our bones in this small space, to which we are now confined.

BROTHERS;—We shall be persuaded that you mean to do us justice if you agree, that the Ohio, shall remain the boundary line between us, if you will not consent thereto, our meeting will be altogether unnecessary.

This is the great point which we hoped would have been explained, before you left your homes, as our message last Fall was principally directed to obtain that information.

Epilogue: Outcomes

In addition to the accounts of Native American egalitarianism, there were two social solutions to poverty offered in the above documents. Thomas Paine's ideas of a "natural inheritance" for youth and for a social insurance plan for the elderly were not implemented in his lifetime. However, Paine's proposal is widely recognized today as the first U.S. plan for an old-age pension, and thus is credited with playing an important role in the development of Social Security. Furthermore, an adaptation of Paine's idea for providing young men and women with "assets" has recently been put forward as a way to replace the U.S. social welfare system, which is based on income, with an assets-based model.

The United States did not implement the Council of Indians' suggestion to give the large amount of money promised to the Wabash Indians for their homeland instead to the poverty-stricken settlers. The United States refused this offer and chose military action against the Wabash. After a four-year war, which included one of the worst defeats ever for the U.S. Army by Native Americans (900 U.S. soldiers dead), the army defeated the Wabash tribes in the Battle of Fallen Timbers. In 1795, after having their villages burned and food stock destroyed, the Native Americans ceded most of their land to the United States.[12]

Poorhouse residents climbing a treadmill as part of their work requirement

Chapter 2

The Early Republic and Pre–Civil War America

Moral Cures, Poorhouses, and Structural Solutions

Prologue: Social Context and Overview of Solutions

In the early republic, poverty was one of the most urgent social issues facing the new nation. Poor people did not have access to the basic necessities of life: adequate housing, food, employment, education, and health care. Historians have estimated that the proportion of people living in poverty in the American colonies was as high as 33 percent of the population. Historian Gary Nash reported that on the eve of the American Revolution, poverty "blighted the lives of a large part of the population." Urban poverty received the most amount of attention, but rural America, where more than 90 percent of the population lived in the late eighteenth century, was also home to widespread poverty.[1]

After the revolution, the crisis of poverty, particularly in the cities, deepened decade by decade. The growing level of poverty can be seen in the public relief records and the tax rate. For example, the tax expenditure for assisting the poor increased in Massachusetts from $28,000 in 1800 to $72,000 in 1821, and to $138,539 by 1834. For some cities, like Salem, nearly 50 percent of the entire city budget was spent on assisting the poor in 1816. In the state of New York, total public assistance doubled to $535,000 between 1815 and 1822; by 1830, 10 percent of the population of New York City received government relief.[2]

Although there was disagreement about the causes of poverty and its potential solutions, there was widespread agreement that local government relief programs and private charity had failed to deal with this growing crisis. Although the revolutionary-era ideology of equality, with its belief that all white men should have a fair opportunity in the social and political life of the republic, inspired many to focus on changing political, economic, and educational structures, an additional and competing ideology—that of liberty—had also developed. Many early Americans interpreted liberty to mean that private property was sacrosanct, individual initiative was the key to success, and that a small and decentralized government was the best way to maintain freedom. Throughout American history, this rugged individualistic interpretation of liberty has hindered social reformers and structural change advocates from redistributing wealth; at the same time, this vision inspired other social reformers to promote the poorhouse, which became one of the major social institutions of the nineteenth century.[3]

The Causes of Poverty

In their attempts to discover the causes of poverty, early American thinkers separated various groups of poor people into two main groups: the worthy poor, who deserved relief, and the unworthy poor, who did not. In 1821, a committee for the General Court (state legislature) of the Commonwealth of Massachusetts, which was chaired by Josiah Quincy and composed of prominent citizens, argued that infants, the elderly, the sick, and the disabled were all part of the "impotent poor." The Quincy committee contended that since the impotent poor were incapable of work and were poor through no fault of their own, they should be granted relief by the local government. However, the committee took issue with people it labeled "able poor" since its members believed that those who could work were taking advantage of a relief system that encouraged idleness. Generally, the "able poor" were seen as drunk, lazy, or lacking religiosity, and thus, their poverty was a result of their own bad choices.[4]

Although many in the early republic agreed with this perspective in theory, in practice they found it difficult to distinguish between the impotent and the able poor. Secretary of State John Yates of New York attempted in his 1824 report on poor relief to distinguish between these two groups by labeling them the "temporary or occasional poor" and the "permanent poor." Soon after, Charles Burroughs, rector of St. John's Church, made a moral distinction by claiming that there was a difference between poverty and pauperism. Poverty was a "misfortune" and "unavoidable evil" that afflicts the "insane, the aged and the maimed, the helpless and infirm." Burroughs felt that everything should be done to assist this group. However, pauperism was a sin and "the consequence of willful error, of shameful indolence, of vicious habits," and relief should be withheld. These categories became the basis of modern notions of the deserving and undeserving poor.[5]

In contrast to this perspective, some Americans looked to structural explanations for the increase in poverty. They argued it was the result of the mechanization of agriculture, seasonality of farm labor, low wages, lack of work, and a loss of home manufacturing—particularly for women—due to industrialization. People observed that as industrialization increased, laborers were becoming deskilled, consigned to boring and repetitive jobs in the new capitalist order. With no minimum wage and strong competition between ex-journeymen, immigrants, women, and children for these menial jobs, wages began to decrease. Matthew Carey, one of the early republic's most renowned printers and editors, made the case that it was impossible to buy the necessities of life on the average wage of an industrial worker. Carey demonstrated that a couple's total pay for a month's work was $143, while monthly expenses were $146. Carey concluded that poverty was not the result of personal failure, but of an unjust distribution of wealth. He declared, "We must never forget, that THE LOW RATE OF WAGES IS THE ROOT OF THE MISCHIEF; and that unless we can succeed in raising the price of labour, our utmost efforts will do little towards bettering the condition of the industrious classes."[6]

Several early nineteenth-century writers put this unjust distribution of wealth into the context of the American Revolution. Wilson Pierson and George Mc-Farlan, two members of the Association of Working People, lamented the fact that the poor had no laws to implement the revolution's goals of equality and freedom since "the laws are made by the rich, and of course *for* the rich." Thomas Skidmore, a machinist who helped to begin the New York Workingman's Party, also discussed inequality and poverty in the context of the revolution. Deeply influenced by Native American egalitarianism and Paine's belief in "natural inheritance," Skidmore asked how it was possible for a person to be created equal as stated in the Declaration of Independence when the rich and the poor were born into unequal circumstances. In his 1829 book, Skidmore concluded that "as long as property is unequal; or rather, as long as it is so enormously unequal, as we see it at present, that those who possess it *will* live on the labor of others."[7]

It must also be remembered that in the early republic, American policies and practices such as enslavement, removal and relocation, and discrimination caused poverty among African Americans, Native Americans, immigrants, and women. In 1800, there were 1 million African Americans who were kept in poverty through enslavement. The number of enslaved African Americans rose to 2 million by 1830, and to 4 million by the beginning of the Civil War. In addition, tens of thousands of Indians were forced into a state of persistent poverty in the nineteenth century because of the U.S. policy of removal and relocation. With the passing of the Indian Removal Act of 1830, Indians were forcibly removed east of the Mississippi, causing widespread death and suffering. This removal policy, which resulted in the largest forced migration in human history, settled and quarantined Native Americans on reservations that contained little productive land. Additionally, Irish Catholic immigrants experienced severe prejudice in the workplace and larger society, forcing many into poverty. In the 1820s, 25 percent of all people living in poorhouses in New York and Baltimore were Irish immigrants. Also, women experienced poverty at much higher rates than men because they were not allowed to own property and were compensated less for their labor than were men. The average poor woman was between the ages of 25 and 50 and had no support from a partner.[8]

Solutions to Poverty

The United States had inherited from its colonial days a system of "outdoor relief" to help poor widows, children, elderly people, and people with disabilities. People in the local communities provided outdoor relief to the destitute in the form of wood, food, or money, and this allowed many poor people to remain in their homes. This practice was seen as a public responsibility and was managed by men called "Overseers of the Poor." The Overseers, relying heavily on English custom, (a) helped only local people; (b) required people who were able to work to do manual labor such as cut wood and maintain roads;

(c) denied relief if relatives were able to contribute the necessary care; and (d) auctioned poor children as apprentices to farmers and artisans. However, with the increase in poverty in the early republic, elite society began to argue that outdoor relief was financially inefficient at best and inhumane at worst, since poor people were shuffled around from community to community, sometimes in the bitter cold, in an attempt to identify their home town. In addition, the practice of auctioning children was seen as cruel, since many of the buyers ended up mistreating the children.[9]

Logically, the solutions to poverty developed in the early to mid-nineteenth century—moral cures, poorhouses, and structural solutions—were based on what people thought of as the causes of poverty. People who believed that individuals were poor because of their own immoral conduct advocated transformation of character through Christianity. The Second Great Awakening, a Christian revival based on the notion that Christ died for all, and that humans were called to use their free will for self-improvement and social reform, spread from the frontier to the East Coast during the 1780s to the 1830s. Charity had always played an important role in Christianity, but the message of social reform in general and serving the poor specifically was revived by this Christian movement. In a clear break from the Calvinist doctrine of predestination and human sinfulness, many of these Christian social reformers believed that it was possible not only to eradicate poverty and other social ills, but also to eliminate all human sin.

This belief that the poor needed to be evangelized can be seen in the New York Female Missionary Society's Second Annual Report, which stated that "the poor of this city … either on account of their poverty, their wickedness, or their ignorance, are destitute of the common ordinances of the Gospel." Similarly, the New York Society for the Prevention of Pauperism claimed that "every citizen should remember that intemperance, ignorance, and idleness are the prolific parents of pauperism, and that every exertion should be made to exterminate those dangerous vices by inculcating religion, morality, sobriety, and industry and by diffusing useful knowledge among the indigent and laboring people." For the Christian social reformers, poverty and sin became almost synonymous.[10]

In order to evangelize the poor, Christian volunteers went into poor neighborhoods to distribute Bibles and tracts (short essays on Christian teachings) in the hopes of transforming their "characters." Organizations like the Boston Society for the Moral and Religious Instruction of the Poor believed that spiritual salvation and material prosperity would result from the distribution of these texts. For the Christian volunteers, many of whom were upper- and middle-class women, this was their first close contact with poor people, and not surprisingly, they brought upper-middle-class attitudes to the situations they witnessed. Thus, the volunteers applied their moral judgments to such issues as public begging, drunkenness, infidelity, and abandonment. As these reformers developed their own private relief organizations, issues of "character" played a central role in determining if such aid as food, clothes, fuel, and money were to be provided.[11]

People who felt that poverty came from lack of effort on the part of the poor offered the poorhouse as the best solution. Poorhouse advocates believed that the main cause of the increase in poverty was the generosity of public relief and private charity, which was undermining the work ethic. Poorhouse supporters felt that this aid, while well intentioned, was encouraging poor people to depend on others to provide life's necessities. Yates argued that "our poor laws are manifestly defective in principle, and mischievous in practice, and that under the imposing and charitable aspect of affording relief exclusively to the poor and infirm, they frequently invite the able-bodied vagrant to partake of the same bounty." Additionally, poorhouse advocates believed the generosity of public outdoor relief and private charity demoralized the working class and encouraged begging. According to Quincy, who was the Overseer of the Poor in Beverly, Massachusetts, outdoor relief was responsible for "diminishing the industry, destroying the economical habits, and eradicating the providence of the labouring class of society." These rugged individualists had the goal of reducing public relief as much as possible.[12]

Several larger towns and cities had built poorhouses, also known as almshouses or houses of industry, by the early 1700s. However, with the increase in poverty in the early 1800s and the corresponding increase in taxes, even more local governments turned to the poorhouse as the most expedient response to poverty. Poorhouses were seen as a cost-effective alternative to public and private relief as they provided room and board for the "worthy poor," encouraged the work ethic of the "able-bodied poor," and reduced tax money spent on individual relief.

Poorhouses were generally built on land adjacent to farms in order to provide an environment that was both compassionate for the "impotent poor" and physically demanding for the "able-bodied poor." There was a mandatory work requirement for all inmates who were fit and strong enough. Alcohol and begging were illegal, and the children were to be schooled. As the historian Seth Rockman noted, the poorhouse followed a strict routine: "Although almshouses were not penal institutions like jails or penitentiaries, they served a disciplinary purpose. Indeed, many localities tried to make their almshouses as inhospitable as possible to discourage the poor from living at the public's expense. Most almshouses regulated the waking hours of their inhabitants, mandating strenuous labor, stipulating a diet of bland food, and limiting opportunities for relaxation." People who supported poorhouses hoped that this physically difficult regimen would frighten away the "undeserving" poor and encourage them to make a living through work. Eventually, by discouraging the able-bodied poor from staying at the poorhouse, taxes would also be reduced. In contrast to Christian social reformers, poorhouse advocates believed that their reforms would not eliminate poverty but would greatly reduce it.[13]

The poorhouse was part of a larger movement to develop secular institutions to deal with the social issues of the day. By the mid-nineteenth century, many specialized institutions were developed to educate youth, reform juvenile delinquents, support the deaf and blind, and provide care for the mentally ill. All of these secular institutions were based on the belief that environmental factors had altered the individual's personality and that if a person was isolated from these negative forces, he or she could be rehabilitated. The rise of these secular institutions coincided with the rise of capitalism, which relied on punctual, predictable, and steady work; no longer were decisions left to the individual about when to work and for how long, as in precapitalist days. Accordingly, these secular institutions mirrored this new work pattern; the poorhouses promoted the work ethic, schools focused on punctuality and regular attendance, and mental hospitals tried to establish order and predictability to promote health.[14]

This focus on reducing poverty through the elimination of sin and sloth tended to obscure arguments for structural solutions. In the 1820s and 1830s, working-class and poor people and their supporters promoted solutions to poverty that focused on political, economic, and educational structures. For example, labor activists like Wilson Pierson and George McFarlane felt that the way to solve poverty was through "union among the working people." They advocated for working-class people to utilize the newly gained right to vote by supporting candidates who promoted working-class interests. However, Pierson and McFarlane were aware that working-class people did not have the benefits of a liberal education, so they called for the development of a national education system where rich and poor received the same education. Frances Wright, editor of the working-class newspaper *Free Enquiry,* called for the development of an education system that went beyond the New England common school curriculum by incorporating all branches of intellectual knowledge, not just reading and writing. As an alternative to solving poverty through education, Matthew Carey proposed paying workers enough to secure the necessities of life (an early version of a living wage proposal). And Thomas Skidmore argued that in order to bring about the equality the American Revolution promised, the inheritance of land should be abolished; when people died, their property should be given to the state in order to be divided up equally among its citizens, thereby redistributing wealth.[15]

Native Americans also advocated for structural change. Many Native Americans had concluded that they were destined to live in poverty if they did not retain their land. Some, like the Shawnee Tecumseh, advocated armed resistance against white encroachment on their lands. Tecumseh traveled from Mississippi to Canada to encourage Native Americans to band together against the white land grab. Tecumseh warned in an 1811 speech to the Choctaws and Chickasaws, "The white usurpation in our common country must be stopped, or we, its rightful owners, be forever destroyed and wiped out as a race of people." For Native Americans, the solution to poverty was to retain control of their land.

Third Annual Report (1819)

Boston Society for the Moral and Religious Instruction of the Poor

The Third Annual Report *concludes with this passage. Previously, the report discussed the Society's state of affairs, such as activities from their five Sabbath schools, distribution of Bibles and tracts, and a financial statement.*

RESPECTED INHABITANTS OF BOSTON,

You have seen, in the preceding pages, what has been attempted for different classes of your townsmen; for seamen, for children of the poor, and for those, whom ignorance and vice have debarred from the blessings of that Christian community, in which a kind Providence has placed their lot. You will not refuse a hearty assent to the following propositions which may be received with the confidence due to great moral and political axioms.

1. Among an ignorant and neglected population, the tendency to vice, crimes, poverty and wretchedness, is strong and rapid.
2. If this tendency be not checked, it not only destroys vast numbers by its direct influence, but endangers the peace and security of every member of society.
3. It is much wiser to prevent crimes by a salutary moral influence, than to rely solely upon punishment.
4. The mere dread of legal punishment never yet effectually deterred abandoned men from the perpetration of gross crimes.

5. But a judicious moral influence has saved multitudes from becoming abandoned; and has thus preserved society from numberless outrages, to which it would otherwise have been exposed.

6. Hence, a wise economy, and a regard to the protection and security of property, require, that the means of moral and religious instruction be furnished to all classes of the community, but especially to the poor.

7. Nine tenths of the pauperism in our country is occasioned by vice; and much the greater part of the public expenses for the support of the poor would be saved, if a great and general effort were made to instruct the ignorant, to encourage industry, and to restrain from the most noxious vices.

8. Under the influence of true benevolence and enlightened public spirit, the inhabitants of a large and wealthy town will provide, by private subscriptions and donations, if either means are not at hand, for the education of poor children, and the stated dissemination of religious truth.

With these things in view is it necessary to urge the claims of the Society, which now addresses you? Is there room for doubt, or hesitation, as to the point, whether the labors of this Society shall be extended, or suffered to languish for want of countenance and support? Rather let it be presumed, that the spontaneous and abundant liberality of the people of this ancient and opulent town will furnish ample means for carrying the benefits of instruction into every destitute neighborhood, and the comforts of industry, peace, and virtue to every fire-side.

Report of the Committee on the Pauper Laws of This Commonwealth (1821)

Quincy Committee

The Quincy Committee was given the task to consider the pauper laws of Massachusetts, and to recommend any changes.

... It was impossible for your Committee, while contemplating the effect of the existing system of poor laws in Massachusetts, not to turn their attention to the state of the same subject, in England. In this part of the British nation, a system of pauper laws prevails, having the same original, and a similar principle with our own; and it will be found not only that the results of her experience are, in a remarkable degree, similar to our own, but, also, that the reasonings and opinions of her statesmen and writers on public economy, founded on that experience, are singularly coincident with the facts detailed, and the opinions expressed, in almost every important document obtained from the returns of the Overseers of the Poor in Massachusetts.

In contemplating these coincidences, the anxiety of your Committee was not allayed, but on the contrary their sense of the vital importance to Massachusetts of adopting a just system upon this subject, was in an extreme degree augmented, by a comparison of the effects of their common pauper system, upon the pecuniary resources of England and upon those of this Commonwealth. The returns of the towns, under the request of the Legislature at their last session, being in point of number but a little more than half of all the towns in the Commonwealth, it is impossible for your Committee to compare the gross aggregate of all the pauper expences of this Commonwealth, with those of Great Britain. But if the proportion of the increase of the payments out of the Treasury of this Commonwealth, for the last twenty years, be taken as an evidence of the proportion of the increase of the pauper burden on Massachusetts, then the proportion of the increase of the pauper burden on Massachusetts has exceeded, in a given number of years, the proportion of the increase of the pauper burden of Great Britain. It appears by an official statement made in the year 1816, to the House of Commons, and published in a report of a select Committee of that House, on the Poor laws, that the proportion of the increase of the British poor rate, between the years 1785 and 1815, was, in round numbers from two millions sterling to five millions; in other words, there was an *increase of three fifths in thirty years.* According to an annexed statement of the Treasurer of Massachusetts, it appears that the increase of the payments out of the Treasury of this State, on pauper accounts, between the years 1801 and 1820, was, in round numbers, from twenty eight thousand dollars, to seventy two thousand;—in other words, *an increase of three fifths in twenty years.* Without pretending to assert that the state of the payments out of the Treasury of the State is a true criterion of the increase of the whole amount of pauper burden, in Massachusetts, your Committee do consider themselves justified by the fact, in concluding that the pernicious consequences of the existing system are palpable, that they are increasing, and that they imperiously call for the interference of the Legislature, in some manner, equally prompt and efficacious.

It is well known to the General Court, that the evils of pauperism, in Great Britain, have of late years, become so desperate and malignant in their nature, as to have been a subject of parliamentary investigation, and that the causes of those evils and their remedies, have been the source of more controversy, and given rise to as great a number of publications, in that nation, as perhaps any other subject whatsoever.

Your Committee, as far as they have had opportunity, have availed themselves of all the light to be derived from those sources, in the prosecution of their researches, and without availing themselves, intentionally, of the language, or particular course of thought of any of the English writers; they ask leave to state, in a very short and abstract way, their general view of the light, derived from these sources, as it concentrates upon, and illustrates certain particular and important points, in the actual condition of pauperism in Massachusetts.

The principle of pauper laws is that of a state, or public, or, as sometimes called, a compulsory provision for the poor. The poor are of two classes. 1. The impotent poor; in which denomination are included all, who are wholly incapable of work, through old age, infancy, sickness or corporeal debility. 2. The able poor; in which denomination are included all, who are capable of work, of some nature, or other; but differing in the degree of their capacity, and in the kind of work, of which they are capable.

With the respect to the first class; that of poor, absolutely impotent, were there none other than this class, there would be little difficulty, either as to the principle, or as to the mode of extending relief.

But another class exists; that of the able poor; in relation to which, and from the difficulty of discriminating between this class and the former, and of apportioning the degree of public provision to the degree of actual impotency, arise all the objections to the principle of the existing pauper system. The evils, also, which are attributed to this system, of diminishing the industry, destroying the economical habits and eradicating the providence of the labouring class of society may all be referred to the same source;—the difficulty of discriminating between the able poor and the impotent poor and of apportioning the degree of public provision to the degree of actual impotency.

This difficulty, cannot, apparently, be removed by any legislative provision. There must be, in the nature of things, numerous and minute shades of difference between, the pauper, who, through impotency, can do absolutely nothing, and the pauper, who is able to do something, but that, very little. Nor does the difficulty of discrimination, proportionally, diminish as the ability, in any particular pauper, to do something, increases. There always must exist, so many circumstances of age, sex, previous habits, muscular, or mental, strength, to be taken into the account, that society is absolutely incapable to fix any standard, or to prescribe any rule, by which the claim of right to the benefit of the public provision shall absolutely be determined. The consequence is that the admission, or rejection, of the claim to such relief is necessarily left to the discretion of Overseers; or to those, who are entrusted by law, with the distribution of the public charity.

The necessity of entrusting this discretion, the class of society to which it must be entrusted, and the circumstances and feelings, under which such distribution must be made, are the proximate causes of the evils, resulting from a public, or compulsory, provision for the poor.

From the nature of things, this discretion will always be entrusted to men in good, generally in easy, circumstances; that is, to the prosperous class of society. "The humanity natural to this class, will never see the poor, in any thing like want, when that want is palpably and visibly brought before it, without extending relief." Much less will this be the case, when they have means, placed in their hands by society itself, applicable to this very purpose. In executing the trust, they will, almost unavoidably, be guided by sentiments of pity and compassion, and be very little influenced by the consideration of the effect of the facility, or fullness, of provision, to encourage habits of idleness, dissipation, and extravagance among the class, which labor. "They first give necessaries, then comforts; and often, in the end, pamper, rather than relieve."

If the means, placed under their control, are confined to provision for the poor, in public poor, or alms houses, the effect of these dispositions and feelings appears in the ease, with which admission is obtained; the kindness with which the poor are treated, during their residence, and in the superiority of the food of the public table, to that, to which they have been accustomed. If those means consist in funds, the same temper and feelings predominate, in their distribution. It is laborious to ascertain the exact merit of each applicant. Supply is sometimes excessive; at others misplaced. The poor begin to consider it as a right; next, they calculate upon it as an income. The stimulus to industry and economy is annihilated, or weakened; temptations to extravagance and dissipation are increased, in proportion as public supply is likely, or certain, or desirable. The just pride of independence, so honorable to man, in every condition, is thus corrupted by the certainty of public provision; and is either weakened, or destroyed according to the facility of its attainment, or its amount.

Views of this kind, connected with the experience of England, under the operation of her poor laws, have led some of her most distinguished statesmen and writers on public economy, to denounce all public, or compulsory provision for the poor, as increasing the evil they pretend to remedy, and augmenting the misery they undertake to prevent. Thus the Earl of Sheffield, in his observations on the English poor laws, published in 1818, declares, that "the tendency of all parochial relief is to encourage the worthless and audacious; to suppress the feelings of pity towards the poor; to lessen their honest exertions; to deprave their morals; to destroy the notions of a provident spirit; to multiply their number; offering a premium for indolence, prodigality, and vice; and stopping that course of things, by which want leads to labor, labor to comfort, the knowledge of comfort to industry, and its consequent virtues, and neglecting that respectable poverty, which shrinks from public view; it encourages all those abominable arts, which make beggary and parish relief a better trade than labor."

The celebrated Henry Brougham, also, in a letter to Sir Samuel Romilly, published in the same year, on the abuse of public charities, lays it down as "a principle, which will admit of no contradiction, that the existence of any permanent fund for the support of the poor, the appropriation of any revenue, however raised, which must be peremptorily expended, in maintaining such as have no other means of subsistence, has, upon the whole, a direct tendency to increase their numbers." To the class of funds "directly productive of paupers," he refers "all revenues of alms houses, hospitals, and schools, where children are supported as well as educated; all yearly sums to be given away to mendicants, or poor families; and above all, the statutory provision for the poor itself."

Your Committee in placing, in this strong light the objections to the entire principle of our existing pauper laws, have had no intention to recommend, nor any idea that their investigations would ultimately result in, an abolition of those laws altogether in Massachusetts. But they have been induced to this statement from a consideration that to any effectual attempt to ameliorate the present system of the Pauper laws a distinct apprehension of the nature of the objections to them should be attained; and the real nature of the evils as well as the manner, in which the causes, which induce them, operate, should be known and made familiar to our fellow citizens. It is apparent, also, not only from the remarks of the Overseers of the Poor, of the Town of Richmond, in the document annexed, but also from expressions in returns from other towns, that a similar train of thoughts exists in some parts of this Commonwealth.

Taking it for granted, therefore, that the present system of making some public, or compulsory provision for the poor is too deeply rivetted in the affections, or the moral sentiment of our people to be loosened by theories, however plausible, or supported by, however high names, or at authority; your Committee next turned their attention to the various modes, which, it appeared by the returns from the various Overseers of the Poor in this Commonwealth, had been adopted in different towns and compared the results of their experience, with that of Great Britain; so far as they had the means of such comparison. Your Committee found these modes to be four.

1. Provision for the poor, by letting them out to the lowest bidder, in families at large, within the town.

2. Provision, by letting them to the lowest bidder, together; that is, all to one person.
3. Provision, by supplies, in money, or articles, at their own houses.
4. Provision, by poor, or alms, houses.

As to the first mode, your Committee do not consider it as of a nature to require much examination, or analysis. It is obviously applicable only to very small towns. That it is exceptionable, in its principle, is well illustrated, by the reflections of the Overseers of the Poor of the Town of Danvers, annexed to this report. And how liable to abuses it is, may be gathered from the remarks of those of the Town of Chilmark, who state, "that in that town the average expense of supporting adults and children is about one dollar and thirty cents per head, per week; this," they add, "we consider a large sum, but *the poor being sometimes boarded with those, who are in want themselves, it is not lost to the town.*"

As to the second mode, it partakes of the character of the preceding. It is also, as is well observed by the Overseers of the Town of Sutton, "an approximation to the method of supporting them in a poor house and is a diminution of the expense." It is obviously more unexceptionable, in other respects, than boarding them to the lowest bidder at large.

As to the third mode, provision for the poor, by supplies of money, or articles, at their own houses, the result of the experience of England is unequivocally stated to be, that "the discretion of the Overseers of the Poor, exercised in this way has been the source of abuse, mismanagement and waste; that supplies, if given in money, are mischievous and often misapplied; when given for necessaries, as expended by the men, in ale, and by the women, for tea and sugar; that when given in articles of food and clothing, they were often sold to obtain luxuries, encouraged other applications, checked exertion and promoted habits of indolence and dissipation; and that the great object of English policy ought to be to eradicate this mode of parish support." ...

As to the fourth and last mode: Provision by poor, or alms, houses, the experience of England has resulted in this, that "in every case, where means of work were connected with such houses, in united districts, and when they have been superintended by the principal inhabitants, they have been greatly beneficial. This has been done in various parts of England, by a number of parishes being united into one district, with evident good effect, both as it respects the better condition of the poor, and also as to the reduction of the expense." ...

Upon the whole, your Committee apprehend that the experience both of England and of Massachusetts concur in the five following results, which may be well adopted as principles, in relation to the whole subject.

1. That of all modes of providing for the poor, the most wasteful, the most expensive, and most injurious to their morals and destructive of their industrious habits is that of supply in their own families.
2. That the most economical mode is that of Alms Houses; having the character of Work Houses, or Houses of Industry, in which work is provided for every degree of ability in the pauper; and thus the able poor made to provide, partially, at least for their own support; and also to the support, or at least the comfort of the impotent poor.
3. That of all modes of employing the labor of the pauper, agriculture affords the best, the most healthy, and the most certainly profitable; the poor being thus enabled, to raise, always, at least their own provisions.
4. That the success of these establishments depends upon their being placed under the superintendance of a Board of Overseers, constituted of the most substantial and intelligent inhabitants of the vicinity.
5. That of all causes of pauperism, intemperance, in the use of spirituous liquors, is the most powerful and universal....

While, therefore, your Committee on the one hand are of opinion, that no subject more imperiously claims the attention and solicitude of the Legislature:—that it is the duty of society by general arrangements, to attempt to diminish the increase of pauperism, as well as to make provision for that which is inevitable;—that diminution of the evil, is best, and most surely to be effected by making Alms Houses, Houses of Industry, and not abodes of idleness, and denying for the most part all supply from public provision, except on condition of admission into the public institution;—and that of all modes of employing the industry of the poor, the best is in agriculture; yet on the other hand, they are also of opinion, that no ultimate system should be founded upon these principles, until they have been laid before their fellow citizens, for their contemplation. Certainty and general satisfaction, being, in cases of this nature, much more important than expedition....

Address of the Association of Working People (1829)

Wilson Pierson and George McFarlane

This article appeared in the Free Enquirer, *a working-class newspaper.*

FELLOW CITIZENS AND FELLOW LABORERS,

The Association of Working People having at length become organised, have deemed it expedient to address you, with a view of making known to you their intentions and at the same time engaging your assistance in carrying their views into effect.

The Working People have been emphatically denominated the "bone and sinew" of the body politic; and this is true, inasmuch as they are the most numerous and at the same time the most useful of all classes into which men are divided; it being by them that all things are made, that are made for the use of man, by the power of art in peace; and they forming in war their country's principal and sure defence; while to say the least, *some* of the other classes are mere drones in the hive, who not only live upon the product of the working man's labor, but in fact, appropriate a much larger share to themselves, than the producer himself is able to enjoy.

And, Fellow Citizens, why are these things so? Why is it that one class of men are sunk so far below the rest, in a country which has declared to the universe, that "all men are created free and equal?" Have we not laws to secure to us that "Freedom and Equality" to obtain which our forefathers opposed the legions of Britain in the dark days of the Revolution? No! the poor have no laws; the laws are made by the rich, and of course *for* the rich.

It is a lamentable fact, that though we are nominally a "governing and self governed people," still there are a privileged few who lord it over us as though we were not fit to claim an equality with them, treating us as though we were made of different and less costly materials than they, even while we have been the means of their advancement; making us, as it were, the ladder by which they climb into office; and when they have arrived at the desired height, kicking the ladder down.

The question that naturally arises is, how are these things to be remedied? We answer by *union among the working people.* Too long have we slumbered! and "remember that it was while sleeping that Sampson was shorn of his locks." Too long have ye been the willing dupes of the demon, party spirit; too long have ye neglected your own interest and suffered yourselves to be led away by the "magic of a name;" giving your suffrages to men who have looked down from the height to which you exalted them, with the most sovereign contempt for your blindness to your own interests.

Arise then in your strength, and when called upon to exercise the distinctive privilege of a *freeman*, the "elective franchise," give your votes to no man who is not pledged to support your interests. You will ask where are we to find such men? Are not the interests of the non-producing classes in direct opposition to the interests of the laborer? And is it not in the ranks of these classes, that we are accustomed to find men best qualified for the office of Legislators, as but few of our own class have received the benefits of a liberal education?

We can but answer, True: and pity, that it is true. But at the same time we ask again, why are these things so? Is it not because the funds that should have been appropriated to a rational system of general education at the expense of the state, have been shamefully squandered and misapplied, and instead of being expended in the cause of true Internal Improvement, in the improvement of the minds of the rising generation, they have been lavished for purposes of minor importance, while what little has been done towards a system of General Education, has been handed out as the dole of charity, and as such has been refused by all who though poor in worldly goods, are rich in an *independent republican spirit* which scorns to receive as a favor what it should demand as a right.

Let us then, Fellow Citizens, shake off the torpor of sloth and inactivity, which has so long held us in ignominious thraldom; let every man come forward and use his utmost exertions to produce a system of instruction where the children of the rich and the poor shall be placed upon a level, and shall receive a National Education calculated to make *republicans* and banish *aristocrats,* which will never be the case, while our State Legislatures erect and endow Seminaries, Colleges and Academies, for the rich, and dole out charity schools for the poor....

Now! then, is the accepted time, and now is the day of your political salvation. Come forward with one accord, and show to the world, that you are in very deed what you profess to be, FREEMEN; and woe! to the traitor who would wish to brand you SLAVES.

Existing Evils and Their Remedy (1829)

Frances Wright

In addition to being an editor of the Free Enquirer, *Wright was renowned for being an outspoken lecturer when women were not supposed to speak in public, and the first to advocate for free public schools for all children.*

... I am addressing the people of Philadelphia—the people of a city where Jefferson penned the glorious declaration which awoke this nation and the world—the city, where the larum so astounding to tyranny, so fraught with hope, and joy, and exulting triumph to humankind, was first sounded in the ears of Americans. I speak to the descendants of those men who heard from the steps of their old state house the principles of liberty and equality first proclaimed to man. I speak to the inhabitants of a city founded by the most peaceful, the most humane, and the most practical of all Christian sects. I speak to mechanics who are uniting for the discovery of their interests and the protection of their rights. I speak to a public whose benevolence has been long harrowed by increasing pauperism, and whose social order and social happiness are threatened by increasing vice. I speak to sectarians who are weary of sectarianism. I speak to honest men who tremble for their honesty. I speak to the dishonest whose integrity has fallen before the discouragements waiting upon industry; and who, by slow degrees, or in moments of desperation, have forsaken honest labor, because without a reward, for fraudulent speculation, because it promised one chance of success to a thousand chances of ruin. I speak to parents anxious for their offspring—to husbands who, while shortening their existence by excess of labor, foresee, at their death, not sorrow alone, but unrequited industry and hopeless penury, involving shame and perhaps infamy, for their oppressed widows and unprotected children. I speak to human beings surrounded by human suffering—to fellow citizens pledged to fellow feeling—to republicans pledged to equal rights, and, as a consequent, to equal condition and equal enjoyments; and I call them—oh, would that my voice were loud to reach every ear, and persuasive to reach every heart!—I call them TO UNITE; and to unite for the consideration of the evils around us—for the discovery and application of their remedy.

Dreadful has been the distress exhibited during the past year, not in this city only, but in every city throughout the whole extent of this vast republic. Long had the mass of evil been accumulating ere it attracted attention, and, would we understand how far the plague spot is to spread, or what is to be its termination, we must look to Europe.

We are fast travelling in the footsteps of Europe, my friends; for her principles of action are ours. We have in all our habits and usages the same vices, and, with these same vices, we must have, as we see we have, the same evils.

The great principles stamped in America's declaration of independence are true, are great, are sublime, and are *all her own.* But her usages, her law, her religion, her education, are false, narrow, prejudiced, ignorant, and are the relic of dark ages—the gift and bequeathment of king-governed, priest-ridden nations, whose supremacy, indeed, the people of America have challenged and overthrown, but whose example they are still following....

Sparta, when she conceived her democracy, commenced with educational equality; when she aimed at national union, she cemented that union in childhood—at the public board, in the gymnasium, in the temple, in the common habits, common feelings, common duties, and common condition. And so, not-withstanding all the errors with which her institutions were fraught, and all the vices which arose out of those errors, did she present for ages, a wondrous sample of democratic union, and consequently of national prosperity?

What, then, is wanted here? What Sparta had—*a national education*. And what Sparta, in many respects, had not—*a rational education*.

Hitherto, my friends, in government as in every branch of morals, we have but too much mistaken words for truths and forms for principles. To render men free, it sufficeth not to proclaim their liberty; to make them equal, it sufficeth not to call them so. True, the 4th of July '76 commenced a new era for our race. True, the sun of promise then rose upon the world. But let us not mistake for the fulness of light what was but its harbinger. Let us not conceive that man in signing the declaration of his rights secured their possession; that having framed the theory he had not, and hath not still, the practice to seek.

Your fathers, indeed, on the day from which dates your existence as a nation, opened the gates of the temple of human liberty. But think not they entered, nor that you have entered, the sanctuary. They passed not, nor have you passed, even the threshold.

Who speaks of liberty while the human mind is in chains? Who of equality while the thousands are in squalid wretchedness, the millions harrassed with health-destroying labor, the few afflicted with health-destroying idleness, and all tormented by health-destroying solicitude? Look abroad on the misery which is gaining on the land! Mark the strife, and the discord, and the jealousies, the shock of interests and opinions, the hatreds of sect, the estrangements of class, the pride of wealth, the debasement of poverty, the helplessness of youth unprotected, of age uncomforted, of industry unrewarded, of ignorance un-enlightened, of vice unreclaimed, of misery unpitied, of sickness, hunger, and nakedness unsatisfied, unalleviated, and unheeded. Go! mark all the wrongs and the wretchedness with which the eye and the ear and the heart are familiar, and then echo in triumph and celebrate in jubilee the insulting declaration—*all men are free and equal!* ...

In this nation, any more than in any other nation, the mass has never re-flected for the mass; the people, as a body, have never addressed themselves to the study of their own condition, and to the just and fair interpretation of their common interests. And, as it was with their national independence, shall it be with their national happiness—it shall be found only when the mass shall seek it. No people have ever received liberty *in gift*. Given, it were not appreci-ated; it were not understood. Won without exertion, it were lost as readily. Let the people of America recal the ten years of war and tribulation by which they purchased their national independence. Let efforts as strenuous be now made, not with the sword of steel, indeed, but with the sword of the spirit, and their farther enfranchisement from poverty, starvation, and dependence must be equally successful.

Great reforms are not wrought in a day. Evils which are the accumulated results of accumulated errors, are not to be struck down at a blow by the rod of a magician. A free people may boast that all power is in their hands; but no effectual power can be in their hands until knowledge be in their minds.

But how may knowledge be imparted to their minds? Such effective knowledge as shall render apparent to all the interests of all, and demonstrate the simple truths—that a nation to be strong, must be united; to be united, must be equal in condition; to be equal in condition, must he similar in habits and in feeling; to be similar in habits and in feeling, *must be raised in national institutions as the children of a common family, and citizens of a common country.* ...

The noble example of New England has been imitated by other states, until all not possessed of common schools blush for the popular remissness. But, after all, how can common schools, under their best form, and in fullest supply, effect even the purpose which they have in view?

The object proposed by common schools (if I rightly understand it) is to impart to the whole population those means for the acquirement of knowledge which are in common use: reading and writing. To these are added arithmetic, and, occasionally perhaps, some imperfect lessons in the simpler sciences. But, I would ask, supposing these institutions should even be made to embrace all the branches of intellectual knowledge, and, thus, science offered gratis to all the children of the land, how are the children of the very class, for whom we suppose the schools instituted, to be supplied with food and raiment, or instructed in the trade necessary to their future subsistence, while they are following these studies? How are they, I ask, to be fed and clothed, when, as all facts show, the labor of the parents is often insufficient for their own sustenance, and, almost universally, inadequate to the provision of the family without the united efforts of all its members? In your manufacturing districts you have children worked for twelve hours a day; and, in the rapid and certain progress of the existing system, you will soon have them, as in England, *worked to death,* and yet unable, through the period of their miserable existence, to earn a pittance sufficient to satisfy the cravings of hunger. ...

In the beginning, and until all debt was cleared off and so long as the same should be found favorable to the promotion of these best palladiums of a nation's happiness, a double tax might be at once expedient and politic.

First, a moderate tax per head for every child, to be laid upon its parents conjointly or divided between them, due attention being always paid to the varying strength of the two sexes, and to the undue depreciation which now rests on female labor. The more effectually to correct the latter injustice, as well as to consult the convenience of the industrious classes generally, this parental tax might be rendered payable either in money, or in labor, produce, or domestic manufactures, and should be continued for each child until the age when juvenile labor should be found, on the average, equivalent to the educational expenses, which, I have reason to believe, would be at twelve years.

This first tax on parents to embrace equally the whole population; as, however moderate, it would inculcate a certain forethought in all the human family; more especially where it is most wanted—in young persons, who, before they assumed the responsibility of parents, would estimate their fitness to meet it.

The second tax to be on property, increasing in percentage with the wealth of the individual. In this manner I conceive the rich would contribute according to their riches, to the relief of the poor, and to the support of the state, by raising up its best bulwark—an enlightened and united generation....

The Rights of Man to Property! (1829)

Thomas Skidmore

This piece has been excerpted from Thomas Skidmore's book of the same title.

Plan

Let a new State-Convention be assembled. Let it prepare a new Constitution, and let that Constitution, after having been adopted by the people, decree an abolition of all debts; both at home and abroad, between citizen and citizen; and between citizen and foreigner. Let it renounce all property belonging to our citizens, without the State. Let it claim all property within the State, both real and personal, of whatever kind it may be, with the exception of that belonging to resident aliens, and with the further exception of so much personal property, as may be in the possession of transient owners, not being citizens. Let it order an equal division of all this property among the citizens, of and over the age of maturity, in manner yet to be directed. Let it order all transfers or removals of property, except so much as may belong to transient owners, to cease, until the division is accomplished....

Nor is it to be said, even as things are now, that it is the dead who ever give property to their successors, after all. IT IS NOT THEY WHO GIVE: they have power to do nothing: for, if they had, many of them would carry it away with them to another world, if any such there be. It is THE LIVING who give the present holders of property the possession of it; *it is we ourselves,* (for in us and us alone, rests the title,) who have done it; and who yet allow it to be said, and hardly without contradiction from us, that others have done it: it is a mistake: IT IS NONE BUT THE GENERATION PRESENT,—that gives, to what are called heirs, the possessions they enjoy; without this gift, this unjust and undeserved gift, they could not and would not have it at all! It is in OUR POWER, then, to CALL BACK the gift, whenever we shall think fit! That NOW IS THE TIME, need not further be shown; for in showing that ALL MEN HAVE EQUAL RIGHTS, as well TO PROPERTY, as to life and liberty, every thing is shown that is requisite. The time for *acting* on these principles is, when they are seen to be true; whenever they find a confirmation of their correctness in every human breast.

It remains then now, to speak more particularly of the methods which will be found most convenient in practice, to bring about the General Division in question. It may appear at first view, to be a matter of great difficulty to do it, however just and proper it may, in itself, be.

But on examination, it will be found to be of very easy execution, although it is a subject interwoven with the concerns, with the multiplex concerns, of more than two millions of people. But when so important an object as the re-possession of man's rights, is to be achieved, means will be found which were scarcely imagined to be in existence. And that so great a work, can be so easily done, is, I think, one of the strongest proofs of the genuine character of the rights in question.

I shall suppose, however, that the course I recommend to be pursued, is the one which shall be adopted, and that the details necessary to execute it, will be much of the character, which I now proceed to describe. If the reader shall think that the measure of disavowing all debts, &c. &c. is too bold and daring, let him suspend his opinion, till I have an opportunity to show him, that both justice and policy demand it; that in its operation it will be found to injure no one's just rights; and that it is the cheapest, surest, readiest way in which he can obtain his own rights. The first of these details consists in an universal suspension of all business, except in so much as is necessary for subsistence, until the whole can be accomplished. All persons having domicil or residence, will remain where they are. Those who have not any fixed residence, and many unhappily there are, especially in cities; a grievous evil, this, growing out of the present system of the rights of property, will have such residence provided for them. All without distinction will have food and fire, (perhaps after the manner of rations) furnished to them, at the expense of the State, until the division is accomplished....

If a man were to ask me, to what I would compare the unequal distribution of property which prevails in the world, and has ever prevailed, I would say, that it reminds me of a large party of gentlemen, who should have a common right to dine at one and the same public table; a part of whom should arrive first, sit down and eat what they chose; and then, because the remaining part came later to dinner, should undertake to monopolize the whole; and deprive them of the opportunity of satisfying their hunger, but upon terms such as those who had feasted, should be pleased to prescribe.

Such, now, is the actual condition of the whole human race. Those who have gone before us, have been the first to sit down to the table, and to enjoy themselves, without interruption, from those who came afterwards; and not content with this enjoyment, they have disposed of the whole dinner, in such a manner, that nine-tenths of the beings that now people this globe, have not wherewith to dine, but upon terms such as these first monopolisers, or those to whom they pretend they have conferred their own power as successors, shall choose to dictate. It is, as if, after dining till they were satisfied, a general scramble ensued, for what remained on the table; and those who succeeded in filling their pockets and other receptacles, with provisions, should have something to give to their children; but those who should have the misfortune to get none, or having got it, should lose it again, through fraud, calamity, or force, should have none for theirs, to the latest generation....

It has been shown already, throughout these pages, that *title* to property exists for all; and for all alike; not because others have been; nor because they have *not* been; not because they had a certain being for a parent, rather than another being; not because they appear later, or earlier, on the stage of life, than others; not because of purchase, of conquest, of preoccupancy, or what not; but BECAUSE THEY ARE: BECAUSE THEY EXIST. I AM; THEREFORE IS PROPERTY MINE; as much so as any man's, and that without asking any man's permission; without paying any man price; without knowing or caring farther than as my equal right extends, whether any other human being exists, or not. Such is the language of nature; such is the language of right; and such are the principles which will justify any people in pulling down any government; which denies, even to a *single* individual of the human race, his possession, his real tangible possession, of this unalienable right of nature; or its unquestionable equivalent. How much more so, then, is it the duty of any such people, to destroy their own government, when *more than nine-tenths*, it may be, are deprived of rights which the Creator gave them, when he gave them existence? ...

Take away from the possessors of the world their dividends, their rents, their profits; in one word, that which they receive for the *use* of it, and which belongs, freely belongs, to one as much as another; and what would become of the present miserable condition of the human race? It would be annihilated forever. But these dividends, these rents, these profits, these prices paid for the use of the world, or of the world's materials, will never cease to be paid, till the *possession* of these materials is made equal, or substantially equal, among all men; till there shall be no lenders, no borrowers; no landlords, no tenants; no masters, no journeymen; no Wealth, no Want....

I approach, then, the close of this Work. I hasten to commit it to the hands, the heads and the hearts of those for whose benefit it is written. It is to them that I look, for the *power* necessary, to bring the system it recommends into existence. If they shall think I have so far understood myself, and the subject I have undertaken to discuss, as to have perceived, and marked out the path that leads them to the enjoyment of their rights, their interests and their happiness, IT WILL BE FOR THOSE WHO ARE SUFFERING THE EVILS, of which I have endeavored to point out the causes and the remedies, TO LEAD THE WAY. Those who are enjoying the sweets of the labor of others, will have no hearts to feel for the misery which the present system occasions. And the first throe of pain, which they *will* feel, will be that of *alarm,* that they are soon to be ordered to riot on the toils of others no more for ever! But those who *suffer,* will feel no cause of alarm. The very intensity of their sufferings, since now they understand their origin and cure, will add double vigor to their exertions to recover their rights. But let them understand, that much is to be done, to accomplish this recovery. IT IS TO BE THE RESULT OF THE COMBINED EXERTIONS, OF GREAT NUMBERS OF MEN. These, by no means, *now* understand their true situation; but when they do, they will be ready and willing to do what belongs to their happiness. If, then, there be truth; if there be reason; if there be force of argument, in the work which I thus commit to the hands of those for whose benefit it is written; let them read; let it be read; let it be conversed about, in the hearing of those whose *interest* it is, to hear whatever of truth, of reason, and argument it may contain; and *as often,* too, as there may be opportunity. Let them awake to a *knowledge* of their rights, and how they may be obtained, and they will not be slow (since it will *then* be so easy) to reclaim them.

Let the poor and middling classes understand that their oppressions come from the overgrown wealth that exists among them, on the one hand, and from entire destitution on the other; and that as this overgrown wealth is continually augmenting its possessions, in a rapid ratio, the public sufferings are continually augmenting also; and must continue to augment, until the equal and unalienable rights of the people shall order otherwise. Let the parent reflect, if he be now a man of toil, that his children must be, ninety-nine cases in a hundred, slaves, *and worse,* to some rich proprietor; and that there is no alternative, but the change proposed. Let him not cheat himself with empty pretensions; for, *he who commands the property of a State, or even an inordinate portion of it,* HAS THE LIBERTY AND THE HAPPINESS OF ITS CITIZENS IN HIS OWN KEEPING. And if there be some dozen, or fifty, or five hundred of these large proprietors, they are neither more nor less than so many additional keepers. He who can feed me, or starve me; give me employment, or bid me wander about in idleness; is my master; and it is the utmost folly for me to boast of being any thing but a slave.

In fine, let the people awake to their rights; let them understand in what they consist; let them see the course they must pursue to obtain them; let them follow up that course, by informing each as many as he can, his fellow citizens, of the truth which this Work contains; let all co-operate, in the early and effectual accomplishment of the objects it recommends, and these objects will easily and speedily be achieved, and none will have labored in vain....

Sleep Not Longer, O Choctaws and Chickasaws (1811)

Tecumseh

Tecumseh delivered this speech in the hopes of attracting Choctaws and Chickasaws to fight alongside other Native Americans against the United States.

"In view of questions of vast importance, have we met together in solemn council to-night. Nor should we here debate whether we have been wronged and injured, but by what measures we should avenge ourselves; for our merciless oppressors, having long since planned out their proceedings, are not about to make, but have and are still making attacks upon those of our race who have as yet come to no resolution. Nor are we ignorant by what steps, and by what gradual advances, the whites break in upon our neighbors. Imagining themselves to be still undiscovered they show themselves the less audacious because you are insensible. The whites are already nearly a match for us united, and too strong for any one tribe alone to resist; so that unless we support one another with our collective and united forces; unless every tribe unanimously combines to give a check to the ambition and avarice of the whites, they will soon conquer us apart and disunited, and we will be driven away from our native country and scattered as autumnal leaves before the wind.

"But have we not courage enough remaining to defend our country and maintain our ancient independence? Will we calmly suffer the white intruders and tyrants to enslave us? Shall it be said of our race that we knew not how to extricate ourselves from the three most to be dreaded calamities—folly, inactivity and cowardice? But what need is there to speak of the past? It speaks for itself and asks, 'Where to-day is the Pequod? Where the Narragansetts, the Mohawks, Pocanokets, and many other once powerful tribes of our race? They have vanished before the avarice and oppression of the white men, as snow before a summer sun. In the vain hope of alone defending their ancient possessions, they have fallen in the wars with the white men. Look abroad over their once beautiful country, and what see you now? Naught but the ravages of the pale-face destroyers meet your eyes. So it will be with you Choctaws and Chickasaws! Soon your mighty forest trees, under the shade of whose wide spreading branches you have played in infancy, sported in boyhood, and now rest your wearied limbs after the fatigue of the chase, will be cut down to fence in the land which the white intruders dare to call their own. Soon their broad roads will pass over the grave of your fathers, and the place of their rest will be blotted out forever. The annihilation of our race is at hand unless we unite in one common cause against the common foe. Think not, brave Choctaws and Chickasaws, that you can remain passive and indifferent to the common danger, and thus escape the common fate. Your people too, will soon be as falling leaves and scattering clouds before their blighting breath. You too will be driven away from your native land and ancient domains as leaves are driven before the wintry storms."

These were corroding words; and well might terrible thoughts of resistance pass through the minds of those freemen and patriots, as, by the light of the burning heap gleaming through the darkness of the night, they in admiring silence gazed upon the face of Tecumseh and listened to his untaught eloquence, which thrilled and swayed their hearts and moved the deep waters of their souls, as he plead the cause of right from the vindications of his own heart upon which was written the statute—"A favor for a favor, an injury for an injury."

"Sleep not longer, O Choctaws and Chickasaws," continued the indefatigable orator, "in false security and delusive hopes. Our broad domains are fast escaping from our grasp. Every year our white intruders become more greedy, exacting, oppressive and overbearing. Every year contentions spring up between them and our people and when blood is shed we have to make atonement whether right or wrong, at the cost of the lives of our greatest chiefs, and the yielding up of large tracts of our lands. Before the pale-faces came among us, we enjoyed the happiness of unbounded freedom, and were acquainted with neither riches, wants, nor oppression. How is it now? Wants and oppressions are our lot; for are we not controlled in everything, and dare we move without asking, by your leave? Are we not being stripped day by day of the little that remains of our ancient liberty? Do they not even now kick and strike us as they do their black-faces? How long will it be before they will tie us to a post and whip us, and make us work for them in their corn fields as they do them? Shall we wait for that moment or shall we die fighting before submitting to such ignominy?"

At this juncture a low, muffled groan of indignation forced its way through the clinched teeth running through the entire assembly, and some of the younger warriors, no longer enabled to restrain themselves, leaped from their seats upon the ground, and, accompanying the act with the thrilling war-whoops of defiance, flourished their tomahawks in a frenzy of rage. Tecumseh turned his eyes upon them with a calm but rebuking look, which spoke but too well his disapproval of such an undignified and premature display of feelings, which had interrupted him; then with a gentle wave of the hand, the interpretation of which was not very difficult, he again continued: "Have we not for years had before our eyes a sample of their designs, and are they not sufficient harbingers of their future determinations? Will we not soon be driven from our respective countries and the graves of our ancestors? Will not the bones of our dead be plowed up, and their graves be turned into fields? Shall we calmly wait until they become so numerous that we will no longer be able to resist oppression? Will we wait to be destroyed in our turn, without making an effort worthy our race? Shall we give up our homes, our country, bequeathed to us by the Great Spirit, the graves of our dead, and everything that is dear and sacred to us, without a struggle? I know you will cry with me, Never! Never! Then let us by unity of action destroy them all, which we now can do, or drive them back whence they came. War or extermination is now our only choice. Which do you choose? I know your answer. Therefore, I now call on you, brave Choctaws and Chickasaws, to assist in the just cause of liberating our race from the grasp of our faithless invaders and heartless oppressors. The white usurpation in our common country must be stopped, or we, its rightful owners, be forever destroyed and wiped out as a race of people. I am now at the head of many warriors backed by the strong arm of English soldiers. Choctaws and Chickasaws, you have too long borne with grievous usurpation inflicted by the arrogant Americans. Be no longer their dupes. If there be one here to-night who believes that his rights will not sooner or later, be taken from him by the avaricious American pale-faces, his ignorance ought to excite pity, for he knows little of the character of our common foe. And if there be one among you mad enough to undervalue the growing power of the white race among us, let him tremble in considering the fearful woes he will bring down upon our entire race, if by his criminal indifference he assists the designs of our common enemy against our common country. Then listen to the voice of duty, of honor, of nature and of your endangered country. Let us form one body, one heart, and defend to the last warrior our country, our homes, our liberty, and the graves of our fathers."

Choctaws and Chickasaws, you are among the few of our race who sit indolently at ease. You have indeed enjoyed the reputation of being brave, but will you be indebted for it more from report than fact? Will you let the whites encroach upon your domains even to your very door before you will assert your rights in resistance? Let no one in this council imagine that I speak more from malice against the pale-face Americans than just grounds of complaint. Complaint is just toward friends who have failed in their duty; accusation is against enemies guilty of injustice. And surely, if any people ever had, we have good and just reasons to believe we have ample grounds to accuse the Americans of injustice; especially when such great acts of injustice have been committed by them upon our race, of which they seem to have no manner of regard, or even to reflect. They are a people fond of innovations, quick to contrive and quick to put their schemes into effectual execution, no matter how great the wrong and injury to us; while we are content to preserve what we already have. Their designs are to enlarge their possessions by taking yours in turn; and will you, can you longer dally, O Choctaws and Chickasaws? Do you imagine that that people will not continue longest in the enjoyment of peace who timely prepare to vindicate themselves, and manifest a determined resolution to do themselves right whenever they are wronged? Far otherwise. Then haste to the relief of our common cause, as by consanguinity of blood you are bound; lest the day be not far distant when you will be left single-handed and alone to the cruel mercy of our most inveterate foe."

Though the North American Indians never expressed their emotions by any audible signs whatever, yet the frowning brows, and the flashing eyes of that mighty concourse of seated and silent men told Tecumseh, as he closed and took his seat upon the ground among his warriors, that he had touched a thousand chords whose vibrations responded in tones that were in perfect unison and harmony with his own, and he fully believed, and correctly too, that he had accomplished the mission whereunto, he was sent, even beyond his most sanguine hopes and expectations....

Epilogue: Outcomes

Moral reformers were unsuccessful in reducing poverty during the Second Great Awakening. In the face of this failure, moral reformers turned toward patriarchal, professional, and bureaucratic solutions. As historian Michael Katz put it, the "evangelical, feminine tone had been transmuted into a harsher, moralistic, bureaucratic, male proto-professional campaign aimed more at the behavior of the poor than at their souls." Men began to take over responsibility for fund-raising and operating the day-to-day activities of formerly women-run Christian associations that served the poor. Male full-time staff replaced female volunteers and part-time staff; when women did participate, it was in a secondary role.[16]

The poorhouse, the most prominent response to poverty by local governments, was initially seen as a great success. Indeed, the states that had most aggressively built poorhouses in the early 1800s—Pennsylvania, Delaware, Rhode Island, and Virginia—all reported a reduction in the number of "paupers." In addition, tax savings were reported; for example, one local community in New York had reduced its spending on the poor by one-third. However, by mid-century, there was growing concern that poorhouses were not living up to their promise as a humane, reformatory institution. In South Carolina in 1857, commissioners of the poor were shocked to see the Charleston poorhouse in a state of filth and neglect, the beds filled with vermin, the bathrooms covered in filth, and the floors unwashed. At the same time, a select committee from the New York Senate reported that "the poorhouses throughout the State may be generally described as badly constructed, ill-arranged, ill-warmed, and ill-ventilated. The rooms are crossed with inmates; and the air, particularly in the sleeping apartments, is very noxious, and to casual visitors, almost insufferable. In some cases, as many as forty-five inmates occupy a single dormitory, with low ceilings and sleeping boxes arranged in three tiers one above another. Good health is incompatible with such arrangements. They make it an impossibility."[17]

Moreover, the poorhouse was unsuccessful at reducing "pauperism," the need for relief, and alcoholism. In the state of New York, between 1840 and 1860, the number of people in poorhouses increased from 14,315 to 39,563, and the number of people needing outdoor relief increased from 11,037 to 174,403. Alcohol was easily accessible at the poorhouse; doctors prescribed it as medicine, employees smuggled it in to sell to inmates, and liquor cabinets were repeatedly broken into. Poorhouses did not promote industry, as there was not enough useful work to do, especially in the winter months when it was impossible to farm. Many times, work rules were arbitrarily enforced on inmates, coercing people to do meaningless work like moving wood from one part of the compound to another and then back again. In the summer, the men who could work mostly left the poorhouse to get jobs, but the sick, disabled, and old could not work in the fields any time of the year.[18]

In 1890, Amos Warner's study reported on the dilapidated state of poorhouses: the lack of funds to provide healthy food, appropriate buildings, heat, and clothing; the supervisors' brutal treatment of inmates; and the failure to separate the insane, disabled, elderly, children, widows, prostitutes, or alcoholics, which made it impossible to meet the various needs of each group. Instead of being a compassionate environment for the deserving poor, the poorhouse turned into a place to be feared. By 1920, the poorhouse was seen as a human dumping ground. Poorhouses eventually transformed themselves into nursing homes. However, although the poorhouse movement eventually came to an end, its legacy of dividing the poor into deserving and undeserving categories has remained a dominant characteristic of American discourse on poverty up to the present.[19]

The various proposals of Wilson Pierson and George McFarlane, Frances Wright, Thomas Carey, and Thomas Skidmore were not enacted during this period. Interestingly, Wright's plan for state-run boarding schools and Skidmore's proposal to ban inheritance did not stimulate much support in working-class communities. However, Wright's idea of using education as a tool to lift the poor out of poverty would be promoted by educators from the Progressive era to the present day. The same can be said about Thomas Carey's proposal to pay workers enough to secure the "indispensable necessaries of life." While it was not successful in his day, the call for a "living wage" has continued to inspire workers. Pierson and McFarlane's idea for using the vote to advocate for working-class interests would prove to be somewhat successful in the Progressive and New Deal eras. But these proposals would have to wait, as the labor movement was decimated during the depression of 1837, and workingmen's parties and unions fell apart. For the next twenty years, the labor movement was in a weak position.[20]

Tecumseh's call to the Choctaws and Chickasaws to fight for their land was appealing to some, but was not acted upon that day because Pushmataha, the chief of the Choctaws, gave an eloquent rebuttal at the same meeting. Tecumseh did attract 3,000 Native Americans to join his campaign, and he led them into war in 1812. However, Tecumseh was killed in the Battle of Thames in 1813, and his movement fell apart. With the Indian Removal Act of 1830, all Indian tribes, from New England to Georgia to the Northwest Territories, were moved west of the Mississippi River. By the mid-nineteenth century, the U.S. government described its acquisiton of Indian land as well as Mexican land as "Manifest Destiny," the racist belief that it was God's will for whites to expand their territory from the East to the West Coast. White people claimed that Manifest Destiny brought Christianity, democracy, and technological progress to a land inhabited by supposedly inferior people. Much of this stolen land was given to white settlers as part of the Homestead Act of 1862 and the Dawes Act of 1887, playing a major role in the social mobility and wealth creation of many whites and the impoverishment of many Indians.[21]

Freedmen's Bureau school started under Reconstruction

Chapter 3

After the Civil War: The Rise of Labor and Scientific Charity

Prologue: Social Context and Overview of Solutions

As the United States emerged from the Civil War, the social conditions of the four million newly freed African Americans were desperate. The victory of the North, with the support of 200,000 black soldiers, provided African Americans with their freedom. Yet, this new liberty included no widespread land redistribution or monetary settlement for 246 years of free labor. At the same time, many white citizens connected the enslavement of African Americans to the "wage slavery" of the new industrial factories. As a result of workers' dissatisfaction with the low wages, ten- to eleven-hour workdays six days a week,

61

and dangerous working conditions, the labor movement became increasingly organized and powerful. This increased labor activity led to the railroad strike of 1877 and the Haymarket tragedy in 1886, which were the most widespread and violent strikes in U.S. history. In the face of high levels of poverty in U.S. cities and an undeferential labor movement, a new theory called scientific charity, which focused on private charities working closely together, was developed to try once again to reduce outdoor relief.[1]

Wards of the State

As the Union army began moving through the South, African Americans came out to greet the liberating forces. As this trickle of desperate human beings became a flood, the question became what to do with emancipated blacks. Initially, African Americans congregated at Union fortresses throughout the South. The federal government put out a call to help the freed blacks, and new associations, as well as established charities, responded with clothes, money, schoolbooks, and teachers. Within a short time, it became clear that this was a national issue that demanded a national response. The federal government responded with the Freedmen's Bureau to provide African Americans with food, health care, schools, and land. This massive attempt to lift almost an entire people out of destitution made the emancipated blacks the wards, or responsibility, of the nation.[2]

Native Americans had also become wards of the nation as a result of the U.S. removal and relocation policy. Initially, tribes were treated as sovereign nations who were able to negotiate with the U.S. government in "agreements between equals." From 1787 to 1871, more than 600 treaties were signed between Indian tribes and the U.S. government. At the same time, Indians were treated as wards of the state, much like children, with the president and Congress having ultimate responsibility for them. In legal terms, the United States had the "duty of protection" of Native Americans. However, in 1871, Congress passed legislation abolishing the power of American Indians to make treaties and assumed "plenary power" over Indians, which allowed the federal government to terminate official recognition and to confiscate land.[3]

Sitting Bull (Tatanka Iyotanka), the renowned head chief, argued that the Lakota Sioux tribes were both a ward of the state and a sovereign nation that had signed treaties with the United States. In his 1883 presentation to a U.S. Senate committee, Sitting Bull reminded the "Great Father" (the president) that he had a responsibility to take care of the Lakota. At the same time, he demanded that the "Great Father" live up to previous treaties the U.S. government had signed promising monetary payment, clothing, agricultural tools, and livestock. Without these resources, Sitting Bull believed, the Lakota would not escape poverty.

Other Native American tribes fared better than the Lakota. The Cherokees, after the Long Walk of 1838, which had relocated them from their homelands in Georgia, Alabama, Tennessee, and North Carolina to "Indian territory" (what is now Oklahoma) at the cost of 8,000 lives, had by 1880 rebuilt their civilization. After visiting the Cherokee nation in the early 1880s, Senator Henry Dawes of Massachusetts described Cherokee social development in glowing terms. Dawes stated that "there was not a family in that whole nation that had not a home of its own. There was not a pauper in that nation, and the nation did not owe one dollar. It built its own capitol, in which we had this examination, and built its schools and its hospitals." However, Dawes found a fundamental flaw in the Cherokee social system, describing it in this fashion: "Yet the defect of the system was apparent. They have got as far as they can go, because they own their land in common. It is Henry George's system, and under that there is no enterprise to make your home any better than that of your neighbors. There is no selfishness, which is at the bottom of civilization. Till this people will consent to give up their lands, and divide them among their citizens so that each can own the land he cultivates, they will not make much more progress."[4]

Because of this "defect" and U.S. interest in obtaining Indian land, Dawes proposed to alter the Native American social system. In 1887, Dawes cosponsored the General Allotment Act, which divided communally owned lands of American Indians into small, individually owned parcels, with the "surplus" land to be sold or leased to whites. This policy, which has become known as the Dawes Act, was designed to make the Indians into independent farmers and ranchers. Native Americans who were allotted land became U.S. citizens and received farming tools. The goals of this assimilation process were to "Americanize" the Indians and to annul tribal governments and disperse communal landholdings so that Indians would live under the same conditions of "freedom" and taxation as whites. Under the Dawes Act and other legislation from this time period, the federal government attempted to diminish significantly the relationship and responsibility between itself and Native American tribes.[5]

Labor and the New Economy

Between the end of the Civil War and the turn of the nineteenth century, an economic revolution occurred in the United States. With the formation of a national market supported by the completion of the transcontinental railroad in 1869, the relative ease of peacetime, generous mineral resources, and rich farmland (seized from Native Americans), industrial capitalism flourished. This new economic system was based in laissez faire capitalism, which justified its existence and perspective by pointing to the early American vision of liberty based on private property, individual initiative, and a national government that kept its hands off the economy. In a very short time, a new capitalist elite emerged, and along with them, a modern working class. In the industrial age, merchants, farmers, and small-town artisans no longer controlled the destiny of the country.[6]

This national market brought about an explosion of economic growth as well as instability. In 1860, the United States employed 1.3 million factory workers and invested $1 billion in manufacturing plants; by 1900, the number of workers had grown to 5.5 million and investment had reached $12 billion. Historians Mary and Charles Beard noted that "twenty-years after the death of Lincoln, America had become, in the quantity and value of her products, the first manufacturing nation in the world. What England had once accomplished in a hundred years, the United States had achieved in half the time." By 1894, the United States was the leading industrial power in the world, producing more manufactured goods than England, France, and Germany combined.[7]

At the same time, the new economy generated a great deal of instability and suffering, which led to widespread poverty alongside the great wealth. The problem was that early capitalist development was highly unstable. The emerging industrial capitalist system not only boomed, it also busted, alternating between rapid growth and depression. The depression of 1873, which began with the failure of a brokerage house followed by the collapse of thirty-seven banks and investment firms due to overspeculation and inflated stock prices, lasted five years. The 1873 depression led to the unemployment of 1 million workers, the closing of 50,000 businesses, and the threat of starvation for many. From January to March of 1874, 90,000 workers, almost half of them women, were forced to sleep in police stations. The U.S. economy started to grow again in the late 1870s, but it was once again hit by depression from 1882 to 1885, which left 2 million unemployed.[8]

These economic downturns led many to wander the country looking for work and food. Instead of seeing the structural reasons for their unemployment and poverty, people called them the derogatory term "tramp." Anyone who was traveling on the road and without a job could be stigmatized as a tramp and thrown into jail under vagrancy laws. Tramps became the new undeserving poor, and the affluent depicted them as a menace to be feared. This led the upper class, which had benefited greatly from industrialization, to become fearful of the central cities, where both the unemployed and new immigrants lived.

Between 1861 and 1890, 10 million immigrants, mostly from Germany, Ireland, and Britain but also from Italy, China, and Scandinavia, arrived in the United States and moved into the cities. Although these new waves of immigrants provided the United States with a steady supply of cheap labor for the new industrial factories, they also put enormous stress on city systems because of the high rates of poverty, disease, and illiteracy. As a result, the affluent abandoned the cities for the outlying suburbs. The result was that the rich and poor lived near each other, but in separate worlds.[9]

The increasing demands of the working class also caused social instability. The new economic system left the nation's modes of production and resources in the hands of a small group of white wealthy men, while the factory workers lived and worked in miserable conditions. Investigations conducted into the living conditions of the working class found three to four families in a single room, with the children slowly freezing and starving to death. Fueled by wage cuts in mining and manufacturing in 1874, labor protest increased. When the owners of the railroads tried to cut workers' wages by 10 percent in 1877, workers went out on strike and shut down the railroads in Baltimore, Pittsburgh, St. Louis, Martinsburg (West Virginia), and Reading (Pennsylvania). This strike involved 100,000 workers and led to the death of more than 100 people and the incarceration of 1,000. To stop the striking workers, the federal government sent in the army. Importantly, the 1877 railroad strike was a forerunner to the labor unrest of the 1880s, which averaged approximately 500 strikes from 1881 to 1885 and involved 150,000 strikers per year. In 1886, labor protest peaked with 1,500 strikes involving 400,000 workers.[10]

Labor advocates pushed for structural solutions to the capitalist system, advocating for such social reforms as the eight-hour workday and increased pay, with some going so far as to call for the replacement of capitalism with socialism. Clearly, the labor movement looked for more collective solutions, embracing mutual action rather than individualism, while the capitalists promoted the idea of acquisitive individualism, free markets, and the survival of the fittest and were opposed to social reforms and to the more radical proposals. A Detroit banner summed up the differences between the two camps: "Each for himself is the bosses' plea; Union for all will make you free."[11]

The Knights of Labor, founded in 1869, worked to reform the capitalist system. At its height, the Knights had 702,000 members. It was an inclusive organization, with membership open to skilled and unskilled labor, whites and blacks, men and women, citizens and immigrants, and even employers who treated workers humanely. In the preamble to the Knights' constitution, they stated their position: "The recent alarming development and aggression of aggregated wealth, which, unless checked, will inevitably lead to the pauperization and hopeless degradation of the toiling masses, render it imperative, if we desire to enjoy the blessing of life, that a check should be placed upon its power and upon unjust accumulation, and a system adopted which will secure to the laborer the fruits of his toil."

The preamble also listed the Knights' goals, which included securing for workers a proper share of the wealth that they created, substituting arbitration for strikes, securing for both sexes equal pay for equal work, and reducing the workday to eight hours. Although it strove to improve the pay and conditions of workers, it also argued that this was not the end goal; rather these improvements were just stepping-stones toward reaching the highest and noblest human capacity for good.[12]

Terrence Powderly, the leader of the Knights in the 1880s, believed that the working class and poor could achieve their goals without resorting to violence because the workers had access to the ballot. Susan B. Anthony, who was at the forefront of the first wave of feminism, was pushing for this same right for women that white working-class men received in the early 1820s. Anthony argued that women, who made only 50 percent of men's wages, were "in a position of the pauper" and were without the means to change their material conditions and social location without access to the ballot. She asserted that with the right to vote, the 3 million wage-earning women would change their low economic status as well as help poor men raise their salary since the capitalists would no longer be able to use women's wages as a downward pressure on male earnings.[13]

Not all labor activists believed in social reform; other labor advocates believed that the only way to reduce poverty was to change the entire capitalist system. Albert Parsons, a twenty-year veteran labor advocate, called for the replacement of capitalism with socialism and anarchism. Parsons was a leader of the nationwide strike for the eight-hour workday that occurred in the spring of 1886. On May 1 of that year, some 350,000 workers in 11,562 businesses went out on strike across the United States. In Parsons's hometown of Chicago, 40,000 workers struck, closing the railroads and bringing city business to a standstill. During an evening rally at Haymarket Square, 3,000 people had gathered to protest the death of four striking workers who were killed by police. At the end of the rally, people were starting to leave when a bomb was detonated near the police, killing seven officers and wounding 200 people. The next day, Albert Parsons and seven others were arrested. Even though Parsons was not present at Haymarket Square at the time of the bombing, he was charged with murder, since under Illinois law, a person who incited murder was guilty of murder. At his trial, Parsons was asked if he had anything to say regarding why the sentence of death should not be passed upon him. Given this opportunity, Parsons launched into a defense of socialism and anarchism, with their respective tenets that workers should control the mode of production and that the government should be eliminated.[14]

Two years after the Haymarket uprising, Edward Bellamy published *Looking Backward*, a utopian novel about an American who fell asleep in 1887 and woke up in the year 2000 to find that he was living in a socialist society where people lived and worked cooperatively. The book provided the reader with vivid imagery of a nation that "guarantees the nurture, education, and comfortable maintenance of every citizen from cradle to the grave" and grants its citizens an equal share of its wealth. In the book, when Julian West, the nineteenth-century man who had slept for 113 years, suggested to Dr. Leete, the twentieth-century man who hosted him, that the change to socialism must have caused great bloodshed, Dr. Leete replied, "On the contrary... there was absolutely no violence. The change had been foreseen. Public opinion had become fully ripe for it, and the whole mass of the people was behind it. There was no more possibility of opposing it by force than by argument."[15] With this novel, Bellamy argued that a socialist society could be brought about in the United States.

Another proposal that caused great excitement in the late nineteenth century was Henry George's single tax plan, outlined in his book *Progress and Poverty*. George believed that poverty with progress was the great paradox of his time, and he offered a simple strategy to solve it. He called for the elimination of all taxes, replacing them with a single tax on land, which would be reassessed as the value increased or decreased. George felt that this was logical, arguing that "the value of a building, like the value of goods, or of anything properly styled wealth, is produced by individual exertion, and therefore properly belongs to the individual; but the value of land only arises with the growth and improvement of the community, and therefore properly belongs to the community." According to George, the single tax would increase the production of wealth since it removed the burdens on capitalists and working people, ended land speculation, freed up land for the common citizen, and eliminated tax collectors.[16]

Scientific Charity

In contrast to these structural solutions to poverty, a proposal to privatize relief was put forward by civic leaders. As the number of people asking for relief in the cities continued to grow in the 1870s, civic leaders began to worry that the poor had come to see relief as a right rather than a privilege, and they were determined to change this. Just as the elite class tried to squelch the right of workers to unionize, alter working conditions, and control the mode of production, civic leaders (many of whom were from the upper class or sympathetic to capitalism) tried to stifle the right of "tramps" to outdoor relief. Civic leaders attempted to replace the demand of the poor for outdoor relief with Charity Organization Societies (COS) with the goal of making charity rational and systemic. This new movement was entitled "scientific charity."[17]

Scientific charity built on Americans' notion of self-reliance, limited government, and economic freedom. Proponents of scientific charity shared the poorhouse advocates' goals of cutting relief expenses and reducing the number of able-bodied who were receiving assistance, as well as the moral reformers' goal of uplifting people from poverty through discipline and religious education via private charity. In this model, individuals responded to charity and the government stayed out of the economic sphere. Individuals were seen as rational actors who freely made decisions based on their own self-interest and who were responsible for how they fared economically. Scientific charity fit well with the post–Civil War concept of social Darwinism, which held that humans were in competition and the strong survived and thrived while the weak did not. Not surprisingly, Charity Organization Societies were generally opposed to unions.[18]

Two of the leading advocates for Charity Organization Societies were Josephine Lowell and S. Humphrey Gurteen. Lowell, who was from a radical abolitionist family, believed that idleness was a major cause of poverty, and she advocated giving those who requested relief a labor test (such as breaking stones or chopping wood) before they received private charity. During her life, she developed several principles to guide her social reform work. One of her key principles was that "charity must tend to develop the m ɔ ral nature of those it helps." Lowell opposed both local government relief and almsgiving (individual giving directly to the poor) since she felt this practice did not morally uplift the people and created dependency. She felt that charity agents and visitors could provide a personal relationship conducive to helping needy individuals instead of treating them as "cases." Lowell thought "that each case must be dealt with radically and a permanent means of helping it to be found, and that the best way to help people is to help them to help themselves."[19]

Gurteen provided many practical ideas to implement organized Charity Organization Societies. Gurteen's plan was to have various groups already providing services to the poor coordinate their efforts. There would be a central office that served as a charity clearinghouse where "friendly visitors" (COS agents) involved in investigating the poor would meet to compare notes to determine who was worthy of relief and who was an imposter. This collaboration would result in a complete registry of every person in the city who was receiving public or private assistance. The goal of this organized approach was to stop providing relief to the undeserving poor but continue to provide the deserving poor with the assistance to solve their own problems. Gurteen believed that COS would end outdoor relief, stop pauperism, and reduce poverty to its lowest possible level.[20]

The Freedmen's Bureau (1901)

W. E. B. Du Bois

This article was part of Du Bois's work to reevaluate the Reconstruction Era.

The problem of the twentieth century is the problem of the color line; the relation of the darker to the lighter races of men in Asia and Africa, in America and the islands of the sea. It was a phase of this problem that caused the Civil War; and however much they who marched south and north in 1861 may have fixed on the technical points of union and local autonomy as a shibboleth, all nevertheless knew, as we know, that the question of Negro slavery was the deeper cause of the conflict. Curious it was, too, how this deeper question ever forced itself to the surface, despite effort and disclaimer. No sooner had Northern armies touched Southern soil than this old question, newly guised, sprang from the earth,—What shall be done with slaves? Peremptory military commands, this way and that, could not answer the query; the Emancipation Proclamation seemed but to broaden and intensify the difficulties; and so at last there arose in the South a government of men called the Freedmen's Bureau, which lasted, legally, from 1865 to 1872, but in a sense from 1861 to 1876, and which sought to settle the Negro problems in the United States of America.

It is the aim of this essay to study the Freedmen's Bureau,—the occasion of its rise, the character of its work, and its final success and failure,—not only as a part of American history, but above all as one of the most singular and interesting of the attempts made by a great nation to grapple with vast problems of race and social condition.

No sooner had the armies, east and west, penetrated Virginia and Tennessee than fugitive slaves appeared within their lines. They came at night, when the flickering camp fires of the blue hosts shone like vast unsteady stars along the black horizon: old men, and thin, with gray and tufted hair; women with frightened eyes, dragging whimpering, hungry children; men and girls, stalwart and gaunt,—a horde of starving vagabonds, homeless, helpless, and pitiable in their dark distress....

Then the long-headed man, with care-chiseled face, who sat in the White House, saw the inevitable, and emancipated the slaves of rebels on New Year's, 1863. A month later Congress called earnestly for the Negro soldiers whom the act of July, 1862, had half grudgingly allowed to enlist. Thus the barriers were leveled, and the deed was done. The stream of fugitives swelled to a flood, and anxious officers kept inquiring: "What must be done with slaves arriving almost daily? Am I to find food and shelter for women and children?"

It was a Pierce of Boston who pointed out the way, and thus became in a sense the founder of the Freedmen's Bureau. Being specially detailed from the ranks to care for the freedmen at Fortress Monroe, he afterward founded the celebrated Port Royal experiment and started the Freedmen's Aid Societies. Thus, under the timid Treasury officials and bold army officers, Pierce's plan widened and developed. At first, the able-bodied men were enlisted as soldiers or hired as laborers, the women and children were herded into central camps under guard, and "superintendents of contrabands" multiplied here and there. Centres of massed freedmen arose at Fortress Monroe, Va., Washington, D.C., Beaufort and Port Royal, S.C., New Orleans, La., Vicksburg and Corinth, Miss., Columbus, Ky., Cairo, Ill., and elsewhere, and the army chaplains found here new and fruitful fields.

Then came the Freedmen's Aid Societies, born of the touching appeals for relief and help from these centres of distress. There was the American Missionary Association, sprung from the Amistad, and now full grown for work, the various church organizations, the National Freedmen's Relief Association, the American Freedmen's Union, the Western Freedmen's Aid Commission,—in all fifty or more active organizations, which ̇sent clothes, money, school-books, and teachers southward. All they did was needed, for the destitution of the freedmen was often reported as "too appalling for belief," and the situation was growing daily worse rather than better.

And daily, too, it seemed more plain that this was no ordinary matter of temporary relief, but a national crisis; for here loomed a labor problem of vast dimensions. Masses of Negroes stood idle, or, if they worked spasmodically, were never sure of pay; and if perchance they received pay, squandered the new thing thoughtlessly. In these and in other ways were camp life and the new liberty demoralizing the freedmen. The broader economic organization thus clearly demanded sprang up here and there as accident and local conditions determined....

Meantime the election took place, and the administration, returning from the country with a vote of renewed confidence, addressed itself to the matter more seriously. A conference between the houses agreed upon a carefully drawn measure which contained the chief provisions of Charles Sumner's bill, but made the proposed organization a department independent of both the War and Treasury officials. The bill was conservative, giving the new department "general superintendence of all freedmen." It was to "establish regulations" for them, protect them, lease them lands, adjust their wages, and appear in civil and military courts as their "next friend." There were many limitations attached to the powers thus granted, and the organization was made permanent. Nevertheless, the Senate defeated the bill, and a new conference committee was appointed. This committee reported a new bill, February 28, which was whirled through just as the session closed, and which became the act of 1865 establishing in the War Department a "Bureau of Refugees, Freedmen, and Abandoned Lands."

This last compromise was a hasty bit of legislation, vague and uncertain in outline. A Bureau was created, "to continue during the present War of Rebellion, and for one year thereafter," to which was given "the supervision and management of all abandoned lands, and the control of all subjects relating to refugees and freedmen," under "such rules and regulations as may be presented by the head of the Bureau and approved by the President." A commissioner, appointed by the President and Senate, was to control the Bureau, with an office force not exceeding ten clerks. The President might also appoint commissioners in the seceded states, and to all these offices military officials might be detailed at regular pay. The Secretary of War could issue rations, clothing, and fuel to the destitute, and all abandoned property was placed in the hands of the Bureau for eventual lease and sale to ex-slaves in forty-acre parcels.

Thus did the United States government definitely assume charge of the emancipated Negro as the ward of the nation. It was a tremendous undertaking. Here, at a stroke of the pen, was erected a government of millions of men,—and not ordinary men, either, but black men emasculated by a peculiarly complete system of slavery, centuries old; and now, suddenly, violently, they come into a new birthright, at a time of war and passion, in the midst of the stricken, embittered population of their former masters. Any man might well have hesitated to assume charge of such a work, with vast responsibilities, indefinite powers, and limited resources. Probably no one but a soldier would have answered such a call promptly; and indeed no one but a soldier could be called, for Congress had appropriated no money for salaries and expenses.

Less than a month after the weary emancipator passed to his rest, his successor assigned Major General Oliver O. Howard to duty as commissioner of the new Bureau. He was a Maine man, then only thirty-five years of age. He had marched with Sherman to the sea, had fought well at Gettysburg, and had but a year before been assigned to the command of the Department of Tennessee. An honest and sincere man, with rather too much faith in human nature, little aptitude for systematic business and intricate detail, he was nevertheless conservative, hard-working, and, above all, acquainted at first-hand with much of the work before him. And of that work it has been truly said, "No approximately correct history of civilization can ever be written which does not throw out in bold relief, as one of the great landmarks of political and social progress, the organization and administration of the Freedmen's Bureau."

On May 12, 1865, Howard was appointed, and he assumed the duties of his office promptly on the 15th, and began examining the field of work. A curious mess he looked upon: little despotisms, communistic experiments, slavery, peonage, business speculations, organized charity, unorganized almsgiving,—all reeling on under the guise of helping the freedman, and all enshrined in the smoke and blood of war and the cursing and silence of angry men. On May 19 the new government—for a government it really was—issued its constitution; commissioners were to be appointed in each of the seceded states, who were to take charge of "all subjects relating to refugees and freedmen," and all relief and rations were to be given by their consent alone. The Bureau invited continued cooperation with benevolent societies, and declared, "It will be the object of all commissioners to introduce practicable systems of compensated labor," and to establish schools. Forthwith nine assistant commissioners were appointed. They were to hasten to their fields of work; seek gradually to close relief establishments, and make the destitute self-supporting; act as courts of law where there were no courts, or where Negroes were not recognized in them as free; establish the institution of marriage among ex-slaves, and keep records; see that freedmen were free to choose their employers, and help in making fair contracts for them; and finally, the circular said, "Simple good faith, for which we hope on all hands for those concerned in the passing away of slavery, will especially relieve the assistant commissioners in the discharge of their duties toward the freedmen, as well as promote the general welfare."

No sooner was the work thus started, and the general system and local organization in some measure begun, than two grave difficulties appeared which changed largely the theory and outcome of Bureau work. First, there were the abandoned lands of the South. It had long been the more or less definitely expressed theory of the North that all the chief problems of emancipation might be settled by establishing the slaves on the forfeited lands of their masters,—a sort of poetic justice, said some. But this poetry done into solemn prose meant either wholesale confiscation of private property in the South, or vast appropriations. Now Congress had not appropriated a cent, and no sooner did the proclamations of general amnesty appear than the 800,000 acres of abandoned lands in the hands of the Freedmen's Bureau melted quickly away. The second difficulty lay in perfecting the local organization of the Bureau throughout the wide field of work. Making a new machine and sending out officials of duly ascertained fitness for a great work of social reform is no child's task; but this task was even harder, for a new central organization had to be fitted on a heterogeneous and confused but already existing system of relief and control of ex-slaves; and the agents available for this work must be sought for in an army still busy with war operations,—men in the very nature of the case ill fitted for delicate social work,—or among the questionable camp followers of an invading host. Thus, after a year's work, vigorously as it was pushed, the problem looked even more difficult to grasp and solve than at the beginning. Nevertheless, three things that year's work did, well worth the doing: it relieved a vast amount of physical suffering; it transported 7000 fugitives from congested centres back to the farm; and, best of all, it inaugurated the crusade of the New England schoolma'am.

The annals of this Ninth Crusade are yet to be written, the tale of a mission that seemed to our age far more quixotic than the quest of St. Louis seemed to his. Behind the mists of ruin and rapine waved the calico dresses of women who dared, and after the hoarse mouthings of the field guns rang the rhythm of the alphabet. Rich and poor they were, serious and curious. Bereaved now of a father, now of a brother, now of more than these, they came seeking a life work in planting New England schoolhouses among the white and black of the South. They did their work well. In that first year they taught 100,000 souls, and more....

The act of 1866 gave the Freedmen's Bureau its final form,—the form by which it will be known to posterity and judged of men. It extended the existence of the Bureau to July, 1868; it authorized additional assistant commissioners, the retention of army officers mustered out of regular service, the sale of certain forfeited lands to freedmen on nominal terms, the sale of Confederate public property for Negro schools, and a wider field of judicial interpretation and cognizance. The government of the un-reconstructed South was thus put very largely in the hands of the Freedmen's Bureau, especially as in many cases the departmental military commander was now made also assistant commissioner. It was thus that the Freedmen's Bureau became a full-fledged government of men. It made laws, executed them and interpreted them; it laid and collected taxes, defined and punished crime, maintained and used military force, and dictated such measures as it thought necessary and proper for the accomplishment of its varied ends. Naturally, all these powers were not exercised continuously nor to their fullest extent; and yet, as General Howard has said, "scarcely any subject that has to be legislated upon in civil society failed, at one time or another, to demand the action of this singular Bureau." ...

Here, then, was the field of work for the Freedmen's Bureau; and since, with some hesitation, it was continued by the act of 1868 till 1869, let us look upon four years of its work as a whole. There were, in 1868, 900 Bureau officials scattered from Washington to Texas, ruling, directly and indirectly, many millions of men. And the deeds of these rulers fall mainly under seven heads,—the relief of physical suffering, the overseeing of the beginnings of free labor, the buying and selling of land, the establishment of schools, the paying of bounties, the administration of justice, and the financiering of all these activities. Up to June, 1869, over half a million patients had been treated by Bureau physicians and surgeons, and sixty hospitals and asylums had been in operation. In fifty months of work 21,000,000 free rations were distributed at a cost of over $4,000,000,—beginning at the rate of 30,000 rations a day in 1865, and discontinuing in 1869. Next came the difficult question of labor. First, 30,000 black men were transported from the refuges and relief stations back to the farms, back to the critical trial of a new way of working. Plain, simple instructions went out from Washington,—the freedom of laborers to choose employers, no fixed rates of wages, no peonage or forced labor. So far so good; but where local agents differed *toto coelo* in capacity and character, where the personnel was continually changing, the outcome was varied. The largest element of success lay in the fact that the majority of the freedmen were willing, often eager, to work. So contracts were written,—50,000 in a single state,—laborers advised, wages guaranteed, and employers supplied. In truth, the organization became a vast labor bureau; not perfect, indeed,—notably defective here and there,—but on the whole, considering the situation, successful beyond the dreams of thoughtful men. The two great obstacles which confronted the officers at every turn were the tyrant and the idler: the slaveholder, who believed slavery was right, and was determined to perpetuate it under another name; and the freedman, who regarded freedom as perpetual rest. These were the Devil and the Deep Sea.

In the work of establishing the Negroes as peasant proprietors the Bureau was severely handicapped, as I have shown. Nevertheless, something was done. Abandoned lands were leased so long as they remained in the hands of the Bureau, and a total revenue of $400,000 derived from black tenants. Some other lands to which the nation had gained title were sold, and public lands were opened for the settlement of the few blacks who had tools and capital. The vision of landowning, however, the righteous and reasonable ambition for forty acres and a mule which filled the freedmen's dreams, was doomed in most cases to disappointment. And those men of marvelous hind-sight, who to-day are seeking to preach the Negro back to the soil, know well, or ought to know, that it was here, in 1865, that the finest opportunity of binding the black peasant to the soil was lost. Yet, with help and striving, the Negro gained some land, and by 1874, in the one state of Georgia, owned near 350,000 acres.

The greatest success of the Freedmen's Bureau lay in the planting of the free school among Negroes, and the idea of free elementary education among all classes in the South. It not only called the schoolmistress through the benevolent agencies, and built them schoolhouses, but it helped discover and support such apostles of human development as Edmund Ware, Erastus Cravath, and Samuel Armstrong. State superintendents of education were appointed, and by 1870 150,000 children were in school. The opposition to Negro education was bitter in the South, for the South believed an educated Negro to be a dangerous Negro. And the South was not wholly wrong; for education among all kinds of men always has had, and always will have, an element of danger and revolution, of dissatisfaction and discontent. Nevertheless, men strive to know. It was some inkling of this paradox, even in the unquiet days of the Bureau, that allayed an opposition to human training, which still to-day lies smouldering, but not flaming. Fisk, Atlanta, Howard, and Hampton were founded in these days, and nearly $6,000,000 was expended in five years for educational work, $750,000 of which came from the freedmen themselves....

Such was the work of the Freedmen's Bureau. To sum it up in brief, we may say: it set going a system of free labor; it established the black peasant proprietor; it secured the recognition of black freedmen before courts of law; it founded the free public school in the South. On the other hand, it failed to establish good will between ex-masters and freedmen; to guard its work wholly from paternalistic methods that discouraged self-reliance; to make Negroes landholders in any considerable numbers. Its successes were the result of hard work, supplemented by the aid of philanthropists and the eager striving of black men. Its failures were the result of bad local agents, inherent difficulties of the work, and national neglect. The Freedmen's Bureau expired by limitation in 1869, save its educational and bounty departments. The educational work came to an end in 1872, and General Howard's connection with the Bureau ceased at that time....

The most bitter attacks on the Freedmen's Bureau were aimed not so much at its conduct or policy under the law as at the necessity for any such organization at all. Such attacks came naturally from the border states and the South, and they were summed up by Senator Davis, of Kentucky, when he moved to entitle the act of 1866 a bill "to promote strife and conflict between the white and black races... by a grant of unconstitutional power." The argument was of tremendous strength, but its very strength was its weakness. For, argued the plain common sense of the nation, if it is unconstitutional, unpracticable, and futile for the nation to stand guardian over its helpless wards, then there is left but one alternative: to make those wards their own guardians by arming them with the ballot. The alternative offered the nation then was not between full and restricted Negro suffrage; else every sensible man, black and white, would easily have chosen the latter. It was rather a choice between suffrage and slavery, after endless blood and gold had flowed to sweep human bondage away. Not a single Southern legislature stood ready to admit a Negro, under any conditions, to the polls; not a single Southern legislature believed free Negro labor was possible without a system of restrictions that took all its freedom away; there was scarcely a white man in the South who did not honestly regard emancipation as a crime, and its practical nullification as a duty. In such a situation, the granting of the ballot to the black man was a necessity, the very least a guilty nation could grant a wronged race. Had the opposition to government guardianship of Negroes been less bitter, and the attachment to the slave system less strong, the social seer can well imagine a far better policy: a permanent Freedmen's Bureau, with a national system of Negro schools; a carefully supervised employment and labor office; a system of impartial protection before the regular courts; and such institutions for social betterment as savings banks, land and building associations, and social settlements. All this vast expenditure of money and brains might have formed a great school of prospective citizenship, and solved in a way we have not yet solved the most perplexing and persistent of the Negro problems.

That such an institution was unthinkable in 1870 was due in part to certain acts of the Freedmen's Bureau itself. It came to regard its work as merely temporary, and Negro suffrage as a final answer to all present perplexities. The political ambition of many of its agents and proteges led it far afield into questionable activities, until the South, nursing its own deep prejudices, came easily to ignore all the good deeds of the Bureau, and hate its very name with perfect hatred. So the Freedmen's Bureau died, and its child was the Fifteenth Amendment.

The passing of a great human institution before its work is done, like the untimely passing of a single soul, but leaves a legacy of striving for other men. The legacy of the Freedmen's Bureau is the heavy heritage of this generation. Today, when new and vaster problems are destined to strain every fibre of the national mind and soul, would it not be well to count this legacy honestly and carefully? For this much all men know: despite compromise, struggle, war, and struggle, the Negro is not free. In the backwoods of the Gulf states, for miles and miles, he may not leave the plantation of his birth; in well-nigh the whole rural South the black farmers are peons, bound by law and custom to an economic slavery, from which the only escape is death or the penitentiary. In the most cultured sections and cities of the South the Negroes are a segregated servile caste, with restricted rights and privileges. Before the courts, both in law and custom, they stand on a different and peculiar basis. Taxation without representation is the rule of their political life. And the result of all this is, and in nature must have been, lawlessness and crime. That is the large legacy of the Freedmen's Bureau, the work it did not do because it could not.

I have seen a land right merry with the sun; where children sing, and rolling hills lie like passioned women, wanton with harvest. And there in the King's Highway sat and sits a figure, veiled and bowed, by which the traveler's footsteps hasten as they go. On the tainted air broods fear. Three centuries' thought has been the raising and unveiling of that bowed human heart, and now, behold, my fellows, a century new for the duty and the deed. The problem of the twentieth century is the problem of the color line.

It Is Not Right for Me to Live in Poverty (1883)

Sitting Bull [Tatanka Iyotanka]

Sitting Bull gave this speech at a U.S. Senate committee to study conditions of Native Americans in the territories of Dakota and Montana. Note that a recorder for the U.S. government wrote the comments in the testimony about the reaction to Sitting Bull's words and actions.

By the CHAIRMAN (to the interpreter): Q. Ask Sitting Bull if he has anything to say to the committee.

SITTING BULL. Of course I will speak to you if you desire me to do so. I suppose it is only such men as you desire to speak who must say anything.

The CHAIRMAN. We supposed the Indians would select men to speak for them, but any man who desires to speak, or any man the Indians here desire shall talk for them we will be glad to hear if he has anything to say.

SITTING BULL. Do you not know who I am, that you speak as you do?

The CHAIRMAN. I know that you are Sitting Bull, and if you have anything to say we will be glad to hear you.

SITTING BULL. Do you recognize me; do you know who I am?

The CHAIRMAN. I know you are Sitting Bull.

SITTING BULL. You say you know I am Sitting Bull, but do you know what position I hold?

The CHAIRMAN. I do not know any difference between you and the other Indians at this agency.

SITTING BULL. I am here by the will of the Great Spirit, and by his will I am a chief. My heart is red and sweet, and I know it is sweet, because whatever passes near me puts out its tongue to me; and yet you men have come here to talk with us, and you say you do not know who I am. I want to tell you that if the Great Spirit has chosen any one to be the chief of this country it is myself.

The CHAIRMAN. In whatever capacity you may be here to-day, if you desire to say anything to us we will listen to you; otherwise we will dismiss this council.

SITTING BULL. Yes; that is all right. You have conducted yourselves like men who have been drinking whisky, and I came here to give you some advice. [Here Sitting Bull waved his hand and at once the Indians left the room in a body.]

After the council had been broken up by the action of Sitting Bull some of the Yanktonnais chiefs, from the northern portion of the reservation, sent the interpreter to ask the committee if they could have a separate talk; that heretofore the other Indians from the lower portion of the reservation had monopolized the talk and they had been unable to speak of their needs.

The committee granted the request and the council was reconvened.

The CHAIRMAN (to the interpreter, Wells). Say to these Indians that we understand that those who have come here now want to have a separate talk with the committee. Say to them also that if they are going to be controlled by Sitting Bull we do not wish to have any further talk with them.

[At this point several Indians remarked they were very anxious to say a great many things to the committee, but that the other Indians occupied the floor, and when they got up to talk the others left the room, and, of course, they had to go too.]

The CHAIRMAN. We understand that the Indians who have come together here feel as if they had not an opportunity to talk with the committee, and that the reason they did not have an opportunity was because Sitting Bull told the Indians to leave the room, and if you are under the influence of Sitting Bull and are going to talk or leave the room just as Sitting Bull directs we do not want to have any further talk with you. We have not come here to get anything out of you; we have come to try and help you. We want a plain, fair talk with you, and we want you to tell us just what you want us to do for you. But we do not want to talk with such men as Sitting Bull, who makes war upon the Government. If any of you want to say anything to the committee we will be glad to hear you now. Who will talk for you?

A few minutes later:

SITTING BULL spoke as follows: I came in with a glad heart to shake hands with you, my friends, for I feel that I have displeased you; and I am here to apologize to you for my bad conduct and to take back what I said. I will take it back because I consider I have made your hearts bad. I heard that you were coming here from the Great Father's house some time before you came, and I have been sitting here like a prisoner waiting for some one to release me. I was looking for you everywhere, and I considered that when we talked with you it was the same as if we were talking with the Great Father; and I believe that what I pour out from my heart the Great Father will hear. What I take back is what I said to cause the people to leave the council, and want to apologize for leaving myself. The people acted like children, and I am sorry for it. I was very sorry when I found out that your intentions were good and entirely different from what I supposed they were. Now I will tell you my mind and I will tell everything straight. I know the Great Spirit is looking down upon me from above and will hear what I say, therefore I will do my best to talk straight; and I am in hopes that some one will listen to my wishes and help me to carry them out. I have always been a chief, and have been made chief of all the land. Thirty-two years ago I was present at councils with the whiteman, and at the time of the Fort Rice council I was on the prairie listening to it, and since then a great many questions have been asked me about it, and I always said wait; and when the Black Hills council was held, and they asked me to give up that land, I said they must wait. I remember well all the promises that were made about that land because I have thought a great deal about them since that time. Of course I know that the Great Spirit provided me with animals for my food, but I did not stay out on the prairie because I did not wish to accept the offers of the Great Father, for I sent in a great many of my people and I told them that the Great Father was providing for them and keeping his agreements with them, and I was sending the Indians word all the time I was out that they must remember their agreements and fulfill them, and carry them out straight. When the English authorities were looking for me I heard that the Great Father's people were looking for me too. I was not lost. I knew where I was going all the time. Previous to that time, when a Catholic priest called "White Hair" (meaning Bishop Marty) came to see me, I told him all these things plainly. He told me the wishes of the Great Father, and I made promises which I meant to fulfill, and did fulfill; and when I went over into the British possessions he followed me, and I told him everything that was in my heart, and sent him back to tell the Great Father what I told him; and General Terry sent me word afterwards to come in, because he had big promises to make me, and I sent him word that I would not throw my country away; that I considered it all mine still, and I wanted him to wait just four years for me; that I had gone over there to attend to some business of my own, and my people were doing just as any other people would do. If a man loses anything and goes back and looks carefully for it he will find it, and that is what the Indians are doing now when they ask you to give them the things that were promised them in the past; and I do not consider that they should be treated like beasts, and that is the reason I have grown up with the feelings I have. Whatever you wanted of me I have obeyed, and I have come when you called me. The Great Father sent me word that whatever he had against me in the past had been forgiven and thrown aside, and he would have nothing against me in the future, and I accepted his promises and came in; and he told me not to step aside from the white man's path, and I told him I would not, and I am doing my best to travel in that path. I feel that my country has gotten a bad name, and I want it to have a good name; it used to have a good name; and I sit sometimes and wonder who it is that has given it a bad name. You are the only people now who can give it a good name, and I want you to take good care of my country and respect it. When we sold the Black Hills we got a very small price for it, and not what we ought to have received. I used to think that the size of the payments would remain the same all the time, but they are growing smaller all the time. I want you to tell the Great Father everything I have said, and that we want some benefit from the promises he has made to us; and I don't think I should be tormented with anything about giving up any part of my land until those promises are fulfilled—I would rather wait until that time, when I will be ready to transact any business he may desire. I consider that my country takes in the Black Hills, and runs from the Powder River to the Missouri; and that all of this land belongs to me. Our reservation is not as large as we want it to be, and I suppose the Great Father owes us money now for land he has taken from us in the past. You white men advise us to follow your ways, and therefore I talk as I do. When you have a piece of land, and anything trespasses on it, you catch it and keep it until you get damages, and I am doing the same thing now; and I want you to tell all this to the Great Father for me. I am looking into the future for the benefit of my children, and that is what I mean, when I say I want my country taken care of for me. My children will grow up here, and I am looking ahead for their benefit, and for the benefit of my children's children, too; and even beyond that again. I sit here and look around me now, and I see my people starving, and I want the Great Father to make an increase in the amount of food that is allowed us now, so that they may be able to live. We want cattle to butcher—I want to kill 300 head of cattle at a time. That is the way you live, and we want to live the same way. This is what I want you to tell the Great Father when you go back home. If we get the things we want our children will be raised like the white children. When the Great Father told me to live like his people I told him to send me six teams of mules, because that is the way white people make a living, and I wanted my children to have these things to help them to make a living. I also told him to send me two spans of horses with wagons, and everything else my children would need. I also asked for a horse and buggy for my children; I was advised to follow the ways of the white man, and that is why I asked for those things. I never ask for anything that is not needed. I also asked for a cow and a bull for each family, so that they can raise cattle of their own. I asked for four yokes of oxen and wagons with them. Also a yoke of oxen and a wagon for each of my children to haul wood with. It is your own doing that I am here; you sent me here, and advised me to live as you do, and it is not right for me to live in poverty. I asked the Great Father for hogs, male and female, and for male and female sheep for my children to raise from. I did not leave out anything in the way of animals that the white men have; I asked for every one of them. I want you to tell the Great Father to send me some agricultural implements, so that I will not be obliged to work bare-handed. Whatever he sends to this agency our agent will take care of for us, and we will be satisfied because we know he will keep everything right. Whatever is sent here for us he will be pleased to take care of for us. I want to tell you that our rations have been reduced to almost nothing, and many of the people have starved to death. Now I beg of you to have the amount of rations increased so that our children will not starve, but will live better than they do now. I want clothing too, and I will ask for that too. We want all kinds of clothing for our people. Look at the men around here and see how poorly dressed they are. We want some clothing this month, and when it gets cold we want more of it to protect us from the weather. That is all I have to say.

Mr. LOGAN (to the interpreter). I want to say something to that man [pointing to Sitting Bull] before he sits down, and I want you to tell these Indians to listen to all that I will say to him.

Sitting Bull, this committee came here on behalf of the Government, with nothing in view except to ascertain the wants of the Indians, and to inquire into the provisions of the treaty recently made, and whether or not it was satisfactory to the Indians. We invited the Indians to come here to-day for a friendly talk, and they appointed yourself and two others to talk with the committee. When you talked you accused the committee of being drunk, you insulted them; and I understand this is not the first time you have been guilty of an offense of a like kind to a committee of Congress. You said to this committee before insulting them that you were chief of all the people of this country, and that you were appointed chief by the Great Spirit. I want to say to you that you were not appointed by the Great Spirit, nor has any one else been. Appointments are not made in that way. I want to say further that you are not a great chief of this country; that you have no following, no power, no control, and no right to any control. You are on an Indian reservation merely at the suffrance of the Government. You are fed by the Government, clothed by the Government, your children are educated by the Government, and all you have and are today is because of the Government. If it were not for the Government you would be freezing and starving to-day in the mountains. I merely say these things to you to notify you that you cannot insult the people of the United States of America, or its committees. You came here when you were a prisoner, and were told that if you behaved yourself you would be treated well, just as other Indians who behave themselves will be treated. So you will be; but you must not incite these Indians to bad deeds. You must not break up councils; and you have to behave yourself just as any other man; and if you are ever guilty of such a thing again you will be put into the guard-house, and be made to work.

I want to say to these Indians here that this man is not their chief; he has no power; and they must obey the Government and not be governed by the dictates of this man. I want to say further that the Government is willing to be kind to the Indians and take care of them and their children. The Government feeds and clothes and educates your children now, and desires to teach you to become farmers, and to civilize you, and make you as white men; but you have to learn that you are the equals of other men, and no man has a right to break up a council, and insult men who come here to talk with you, and to do you a kindness. And I am glad to say to you that in your presence Sitting Bull, with all his vanity, came before this committee and apologized for the insult he had given them. Now I want to say to you that we came to do you good, and not to do you harm; and to Sitting Bull I want to say that inasmuch as he apologized to the committee we accept his apology, but at the same time notify him that he must never repeat an offense of this character again. That is all I want to say.

The CHAIRMAN. Before this council breaks up I want to say that we will carry back to Washington and to the Great Father all that has been said by both the Indians and the white men; and the Great Father would be very glad to know that you want to become like white men and we want to carry back to him the word from you Indians that you want to do just as white men do, so that you can live as white men live—in houses, and wear warm, comfortable clothing like they do. If you are willing for us to carry that word back we will be glad to do it, and if you are in earnest the Great Father will do all in his power to help you. You must act like white men, though, and they help themselves. If you will do as they do the Great Father will give you agricultural implements, and will do all he can for you.

SITTING BULL. I wish to say a word about my not being a chief, have no authority, am proud, and consider myself a great man in general.

The CHAIRMAN. We do not care to talk any more with you to-night.

SITTING BULL. I would like to speak. I have grown to be a very independent man, and consider myself a very great man.

Mr. LOGAN. You have made your speech, and we do not care to have you continue any further.

SITTING BULL. I have just one more word to say. Of course if a man is a chief, and has authority, he should be proud, and think himself a great man.

The CHAIRMAN. We do not care to have any further conversation with you in regard to your authority. The Great Father considers you like any other Indian here; and so long as you obey the law you will be treated well, but you have no more authority here than any other Indian; and you must understand distinctly that you have no right to give orders to the Indians. You must obey the authorities here or you must suffer punishment for disobedience.

The Army of the Discontented (1890)

Terrence Powderly

As leader of the Knights of Labor, Powderly was one of the primary advocates of an eight-hour workday.

In January, 1884, the following paragraph appeared in one of the daily papers:

"It is estimated that at the present time one million and a half of men are out of employment in the United States; it is safe to predict that, if opportunities were offered to these men to drop into useful occupations, a large majority would not avail themselves of them."

Since then, the number of the unemployed must have increased, for nearly every day we read such items as this:

"The worsted mill connected with the Bigelow Carpet Mills, which employs about three hundred hands, shut down this morning for three weeks. This, with the five per cent. cut down at the Lancaster Gingham Mills, where two thousand five hundred hands are employed, which also went into effect this morning, makes Clinton's business outlook decidedly poor."

In the two years ending December 1, 1884, those employed in and around the coal-mines worked but little over half-time, and for the length of time that they were not at work they must be counted in with the unemployed. If the figures above quoted were correct in January, it is safe to assume that at present the number will not fall short of 2,000,000. The census of 1880 shows that the number of persons engaged in gainful occupations was 17,392,099. Of this number 3,837,112 were engaged in manufacturing, mechanical, and mining pursuits, while 5,183,000 gained a livelihood as laborers (agricultural and otherwise). Thus in 1880 we had in the United States, between laborers, mechanics, miners, and those engaged in manufacturing establishments, 9,020,211 persons.

From a personal experience, I am led to believe that the greater portion of those who are now out of employment comes from occupations that go to make up the 9,020,211. It is safe to assume that the 2,000,000 unemployed persons are discontented with their lot; and not only are they discontented, but those who labor at the same occupations that they previously followed have every reason to be dissatisfied also. With so many men and women seeking employment, the tendency of wages must be downward. It does not follow, because men are out of employment, that such articles as their fellow-workmen produce should decrease in value, or that the profit on the manufactured article, accruing to the owners of the establishments in which they work, should be any less; on the contrary, the expectation is that diminished production will increase the price of the manufactured article, or at least prevent its depreciation when thrown on the market. Notwithstanding the reduction in the expenses of the mining company, we pay the same price for coal that we paid a year ago. It matters not that the carpet mills "suspend three hundred hands," the price of carpeting remains unchanged. The gingham mills and the cotton and woolen mills may reduce the wages of employés five and ten per cent. yet, the price of gingham and calico continues as before. Whether the manufactured article commands the same price in the market or not the employer, knowing that he can secure an abundance of help, reduces the wages of his employés. Those who are out of employment are no longer producers, and they certainly are not consumers to any increased extent. The wages of those employed having been reduced, their powers of consumption are limited. The merchant whose shelves are stocked with goods becomes discontented when he views the rows of men and women that stand in front of his store, peering with hungry-looking eyes through his windows at the goods so temptingly held to view, willing and anxious to buy these goods, but deprived of the means, through enforced idleness or inadequate compensation for services rendered. Ask the business man what the cause of the depression is, and he, parrot-like, will say, "It is all regulated by the law of supply and demand." A moment's reflection would show him that the law of supply and demand, like all other laws, is open to different constructions. On his shelves is a supply of goods; outside of his window is a demand for these goods—a demand that is at all times equal to the supply. Why is it that the demand does not reach forth and secure the supply? The answer comes, "Because the medium of exchange is lacking; because labor is too cheap and plenty, and money too dear and scarce." That a deep-rooted feeling of discontent pervades the masses, none can deny; that there is a just cause for it, must be admitted. The old cry, "These agitators are stirring up a feeling of dissatisfaction among workingmen, and they should be suppressed," will not avail now. Every thinking person knows that the agitator did not throw two millions of men out of employment. The man who reads such paragraphs as this will not lay the blame of it at the door of the agitator.

"Mrs. Sarah Jane Cleary, an English woman, residing in this city, committed suicide a few days since. Her husband is a miner, and owing to the frequent suspensions of business in the mines during the past winter, his meager earnings were insufficient to support the family. The fact preyed on Mrs. Cleary's mind, and she resolved to end her life, that her children might receive her share of the food, otherwise they would go hungry."

The Cincinnati riots, that occurred less than one year ago, were not brought about through the agitation of the labor leader. If the demand for "the removal of unjust technicalities, delays, and discriminations in the administration of justice" had been listened to when first made by the Knights of Labor, Cincinnati would have been spared sorrow and disgrace, and her "prominent citizens" would not have had to lead a mob in order to open the eyes of the country to the manner in which her courts were throttled and virtue and truth were trampled upon in her temples of justice. That the army of the discontented is gathering fresh recruits day by day is true, and if this army should become so large that, driven to desperation, it should one day arise in its wrath and grapple with its real or fancied enemy, the responsibility for that act must fall upon the heads of those who could have averted the blow, but who turned a deaf ear to the supplication of suffering humanity, and gave the screw of oppression an extra turn because they had the power. Workingmen's organizations are doing all they can to avert the blow; but if that day dawns upon us, it will be chargeable directly to men who taunt others with unequal earnings and distort the truth....

It may be said that many of the employés of the manufacturing establishments are minors, and consequently can not perform as great an amount of labor as a corresponding number of adults. That argument might have had some weight years ago, but now it is fruitless. The age and strength of the workman are no longer regarded as factors in the field of production; it is the skill of the operator in managing a labor-saving machine that is held to be the most essential. It is true that a child can operate a machine as successfully as a man, and that muscle is no longer a requisite in accomplishing results. It is also true that less time is required to perform a given amount of labor than heretofore. This being the case, the plea for shorter hours is not unreasonable. Benjamin Franklin said, one hundred years ago, that "if the workers of the world would labor but four hours each day, they could produce enough in that length of time to supply the wants of mankind." While it is true that the means of supplying the wants of man have increased as if by magic, yet man has acquired no new wants; he is merely enabled to gratify his needs more fully. If it were true in Franklin's time that four hours of toil each day would prove sufficient to minister to the necessities of the world's inhabitants, the argument certainly has lost none of its force since then. At that time it took the sailing-vessel three months to cross the ocean; the stage-coach made its thirty or forty miles a day; the electric wire was not dreamt of; and the letter that traveled but little faster than the stage-coach was the quickest medium of communication.

It required six days' labor at the hands of the machinist, with hammer, chisel, and file, to perfect a certain piece of machinery at the beginning of this century. The machinist of the present day can finish a better job in six hours, with the aid of a labor-saving machine. In a yarn mill in Philadelphia the proprietor says that improved machinery has caused a displacement of fifty per cent. of the former employés within five years, and that one person, with the aid of improved machinery, can perform the work that it took upward of one hundred carders and spinners to do with the tools and implements in use at the beginning of this century. In Massachusetts it has been estimated that 318,768 men, women, and children do, with improved machinery, the work that it would require 1,912,468 men to perform if improved machinery were not in use. To insure safety on a passenger train, it is no longer necessary to have a brakeman at each end of the car; the automatic air-brake does the work, while one brakeman can shout "All right here!" for the whole train. The employé that has had a limb cut off in a collision, must beg for bread or turn the crank of a hand-organ and gather his pennies under the legend, "Please assist a poor soldier who lost his leg at Gettysburg." He is no longer stationed, flag in hand, at the switch; the automatic lever directs the course of the train and renders the one-legged switchman unnecessary. It is said that the iron-molder recently invented is capable of performing as much labor as three skilled workmen; while the following dispatch to a Philadelphia paper, from Mahanoy City, shows what is being done in the mines:

For the past three years the reduction in wages has been systematic and steady. When one of the officials of one of the great companies was interviewed on the matter, he replied that the advance in labor-saving machinery had lightened the labor of the men. A miner at one of the Reading collieries says that some months ago he expended a large sum for a patent drill, which enabled him to do five times the usual amount of work. He was employed in driving a gangway, the price paid being $10 a yard; but at the end of the week, when the officials saw the amount of work he had done the rate was reduced to $4.50 a yard.…

A great many remedies are recommended for the ills that I speak of; let me deal with what seems to be the most unimportant—the reduction of the hours of labor to eight a day. Men, women, and children are working from ten to eighteen hours a day, and two million men have nothing to do. If four men, following a given occupation, at which they work ten hours a day, would rest from their labors two hours each day, the two hours taken from the labor of each, if added together, would give the tramp that stands looking on an opportunity of stepping into a position at eight hours a day. It is said that a vast majority of those who are idle would not work if they had work to do. That statement is untrue; but let us admit that five hundred thousand of the two million idle men would not work, we still have a million and a half who are anxious and willing to work. If but six million of the seventeen million producers will abstain from working ten, fifteen, and eighteen hours a day, and work but eight, the one million and a half of idle men that are willing to work can again take their places in the ranks of the world's producers. Need it be said that a million and a half of new hats will be needed; that a corresponding number of pairs of shoes, suits of clothing, and a hundred other things, will be required; that the wants of these men and their families will be supplied; that shelves will be emptied of their goods, and that the money expended will again go into circulation. It would entail hardship on some branches of business to require men employed in them to work eight hours a day. Miners and those working by contract could not very well adopt the eight hour plan without lengthening their hours of labor. Before giving the matter a second thought, many of these men look upon the eight hour agitation as of no consequence to them. If a mechanic is thrown out of employment and can not find anything to do at his trade, he turns toward the first place where an opportunity for work is presented. If he is re-enforced by two million idle men, the number that apply at the mouth of the mine, or seek to secure contracts at lower figures, becomes quite large, and the miner and contract man grumble because so many men are crowding in upon them in quest of work. Every new applicant for work in the mine makes it possible for the boss to let his contract to a lower bidder; therefore it is clearly to the interest of the miner to assist in reducing the hours of labor in shop, mill, and factory, to the end that the idle millions may be gathered in from the streets to self-sustaining positions.

The eight hour system, to be of value to the masses, must be put in operation all over the country, for the manufacturers of one State can not successfully compete with those of other States if they run their establishments but eight hours while others operate theirs ten or twelve hours a day. The movement should be national, and should have the hearty co-operation of all men.

A Scottish clergyman, Dr. Donald Macleod, in a sermon on "The Sin of Cheapness," says that "the craving for cheapness and hunting after bargains is not only economically false, but a cause of great suffering to thousands of men, women, and children." If men worked shorter hours, they would learn that when a man begins to look for cheap bargains he strikes a blow at trade everywhere. The employer looks for a better bargain in labor, and reduces his force or hires cheaper men. His employé must practice enforced economy, which is no saving; he drives sharper bargains for articles manufactured by others; he can not purchase as good an article, or in such quantities, as before; and the effect is felt where these articles are made, taking the shape of a reduction either in the working force or in the wages. When the President of the United States issued his Thanksgiving proclamation in 1884, there were millions of men and women in want of bread, notwithstanding "the abundant harvests and continued prosperity which God hath vouch-safed to this nation," and the cry, not of thanksgiving, went up from millions of farmers of "Too much wheat!" Doubting as to the exact meaning of the Creator in growing so much wheat, they invoked the aid of such institutions as the Chicago Board of Trade, in the hope of thwarting the will of God by cornering wheat. These men invoked blessings on their Thanksgiving dinners, and thanked God for the turkey, while they hoarded the wheat away from those who asked for bread.

Give men shorter hours in which to labor, and you give them more time to study and learn why bread is so scarce while wheat is so plenty. You give them more time in which to learn that millions of acres of American soil are controlled by alien landlords who have no interest in America but to draw a revenue from it. You give them time to learn that America belongs to Americans, native and naturalized, and that the landlord who drives his tenant from the Old World must not be permitted to exact tribute from him when he settles in our country.

Woman Wants Bread, Not the Ballot! (ca. 1870–1880)

Susan B. Anthony

This speech was delivered in most of the major cities in the United States between 1870 and 1880. However, the speech was never written down, and this excerpt was created from notes and newspaper reports.

My purpose tonight is to demonstrate the great historical fact that disfranchisement is not only political degradation, but also moral, social, educational and industrial degradation; and that it does not matter whether the disfranchised class live under a monarchial or a republican form of government, or whether it be white workingmen of England, negroes on our southern plantations, serfs of Russia, Chinamen on our Pacific coast, or native born, tax-paying women of this republic. Wherever, on the face of the globe or on the page of history, you show me a disfranchised class, I will show you a degraded class of labor. Disfranchisement means inability to make, shape or control one's own circumstances. The disfranchised must always do the work, accept the wages, occupy the position the enfranchised assign to them. The disfranchised are in the position of the pauper. You remember the old adage, "Beggars must not be choosers," they must take what they can get or nothing! That is exactly the position of women in the world of work today; they can not choose. If they could, do you for a moment believe they would take the subordinate places and the inferior pay? Nor is it a "new thing under the sun" for the disfranchised, the inferior classes weighed down with wrongs, to declare they "do not want to vote." The rank and file are not philosophers, they are not educated to think for themselves, but simply to accept, unquestioned, whatever comes.

Years ago in England when the workingmen, starving in the mines and factories, gathered in mobs and took bread wherever they could get it, their friends tried to educate them into a knowledge of the causes of their poverty and degradation. At one of these "monster bread meetings," held in Manchester, John Bright said to them, "Workingmen, what you need to bring to you cheap bread and plenty of it, is the franchise"; but those ignorant men shouted back to Mr. Bright, precisely as the women of America do to us today, "It is not the vote we want, it is bread," and they broke up the meeting, refusing to allow him, their best friend, to explain to them the powers of the franchise. The condition of those workingmen was very little above that of slavery. Some of you may remember when George Thompson came over to this country and rebuked us for our crime and our curse of slavery, how the slaveholders and their abettors shouted back to Mr. Thompson.

"Look at home, look into your mines and your factories, you have slavery in England"....

It is said women do not need the ballot for their protection because they are supported by men. Statistics show that there are 3,000,000 women in this nation supporting themselves. In the crowded cities of the East they are compelled to work in shops, stores and factories for the merest pittance. In New York alone, there are over 50,000 of these women receiving less than fifty cents a day. Women wage-earners in different occupations have organized themselves into trades unions, from time to time, and made their strikes to get justice at the hands of their employers just as men have done, but I have yet to learn of a successful strike of any body of women. The best organized one I ever knew was that of the collar laundry women of the city of Troy, N.Y., the great emporium for the manufacture of shirts, collars and cuffs. They formed a trades union of several hundred members and demanded an increase of wages. It was refused. So one May morning in 1867, each woman threw down her scissors and her needle, her starch-pan and flat-iron, and for three long months not one returned to the factories. At the end of that time, they were literally starved out, and the majority of them were compelled to go back, but not at their old wages, for their employers cut them down to even a lower figure.

In the winter following I met the president of this union, a bright young Irish girl, and asked her, "Do you not think if you had been 500 carpenters or 500 masons, you would have succeeded?" "Certainly," she said, and then she told me of 200 bricklayers who had the year before been on strike and gained every point with their employers. "What could have made the difference? Their 200 were but a fraction of that trade, while your 500 absolutely controlled yours." Finally, she said, "It was because the editors ridiculed and denounced us." "Did they ridicule and denounce the bricklayers?" "No." "What did they say about you?" "Why, that our wages were good enough now, better than those of any other workingwomen except teachers; and if we weren't satisfied, we had better go and get married." "What then do you think made this difference?" After studying over the question awhile she concluded, "It must have been because our employers bribed the editors." "Couldn't the employers of the bricklayers have bribed the editors?" She had never thought of that. Most people never do think; they see one thing totally unlike another, but the person who stops to inquire into the cause that produces the one or the other is the exception. So this young Irish girl was simply not an exception, but followed the general rule of people, whether men or women; she hadn't thought. In the case of the bricklayers, no editor, either Democrat or Republican, would have accepted the proffer of a bribe, because he would have known that if he denounced or ridiculed those men, not only they but all the trades union men of the city at the next election would vote solidly against the nominees advocated by that editor. If those collar laundry women had been voters, they would have held, in that little city of Troy, the "balance of political power" and the editor or the politician who ignored or insulted them would have turned that balance over to the opposing party.

My friends, the condition of those collar laundry women but represents the utter helplessness of disfranchisement. The question with you, as men, is not whether you want your wives and daughters to vote, nor with you, as women, whether you yourselves want to vote; but whether you will help to put this power of the ballot into the hands of the 3,000,000 wage-earning women, so that they may be able to compel politicians to legislate in their favor and employers to grant them justice.

The law of capital is to extort the greatest amount of work for the least amount of money; the rule of labor is to do the smallest amount of work for the largest amount of money. Hence there is, and in the nature of things must continue to be, antagonism between the two classes; therefore, neither should be left wholly at the mercy of the other....

I believe that by nature men are no more unjust than women. If from the beginning women had maintained the right to rule not only themselves but men also, the latter today doubtless would be occupying the subordinate places with inferior pay in the world of work; women would be holding the higher positions with the big salaries; widowers would be doomed to a "life interest of one-third of the family estate"; husbands would "owe service" to their wives, so that every one of you men would be begging your good wives, "Please be so kind as to 'give me' ten cents for a cigar." The principle of self-government cannot be violated with impunity. The individual's right to it is sacred—regardless of class, caste, race, color, sex or any other accident or incident of birth. What we ask is that you shall cease to imagine that women are outside this law, and that you shall come into the knowledge that disfranchisement means the same degradation to your daughters as to your sons.

Governments cannot afford to ignore the rights of those holding the ballot, who make and unmake every law and law-maker. It is not because the members of Congress are tyrants that women receive only half pay and are admitted only to inferior positions in the departments. It is simply in obedience to a law of political economy which makes it impossible for a government to do as much for the disfranchised as for the enfranchised. Women are no exception to the general rule. As disfranchisement always has degraded men, socially, morally and industrially, so today it is disfranchisement that degrades women in the same spheres.

Again men say it is not votes, but the law of supply and demand which regulates wages. The law of gravity is that water shall run down hill, but when men build a dam across the stream, the force of gravity is stopped and the water held back. The law of supply and demand regulates free and enfranchised labor, but disfranchisement stops its operation. What we ask is the removal of the dam, that women, like men, may reap the benefit of the law. Did the law of supply and demand regulate work and wages in the olden days of slavery? This law can no more reach the disfranchised than it did the enslaved. There is scarcely a place where a woman can earn a single dollar without a man's consent.

There are many women equally well qualified with men for principals and superintendents of schools, and yet, while three-fourths of the teachers are women, nearly all of them are relegated to subordinate positions on half or at most two-thirds the salaries paid to men. The law of supply and demand is ignored, and that of sex alone settles the question. If a business man should advertise for a book-keeper and ten young men, equally well qualified, should present themselves and, after looking them over, he should say, "To you who have red hair, we will pay full wages, while to you with black hair we will pay half the regular price," that would not be a more flagrant violation of the law of supply and demand than is that now perpetrated upon women because of their sex.

And then again you say, "Capital, not the vote, regulates labor." Granted, for the sake of the argument, that capital does control the labor of women, Chinamen and slaves; but no one with eyes to see and ears to hear, will concede for a moment that capital absolutely dominates the work and wages of the free and enfranchised men of this republic. It is in order to lift the millions of our wage-earning women into a position of as much power over their own labor as men possess that they should be invested with the franchise. This ought to be done not only for the sake of justice to the women, but to the men with whom they compete; for, just so long as there is a degraded class of labor in the market, it always will be used by the capitalists to checkmate and undermine the superior classes....

We recognize that the ballot is a two-edged, nay, a many-edged sword, which may be made to cut in every direction. If wily politicians and sordid capitalists may wield it for mere party and personal greed; if oppressed wage-earners may invoke it to wring justice from legislators and extort material advantages from employers; if the lowest and most degraded classes of men may use it to open wide the sluice-ways of vice and crime; if it may be the instrumentality by which the narrow, selfish, corrupt and corrupting men and measures rule—it is quite as true that noble-minded statesmen, philanthropists and reformers may make it the weapon with which to reverse the above order of things, as soon as they can have added to their now small numbers the immensely larger ratio of what men so love to call "the better half of the people." When women vote, they will make a new balance of power that must be weighed and measured and calculated in its effect upon every social and moral question which goes to the arbitrament of the ballot-box. Who can doubt that when the representative women of thought and culture, who are today the moral backbone of our nation, sit in counsel with the best men of the country, higher conditions will be the result? ...

We Seek Liberty for the Slave (1886)

Albert Parsons

Albert Parsons gave this speech in court as he was about to be sentenced to death for his supposed role in the Haymarket affair.

... Your honor: if there is one distinguishing characteristic which has made itself prominent in the conduct of this trial, it has been the passion, the heat, and the anger, the violence both to sentiment and to person, of everything connected with this case. You ask me why sentence of death should not be pronounced upon me, or, what is tantamount to the same thing, you ask me why you should give me a new trial in order that I might establish my innocence and the ends of justice be subserved. I answer you and say that this verdict is the verdict of passion, born in passion, nurtured in passion, and is the sum total of the organized passion of the city of Chicago. For this reason I ask your suspension of the sentence and the granting of a new trial....

In order that I may place myself properly before you, it is necessary, in vindication of whatever I may have said or done in the history of my past life, that I should enter somewhat into details, and I claim, even at the expense of being lengthy, the ends of justice require that this shall be done.

For the past twenty years my life has been closely identified with, and I have actively participated in, what is known as the labor movement in America. I have some knowledge of that movement in consequence of this experience and of the careful study which opportunity has afforded me from time to time to give to the matter, and what I have to say upon this subject relating to the labor movement or to myself as connected with it in this trial and before this bar—I will speak the truth, the whole truth, be the consequences what they may.

The United States census for 1880 reports that there are in the United States 16,200,000 wage workers. These are the persons who, by their industry, create all the wealth of this country. And now before I say anything further it may be necessary in order to clearly understand what I am going to state further on, for me to define what I mean and what is meant in the labor movement by these words, wage worker. Wage workers are those who work for wages and who have no other means of subsistence than the selling of their daily toil from hour to hour, day to day, week to week, month to month, and year to year, as the case may be. Their whole property consists entirely of their labor—strength and skill or, rather, they possess nothing but their empty hands. They live only when afforded an opportunity to work, and this opportunity must be procured from the possessors of the means of subsistence—capital—before their right to live at all or the opportunity to do so is possessed. Now, there are 16,200,000 of these people in the United States, according to the census of 1880. Among this number are 9,000,000 men, and reckoning five persons to each family, they represent 45,000,000 of our population. It is claimed that there are between eleven and twelve million voters in the United States. Now, out of these 12,000,000 voters, 9,000,000 are wage workers. The remainder of the 16,200,000 is composed of the women and children employed in the factories, the mines and the various avocations of this country. This class of people—the working class who alone do all the useful and productive labor of this country are the hirelings and dependents of the propertied class....

Now, the money makers, the business men, those people who deal in stocks and bonds, the speculators and employers, all that class of men known as the money making class, have no conception of this labor question; they don't understand what it means. To use the street parlance, with many of them it is a difficult matter to "catch onto" it, and they are perverse also; they will not have knowledge of it. They don't want to know anything about it, and they won't hear anything about it, and they propose to club, lock up, and, if necessary, strangle those who insist on their hearing this question. Can it any longer be denied that there is such a thing as the labor question?

I am an Anarchist. Now strike! But hear me before you strike. What is Socialism, or Anarchism? Briefly stated, it is the right of the toiler to the free and equal use of the tools of production, and the right of the producers to their product. That is Socialism. The history of mankind is one of growth. It has been evolutionary and revolutionary. The dividing line between evolution and revolution, or that imperceptible boundary line where one begins and the other ends can never be designated. Who believed at the time that our fathers tossed the tea into Boston harbor that it meant the first act of the revolution separating this continent from the dominion of George III and founding this republic here in which we, their descendants, live today. Evolution and revolution are synonymous. Evolution is the incubatory state of revolution. The birth is the revolution—its process the evolution.

What is the history of man with regard to the laboring classes? Originally the earth and its contents were held in common by all men. Then came a change brought about by violence, robbery and wholesale murder, called war. Later, but still way back in history, we find that there were but two classes in the world—slaves and masters. Time rolled on and we find a labor system of serf-dom. This serf labor system existed in the sixteenth and seventeenth centuries, and throughout the world the serf had a right to the soil on which he lived. The lord of the land could not exclude him from its use. But the discovery of America and the developments which followed that discovery and its settlement, a century or two afterwards, the gold found in Peru and Mexico by the invading hosts of Pizarro and Cortez, who carried back to Europe this precious metal, infused new vitality into the commercial stagnant blood of Europe and set in motion those wheels which have rolled on and on, until today commerce covers the face of the earth; time is annihilated and distance is known no more. Following the abolition of the serfdom system was the establishment of the wage labor system. This found its fruition, or birth, rather, in the French Revolutions of 1789 and 1793. It was then for the first time that civil and political liberty was established in Europe. We see, by a mere glance back into history, that the sixteenth century was engaged in a struggle for religious freedom and the right of conscience—mental liberty. Following that in the seventeenth and eighteenth centuries was the struggle throughout France which resulted in the establishment of the republic and the founding of the right of political liberty. The struggle today, which follows on in the line of progress and in the logic of events, is the industrial problem, of which we were the representatives, as the State's attorney has said we were, selected by the grand jury because we were leaders, and are to be punished and consigned to an ignominious death for that reason, that the wage slaves of Chicago and of America may be horrified, terror-stricken, and driven like rats back to their holes, to hunger, slavery, misery and death. The industrial question, following on in the natural order of events, the wage system of industry is now up for consideration; it presses for a hearing; it demands a solution; it cannot be throttled by this district attorney, nor all the district attorneys upon the soil of America.

Now, what is this labor question which these gentlemen treat with such profound contempt, for advocating which these distinguished "honorable" gentlemen would throttle and put us to an ignominious death and hurry us like rats into our holes? What is it? You will pardon me if I exhibit some feeling. I have sat here for two months, and these men have poured their vituperations out upon my head and I have not been permitted to utter a single word in my own defense. For two months they have poured their poison upon me and upon my colleagues. For two months they have sat here and spat like adders the vile poison of their tongues, and if men could have been placed in a mental inquisition and tortured to death, these men would have succeeded here now, for we have been vilified, misrepresented, held in loathsome contempt, without a chance to speak or contradict a word. Therefore, if I show emotion, it is because of this, and if my comrades and colleagues with me here have spoken in such strains as these, it is because of this. Pardon us. Look at it from the right standpoint. What is this labor question? It is not a question of emotion; the labor question is not a question of sentiment; it is not a religious matter; it is not a political problem; no, sir, it is a stern economic fact, a stubborn and immovable fact. It has, it is true, its emotional phase; it has its sentimental, religious, political aspects; but the sum total of this question is the bread and butter question, the how and why we shall live and earn our daily bread. This is the labor movement, it has a scientific basis. It is founded upon fact, and I have been to considerable pains in my researches of well known and distinguished authors on this question to collect and present to you briefly what this question is and what it springs from. I will first explain to you briefly what capital is:

Capital is the stored up and accumulated surplus of past labor; capital is the product of labor. The function of capital is to appropriate or confiscate for its own use and benefit the "surplus" labor product of the wage laborer. The capitalistic system originated in the forcible seizure of natural opportunities and rights by a few, and then converting those things into special privileges which have since become vested rights, formally entrenched behind the bulwarks of statute law and government. Capital could not exist unless there also existed a majority class who were propertyless, that is, without capital, a class whose only mode of existence is the selling of their labor to capitalists. Capitalism is maintained, fostered, and perpetuated by law; in fact, capital is law—statute law—and law is capital. Now, briefly stated, for I will not take your time but for a moment, what is labor? Labor is a commodity and wages is the price paid for it. The owner of this commodity sells it, that is, himself, to the owner of capital in order to live. Labor is the expression of energy, the power of the laborer's life. This energy or power he must sell to another person in order to live. It is his only means of existence. He works to live, but his work is not simply a part of his life; it is the sacrifice of it. His labor is a commodity which under the guise of free labor he is forced by necessity to hand over to another party. The whole of the wage laborer's activity is not the product of his labor—far from it. The silk he weaves, the palace he builds, the ores he digs from out the mines, are not for him. The only thing he produces for himself is his wages, and the silk, the ores, and the palace which he built, are simply transformed for him into a certain kind of means of existence, namely, a cotton shirt, a few pennies, and the mere tenancy of a lodging house. In other words, his wages represent the bare necessities of his existence, and the unpaid-for or "surplus" portion of his labor product constitutes the vast superabundant wealth of the non-producing or capitalist class.

That is the capitalist system defined in a few words. It is this system that creates these classes, and it is these classes that produce this conflict. This conflict intensifies as the power of the privileged classes over the nonpossessing or propertyless classes increases and intensifies, and this power increases as the idle few become richer and the producing many become poorer; and this produces what is called the labor movement. This is the labor question. Wealth is power; poverty is weakness.

If I had time I might stop here to answer some suggestions that probably arise in the minds of some persons, or perhaps of your honor, not being familiar with this question. I imagine I hear your honor say, "Why, labor is free. This is a free country." Now, we had in the southern states for nearly a century a form of labor known as chattel slave labor. That has been abolished, and I hear you say that labor is free; that the war has resulted in establishing free labor all over America. Is this true? Look at it. The chattel slave of the past—the wage slave of today; what is the difference? The master selected under chattel slavery his own slaves. Under the wage slavery system the wage slave selects his master, and he has got to find one or else he is carried down here to my friend, the jailer, and occupies a cell along side of myself. He is compelled to find one. So the change of the industrial system, in the language of Jefferson Davis, ex-president of the Southern Confederacy, in an interview with the New York *Herald* upon the question of the chattel slave system of the South and that of the so-called "free laborer," and their wages—Jefferson Davis stated positively that the change was a decided benefit to the former chattel slave owners who would not exchange the new system of wage labor at all for chattel labor, because now the dead had to bury themselves and the sick take care of themselves, and now they don't have to employ overseers to look after them. They give them a task to do—a certain amount to do. They say: "Now, here, perform this piece of work in a certain length of time," and if you don't (under the wage system, says Mr. Davis), why, when you come around for your pay next Saturday, you simply find in the envelope which contains your money, a note which informs you of the fact that you have been discharged. Now, Jefferson Davis admitted in his statement that the leather thong dipped in salt brine, for the chattel slave, had been exchanged under the wage system for the lash of hunger, an empty stomach and the ragged back of the wage slave of free born American sovereign citizens, who, according to the census of the United States for 1880, constitute more than nine-tenths of our entire population.

But you say the wage slave had advantages over the chattel slave. The chattel slave couldn't get away from it. Well, if we had the statistics, I believe it could be shown that as many chattel slaves escaped from bondage with the bloodhounds of their masters after them as they tracked their way over the snow-beaten rocks of Canada, and via the underground grape vine road—I believe the statistics would show that as many chattel slaves escaped from their bondage under that system as can and do escape today from wage bondage into capitalistic liberty.

I am a Socialist, I am one of those, although myself a wage slave, who holds that it is wrong, wrong to myself, wrong to my neighbor, and unjust to my fellowmen for me, wage slave that I am, to undertake to make my escape from wage slavery by becoming a master and an owner of slaves myself. I refuse to do it; I refuse equally to be a slave or the owner of slaves. Had I chosen another path in life, I might be upon the avenue of the city of Chicago today, surrounded in my beautiful home with luxury and ease, with slaves to do my bidding. But I chose the other road, and instead I stand here today upon the scaffold. This is my crime. Before high heaven this and this alone is my crime. I have been false and a traitor to the infamies that exist today in capitalistic society. If this is a crime in your opinion I plead guilty to it.

Now, be patient with me; I have been with you, or rather, I have been patient with this trial. Follow me, if you please, and look at the oppressions of this capitalistic system of industry. As was depicted by my comrade Fielden, this morning, every new machine that comes into existence comes as a competitor with the man of labor; as a drag and menace and a prey to the very existence of those who have to sell their labor in order to earn their bread. The man is turned out to starve, and whole occupations and pursuits are revolutionized and completely destroyed by the introduction of machinery, in a day, in an hour as it were. I have known it to be the case in the history of my own life—and I am yet a young man—that whole pursuits and occupations have been wiped out by the invention of machinery.

What becomes of these people? Where are they? They become competitors of other laborers and are made to reduce wages and increase the work hours. Many of them are candidates for the gibbet, they are candidates for your prison cells. Build more penitentiaries; erect new scaffolds, for these men are upon the highway of crime, of misery, of death. Your honor, there never was an effect without a cause. The tree is known by its fruit. Socialists are not those who blindly close their eyes and refuse to look, and who refuse to hear, but having eyes to see, they see, and having ears to hear, they hear. Look at this capitalistic system; look at its operation upon the small business men; the small dealers, the middle class. *Bradstreet's* tells us in last year's report that there were 11,000 small business men financially destroyed during the past twelve months. What became of those people? Where are they, and why have they been wiped out? Has there been any less wealth? No; that which they possessed has simply been transferred into the hands of some other person. Who is that other? It is he who has greater capitalistic facilities. It is the monopolist, the man who can run corners, who can create rings and squeeze these men to death and wipe them out like dead flies from the table into his monopolistic basket. The middle classes destroyed in this manner join the ranks of the proletariat. They become what? They seek out the factory gate, they seek in the various occupations of wage labor employment. What is the result? Then there are more men upon the market. This increases the number of those who are applying for employment. What then? This intensifies the competition, which in turn creates greater monopolists, and with it wages go down until the starvation point is reached, and then what? Your honor, Socialism comes to the people and asks them to look into this thing, to discuss it, to reason, to examine it, to investigate it, to know the facts, because it is by this, and this alone, that violence will be prevented and bloodshed will be avoided; because, as my friend here has said, men in their blind rage, in ignorance, not knowing what ails them, knowing that they are hungry, that they are miserable and destitute, strike blindly, and do as they did with Maxwell here, and fight the labor saving machinery. Imagine such an absurd thing, and yet the capitalistic press has taken great pains to say that Socialists do these things; that we fight machinery; that we fight property. Why, sir, it is an absurdity; it is ridiculous; it is preposterous. No man ever heard an utterance from the mouth of a Socialist to advise anything of the kind. They know to the contrary. We don't fight machinery; we don't oppose the thing. It is only the manner and methods of employing them that we object to. That is all. It is the manipulations of these things in the interests of a few; it is the monopolization of them that we object to. We desire that all the forces of nature, all the forces of society, of the gigantic strength which has resulted from the combined intellect and labor of the ages of the past shall be turned over to man, and made his servant, his obedient slave forever. This is the object of Socialism. It asks no one to give up anything. It seeks no harm to anybody. But, when we witness this condition of things, when we see little children huddling around the factory gates, the poor little things whose bones are not yet hard; when we see them clutched from the hearthstone, taken from the family altar, carried to the bastiles of labor and their little bones ground up into gold dust to bedeck the form of some aristocratic Jezebel, then it stirs us and we speak out. We plead for the little ones; we plead for the helpless; we plead for the oppressed; we seek redress for those who are wronged; we seek knowledge and intelligence for the ignorant; we seek liberty for the slave. Socialism secures the welfare of every human being....

What is Anarchy? What are its doctrines ... for which I am called upon to die. First and foremost, it is our opinion, or the opinion of an Anarchist, that government is despotism; government is an organization of oppression, and law, statute law, is its agent. Anarchy is anti-government, anti-rulers, anti-dictators, anti-bosses and drivers. Anarchy is the negation of force; the elimination of all authority in social affairs; it is the denial of the right of domination of one man over another. It is the diffusion of rights, of power, of duties, equally and freely among all the people. But Anarchy, your honor, like many other words, is defined by Webster's dictionary as having two meanings. In one place it is defined to mean, "without rulers or governors." In another place it is defined to mean, "disorder and confusion." Now, this latter meaning is what we call "capitalistic Anarchy," such as is now witnessed in all portions of the world and especially in this court room; the former, which means without rulers, is what we denominate Communistic Anarchy, which will be ushered in with the social revolution.

Socialism is a word which covers the whole range of human progress and advancement. Socialism is defined by Webster—I think I have a right to speak of this matter, because I am tried here as a Socialist. I am condemned as a Socialist, and it has been of Socialism that my friend Grinnell and these men had so much to say, and I think it right to speak before the country, and be heard in my own behalf, at least. If you are going to put me to death, then let the people know what it is for. Socialism is defined by Webster as "a theory of society which advocates a more precise, more orderly, and more harmonious arrangement of the social relations of mankind than has hitherto prevailed." Therefore everything in the line of progress, in civilization, in fact, is Socialistic. There are two distinct phases of Socialism in the labor movement throughout the world today. One is known as Anarchism, without political government or authority, the other is known as State Socialism or paternalism, or governmental control of everything. The State Socialist seeks to ameliorate and emancipate the wage laborers by means of law, by legislative enactments. The State Socialists demand the right to choose their own rulers. Anarchists would have neither rulers nor law makers of any kind. The Anarchists seek the same ends by the abrogation of law, by the abolition of all government, leaving the people free to unite or disunite, as fancy or interest may dictate, coercing no one, driving no party....

You accuse the Anarchists of using or advising the use of force; it is false. "Out of your own mouth you stand condemned." The present existing state of society is based upon and maintained and perpetuated by force. This capitalistic system that we have today would not exist twenty-four hours if it were not held together by the bayonets and the clubs of the militia and police. No, sir, it would not! Now, sir, we object to this. We protest against it. But you accuse us, or the prosecution here accuses us, of that very thing which they themselves are guilty of. It is the old, old story of Aesop's fable, the lamb standing in the water and the wolf above him; he looks up; the water has run down, the wolf stands above him; he looks down there toward the lamb, and says, "Ho, there! you are making the water muddy." The lamb observes, "My friend, I am below you in the stream." "That doesn't matter; you are my meat, anyhow." And he goes for him and eats him up. That is just the way of the capitalist toward the Anarchist. You are doing the very thing you accuse us of, and against which we protest. Now, any institution that is based upon force is self-condemned; it does not need any argument, in my opinion, to prove it....

Socialism, your honor, means the abolition of wage slavery, because it allows the people to carry on production and consumption by means of a system of universal co-operation. That is what I said at the Haymarket. I pointed out at the Haymarket the fact that the workingmen were being deprived, according to Colonel Wright, the commissioner of the Bureau of Labor Statistics of the United States. He proves by the statistics that they were producing values to the extent of $10 a day, and receiving $1.15; that they were being deprived of $8.85. Now, I said to them: "Here," said I, "Socialism will give you that $8.85; under Socialism you would get that whole $10, whereas under the wage system you receive $1.15 of it. But that is not all: Socialism will make your labor saving machinery a blessing instead of a curse to you; by it wealth will be increased, and drudgery diminished indefinitely. Socialism is simple justice, because wealth is a social, not an individual product, and its appropriation by a few members of society creates a privileged class—a class who monopolize all the benefits of society by enslaving the producing class." Now, your honor, this is what makes the monopolists mad at the Anarchists. This angers the corporation men. See what they say. The result is that a verdict must be brought against Socialism; because, as the district attorney states here, the law, and the government, and Anarchy are upon trial. That is the reason. Not for what I did, but it is for what I believe. It is what I say that these men object to. The verdict was against Socialism....

Charity Organization and the Buffalo Plan (1882)

S. Humphreys Gurteen

Gurteen was the main person to apply scientific charity in the creation of the Charity Organization Society.

The plan for the Organization of Charities, which we are about to describe, has now stood the test of more than eleven years in leading cities of England, and for over four years past has been in successful operation in the city of Buffalo, N.Y.; indeed, we feel convinced, that it is the only plan, so far devised, for dealing effectively with the great question of pauperism. Before, however, entering upon the main question, we would call attention to two important facts:

First. In every one of our large cities, we see poverty, distress and want in a hundred different forms, from the temporary distress of the honest *poor* who prefer to work rather than to beg, to the chronic indigence of the *pauper* who prefers to beg rather than to work; and so down to the criminal who has qualified by dissipation and lawlessness for the reformatory or prison.

Second. At the same time we see in these same cities various agencies, official and private, for the relief of this wide-spread suffering and destitution—asylums, benevolent societies, hospitals and reformatories for the giving of food, clothing or medicine, or for the reclaiming of the erring.

Yet, in spite of all that is being done in the way of charitable relief, it is found on all hands:

1. That pauperism is steadily on the increase in almost every city in the land.
2. That the most truly deserving are those who do not seek, and, therefore, very often do not get relief.
3. That the pauper, the impostor and the fraud of every description carry off at least one-half of all charity, public and private, and hence there is a constant and deplorable waste in the alms-fund of every large city.
4. That by far the larger part of all that is given, even to the honest poor, in the name of charity, is doing positive harm by teaching them to be idle, shiftless and improvident.
5. That but little effort is made, as a rule, to inculcate provident habits among the poor, or to establish provident schemes based on sound business principles, so as to aid the poor to be self-supporting.
6. That little, if anything, is being done to check the evils arising from overcrowded and unhealthy tenements, or to suppress the curses of bastardy, baby-farming and other evils peculiar to the individual city.

Now, we say, without fear of contradiction, that no single parish, no single church, no single benevolent society, no single association ever has or ever can accomplish any permanent reform in this matter of pauperism, with all its attendant evils; and that so long at least as a community divided up, as every community is, into opposing creeds and parties, refuses to work on some common principles which all can adopt, no reform can be expected. On the contrary, the very fact of the existence of various conflicting interests preventing band-work, preventing union, preventing harmonious co-operation, can but tend to aggravate the evils which it is the object of each to eradicate.

Besides, in the suppression of some of the grosser evils which we have mentioned, not even the first step in reform can be taken except by the co-operation of all classes, all creeds, all parties in the community; unless all band together for the attainment of a common object. So firmly rooted have the abuses become, that nothing short of the banded strength of the whole community can ever suppress them.

Now, Charity Organization means the banding together of all the various interests of the city for mutual protection against imposition; for effective working in the matter of relief; for the economic disbursement of the alms-fund of the city; for the improvement of the condition of the poor, and for the reform of abuses which at present are known, perhaps, only to the few.

It means the co-operation of the Mayor, the Chief of Police and the Poor-master, as far as *official* relief-work is concerned.

It means the co-operation of every church, every asylum, every benevolent society, fraternity or citizen, as far as *private* relief-work is concerned.

Moreover, to make such co-operation effective, there must be the adoption of the rules of political economy and of business principles in this subject of charity, which hitherto has been regarded as belonging solely to the sphere of religion or philanthropy.

A Charity Organization *Society* is thus a centre of intercommunication between the various charities and charitable agencies of any given city; an intermediary acting on behalf of each and for the welfare of each, and, from its neutral character, making possible a degree of co-operation which would be impossible apart from such organized action.

Now, the principles which the Society lays down in order to effect the full and complete co-operation of which we have spoken, and apart from which no lasting co-operation is possible, are the following:

1. *There must be no exclusion of any person or body of persons on account of religious creed, politics or nationality.*

These are the subjects which chiefly divide public and private sentiment in any community; they are the chief causes of dissension, and it is absolutely necessary, therefore, that these should be avoided in any scheme of co-operation which appeals to the public at large. Accordingly, the Charity Organization Society, as started in this country in 1877, laid it down as a fundamental principle that the Society should recognize in its operations no form of religious belief, no political affiliations and no national distinctions. All cases were to be investigated impartially and decided on their merits, independently of the altar at which the applicant worshipped, the political party to which he belonged, or the nationality which had given him birth. When the Society, however, had performed its duty in the premises, then the case might be *referred for relief* to any benevolent association, religious or secular, according to the nature of the case. But the Society, as a Society, *i.e.*, in the persons of its Council, District Committees, Agents and Volunteer Visitors in each and every part of its work, was to ignore all questions of this nature.

The practical working of this "golden rule," in the City of Buffalo, where the Society started, has been eminently successful, and has enlisted the co-operation of all creeds to a degree which has surprised even the most sanguine advocates of the scheme.

2. There must be no attempt at proselytism on the part of the Agents or others employed by the Organization.

This rule of the Society is one of highest importance, if hearty and universal co-operation is to be secured. Should the Society countenance any attempt, on the part of those *officially* connected with it, to tamper with the religious faith of those whose social and moral condition it seeks to improve and elevate, it would meet with deserved opposition from men of every creed and every shade of religious belief. The Society advocates, it is true, the complete severance of charitable relief from all considerations of religion, even on the part of those who co-operate, but are not officially connected with it; but the Society does not expect, at once, to overcome traditional exclusiveness in charity, or induce the majority of people to give, simply because a fellow-creature is *poor,* and with no secret hope of finally making a proselyte. The Society, however, allows no proselytizing, whatsoever, in any work of which it has the control.

3. There must be no interference with any existing benevolent societies; each society must retain its autonomy intact; its rules, funds, modes of operation and everything which gives it individuality.

One of the most formidable obstacles that the Society has had to contend against, especially in the older cities, is the unreasoning prejudice of long-established charitable institutions and benevolent societies. Many of these have run away with the idea that, if they join in the organization or banding together of the charities of a city, they will lose their individuality and their work will be rendered, thereby, less effective. A more erroneous impression than this, it would be difficult to conceive. The Society interferes in no way, shape or manner with any existing institution, provided its operations tend to better and not to degrade the condition of the poor. Were it otherwise, the Society could not expect to succeed. Once let the salient point be firmly fixed in the mind, that the object of the Society is simply mutual protection and more effective work, mutual help and free interchange of information, and their hearty co-operation will be easily gained.

4. *There must be no relief given by the Organization itself, except in very urgent cases.*

This is one of the Society's most striking features, that it refuses absolutely to be the dispenser of alms in any shape whatsoever, unless in very exceptional cases. It leaves the sacred duty of alms-giving where it belongs, viz., to the Church or the benevolent Society, or the individual citizen. Not only would the Society fail to gain the co-operation of all religious and benevolent associations if it attempted to interfere in such a matter as this, it would, moreover, expose itself to charges of partiality and unfair dealing, which, whether just or unjust, would inevitably bring the Society's career to a speedy and ignominious ending. But apart from such considerations as these, it is the object of the Organization to help the poor, ultimately, to do without relief, whether official or private. It is true that there are many cases of helpless poverty in every part of the country, which demand at our hands, liberal and wise assistance, but in the vast majority of cases, the poor and the pauper need only such provident help as the Society advocates, to place them in a position of self-support and honorable independence.

5. *There must be no sentiment in the matter. It must be treated as a business scheme, if success is to attend its operations.*

If we keep in mind the *objects* of Charity Organization, that its aims are (1) the repression of pauperism, (2) the improving of the condition of the honest poor, (3) the promotion of provident schemes to aid the struggling poor to be self-supporting, and (4) the reform of social abuses which, at present, are swelling the ranks of pauperism—if we keep in mind the important fact that the Society refrains from interfering in the matter of alms-giving, and is simply an organization of existing charities for the wise administration of charity—it will be seen at once that what is especially needed, in order to effect success, is that the business men of the community take the matter in hand, devoting their business experience to the scheme, and conducting the Society with the same energy and foresight and determination which they evince in commercial life. The control of the Society should never be in the hands of the clergy. Indeed, it is far better that no clergyman should be in the Council. The Society affords ample opportunities for clerical co-operation apart from the direction of its affairs. It is to the business men and professional men (not clergymen) that we must look for the successful working of our Societies.

These are the cardinal principles of successful Organization. Let any one of these "five points" be disregarded, and, sooner or later, Organization will end in total failure....

But the further question remains, how are we to interest the citizens at large?

The first thing to be done is to show the community, in very plain language, the following facts:

1. That Organization renders most efficient aid to the clergy, benevolent societies, institutions, benevolent individuals and the city almoner, by investigating, *free of charge,* all cases applying for relief; thus removing a great burden and a great expense from the shoulders of the benevolent, who desire to give and to give wisely; also by instituting a method of *thorough* investigation, which it is utterly impossible for any single person or society to carry out; and, finally, by supplementing the Poormaster's investigations, by information which even he could not otherwise obtain.

2. That, wherever Organization has been started, it has, without a single exception, either abolished out-door city relief altogether or has reduced the amount, hitherto annually expended, within comparatively reasonable limits. In Brooklyn, out-door city relief was shown to be illegal and has been discontinued. In Philadelphia, the sum required for this purpose was reduced in a single year from $50,000 to $7,000, and today out-door city relief is wholly abolished. In Buffalo, the saving in one year alone was $48,000, while the average saving during the past three years has been $50,000 per annum. Even if the public poor office is honestly and economically administered, the Organization plan keeps taxation down to the lowest possible figure, and this without any unkindness to the poor; since in every case where either a person is cut off from receiving official aid, or is prevented from applying for it, *work* is invariably procured by the Society in order to make up for the degrading official dole which has been withheld or withdrawn.

3. That beggars and cripples are removed from the streets, and, if able to work, are compelled to do so; if not, they are provided for in some less degrading way. That street-begging disappears and private benevolence being directed only to honest cases, can relieve, more effectually, distress which is known to be genuine.

4. That the poor are gradually but surely led from a state often bordering on pauperization to love self-dependence; while in many cases, actual paupers are reclaimed, and brought to acknowledge the true kindness of the Society's plan, as it rekindles their all but extinct sense of independence.

These results are not imaginary or supposititious; they are results already attained; they are facts which can be shown and proved; so that, as Mr. David Gray, the able editor of the "Buffalo Courier," said a short time ago, the results of the working of the plan of the Charity Organization Society are to-day as fully demonstrated as a proposition in mathematics.

With such facts placed prominently before the public, it is not a very difficult matter to gain the hearty co-operation of a community. The chief thing necessary to success, is to place these facts before all of the citizens in such a way that they cannot fail to understand them; to do so by the press and the pulpit, by circulars, by meetings, by private conversation; and this is not an easy thing to do and to do well, since it demands from those interested, a great deal of time, labor and patience....

Epilogue: Outcomes

The federal government's commitment to uplift African Americans after the Civil War lasted seven years. Under pressure from white Southerners who felt it was an intrusion into their affairs, and lacking support from Northerners who lost their focus on reconstruction, Congress terminated the Freedmen's Bureau in 1872. The legacy of the Freedmen's Bureau to reduce poverty is filled with success and failure. Positively, the Freedmen's Bureau provided 21 million meals and gave medical assistance to (including building hospitals) more than 1 million freed people. In addition, the Freedmen's Bureau founded free and integrated public schools in the South, building more than 1,000 schools and spending more than $400,000 on teacher training. In addition, all of today's major black colleges were either founded by, or received aid from, the Freedmen's Bureau. Clearly, the Freedmen's Bureau demonstrated that the federal government could make a difference in the lives of the poor. At the same time, it had no impact on the nation's overall social welfare policy, and the nation would have to wait seventy years before the federal government would develop a national plan to reduce poverty.[21]

Negatively, the Freedmen's Bureau provided little land to emancipated blacks. Special Field Order No. 15, written by General William Tecumseh Sherman in January of 1865, which gave all land thirty miles inland on the coasts of South

Carolina, Georgia, and Florida to freedmen in forty-acre parcels, was rescinded by President Andrew Johnson nine months later. Johnson was determined to return all confiscated land to southern whites, and thus the 40,000 blacks who had already moved onto the land were forced off. Some tax-delinquent white-owned lands were expropriated for freedmen. However, the vast majority of African Americans were forced into working for wages for whites or in sharecropping, both of which proved to be oppressive. As ex-slave Thomas Hall reported, "Lincoln got the praise for freeing us, but did he do it? He gave us freedom without giving us any chance to live to ourselve [sic] and we still had to depend on the southern white man for work, food, and clothing, and he held us out of necessity and want in a state of servitude but little better than slavery." To make matters worse, whites threatened and intimidated blacks with a terror campaign intended to force them to submit to Jim Crow segregation and second-class citizenship. From 1882 to 1930, 2,500 black people were lynched in the ten southern states. On average, a black person was lynched by a white mob once a week, every week, for fifty years. Even though the murderers were often well-known in the community, virtually no white person was ever arrested or convicted of these crimes.[22]

As African Americans saw their hopes fade with the failure of the U.S. government to secure land for them and with the increase of Jim Crow tactics, Native Americans were struggling to survive on unproductive and isolated reservation land. As Indian leaders like Sitting Bull called on the United States government to live up to its treaties and provide the necessary monetary payments, tools, and livestock they needed to survive and flourish, the U.S. response was dismal. From 1870 to 1900, Congress did not provide enough government assistance for the "transition to civilization." Starvation was part of the so-called civilizing experience as self-supporting indigenous people became paupers. In 1872, 31,000 Native Americans relied entirely on government assistance for survival, while another 84,000 relied on partial aid. Additionally, the Dawes Act led to the loss of two-thirds of all native land. In 1887, Native Americans owned 140 million acres of land collectively; by 1934, when the Dawes Allotment policy was abandoned, Native Americans controlled only 50 million acres. As native land was lost to whites through tax foreclosures, real estate fraud, and the need to sell it for money, thousands of Indians died as they lost their means of subsistence. Ironically, the federal government justified this land takeover as part of the Revolutionary War–era ideology of equality championed by Paine and Jefferson, with its belief that all white men should have a fair footing in the republic.

In the cities, workers' attempts to assert egalitarian ideas had mixed results. In the short term, 42,000 workers forced management to accept the eight-hour workday in 1886, and many other strikers won shorter workdays. The workers were also successful in bringing the nation's attention to the plight of the working class and poor. Unfortunately, Albert Parsons was hanged along with three of his associates, and a fourth committed suicide the day before the execution. Six years after the Parsons execution, Governor John Altgeld, governor of Illinois, pardoned three of the Haymarket anarchists on the grounds that the trial was unjust.

The labor strikes of 1877 and 1886 had frightened many in the middle and upper classes, and their anxiety grew about the rising power of the working class. The capitalists' response was to attempt to destroy the eight-hour workday movement through a variety of means, which included locking out workers who joined unions, blacklisting labor activists, infiltrating labor organizations, hiring different ethnic groups so the workers had difficulty communicating with one another, and using the law to intimidate workers by leveling charges such as incitement to riot and obstructing the streets. In fact, many capitalists just stopped negotiating with strikers, as they realized that sitting down with the workers actually encouraged unionization and militancy. These tactics took their toll, as the percentage of workers belonging to organized labor groups dropped from 8.9 in 1886 to 2.4 in 1890. In 1896, the average work schedule was ten hours a day, six days a week; by 1910, it had been reduced to nine hours a day (or fifty-four hours a week). Workers would have to wait until 1938, fifty-two years after the Haymarket tragedy, for the maximum federal workweek to be set at forty hours per week. Interestingly, a thirty-hour workweek was proposed in the early 1930s as a way to increase employment, which was at the heart of the Powderly plan. The bill passed the Senate in 1933, but neither the House of Representatives nor President Roosevelt supported the proposed thirty-hour workweek.[23]

Parsons's radical vision continued to inspire other labor organizers over the next forty years, with the creation of the International Workers of the World, the Socialist Party, and Unemployment Councils. Today, people all over the world observe May 1 as Labor Day in commemoration of the struggle for the eight-hour workday and the Haymarket tragedy. Interestingly, the United States and Canada are the two nations that do not celebrate May 1 as Labor Day, and this is due to that date's connection with socialism.

The eight-hour workday was not the only social issue that took time to change. Some fifty years after Susan Anthony toured the nation with her "Woman Wants Bread" speech, the United States finally ratified the Nineteenth Amendment, guaranteeing women the right to vote. However, the ability to vote did not lead to a change in material conditions for women as predicted by Anthony. The main reason for the lack of change was that women did not unite and vote in a block.

Women turned out to be divided—just as men were—by social class, ethnicity, religion, and region. Another reason for the lack of change was low voter turnout. For example, the number of women registered to vote in 1928 was 31 percent in Louisiana, 43 percent in Chicago, and 47 percent in Vermont. The political role of women would change in this country, but it would have to wait until women gained more independence within economic and family structures.[24]

Edward Bellamy's book *Looking Backward* sold 1 million copies by the early 1890s. As a result of the book, more than a hundred socialist groups formed in the United States. Although a socialist society was not built during Bellamy's time, the book did have a significant influence on people such as Eugene Debs, founder of the Socialist Party. Henry George's idea for a single tax also generated widespread support in the country, and some have argued that it would have been adopted if it had not been for the strong opposition of the wealthy capitalists. George went on to run for governor of New York in 1886, where he finished in second place, ahead of Theodore Roosevelt, with 31 percent of the vote.[25]

Scientific charity fundamentally altered relief to the poor. Charity Organization Societies were set up in nearly all major cities and eventually in many smaller cities throughout the country, adapting their design to the local conditions. By 1890, COS had achieved one of its goals: the sharp reduction of outdoor relief. In ten large cities, outdoor relief by local governments was completely banned. Moreover, with the COS focus on work, the able-bodied poor were forced out of poorhouses. With few options, the poor turned to cheap hotels, flophouses, and police stations. In fact, police stations provided shelter to more men than did poorhouses in the late nineteenth century. One report put the total number of Americans with at least one family member who had slept at a police station at 10 to 20 percent of the population.

Some of the more established private relief organizations resisted scientific charity. Some were reluctant to work with other private charities and religious institutions; some criticized them for providing no services, and others criticized them for invading the privacy of the poor through intrusive investigations. Then, the depression of 1893 struck and COS were completely overwhelmed, unable to respond to the great need of the poor. By the mid-1890s, most public officials and social welfare professionals had come to the conclusion that scientific charity had failed. However, this did not mean the end of three core components of the COS vision—that local, private charities, moral education, and limited outdoor relief reduce poverty. Even though this poverty reduction strategy was shown to be ineffective, it has continued to play an important role in American ideology and is still central to the poverty debate today, as can be seen by George W. Bush's call for "compassionate conservatism."[26]

Coxey's army of the unemployed marching to Washington, D.C.

Chapter 4

The (Un)Progressive Era

Prologue: Social Context and Overview of Solutions

In the late nineteenth century, industrial capitalism created immense wealth and massive poverty. As a result, the poor and the working class generally lived in substandard housing, lacked basic medical care, and received inadequate education. To make matters worse, the depression of 1893 caused the unemployment rate to soar to 18 percent of the workforce. Compounding the unemployment problem was the large influx of immigrants. This human suffering overwhelmed the Charitable Organization Societies. A group of citizens under the banner of "progressivism" set out to improve the material conditions of the working class and poor by reforming capitalism. At the same time, labor organizations kept up their demand for better pay and working conditions, and some continued to call for the replacement of capitalism with socialism. The capitalist class continued its repression of labor organizations, although some of its more enlightened leaders called for cooperation between business and labor under the banner of "welfare capitalism."

The Depression of 1893 and a New Wave of Immigrants

The 1893 depression was the fourth major economic downturn in fifty-six years. The depression lasted for five years and was the largest of the century, with the unemployment rate climbing to 25 percent in Pennsylvania, 35 percent in New York, and 44 percent in Michigan. Charitable Organization Societies, with its focus on coordination, investigation, and "friendly visits," as well as its individualistic approach of helping people to help themselves, proved ineffective in the face of massive unemployment. No longer did COS concentrate its efforts on opposing outdoor relief, and once again public and private agencies increased this form of assistance. As COS was unable to provide a viable solution to the increase in poverty, it lost its standing as a cutting-edge social reform organization.

To deal with the immediate crisis of the depression, local governments for the first time on a large scale utilized public works projects as a main component of relief. These public works projects included street sweeping, street paving, and sewer construction. Private charity agencies contributed to this "work relief" by collecting donations and turning them over to the city in order to employ people. Private agencies also expanded soup kitchens and free lodging houses, and cities offered people small plots of land to grow vegetables.[1]

The employment problem was exacerbated by the immigration of 22 million people into the United States from 1891 to 1930. Entering from the east were Europeans, with close to 50 percent coming from southern and eastern Europe, and from the west, the Chinese and Japanese. From 1850 to 1882, 300,000 Chinese men were recruited to work as low-wage workers and to replace white workers on strike. Confronted with hostility, the Chinese men built "tongs" or halls, which provided credit and loans, settled disputes, buried the dead, and cared for the young and old. Ethnic associations were also created by other groups that experienced discrimination and enmity, for example the Irish and Jewish immigrants.

In response to white racism and fear of competition for jobs and resources, the United States blocked Chinese immigration in 1882. As the capitalists were still in need of cheap labor, they turned to Japan and recruited more than 80,000 Japanese men from 1882 to 1910, followed by more than 32,000 Japanese women who came as "picture brides." The Japanese worked as farmers, fishers, and in other economic endeavors, but in 1907, they too were blocked from immigrating to the United States because of racism and fear of competition.[2]

The immigrants from southern and eastern Europe were not immune from discrimination, as they too were classified as racially inferior by white Americans, who were originally from northern and western Europe. This belief in their superiority led to the passage of the 1924 Immigration and Nationality Act, which severely restricted southern and eastern Europeans from entering the United States. Still in need of labor, U.S. corporations turned to Mexico, and from 1900 to 1930 recruited 1 million Mexicans to immigrate to the United States to work in the mines, fields, railroads, and factories. Conveniently, Mexicans were not among the ethnic groups restricted from immigrating.[3]

Many from this wave of immigration relocated in cities, which changed the United States from a predominantly rural nation into one that was equally divided between urban and rural populations. A large internal migration also began to increase the urban population. From 1910 to 1920, more than 500,000 African Americans migrated from the rural south to northern cities. During this time, Chicago's black population doubled to 100,000, and New York's 150,000 black residents made it the largest African American community in the country. By 1915, 42 million people lived in U.S. cities, up from 6.2 million in 1860. Yet, white prejudice against African Americans, Chinese, Italians, Japanese, Jews, and Poles forced these groups into ethnically segregated ghettos.[4]

The misery experienced by urban working-class and poor people in the late nineteenth and early twentieth centuries was highlighted in a series of books, including *How the Other Half Lives* by Jacob Riis, *The Shame of the Cities* by Lincoln Steffens, and *The Bitter Cry of the Children* by John Spargo. A short example from Riis's work provides a general understanding of the living conditions of the urban poor:

> Be a little careful, please! The hall is dark and you might stumble over the children pitching pennies back there. Not that it would hurt them; kicks and cuffs are their daily diet. They have little else. Here where the hall turns and dives into utter darkness is a step, and another, another. A flight of stairs. You can feel your way, if you cannot see it. Close? Yes! What would you have? All the fresh air that ever enters these stairs comes from the hall-door that is forever slamming, and from the windows of dark bedrooms that in turn receive from the stairs their sole supply of the elements God meant to be free, but man deals out with such niggardly hand. That was a woman filling her pail by the hydrant you just bumped against. The sinks are in the hallway, that all the tenants may have access—and all be

poisoned alike by their summer stenches. Hear the pump squeak! It is the lullaby of tenement-house babes. In summer, when a thousand thirsty throats pant for a cooling drink in this block, it is worked in vain. But the saloon, whose open door you passed in the hall, is always there. The smell of it has followed you up. Here is a door. Listen! That short hacking cough, that tiny, helpless wail—what do they mean? They mean that the soiled bow of white you saw on the door downstairs will have another story to tell—Oh! a sadly familiar story—before the day is at an end. The child is dying with measles. With half a chance it might have lived; but it had none. That dark bedroom killed it.[5]

The infant mortality rate is a general indicator of community health. In U.S. cities during the late nineteenth and early twentieth centuries, some communities experienced 135 infant deaths (before one year of age) out of 1,000. This high mortality rate was caused by malnourishment, polluted water, contaminated milk, and racial discrimination in health care.[6]

Although the urban poor obtained water from unreliable public hydrants, lived in houses with no heating, received light from kerosene lamps, and cooked on stoves that were heated by scraps of scavenged wood and coal, the homes of the wealthy included such amenities as electricity, indoor plumbing, telephones, natural gas, and central heating. During this period, the rich continued to amass wealth, as the percentage of total net wealth held by the top 1 percent of the population doubled between 1871 and 1913.[7]

Euro-Americans also enjoyed some upward mobility during this time period. A study of New York immigrants reported that between 1905 and 1915, 32 percent of Jews and Italians moved out of the working class into higher strata. Although some immigrants became frustrated and returned home—for example, 73 percent of Italian immigrants left New York during one four-year period—there were enough immigrants who stayed, and they helped to create a growing middle class.[8]

Progressive Reformers

Out of the poverty-stricken slums and wretched factory conditions, a new social reform movement emerged: progressivism. Progressives were not confined to a particular organization or political party; rather, they were united in the belief that the economic and social structures of society were responsible for the problems of the day, and that society's ills could be solved through social reform. Progressives encouraged people to volunteer their time and effort to improve society, but they also looked to the government to be a positive force in the social order, rejecting the laissez-faire policies of capitalists. Progressives were involved in a variety of organizations to reform society, from prohibiting child labor to reducing infant mortality, from improving tenement housing to educating immigrant children. Many of the progressives' reforms focused on children, and these efforts came to be called "child-saving." The child-saving movement offered an alternative paradigm for the social reformers and served as a counterpoint to the more radical ideas espoused by militant labor organizations.[9]

One of the movements most identified with the progressive spirit was the settlement house. Settlement houses were social centers for civic cooperation. The people attracted to live in these communal settings within an urban poor neighborhood were predominantly young, white, moderately well-off college graduates. Residents stayed an average of three years, and their living situation was much like a university dormitory. Settlement house residents moved into poor communities because they believed that the gap between the rich and the poor had grown too large, and that the social classes needed to have interaction to maintain societal cohesion. This strategy of living with the poor differed from COS's strategy of sending "visitors" into poor communities, as the latter were always outsiders in the neighborhood. Settlement house residents saw their efforts as more fraternal than paternal, since they regarded the poor as neighbors and friends, not as receivers of charity. Ideally, such residents would not come in with a remedy based on upper-middle-class values but rather develop solutions out of the desires and needs of the poor themselves.[10]

The first settlement house, Toynbee Hall, was developed in England in 1884. Two years later, Stanley Coit founded the first settlement house in the United States, and by 1910, 400 settlement houses were operating in the nation. In the beginning, settlement houses focused on education (e.g., teaching English) and culture (e.g., art exhibits, readings, and ethnic crafts). However, after the 1893 depression, they began to do political work. This work involved municipal reforms like the implementation of garbage pickup and neighborhood bathhouses. They also worked at the state and federal levels on child labor laws, factory conditions and regulation of hours for women workers, tenement housing, and women's suffrage. These reformers shared the philosophy that neighborhood improvement, not solely individual improvement, created the necessary conditions for a healthy community, thus rejecting rugged individualism. In addition, they were concerned with all the poor people and not just the "deserving poor."

Jane Addams, who is the best-known settlement house advocate, founded "Hull-House" in Chicago in 1889. In her book *Twenty Years at Hull-House,* she described the desperate conditions of city dwellers who slaughtered sheep in the basement, sorted rags collected from the city dumps in front of children, and baked bread in unsanitary areas. Addams also explained why people in general, and women in particular, were responding to the settlement house movement's call for social reform. She believed that there was a yearning among young people to experience directly the sentiment of universal fellowship among all people, which had been lost in modern civilization due to social class divisions. As Addams stated, "Nothing so deadens the sympathies and shrivels the power of enjoyment as the persistent keeping away from the great opportunities for helpfulness and a continual ignoring of the starvation struggle which makes up the life of at least half the race. To shut one's self away from that half of the race life is to shut one's self away from the most vital part of it; it is to live out but half the humanity to which we have been born heir and to use but half our faculties. We have all had longings for a fuller life which should include the use of these faculties."

Addams was particularly concerned that women were prevented from using these faculties. She argued that women should not have the professional path of serving humanity closed to them, as with so many other paths in the early twentieth century. Addams's call to service was answered; college-educated women flocked to the settlement houses because they provided interesting work along with a place to live.[11]

One of these college-educated women was Julia Lathrop, a longtime Hull House resident and a close confidante to Jane Addams. Lathrop would go on to be appointed the first chief of the U.S. Children's Bureau, which was created in 1912 to centralize and organize all information concerning the welfare of children. Lathrop's agency investigated infant mortality, child labor, juvenile delinquency, and mother's pensions. In the Hull House tradition, Lathrop was determined to use social scientific research to solve the various problems caused by poverty. As director of the Children's Bureau, she called for equality of opportunity for all, with a focus on a fair start for infants, children, youth, and young adults. Rather than attacking adult poverty, Lathrop started with the infant and built forward to the adult, which was a classic strategy of the child-saving movement.[12]

If progressive reformers were to be successful, they would have to overcome the reluctance of Americans to have the federal government involved in family and economic decisions. This belief that the government should not be involved in private decisions was a serious block to every reform to reduce or eliminate poverty, malnutrition, exploitation, and racial discrimination. Progressives attempted to resolve the issue by asserting that the U.S. government should be enlightened, decent, fair, classless, and disinterested. At the regional level, the western and midwestern reformers most vigorously supported government involvement in social welfare services and the promotion of economic development since there were few private institutions and no "old money" doing this type of work in their region. The East was far more wary of government involvement due to federal corruption witnessed in the 1880s. The East also had a long history of philanthropy to provide social services and economic development.[13]

Progress for Some, Not for Others

Unfortunately, progressive reforms did little to improve the material conditions of African Americans and Native Americans. In the late nineteenth and early twentieth centuries, African Americans lost many of the economic, social, and political rights they had won during Reconstruction. Laws had been passed to disenfranchise and segregate blacks (called Jim Crow laws), and the U.S. government deliberately purged blacks from federal jobs during the Wilson administration (1913–1921). So, although the progressive era was marked by economic and social mobility for some whites, African Americans remained poor and disempowered.

Many settlement houses reproduced the racism in the larger society by not allowing blacks to live in the communal houses. Some white settlement houses argued that segregated facilities were necessary so that each neighborhood had its own social center; however, in reality they feared that black participation would scare off the white community. Yet some within the settlement house movement, such as Mary White Ovington (from the Greenpoint Settlement in New York), Celia Parker Wooley (from the Frederick Douglass Center in Chicago), and Jane Addams, fought against discrimination both within the settlement house movement and in the larger community.[14]

Out of this social context, two leaders—Booker T. Washington and W. E. B. Du Bois—emerged with very different approaches to the poverty and racism that African Americans were experiencing. Washington, founder of Tuskegee Institute, believed the way for African Americans to escape poverty was through hard work, industrial education, and temporarily renouncing the struggle for political power and civil rights. Washington was convinced that demonstrating the character and intelligence of blacks to the white community was the best strategy to overcome racism and disempowerment.[15]

Du Bois, who cofounded the National Association for the Advancement of Colored People (NAACP), disagreed strongly with Washington's approach. Du Bois felt that Washington's strategy was sacrificing social and political equality for economic gain. Du Bois was opposed to this on ideological and practical grounds. Ideologically, he felt that Washington's approach denied blacks their humanity by keeping them segregated and unable to participate fully in democracy, and practically, he believed the strategy was not workable. He felt, as Susan B. Anthony did, that one cannot separate economic gains from political rights. If blacks were to achieve economic parity with whites, they needed to possess the right to vote along with other civil rights.

Du Bois argued that blacks should focus on ending discrimination and segregation, fighting for the right to vote, and developing a "talented tenth" that would be university educated so as to provide the necessary leadership for equality. In *The Souls of Black Folk*, Du Bois responded directly to Washington's agenda when he stated:

> On the whole the distinct impression left by Mr. Washington's propaganda is, first, that the South is justified in its present attitude toward the Negro because of the Negro's degradation; secondly, that the prime cause of the Negro's failure to rise more quickly is his wrong education in the past; and, thirdly, that his future rise depends primarily on his own efforts. Each of these propositions is a dangerous half-truth. The supplementary truths must never be lost sight of: first, slavery and race-prejudice are potent if not sufficient causes of the Negro's position; second, industrial and common-school training were necessarily slow in planting because they had to await the black teachers trained by higher institutions,—it being extremely doubtful if any essentially different development was possible, and certainly a Tuskegee was unthinkable before 1880; and, third, while it is a great truth to say that the Negro must strive and strive mightily to help himself, it is equally true that unless his striving be not simply seconded, but rather aroused and encouraged, by the initiative of the richer and wiser environing group, he cannot hope for great success.[16]

Du Bois believed that in order to right the great wrongs of the past and present, the responsibility for solving poverty and discrimination should fall on the nation, not solely on the shoulders of blacks.

The other major ethnic group untouched by progressive reforms was Native Americans. The U.S. Indian Wars came to an end in 1890 with the murder of Sitting Bull and the Massacre at Wounded Knee. What had started out as a population of 2 to 5 million Native Americans in what is now the continental United States had been reduced to 250,000 by 1900. In California, the numbers of Native Americans had been reduced from 300,000 in 1770 to 16,000 in 1900. This holocaust involved war, disease, seizure of land, removal, relocation, and the attempted destruction of the Native American way of life.[17]

Some white American "reformers" believed that the remaining Indians needed to be "eased into extinction" through the use of off-reservation boarding schools like the Carlisle School in central Pennsylvania, to eradicate native culture, religion, and language. This approach corresponded to how Native Americans were being treated on the reservations. Luther Standing Bear describes how in the Lakota Nation, Indians were not allowed to travel outside the reservation without permission, celebrate indigenous religious traditions, or share food with other families in need. Basically, all decisions were in the hands of U.S. government agents. Many Native Americans rejected this treatment, and people such as Arthur Parker, or Gawaso Wanneh, a Seneca, called for change. Parker, who was an archaeologist at the New York State Museum, asked that the United States return to the American Indian "seven stolen rights," foremost of which was Indian self-determination, and a return of their spirit. Parker stressed that the political and psychological dimensions of oppression must be dealt with, and that if this was not done, all the "help" to economically and educationally uplift American Indians was useless.[18]

Labor Militancy

As progressives pushed to curb the excesses of industrial capitalism, the working class continued its struggle to reform and change capitalism. Part of the reason for increased labor activity was that so many workers were in such close proximity to one another. In 1880, 2.7 million people worked in manufacturing jobs. By 1900, the number of manufacturing jobs had almost doubled to 4.5 million, and it nearly doubled again to 8.4 million in 1920. The huge factories and the large numbers of people who worked in them made it possible for a new militancy to develop. This militancy can be seen in the approximately 1,000 strikes each year throughout the 1890s. By 1904, the number of strikes per year had quadrupled to 4,000.[19]

Three of the most famous strikes during this time were the Homestead steel strike of 1892, the Pullman railroad strike of 1894, and the Ludlow strike of 1913–1914. The Homestead strike involved the Amalgamated Association of Iron and Steel Workers, an American Federated Labor craft union, against Andrew Carnegie's steel mill in Homestead, Pennsylvania. Carnegie, who was the wealthiest U.S. capitalist of his time, attempted to crush the union by cutting pay up to 60 percent since he wanted a passive and compliant workforce. Even though only 750 of the 3,800 steel workers were union members, 3,000 met and voted overwhelmingly to strike.[20]

Another dramatic strike took place two years later when the American Railway Union (ARU) went on strike against the Pullman Palace Car Company, which built railroad sleeping cars. The ARU was the fastest-growing union at the time, and its model of union organizing allowed for all white workers who had been hired by the railroads to join the union, regardless of the specific job or skill level. As the 1893 depression deepened, George Pullman fired 33 percent of his workforce and cut wages by 25 to 40 percent. In response, the 260,000 ARU members, led by the charismatic Eugene Debs, walked off their jobs and brought much of the nation's rail traffic to a standstill.[21]

The third legendary strike was in Ludlow, Colorado, in 1913–1914, directed at John Rockefeller's Colorado Fuel and Iron Company for refusing to recognize and negotiate with the United Mine Workers of America (UMWA). Eleven thousand Colorado miners struck against Rockefeller's open-shop policy, which attempted to guarantee the right of nonunion members to work in the mines. The UMWA, which had continued the Knights of Labor's legacy of interracial unionism, had built a strong union, and by 1910 one-third of all coal miners were union members in comparison to 10 percent in the general U.S. labor force.[22]

In addition to these strikes, three other critical events were carried out by working people: the march on Washington by "Coxey's army," the rise of the Socialist Party, and the creation of the International Workers of the World (IWW). In response to the 1893 depression, Jacob Coxey and Carl Browne came up with the idea of marching with thousands of unemployed citizens to Washington, D.C., in order to demand that Congress pass legislation to end the unemployment crisis. Their "petition in boots" requested that the federal government provide jobs to the unemployed through construction of roads and new community facilities (libraries, schools, and museums). In the spring of 1894, Coxey and more than one thousand unemployed men marched from Los Angeles, Denver, Chicago, and Massillon (Ohio) to Washington. On May 1, Coxey's army of the unemployed arrived at the nation's capital with the goal of appealing directly to the federal government for action.[23]

In addition to Coxey's army, the working class launched two organizations, the IWW (or Wobblies) and the Socialist Party. Both the IWW and the Socialist Party believed in the abolishment of the wage system, collective ownership of the means of production, and the use of wealth to promote the interests of the workers. However, the IWW and the Socialist Party differed in their strategies to replace capitalism with socialism, and they disagreed about how a socialist system would operate. The IWW, which was formed in 1904, encouraged all workers to join their "One Big Union," regardless of skill, race, or sex, in contrast to the American Federation of Labor (AFL), which was organized by craft, and was racially exclusive. The IWW's method of change was direct action. They believed that the rank and file needed to be engaged in continuous struggle. The IWW did not want to be restricted regarding when to strike, so they did not give much credence to making contracts with individual employers since this limited their ability to act.[24]

Strikes were seen as preparation for a massive general strike that would bring all economic activity to a halt. The general strike was seen as labor's most effective weapon since capital needed labor to do the work. The general strike was also seen as the method of change that would replace capitalism with the least amount of violence. At the conclusion of the general strike, capitalism would be overthrown, and a decentralized, democratic worker-run organization would operate the mines and factories. The industries (coal, lumber, railroad, etc.) would govern the affairs of people. The IWW believed that worker-controlled industries would be much more democratic since they included the voices of women, blacks, immigrants, and youth, all of which had been shut out of democratic capitalism.[25]

The Socialist Party, which was founded in 1901, worked to bring about socialism through the ballot box as opposed to the strike. With Eugene Debs as their leader, the socialists set out to build a political party. Although the Socialist Party initially embraced the militant actions of the IWW and saw no inconsistency between the language of class struggle and socialism through voting, it changed course by 1912 and focused on gradual reform as opposed to immediate class struggle. The Socialist Party also articulated a more bureaucratic and top-down model for controlling the means of production in contrast to the IWW's decentralized model.[26]

The Response of Capitalists

In response to the labor unrest and socialists' political challenge, the business class had a variety of strategies. One of the strategies employed by some in the late nineteenth-century capitalist class was repression, and this continued throughout the progressive era. Another major strategy was to offer alternative reforms under the banner of "welfare capitalism," which attempted to persuade workers of the benefits of capitalism. In order to win over workers, welfare capitalists offered employees such incentives as savings plans, home ownership plans, stock purchase plans, and pensions. By the 1920s, welfare capitalists also offered workers shorter workdays, which served the companies' interests because long hours could negatively affect productivity. Welfare capitalists also argued that the unemployment crisis, which recurred with every generation, had to do with the inability to connect workers to employers, rather than with a defect in the system; therefore, welfare capitalists developed employment agencies to more efficiently reach potential workers.

The National Civic Federation, created and directed by Ralph Easley to support these reforms, promoted the ideas of the company as benefactor and the cooperation of big business with the working class. The federation's board was mostly composed of wealthy businessmen, but its longtime vice president was Samuel Gompers of the AFL. To promote cooperation, Easley argued that it was better to work with the conservative AFL, which only wanted its fair share of the pie for its members, than with the IWW, which wanted the whole pie. In addition, Easley was concerned about the long-term stability of capitalism, and he felt that labor unrest undermined it. Easley tried to promote social stability and downplay labor unrest, stating that "the only unrest in the industrial and social fields that I can discern is that wholesome, normal unrest which comes through the education of the people, a better understanding of their rights as workers and the translation of that knowledge through the labor unions and other social and economic organizations into concrete demands for better living conditions."[27]

Public Activities and Investigations (1911)

Jane Addams

These reflections are from Jane Addams's classic book Twenty Years at Hull-House.

One of the striking features of our neighborhood twenty years ago, and one to which we never became reconciled, was the presence of huge wooden garbage boxes fastened to the street pavement in which the undisturbed refuse accumulated day by day. The system of garbage collecting was inadequate throughout the city but it became the greatest menace in a ward such as ours, where the normal amount of waste was much increased by the decayed fruit and vegetables discarded by the Italian and Greek fruit peddlers, and by the residuum left over from the piles of filthy rags which were fished out of the city dumps and brought to the homes of the rag pickers for further sorting and washing.

The children of our neighborhood twenty years ago played their games in and around these huge garbage boxes. They were the first objects that the toddling child learned to climb; their bulk afforded a barricade and their contents provided missiles in all the battles of the older boys; and finally they became the seats upon which absorbed lovers held enchanted converse. We are obliged to remember that all children eat everything which they find and that odors have a curious and intimate power of entwining themselves into our tenderest memories, before even the residents of Hull-House can understand their own early enthusiasm for the removal of these boxes and the establishment of a better system of refuse collection.

It is easy for even the most conscientious citizen of Chicago to forget the foul smells of the stockyards and the garbage dumps, when he is living so far from them that he is only occasionally made conscious of their existence, but the residents of a Settlement are perforce constantly surrounded by them. During our first three years on Halsted Street, we had established a small incinerator at Hull-House and we had many times reported the untoward conditions of the ward to the city hall. We had also arranged many talks for the immigrants, pointing out that although a woman may sweep her own doorway in her native village and allow the refuse to innocently decay in the open air and sunshine, in a crowded city quarter, if the garbage is not properly collected and destroyed, a tenement-house mother may see her children sicken and die, and that the immigrants must therefore not only keep their own houses clean, but must also help the authorities to keep the city clean.

Possibly our efforts slightly modified the worst conditions, but they still remained intolerable, and the fourth summer the situation became for me absolutely desperate when I realized in a moment of panic that my delicate little nephew for whom I was guardian could not be with me at Hull-House at all unless the sickening odors were reduced. I may well be ashamed that other delicate children who were torn from their families, not into boarding school but into eternity, had not long before driven me into effective action. Under the direction of the first man who came as a resident to Hull-House we began a systematic investigation of the city system of garbage collection, both as to its efficiency in other wards and its possible connection with the death rate in the various wards of the city.

The Hull-House Woman's Club had been organized the year before by the resident kindergartner who had first inaugurated a mothers' meeting. The members came together, however, in quite a new way that summer when we discussed with them the high death rate so persistent in our ward. After several club meetings devoted to the subject, despite the fact that the death rate rose highest in the congested foreign colonies and not in the streets in which most of the Irish American club women lived, twelve of their number undertook in connection with the residents, to carefully investigate the condition of the alleys. During August and September the substantiated reports of violations of the law sent in from Hull-House to the health department were one thousand and thirty-seven. For the club woman who had finished a long day's work of washing or ironing followed by the cooking of a hot supper, it would have been much easier to sit on her doorstep during a summer evening than to go up and down ill-kept alleys and get into trouble with her neighbors over the condition of their garbage boxes. It required both civic enterprise and moral conviction to be willing to do this three evenings a week during the hottest and most uncomfortable months of the year. Nevertheless, a certain number of women persisted, as did the residents, and three city inspectors in succession were transferred from the ward because of unsatisfactory services. Still the death rate remained high and the condition seemed little improved throughout the next winter. In sheer desperation, the following spring when the city contracts were awarded for the removal of garbage, with the backing of two well-known business men, I put in a bid for the garbage removal of the nineteenth ward. My paper was thrown out on a technicality but the incident induced the mayor to appoint me the garbage inspector of the ward.

The salary was a thousand dollars a year, and the loss of that political "plum" made a great stir among the politicians. The position was no sinecure whether regarded from the point of view of getting up at six in the morning to see that the men were early at work; or of following the loaded wagons, uneasily dropping their contents at intervals, to their dreary destination at the dump; of insisting that the contractor must increase the number of his wagons from nine to thirteen and from thirteen to seventeen, although he assured me that he lost money on every one and that the former inspector had let him off with seven; or of taking careless landlords into court because they would not provide the proper garbage receptacles; or of arresting the tenant who tried to make the garbage wagons carry away the contents of his stable.

With the two or three residents who nobly stood by, we set up six of those doleful incinerators which are supposed to burn garbage with the fuel collected in the alley itself. The one factory in town which could utilize old tin cans was a window weight factory, and we deluged that with ten times as many tin cans as it could use—much less would pay for. We made desperate attempts to have the dead animals removed by the contractor who was paid most liberally by the city for that purpose but who, we slowly discovered, always made the police ambulances do the work, delivering the carcasses upon freight cars for shipment to a soap factory in Indiana where they were sold for a good price although the contractor himself was the largest stockholder in the concern.…

Many of the foreign-born women of the ward were much shocked by this abrupt departure into the ways of men, and it took a great deal of explanation to convey the idea even remotely that if it were a womanly task to go about in tenement houses in order to nurse the sick, it might be quite as womanly to go through the same district in order to prevent the breeding of so-called "filth

diseases." While some of the women enthusiastically approved the slowly changing conditions and saw that their housewifely duties logically extended to the
adjacent alleys and streets, they yet were quite certain that "it was not a lady's
job." A revelation of this attitude was made one day in a conversation which
the inspector heard vigorously carried on in a laundry. One of the employees
was leaving and was expressing her mind concerning the place in no measured
terms, summing up her contempt for it as follows: "I would rather be the girl
who goes about in the alleys than to stay here any longer!"

And yet the spectacle of eight hours' work for eight hours' pay, the even-
handed justice to all citizens irrespective of "pull," the dividing of responsibility
between landlord and tenant, and the readiness to enforce obedience to law from
both, was, perhaps, one of the most valuable demonstrations which could have
been made. Such daily living on the part of the office holder is of infinitely more
value than many talks on civics for, after all, we credit most easily that which
we see. The careful inspection, combined with other causes, brought about a
great improvement in the cleanliness and comfort of the neighborhood and one
happy day, when the death rate of our ward was found to have dropped from
third to seventh, in the list of city wards and was so reported to our Woman's
Club, the applause which followed recorded the genuine sense of participation
in the result, and a public spirit which had "made good." But the cleanliness of
the ward was becoming much too popular to suit our all-powerful alderman
and, although we felt fatuously secure under the regime of civil service, he found
a way to circumvent us by eliminating the position altogether. He introduced
an ordinance into the city council which combined the collection of refuse
with the cleaning and repairing of the streets, the whole to be placed under a
ward superintendent. The office of course was to be filled under civil service
regulations but only men were eligible to the examination. Although this latter
regulation was afterward modified in favor of one woman, it was retained long
enough to put the nineteenth ward inspector out of office.

Of course our experience in inspecting only made us more conscious of the
wretched housing conditions over which we had been distressed from the first.
It was during the World's Fair summer that one of the Hull-House residents in
a public address upon housing reform used as an example of indifferent landlordism a large block in the neighborhood occupied by small tenements and
stables unconnected with a street sewer, as was much similar property in the
vicinity. In the lecture the resident spared neither a description of the property
nor the name of the owner. The young man who owned the property was justly
indignant at this public method of attack and promptly came to investigate the
condition of the property. Together we made a careful tour of the houses and

stables and in the face of the conditions that we found there, could not but agree with him that supplying South Italian peasants with sanitary appliances seemed a difficult undertaking. Nevertheless he was unwilling that the block should remain in its deplorable state, and he finally cut through the dilemma with the rash proposition that he would give a free lease of the entire tract to Hull-House, accompanying the offer, however, with the warning remark, that if we should choose to use the income from the rents in sanitary improvements we should be throwing our money away.

Even when we decided that the houses were so bad that we could not undertake the task of improving them, he was game and stuck to his proposition that we should have a free lease. We finally submitted a plan that the houses should be torn down and the entire tract turned into a playground, although cautious advisers intimated that it would be very inconsistent to ask for subscriptions for the support of Hull-House when we were known to have thrown away an income of two thousand dollars a year. We, however, felt that a spectacle of inconsistency was better than one of bad landlordism and so the worst of the houses were demolished, the best three were sold and moved across the street under careful provision that they might never be used for junk-shops or saloons, and a public playground was finally established. Hull-House became responsible for its management for ten years, at the end of which time it was turned over to the City Playground Commission, although from the first the city detailed a policeman who was responsible for its general order and who became a valued adjunct of the House....

Festivities of various sorts were held on this early playground, always a May day celebration with its Maypole dance and its May queen. I remember that one year the honor of being queen was offered to the little girl who should pick up the largest number of scraps of paper which littered all the streets and alleys. The children that spring had been organized into a league, and each member had been provided with a stiff piece of wire upon the sharpened point of which stray bits of paper were impaled and later soberly counted off into a large box in the Hull-House alley. The little Italian girl who thus won the scepter took it very gravely as the just reward of hard labor, and we were all so absorbed in the desire for clean and tidy streets that we were wholly oblivious to the incongruity of thus selecting "the queen of love and beauty." ...

The mere consistent enforcement of existing laws and efforts for their advance often placed Hull-House, at least temporarily, into strained relations with its neighbors. I recall a continuous warfare against local landlords who would move wrecks of old houses as a nucleus for new ones in order to evade the provisions of the building code, and a certain Italian neighbor who was filled with bitterness because his new rear tenement was discovered to be illegal. It seemed impossible to make him understand that the health of the tenants was in any wise as important as his undisturbed rents.

Nevertheless many evils constantly arise in Chicago from congested housing which wiser cities forestall and prevent; the inevitable boarders crowded into a dark tenement already too small for the use of the immigrant family occupying it; the surprisingly large number of delinquent girls who have become criminally involved with their own fathers and uncles; the school children who cannot find a quiet spot in which to read or study and who perforce go into the streets each evening; the tuberculosis superinduced and fostered by the inadequate rooms and breathing spaces. One of the Hull-House residents, under the direction of a Chicago physician who stands high as an authority on tuberculosis and who devotes a large proportion of his time to our vicinity, made an investigation into housing conditions as related to tuberculosis with a result as startling as that of the "lung block" in New York.

It is these subtle evils of wretched and inadequate housing which are often most disastrous. In the summer of 1902 during an epidemic of typhoid fever in which our ward, although containing but one thirty-sixth of the population of the city, registered one sixth of the total number of deaths, two of the Hull-House residents made an investigation of the methods of plumbing in the houses adjacent to conspicuous groups of fever cases. They discovered among the people who had been exposed to the infection a widow who had lived in the ward for a number of years, in a comfortable little house of her own. Although the Italian immigrants were closing in all around her, she was not willing to sell her property and to move away until she had finished the education of her children. In the meantime she held herself quite aloof from her Italian neighbors and could never be drawn into any of the public efforts to secure a better code of tenement-house sanitation. Her two daughters were sent to an eastern college. One June when one of them had graduated and the other still had two years before she took her degree, they came to the spotless little house and to their self-sacrificing mother for the summer holiday. They both fell ill with typhoid fever and one daughter died because the mother's utmost efforts could not keep the infection out of her own house. The entire disaster affords, perhaps, a fair illustration of the futility of the individual conscience which would isolate a family from the rest of the community and its interests.

The careful information collected concerning the juxtaposition of the typhoid cases to the various systems of plumbing and nonplumbing was made the basis of a bacteriological study by another resident, Dr. Alice Hamilton, as to the possibility of the infection having been carried by flies. Her researches were so convincing that they have been incorporated into the body of scientific data supporting that theory, but there were also practical results from the investigation. It was discovered that the wretched sanitary appliances through which alone the infection could have become so widely spread would not have been permitted to remain, unless the city inspector had either been criminally careless or open to the arguments of favored landlords.

The agitation finally resulted in a long and stirring trial before the civil service board of half of the employees in the Sanitary Bureau, with the final discharge of eleven out of the entire force of twenty-four. The inspector in our neighborhood was a kindly old man, greatly distressed over the affair, and quite unable to understand why he should not have used his discretion as to the time when a landlord should be forced to put in modern appliances. If he was "very poor," or "just about to sell his place," or "sure that the house would be torn down to make room for a factory," why should one "inconvenience" him? The old man died soon after the trial, feeling persecuted to the very last and not in the least understanding what it was all about. We were amazed at the commercial ramifications which graft in the city hall involved and at the indignation which interference with it produced. Hull-House lost some large subscriptions as the result of this investigation, a loss which, if not easy to bear, was at least comprehensible. We also uncovered unexpected graft in connection with the plumbers' unions, and but for the fearless testimony of one of their members, could never have brought the trial to a successful issue....

We continually conduct small but careful investigations at Hull-House, which may guide us in our immediate doings such as two recently undertaken by Mrs. Britton, one upon the reading of school children before new books were bought for the children's club libraries, and another on the proportion of tuberculosis among school children, before we opened a little experimental outdoor school on one of our balconies....

We find increasingly, however, that the best results are to be obtained in investigations as in other undertakings, by combining our researches with those of other public bodies or with the State itself. When all the Chicago Settlements found themselves distressed over the condition of the newsboys who, because they are merchants and not employees, do not come under the provisions of the Illinois child labor law, they united in the investigation of a thousand young newsboys, who were all interviewed on the streets during the same twenty-four hours. Their school and domestic status was easily determined later, for many of the boys lived in the immediate neighborhoods of the ten Settlements which had undertaken the investigation. The report embodying the results of the investigation recommended a city ordinance containing features from the Boston and Buffalo regulations, and although an ordinance was drawn up and a strenuous effort was made to bring it to the attention of the aldermen, none of them would introduce it into the city council without newspaper backing. We were able to agitate for it again at the annual meeting of the National Child Labor Committee which was held in Chicago in 1908, and which was of course reported in papers throughout the entire country. This meeting also demonstrated that local measures can sometimes be urged most effectively when joined to the efforts of a national body. Undoubtedly the best discussions ever held upon the operation and status of the Illinois law were those which took place then. The needs of the Illinois children were regarded in connection with the children of the nation, and advanced health measures for Illinois were compared with those of other states....

In the earlier years of the American Settlements, the residents were sometimes impatient with the accepted methods of charitable administration and hoped, through residence in an industrial neighborhood, to discover more cooperative and advanced methods of dealing with the problems of poverty which are so dependent upon industrial maladjustment. But during twenty years, the Settlements have seen the charitable people, through their very knowledge of the poor, constantly approach nearer to those methods formerly designated as radical. The residents, so far from holding aloof from organized charity, find testimony, certainly in the National Conferences, that out of the most persistent and intelligent efforts to alleviate poverty, will in all probability arise the most significant suggestions for eradicating poverty. In the hearing before a congressional committee for the establishment of a Children's Bureau, residents in American Settlements joined their fellow philanthropists in urging the need of this indispensable instrument for collecting and disseminating information which would make possible concerted intelligent action on behalf of children.

Mr. Howells has said that we are all so besotted with our novel reading that we have lost the power of seeing certain aspects of life with any sense of reality because we are continually looking for the possible romance. The description might apply to the earlier years of the American settlement, but certainly the later years are filled with discoveries in actual life as romantic as they are unexpected. If I may illustrate one of these romantic discoveries from my own experience, I would cite the indications of an internationalism as sturdy and virile as it is unprecedented which I have seen in our cosmopolitan neighborhood: when a South Italian Catholic is forced by the very exigencies of the situation to make friends with an Austrian Jew representing another nationality and another religion, both of which cut into all his most cherished prejudices, he finds it harder to utilize them a second time and gradually loses them. He thus modifies his provincialism, for if an old enemy working by his side has turned into a friend, almost anything may happen. When, therefore, I became identified with the peace movement both in its International and National Conventions, I hoped that this internationalism engendered in the immigrant quarters of American cities might be recognized as an effective instrument in the cause of peace. I first set it forth with some misgiving before the Convention held in Boston in 1904 and it is always a pleasure to recall the hearty assent given to it by Professor William James.

I have always objected to the phrase "sociological laboratory" applied to us because Settlements should be something much more human and spontaneous than such a phrase connotes, and yet it is inevitable that the residents should know their own neighborhoods more thoroughly than any other, and that their experiences there should affect their convictions.

Years ago I was much entertained by a story told at the Chicago Woman's Club by one of its ablest members in the discussion following a paper of mine on "The Outgrowths of Toynbee Hall." She said that when she was a little girl playing in her mother's garden, she one day discovered a small toad who seemed to her very forlorn and lonely, although as she did not in the least know how to comfort him, she reluctantly left him to his fate; later in the day, quite at the other end of the garden, she found a large toad, also apparently without family and friends. With a heart full of tender sympathy, she took a stick and by exercising infinite patience and some skill, she finally pushed the little toad through the entire length of the garden into the company of the big toad, when, to her expressible horror and surprise, the big toad opened his mouth and swallowed the little one. The moral of the tale was clear applied to people who lived "where they did not naturally belong," although I protested that was exactly what we wanted—to be swallowed and digested, to disappear into the bulk of the people.

Twenty years later I am willing to testify that something of the sort does take place after years of identification with an industrial community.

Child Welfare Standards: A Test of Democracy (1919)

Julia Lathrop

Lathrop's remarks are from her presidential address to the National Conference of Social Work.

...And now you will pardon me, I trust, if instead of attempting a more general discussion, I address you on the subject with which for some years I have chanced to be especially concerned—the public protection of childhood.

The protection of childhood is costly. The standards we are willing to accept and carry forward are a test of democracy because they are a test of whether it is the popular will to pay the cost of what we agree is essential to the wise and safe bringing up of children.

I can never touch upon this subject without thinking of what John Dewey said twenty years ago in his little book on School and Society: "What the best and wisest parent wants for his own child, that must the community want for all of its children. Any other ideal for our schools is narrow and unlovely; acted upon, it destroys our democracy." This standard for childhood cannot apply only to the school child, it must apply to the child at home before he goes to school, and, strange anomaly, it still applies also to the child at work.

Democracy is that form of government and spirit among men which actively insist that society must exist to give every human being a fair chance.

A fair chance for everyone does not begin with adult life nor with infancy. Its mysterious springs are more and more swathed in mystery as we push backward from the man, the youth, the child, the baby, to the endless line of the generations out of which each living being emerges in his turn. But our responsibility is only with today; tomorrow will take care of itself as did yesterday....

And first, as to infant mortality:—

It is not easy, perhaps it is not decent, to reduce the discussion of human life to terms of money. Yet, acknowledging that human life is too precious to be reckoned by dollars, we may get a sense by money calculations of where we are wasting life unnecessarily and of the added cost required to stop the waste. Will you permit me to refer to the figures of the Children's Bureau showing infant mortality in relation to income: They show that infant mortality lessens as the wages of the fathers increase. Naturally the Bureau took as the sign of family income the earnings of the father since American thinking holds that the earnings of the man should be sufficient to enable him to support the wife and young children. When the father's wages were under $450, the infant death rate was 167. As the wages rose to $1,250, the death rate fell to 59. Fourteen per cent of the babies were born in families where the father earned $450 or less, 10 per cent in families where the father's earnings were $1,250 or more.

These figures were made before the war and in certain industries pay has increased. But figures as to living cost preclude the hope that family living standards are improving at present.

Children are not safe and happy if their parents are miserable, and parents must be miserable if they cannot protect a home against poverty.

Let us not deceive ourselves: The power to maintain a decent family living standard is the primary essential of child welfare. This means a living wage and wholesome working life for the man, a good and skillful mother at home to keep the house and comfort all within it. Society can afford no less and can afford no exceptions. This is a universal need.

Infant mortality can be largely prevented and the lives of mothers safeguarded to this end. And a federal measure is proposed which will be costly in money but economical in life. In large areas of our country, where local taxes are raised with difficulty although the tax rates are high, we are confronted by poverty and by isolation. These are areas far removed from doctors, where the visiting nurse is unknown, where hospitals are inaccessible, where hygiene is not taught, and in these regions mothers and babies suffer and die unattended. There are industrials areas, too, where mothers and children are treated with fatalistic neglect. These mothers and these children need public health nurses, hospitals and medical attention, above all homely lessons in hygiene and how to keep well. These things should be provided as the public schools are provided, to be used by all with dignity and self-respect. Such provisions can be secured by government aid to states on the plan already in operation for aid to agriculture, vocational training, good roads, protection against venereal diseases. Millions will be necessary from the Federal Government to be matched by millions more from the state. Will such expenditures be questioned? Let us look at England. Last August a law was passed by Parliament providing for the public protection of maternity and infancy by grants to be used for purposes analogous to those I have outlined above. It goes farther and provides "home helps" during the mother's incapacity. Such protection will be costly, but it was demanded by popular opinion in England. The experience of New Zealand justifies it. Parliamentary reports of the Commonwealth of Australia emphasize the necessity of such public provision for that country.

But let us suppose that we have pulled through the first year of life the two and one-half million children born annually; let us suppose that they have survived that period severely called by teachers and physicians "the neglected age," in which children are still at home in their mothers' arms, and that they are safely launched in school or are of an age to be so launched. What do they learn? Until the illiteracy figures of the draft startled us we ignored the census warning as to illiteracy in this country. We ignored the census figures showing that rural child labor and adult illiteracy occupy the same territory. The revelation of the draft has created a serious determination to abolish adult illiteracy. But what of the children of today? Shall we begin at once to teach them or shall we wait until they too are grown, their minds dulled and stiffened by disuse of books, and try to teach them then? Certainly the question needs only to be stated in order to be answered, so far as efficiency is concerned. Remember that the United States has itself bred two-thirds of its illiterate population. Aside from the adult illiterate immigrants who form a scant one-third of our illiterate population, the adult illiterates of today are the American child laborers of yesterday—largely the rural child workers, for the rural illiteracy rate is double the urban rate, and three-fifths of our population is rural, and an overwhelming proportion of our child labor is rural.

It does not simplify matters to know that many of these rural child laborers and adult illiterates are colored. Rather the matter becomes more urgent, as we realize that the colored population grown three or four fold in the last 50 years, now spreading over the country, north, east and west, is demonstrating that the welfare of the colored child is a nation-wide problem which no section can ignore with prudence or with honor. If no country is safe part slave and part free, so no country is safe if part is ignorant and part is college-bred. No laws limit the hours of rural child labor nor the ages of the laborers. Only a small proportion of our child laborers are protected by the federal law applying to those in mines, quarries and manufacturing establishments. As to these children, who are in a measure protected, twenty-seven per cent of the group between 14 and 16 to whom the Children's Bureau gave certificates of age under the first federal child labor law, could not sign their names legibly.

The best way to abolish child labor, as Florence Kelley has long said, is by compulsory education. We now can take the greatest forward step in our educational history—we can abolish rural child labor and stop the increase of illiteracy by the same measure—a universal compulsory measure for elementary education. This will be costly, but it is entirely practicable by a federal act extending aid to states for rural education, and making conditions as to type of school and of teaching, length of term and required attendance. Such an Act should reach every child. Do we often think of the children of Porto Rico, Hawaii, the Canal Zone natives, to all of whom our protection is pledged. The Philippines are setting a great example by their new compulsory school law. The promptness with which the federal law in aid of Vocational Education was accepted by the States leaves little doubt that a measure for elementary education would be equally acceptable.

As you know, England's new Education Act has cut the root of rural child labor and of industrial exemptions by providing universal compulsory full time schooling for every child to the age of 14, with increasing provision for continuation school to the age of 18. Complete elementary education will be costly, but with England accepting the cost of the new law which adds many million pounds to her annual school budget, we with far lower tax rates and far greater wealth cannot afford to behave with less public spirit.

I need not waste time in urging here that raising the national living standard, stabilizing employment, protecting by law the universal right to wholesome working conditions, substituting good schools for work for all children, providing adequate care for the health and welfare of all mothers and children will all simplify the problems of amelioration which this Conference considers. We know that the enfeebled in mind or body or moral resistance are found in overwhelming proportion among those whose lives are most barren of comfort and knowledge, and financially on the lowest level. While the tasks of dealing with the wastage and wreckage are perhaps never all to be completed, they are sure to be lessened and performed more wisely as the universal living standard rises. It is really because the Conference accepts this view that it has abandoned its old title to take its present one.

Fruitful attempts to raise national living standards must be based on clear rules of action. Accordingly, as you know, a series of Conferences on child welfare standards have been held this spring under the auspices of the Children's Bureau, but with the cooperation of many people, including the foreign guests whose counsel has helped us greatly, and two of whom you will have the pleasure of hearing tonight. The standards agreed upon in Washington but open to revision, we hope may become the "irreducible minimum standards" which President Wilson said should be set forth as a part of Children's Year. They represent no goal, but rather a point of departure for the next generation if we can do our part now. They require full public provision for maternity and infancy. They require education to 16 and continuation school beyond, and protection for the adolescent at school or at work. They require protection for the health of young persons at work, decent working conditions, fair pay. They require modern care for dependent children, reiterating those true standards of the White House Conference of ten years ago which are yet too far from realization. They require careful discrimination and the scientific method in dealing with all those unfortunate children who are permanently or temporarily out of adjustment. The standards for normal children are framed to give new life a fair start, and to build up the joyous mental and physical vigor to which childhood and youth are entitled, and to afford as fair a start as may be in the working world.

The whole question of putting such standards into operation is this: Are we willing to spend the money? Can we make ourselves spend the money? Will we steadily push forward the new legislation, state and federal, which is needed to give them effect? And let us not forget that the universality of their application is a stern test of our democracy. Without universality the standards are sounding brass. We owe much to the sad children of invaded, war torn Europe, but we shall pay that debt best if we pay at the same time our debts at home. We shall cut a poor figure in leading the world democracy if we fail to put in order our own "vast unswept hearth."

Industrial Education for the Negro (1903)

Booker T. Washington

Washington's article first appeared in the anthology The Negro Problem. One of the most fundamental and far-reaching deeds that has been accomplished during the last quarter of a century has been that by which the Negro has been helped to find himself and to learn the secrets of civilization—to learn that there are a few simple, cardinal principles upon which a race must start its upward course, unless it would fail, and its last estate be worse than its first.

It has been necessary for the Negro to learn the difference between being worked and working—to learn that being worked meant degradation, while working means civilization; that all forms of labor are honorable, and all forms of idleness disgraceful. It has been necessary for him to learn that all races that have got upon their feet have done so largely by laying an economic foundation, and, in general, by beginning in a proper cultivation and ownership of the soil.

Forty years ago my race emerged from slavery into freedom. If, in too many cases, the Negro race began development at the wrong end, it was largely because neither white nor black properly understood the case. Nor is it any wonder that this was so, for never before in the history of the world had just such a problem been presented as that of the two races at the coming of freedom in this country.

For two hundred and fifty years, I believe the way for the redemption of the Negro was being prepared through industrial development. Through all those years the Southern white man did business with the Negro in a way that no one else has done business with him. In most cases if a Southern white man wanted a house built he consulted a Negro mechanic about the plan and about the actual building of the structure. If he wanted a suit of clothes made he went to a Negro tailor, and for shoes he went to a shoemaker of the same race. In a certain way every slave plantation in the South was an industrial school. On these plantations young colored men and women were constantly being trained not only as farmers but as carpenters, blacksmiths, wheelwrights, brick masons, engineers, cooks, laundresses, sewing women and housekeepers.

I do not mean in any way to apologize for the curse of slavery, which was a curse to both races, but in what I say about industrial training in slavery I am simply stating facts. This training was crude, and was given for selfish purposes. It did not answer the highest ends, because there was an absence of mental training in connection with the training of the hand. To a large degree, though, this business contact with the Southern white man, and the industrial training on the plantations, left the Negro at the close of the war in possession of nearly all the common and skilled labor in the South. The industries that gave the South its power, prominence and wealth prior to the Civil War were mainly the raising of cotton, sugar cane, rice and tobacco. Before the way could be prepared for the proper growing and marketing of these crops forests had to be cleared, houses to be built, public roads and railroads constructed. In all these works the Negro did most of the heavy work. In the planting, cultivating and marketing of the crops not only was the Negro the chief dependence, but in the manufacture of tobacco he became a skilled and proficient workman, and in this, up to the present time, in the South, holds the lead in the large tobacco manufactories.

In most of the industries, though, what happened? For nearly twenty years after the war, except in a few instances, the value of the industrial training given by the plantations was overlooked. Negro men and women were educated in literature, in mathematics and in the sciences, with little thought of what had been taking place during the preceding two hundred and fifty years, except, perhaps, as something to be escaped, to be got as far away from as possible. As a generation began to pass, those who had been trained as mechanics in slavery began to disappear by death, and gradually it began to be realized that there were few to take their places. There were young men educated in foreign tongues, but few in carpentry or in mechanical or architectural drawing. Many were trained in Latin, but few as engineers and blacksmiths. Too many were taken from the farm and educated, but educated in everything but farming. For this reason they had no interest in farming and did not return to it. And yet eighty-five per cent of the Negro population of the Southern states lives and for a considerable time will continue to live in the country districts. The charge is often brought against the members of my race—and too often justly, I confess—that they are found leaving the country districts and flocking into the great cities where temptations are more frequent and harder to resist, and where the Negro people too often become demoralized. Think, though, how frequently it is the case that from the first day that a pupil begins to go to school his books teach him much about the cities of the world and city life, and almost nothing about the country. How natural it is, then, that when he has the ordering of his life he wants to live it in the city.…

Some years ago, when we decided to make tailoring a part of our training at the Tuskegee Institute, I was amazed to find that it was almost impossible to find in the whole country an educated colored man who could teach the making of clothing. We could find numbers of them who could teach astronomy, theology, Latin or grammar, but almost none who could instruct in the making of clothing, something that has to be used by every one of us every day in the year. How often have I been discouraged as I have gone through the South, and into the homes of the people of my race, and have found women who could converse intelligently upon abstruse subjects, and yet could not tell how to improve the condition of the poorly cooked and still more poorly served bread and meat which they and their families were eating three times a day. It is discouraging to find a girl who can tell you the geographical location of any country on the globe and who does not know where to place the dishes upon a common dinner table. It is discouraging to find a woman who knows much about theoretical chemistry, and who cannot properly wash and iron a shirt.

In what I say here I would not by any means have it understood that I would limit or circumscribe the mental development of the Negro student. No race can be lifted until its mind is awakened and strengthened. By the side of industrial training should always go mental and moral training, but the pushing of mere abstract knowledge into the head means little. We want more than the mere performance of mental gymnastics. Our knowledge must be harnessed to the things of real life. I would encourage the Negro to secure all the mental strength, all the mental culture—whether gleaned from science, mathematics, history, language or literature that his circumstances will allow, but I believe most earnestly that for years to come the education of the people of my race should be so directed that the greatest proportion of the mental strength of the masses will be brought to bear upon the every-day practical things of life, upon something that is needed to be done, and something which they will be permitted to do in the community in which they reside. And just the same with the professional class which the race needs and must have, I would say give the men and women of that class, too, the training which will best fit them to perform in the most successful manner the service which the race demands.

I would not confine the race to industrial life, not even to agriculture, for example, although I believe that by far the greater part of the Negro race is best off in the country districts and must and should continue to live there, but I would teach the race that in industry the foundation must be laid—that the very best service which any one can render to what is called the higher education is to teach the present generation to provide a material or industrial foundation. On such a foundation as this will grow habits of thrift, a love of work, economy, ownership of property, bank accounts. Out of it in the future will grow practical education, professional education, positions of public responsibility. Out of it will grow moral and religious strength. Out of it will grow wealth from which alone can come leisure and the opportunity for the enjoyment of literature and the fine arts....

I would set no limits to the attainments of the Negro in arts, in letters or statesmanship, but I believe the surest way to reach those ends is by laying the foundation in the little things of life that lie immediately about one's door. I plead for industrial education and development for the Negro not because I want to cramp him, but because I want to free him. I want to see him enter the all-powerful business and commercial world....

Early in the history of the Tuskegee Institute we began to combine industrial training with mental and moral culture. Our first efforts were in the direction of agriculture, and we began teaching this with no appliances except one hoe and a blind mule. From this small beginning we have grown until now the Institute owns two thousand acres of land, eight hundred of which are cultivated each year by the young men of the school. We began teaching wheelwrighting and blacksmithing in a small way to the men, and laundry work, cooking and sewing and housekeeping to the young women. The fourteen hundred and over young men and women who attended the school during the last school year received instruction—in addition to academic and religious training—in thirty-three trades and industries, including carpentry, blacksmithing, printing, wheelwrighting, harnessmaking, painting, machinery, founding, shoemaking, brickmasonry and brickmaking, plastering, sawmilling, tinsmithing, tailoring, mechanical and architectural drawing, electrical and steam engineering, canning, sewing, dressmaking, millinery, cooking, laundering, housekeeping, mattress making, basketry, nursing, agriculture, dairying and stock raising, horticulture.

Not only do the students receive instruction in these trades, but they do actual work, by means of which more than half of them pay some part or all of their expenses while remaining at the school. Of the sixty buildings belonging to the school all but four were almost wholly erected by the students as a part of their industrial education. Even the bricks which go into the walls are made by students in the school's brick yard, in which, last year, they manufactured two million bricks....

Almost from the first Tuskegee has kept in mind—and this I think should be the policy of all industrial schools—fitting students for occupations which would be open to them in their home communities. Some years ago we noted the fact that there was beginning to be a demand in the South for men to operate dairies in a skillful, modern manner. We opened a dairy department in connection with the school, where a number of young men could have instruction in the latest and most scientific methods of dairy work. At present we have calls—mainly from Southern white men—for twice as many dairymen as we are able to supply. What is equally satisfactory, the reports which come to us indicate that our young men are giving the highest satisfaction and are fast changing and improving the dairy product in the communities into which they go. I use the dairy here as an example. What I have said of this is equally true of many of the other industries which we teach. Aside from the economic value of this work I cannot but believe, and my observation confirms me in my belief, that as we continue to place Negro men and women of intelligence, religion, modesty, conscience and skill in every community in the South, who will prove by actual results their value to the community, I cannot but believe, I say, that this will constitute a solution to many of the present political and social difficulties.

Many seem to think that industrial education is meant to make the Negro work as he worked in the days of slavery. This is far from my conception of industrial education. If this training is worth anything to the Negro, it consists in teaching him how not to work, but how to make the forces of nature—air, steam, water, horse-power and electricity—work for him. If it has any value it is in lifting labor up out of toil and drudgery into the plane of the dignified and the beautiful. The Negro in the South works and works hard; but too often his ignorance and lack of skill causes him to do his work in the most costly and shiftless manner, and this keeps him near the bottom of the ladder in the economic world....

I close, then, as I began, by saying that as a slave the Negro was worked, and that as a freeman he must learn to work. There is still doubt in many quarters as to the ability of the Negro unguided, unsupported, to hew his own path and put into visible, tangible, indisputable form, products and signs of civilization. This doubt cannot be much affected by abstract arguments, no matter how delicately and convincingly woven together. Patiently, quietly, doggedly, persistently, through summer and winter, sunshine and shadow, by self-sacrifice, by foresight, by honesty and industry, we must re-enforce argument with results. One farm bought, one house built, one home sweetly and intelligently kept, one man who is the largest tax payer or has the largest bank account, one school or church maintained, one factory running successfully, one truck garden profitably cultivated, one patient cured by a Negro doctor, one sermon well preached, one office well filled, one life cleanly lived—these will tell more in our favor than all the abstract eloquence that can be summoned to plead our cause. Our pathway must be up through the soil, up through swamps, up through forests, up through the streams, the rocks, up through commerce, education and religion!

Coxey and His Aims (1894)

Henry Vincent

Vincent's account of Jacob Coxey and his army of the unemployed was published in the same year as the Washington march.

The great Commonweal movement, which had its birth in Massillon in the latter months of the year 1893, and that first began to attract general attention in the first month of the present year, has at its head a man of resolute courage, who is undaunted of obstacles and persistent of purpose. In order to get a proper estimate of the movement itself, it is needful that the life and character of the man should be known, as well as the objects and aims of his great undertaking.

Jacob Selcher Coxey, president of the Coxey Good Roads Association, is a native of Pennsylvania, where in his early days he spent ten years as a laborer in the iron mills before emigrating west to engage in Ohio, since which time he has owned and operated large interests in farming and stock-raising, making a specialty of blooded racing horses. More recently he has also operated extensive quarries, from which supplies of silica are taken for the glass foundries in Indiana and Pittsburg. He is reputed by his neighbors to be worth two hundred thousand dollars, and his standing in the community is that of a worthy and honest man. It is related of him that in all these years as an employer he has never missed a pay day nor had a strike among his men. Of a generous, open-hearted disposition, intensely in earnest, his money and combined energies are brought into requisition to further any project that appeals to his sense of right. In 1892 he drafted a bill which was introduced before Congress, embodying the same demands as his present good roads measure; and its manner of reception (landing, as usual with bills of that nature, in the waste basket or a pigeon hole) determined him upon a more radical effort. Carl Browne was introduced into the campaign of '93, the acquaintance there formed ripened into a friendship, and together they conceived the march to Washington. Mr. Coxey, with his large business interests, not having the time to devote to arranging details, placed the whole matter in Browne's hands, supplying the money and other necessaries, so that it could be pushed free from embarrassments.

In personal characteristics Mr. Coxey is a very retiring, unassuming gentleman, shrinks from rather than courts applause, and no offers of money or emoluments can divert him from the pursuit of this fixed purpose, as numerous incidents in the course of this narrative will amply demonstrate. During the winter of '93 and '94 Messrs. Browne and Coxey held frequent meetings in and about the city of Massillon agitating these bills and awakening public interest in their contemplated project; a platform was formulated along this line and the city ticket named, which formed the basis for an unusually active winter campaign, particularly so for that region. Very naturally the public looked with a measure of disdain upon the announcement that a march to Washington was to be started, but that did not deter the two movers from pushing ahead their plans.

A few weeks previous to the start a son was born to Mr. Coxey, whom he says he named "Legal Tender," his explanation of which runs as follows: "My idea in naming my boy in this manner," said he, "is that in after years as he grows up people will naturally inquire, 'What is the meaning of that name? What do you mean?' and questions of like import. It will ever be a pertinent reminder of the sovereign right of government to use its own full legal tender as money, and that nothing else is money."

This incident is related to illustrate the characteristic earnestness with which Mr. Coxey enters into everything he takes hold of, and the novel methods he employs for impressing lessons and examples on economic problems.

The objects and aims of Mr. Coxey are those of a very earnest man, who, apparently, has studied them long and earnestly and has adopted them as a sort of religion. These views are set forth and explained by him in a speech which he made at Camp California, Williamsport, Md., April 18 of this year. Referring to his plans, Mr. Coxey said in his characteristic style:

"The aim and object of this march to Washington has been to awaken the attention of the whole people to a sense of their duty in impressing upon Congress the necessity for giving immediate relief to the four million of unemployed people, and their immediate families, consisting of twelve million to fifteen million more. The idea of the march is to attract the attention of the whole people of this country to the greatest question that has ever been presented to them—the money question. Believing that the people can only digest one idea at a time, it was necessary to get up some attraction that would overshadow other matters and have their minds centered upon this one idea and to understand it intelligently.

"Knowing that this march would consume thirty-five days from Massillon to Washington, that it would attract their attention and we could present this money feature to them in an impressive sense and a business manner and thus be able to educate them more in six weeks' time than through any one political party in ten years.

"Our plan is to arrive at Washington by May 1, next, and camp there until Congress takes some action upon the two bills that have been presented to them by Senator Peffer, viz.: 'The Good Roads Bill' and 'The Non-interest Bearing

Bond Bill.' Believing that the unemployed people and the businessmen of this country whose interests are identical will try and get to Washington the first week in May, from three hundred thousand to five hundred thousand strong. In this manner they will bring one strongest impression to bear upon Congress coming through the common people that has ever been made in the history of this country.

"So long as Congress can keep the people isolated from each other all over the land, they will never grant them any relief, but when they come in a body like this, peaceably to discuss their grievances and demanding immediate relief, Congress can no longer turn a deaf ear, but will heed them and do it quickly.

"The full text of the bill before Congress by which to build good roads, according to my plan, is as follows:

"SECTION 1. Be it enacted by the Senate and House of Representatives in Congress assembled: That the Secretary of the Treasury of the United States is hereby authorized and instructed to have engraved and printed, immediately after the passage of this bill, five hundred millions of dollars of treasury notes, a legal tender for all debts, public and private, said notes to be in denominations of one, two, five and ten dollars, and to be placed in a fund to be known as the 'general county road fund system of the United States,' and to be expended solely for said purpose.

"SEC. 2. And be it further enacted, That it shall be the duty of the Secretary of War to take charge of the construction of the said General County Road System in the United States, and said construction to commence as soon as the Secretary of the Treasury shall inform the Secretary of War that the said fund is available; which shall not be later than _____; when it shall be the duty of the Secretary of War to inaugurate the work and expend the sum of twenty millions of dollars per month, pro rata, with the number of miles of roads in each state and territory in the United States.

"SEC. 3. Be it further enacted, That all labor other than that of the Secretary of War, 'whose compensations are already fixed by law,' shall be paid by the day, and that the rate be not less than one dollar and fifty cents per day for common labor, and three dollars and fifty cents per day for team and labor, and that eight hours per day shall constitute a day's labor under the provisions of this bill.

"Now the propositions are, that Congress shall issue and appropriate five hundred million dollars of full legal tender treasury notes to the states and territories, pro rata, with the number of miles of roads in each state and territory at the rate of twenty million dollars per month, for the improvements of the public roads of this country, and to give employment to the unemployed in making these improvements. Another provision of this bill says that all labor shall be generally by the day—no contract labor—and the rate shall be not less than one dollar and fifty cents per day of eight hours.

"This will settle the eight hour question, because it brings into competition the government, which stands ready at all times to employ the idle labor in making public roads at one dollar and fifty cents per day for a day of eight hours, and no employer of labor outside of the government will be able to employ a single man for less than one dollar and fifty cents per day of eight hours, so this will practically settle the eight hour question.

"The other matter under consideration is the Non-interest Bearing Bond Bill, now before Congress, as follows:

"Be it enacted by the Senate and House of Representatives, in Congress assembled, that whenever any state, territory, county, township, municipality, or incorporated town or village deems it necessary to make any public improvements, they shall deposit with the Secretary of the Treasury of the United States a non-interest bearing, twenty-five-year bond, not to exceed one-half the assessed valuation of the property in said state, territory, county, township, municipality, or incorporated town or village, and said bond to be retired at the rate of four per cent per annum.

"Whenever the foregoing section of this act has been complied with, it shall be mandatory upon the Secretary of the Treasury of the United States to have engraved and printed treasury notes in the denominations of one, two, five, ten and twenty dollars each, which shall be a full legal tender for all debts, public and private, to the face value of said bond, and deliver to said state, territory, county, township, municipality, or incorporated town or village ninety-nine per cent of said notes, and retain one per cent for expense of engraving and printing same.

"This non-interest, twenty-five-year bond bill grants to all states, counties, townships, municipalities, towns or villages the right to draw their non-interest, twenty-five-year bond, not to exceed one-half the assessed valuation of their entire property, and to deposit the same with the Secretary of the Treasury at Washington. It will then be mandatory upon him to issue the face value of these bonds in full legal tender treasury notes of the denominations of one, two, five, ten and twenty dollars each, returning ninety-nine per cent of those notes to the states, counties, townships, municipalities, towns or villages depositing these bonds, and the government retaining one per cent for the expense of engraving the treasury notes. The parties so receiving the money agree to repay it back at the rate of four per cent per annum, or in twenty-five annual installments without interest.

"This will enable the states, counties, townships, municipalities, towns or villages to make all the public improvements that they will need for all time to come without paying one cent of tribute to any one in the share of usury. They will be enabled to build their statehouses, their insane asylums, courthouses, infirmaries and schoolhouses. All municipalities can build their own market-houses, public libraries, museums, enginehouses, schoolhouses, and public halls where people can come and discuss all questions that interest them; pave their own streets; own and build their own electric light plants, water works, street railroads, and other public improvements that are a convenience and comfort, and promote the advancement of the whole people....

The Social Elements of the Indian Problem (1916)

Arthur Parker [Gawaso Wanneh]

Parker's article first appeared in the American Journal of Sociology.

Seven Stolen Rights

The people of the United States through their governmental agencies, and through the aggression of their citizens have: (1) robbed the American Indian of freedom of action; (2) robbed the American Indian of economic indepen-dence; (3) robbed the American Indian of social organization; (4) robbed a race of men—the American Indian—of intellectual life; (5) robbed the American Indian of moral standards and of racial ideals; (6) robbed the American Indian of a good name among the peoples of the earth; (7) robbed the American Indian of a definitive civic status.

Each of the factors we have named is an essential of the life of a man or a nation. Picture a citizen of this republic without freedom, intellectual or social life, with limited ability to provide his own food and clothing, having no sure belief in an Almighty Being, no hero to admire, and no ideals to foster, with no legal status, and without a reputable name among men. Picture a nation or a people so unhappy. Yet civilization has conspired to produce in varying degrees all these conditions for the American Indians.

So much for the seven great robberies of the race. We have not even cared to mention the minor loss of territory and of resources—these are small things indeed compared with the greater losses that we have named.

But though the robbery has been committed, the government and great citizens will exclaim, "We have given much to atone for your loss, brother red men!"

Let us examine then the nature of these gifts. The federal government and the kind hearts of friends have (1) given reserved tracts of land where the Indians may live unmolested (but are they unmolested?); (2) given agents and superintendents as guardians, and constituted a division of the Department of the Interior as a special bureau for the protection of the red race (but is the Indian protected?); (3) given schools with splendid mechanical equipment (but is the Indian educated in any adequate degree?); (4) given the ignorant and poor clerks who will think and act for them, and handle their money (does this develop manhood, ability, and good citizenship?); (5) given food, clothing, and peace (has the ration system been honest and adequate?); (6) given a new civilization (and with it a host of alluring evils); (7) given a great religion (but in the light of hypocrisy and a commercial conscience how could the Indian absorb it or be absorbed by it?).

So great and good gifts must have a price, the conqueror thought, for men cannot have these boons without suffering some disability. Measures are necessary to protect the givers and even government itself from the results of its own charity and leniency to a people but lately regarded as enemies. The government therefore as a price has denied the Indians the real benefits of civilization and placed them in a position where they have become the prey of every moral, social, and commercial evil. The Indians have been made the material for exploitation.

The Indians were not at once denied the fundamental rights of human beings, living in an organized, civilized community. It was only as the seven great robberies became more or less complete and the reservation system grew that the great denials took effect. The robberies and the denials are of a subtle psychological character and many there are who will ingeniously argue that the Indians still have all the things we have mentioned, or may have them if they will to, and that the seven gifts are but the gratuities of a charitable government.

But the men who so argue are devoid of finer spiritual perceptions or, perchance, they are unable to see from another man's viewpoint when they have one of their own. They are not wanting men and women who are unable to realize that another man can be hungry when their own stomachs are full. There are men having considerable mental endowments and a knowledge of the world who say, "If I were in his place, I would do thus and so. I would seize opportunity and soon all would be well." Men of this character are still mentally blind and spiritually dull and are the first to deny that any great wrong has been done after all. They are insensible to the fact that the red man has felt his debasement and that his soul and his children's souls are bitter with a grief they cannot express and which they cannot cast out.

The result of such denials of basic human rights to proud men and women is definite and deep. Whether he can express his thoughts in words or not, whether the turmoil in his heart finds voice or not, every American Indian who has suffered the oppression that is worse than death feels that civilization has (1) made him a man without a country; (2) usurped his responsibility; (3) demeaned his manhood; (4) destroyed his ideals; (5) broken faith with him; (6) humiliated his spirit; (7) refused to listen to his petitions....

If these statements seem to tinge of satire and of bitter invective to the civilized man, they are nevertheless very real things to the Indian who knows wherein he is wounded. To him this analysis will seem mild indeed, for it says nothing of a thousand deeds that made the four centuries of contact years of cruel misunderstanding. Yet to him these earlier years were better years than now, for he was then a free man who could boast a nation, who could speak his thought, and who bowed to no being save God, his superior and guardian. Nor will we here mention the awful wars against women and children, the treacherous onslaughts on sleeping Indian villages, the murders of the old and helpless, the broken promises, the stolen lands, the robbed orphans and widows—for all of which men professing civilization and religion are responsible—for this is aside from our argument. We mention what is more awful than the robbery of lands, more hideous than the scalping and burning of Indian women and babies, more harrowing than tortures at the stake—we mean the crushing of a noble people's spirit and the usurpation of its right to be responsible and self-supporting.

Let it be affirmed as a deep conviction that until the American Indian is given back the right of assuming responsibility for his own acts and until his spirit is roused to action that awakened ideals will give him, all effort, all governmental protection, all gifts are of small value to him.

The Indian must be given back the things of which he has been robbed, with the natural accumulation of interest that the world's progress has earned. American civilization and Christianity must return the seven stolen rights without which no race or community of men can live....

The Socialist Party's Appeal (1908)

Eugene Debs

Debs wrote this piece as part of his 1908 presidential campaign.

At a public meeting in New York City some months ago the present Presidential candidate of the Republican party was asked this question: "What is a man to do who is out of work in a financial panic and is starving?"

This is an intensely human as well as a very practical question. It epitomizes the problem of the unemployed and places it in bold relief. It is not too much to say that the future welfare and progress of our country—aye, the fate of civilization itself—depends upon a correct solution of this problem. In view of the supreme importance of the question it might naturally be expected that the Republican party would offer some practical and well-defined method of dealing with it, and one might suppose that the party's standard-bearer would be in a position clearly to expound that method in making reply to his interrogator. But how pitifully inadequate was the answer! It is at least creditable to Mr. Taft's honesty that he frankly replied, "God knows!"

When Mr. Kern, the Vice-Presidential candidate of the Democratic party, was asked recently what his party proposed to do for the relief of the unemployed, he is reported to have answered, "Nothing directly, nothing socialistic. We hope that carrying out the general ideas in our platform will so restore confidence that industry will start up again. But that's about all. In fact, that's enough."

These answers are not cited for any partisan purpose, but because they serve admirably to illustrate the really essential difference between the Socialist party and its most formidable political rivals. The Socialist party does not refer this important problem to the Deity for solution. It recognizes the fact that it is of human creation and must be solved by human effort. It proposes to do something "directly," something "socialistic," for the relief of the unemployed. The Socialist party recognizes the serious nature of the unemployed problem and aims to solve it in the only way it can be solved, namely, by removing its cause. As means of temporary relief, applicable during the period of transition to a collective system of industry, the party proposes "immediate government relief for the unemployed workers by building schools, by reforesting of cut-over and waste lands, by reclamation of arid tracts and the building of canals, and by extending all other useful public works." Both from the standpoint of effectiveness and that of practicability this program may be offered without comment in lieu of Mr. Taft's "God knows!" and Mr. Kern's "hope" of restored confidence.

As a matter of fact, it is an entire impossibility for either the Republican or the Democratic party to offer any practicable solution for our industrial ills, because those ills are the inevitable and perfectly natural outgrowth of the wage system of industry, which system both parties are alike pledged to support and defend. That the economic policy of the Republican party is impotent to stay the periodic recurrence of industrial and financial crises is proved by the existing depression, and as the party's platform utterance in relation to labor pledges it to a continuance of what is denominated "the same wise policy," there is certainly no hope of relief from that quarter. With regard to the Democratic party, the country already has had sufficient experience with its methods of dealing with important economic problems to justify the suspicion that Mr. Kern's "hope" may prove somewhat elusive.

The Socialist party of the United States is part of a great international movement which far overshadows any other movement recorded in history. Its basic idea is the complete and permanent emancipation of labor all over the world....

The Socialist party is the political expression of what is known as "the class struggle." This struggle is an economic fact as old as history itself, but it is only within the past generation that it has become a thoroughly conscious and well-organized political fact. As long as this struggle was confined to its economic aspect the ruling classes had nothing to fear, as, being in control of all the means and agencies of government, they were always able to use their power effectively to suppress uprisings either of chattel slaves, feudal serfs, or free-born and politically equal capitalist wageworkers. But now that the struggle has definitely entered the political field it assumes for the present ruling class a new and sinister aspect. With the whole power of the state—the army, the navy, the courts, the police—in possession of the working class by virtue of its victory at the polls, the death knell of capitalist private property and wage slavery is sounded.

This does not mean, however, that the workers will wrest control of government from the capitalist class simply for the purpose of continuing the class struggle on a new plane, as has been the case in all previous political revolutions when one class has superseded another in the control of government. It does not mean that the workers and capitalists will merely change places, as many poorly informed persons undoubtedly still believe. It means the inauguration of an entirely new system of industry, in which the exploitation of man by man will have no place. It means the establishment of a new economic motive for production and distribution. Instead of profit being the ruling motive of industry, as at present, all production and distribution will be for use. As a consequence, the class struggle and economic class antgonisms as we now know them will entirely disappear. Did the Socialist party have no higher political ideal than the victory of one class over another it would not be worthy of a moment's support from any right-thinking individual. It would, indeed, be impossible for the party to gain any considerable strength or prestige. It is the great moral worth of its ideals that attracts adherents to the Socialist movement even from the ranks of the capitalist class, and holds them to their allegiance with an enthusiasm that suggests a close parallel with the early days of Christianity; and it is the mathematical certainty with which its conclusions are stated that enables the Socialist party to expand and advance with irresistible force to the goal it has in view, in spite of the appalling opposition it has had to encounter. It is this certainty, and the moral worth of its ideals, which moved Mommsen, the venerable German historian, to say that "this is the only great party which has a claim to political respect."

The capitalist was originally a socially useful individual, but the evolution of our industrial system has rendered him a parasite, an entirely useless functionary that must be eliminated if civilization is to endure. It is a leading thought in modern philosophy that in its process of development each institution tends to cancel itself. Born out of social necessity, its progress is determined by repulsions and attractions arising in society, which produce effects tending to negate its original function. Now, that is what has happened to the capitalist. He is no longer useful. He is merely a clog to social progress and must be abolished, just as the feudal lord and chattel slaveholder have been abolished.

The capitalist was originally a manager who worked hard at his business and received what economists call the "wages of superintendence." So long as he occupied that position the capitalist might be restrained and controlled in various ways, but he could not be got rid of. He performed real functions, and as society was not yet prepared to take those functions upon itself, it could not afford to discharge him. But now the capitalist proper has become absolutely useless. Finding it easier to combine with others of his class in a large undertaking, he has abdicated his position of overseer and has put in a salaried manager to act for him. This salaried manager now performs the only social function of the capitalist, while the capitalist himself has become a mere rent or interest receiver. The rent or interest he receives is paid for the use of a monopoly which not he, but a vast multitude of people, created by their joint efforts.

This differentiation between manager and capitalist is a necessary part of the process of capitalistic evolution due to machine industry. As competition led to waste in production, so it also led to the cutting of profits among capitalists. To prevent this the concentration of capital was necessary, by which the large capitalist could undersell his small rivals in the marketing of goods produced by machinery and distributed by agencies initially too costly for any individual competitor to purchase or set on foot. For such massive capitals the contributions of several capitalists are necessary. Hence the joint stock company, the corporation, and finally the trust. Thru the medium of such agencies a person in the United States can own stock in an enterprise in Africa or South America which he has never visited and never intends to visit, and which, therefore, he cannot "superintend" in any way. He and the other stockholders put in a manager with injunctions to be economical. The manager's business is to earn the largest possible dividends for his employers. If he does not do so he is dismissed. To secure high dividends the manager will lower wages. If that is resisted there will probably be either a strike or a lockout. Cheap labor will be imported by the manager, and if the workers resist by intimidation or organized boycotting the forces of the state will be used against them, and in the end they must submit. The old personal relation between the workers and the employer is gone. From the point of view of the corporation owners the workers are simply an extension of the machine of profit production. The workers are not regarded as having human attributes. Their labor is trafficked in as a commodity, like iron and steel, and the only interest the capitalist retains in production is his interest as an idle dividend receiver. Society can get along without the capitalist; it refuses longer to support him in idleness and luxury.

The process of industrial evolution that has rendered the capitalist a useless functionary has at the same time evolved an organization, co-operative in character, whereby industry may be carried on without friction for the benefit of the whole people instead of for the profit of the individual capitalist. The conduct of industry will be entrusted to men who are technically familiar with its processes, precisely as it is now entrusted to managers by the stockholders of a corporation; in short, the whole of industry will represent a giant corporation in which all citizens are stockholders, and the state will represent a board of directors acting for the whole people. Details of organization and performance may well be left to the experts to whose direction the matter will be given when the time comes. It is not the mission of the Socialist party to speculate concerning the manner in which the workers will conduct their affairs when they have come into possession of their inheritance which the ages have prepared for them. Standards of right and justice under the new *régime,* however, may well be indicated.

"Without rights there shall be no duties; without duties no rights." What will be the practical interpretation of this Socialist axiom? Obviously, social parasitism must cease; every man must be a producer, or perform some socially useful function, in order to procure title to any share in the product of the collective industry. The only citizenship held honorable will be economic citizenship, or comradeship in production and in the sharing of product.

The spectacle of strong men walking the streets idle and hungry, vainly begging for a chance to work for the pittance that will suffice to ward off starvation from themselves and their loved ones, will be no more. The cruelty of children of tender years being forced hungry to school in a great city like New York will disappear. No longer will there be a problem of the unemployed, and the capitalist will be elevated from his present condition of parasitism to that of a worker and producer of wealth. The class struggle must necessarily cease, for there will be no classes. Each individual will be his own economic master, and all will be servants of the collectivity. Human Brotherhood, as taught by Christ nineteen centuries ago, will for the first time begin to be realized.

The struggle for working class emancipation, which finds its expression thru the Socialist party, must continue, and will increase in intensity until either the ruling class completely subjugates the working class, or until the working class entirely absorbs the capitalist class. There is no middle ground possible, and it is this fact that makes ludicrous those sporadic reform movements typified by the Populist and Independence parties.

But the subjugation of the working class is out of the question. Intelligence has gone too far for that; it is the capitalist class that is doomed. Hence the only possible outcome of the present struggle is victory for the working class and the absorption by that class of all other classes.

When the present Socialist party has accomplished its mission of uniting the workers of the world into a solid political phalanx the end of capitalist domination is at hand, and the era of industrial peace so long wished for by philanthropists and seers will dawn upon the world.

Epilogue: Outcomes

There are two major schools of thought about the effectiveness of the progressive reforms. One is that progressivism helped to correct the worst abuses of the capitalist system, and thus marked the beginning of a new age where government was more willing to become involved in the economic and social sphere. The other is that progressivism was a necessary correction allowed by the business class in order to bring stability to the economy, to undermine the more radical demands of labor unions, and to maintain ultimate control of the market. There is evidence for both of these perspectives.[28]

Examining the first line of thought, there can be little doubt that progressivism had a profound effect on the United States. Although progressives did not achieve all they wanted, they did have victories. For example, child labor laws were enacted in thirty-eight states by 1912. In Illinois, the state legislature banned labor for children fourteen and under and mandated an eight-hour workday for women after Florence Kelley, a settlement house resident, conducted a study of the sweatshop conditions in the factories. Progressives also helped to pass two federal laws outlawing some forms of child labor in 1916 and 1918. Unfortunately, the U.S. Supreme Court, which historically has sided with big business, overturned the two federal laws. In addition, many of the state laws banning child labor were not well enforced. However, these victories did shift public opinion against child labor.[29]

Progressives also made improvements to the public health system. In Philadelphia in 1870, 175 infants out of 1,000 died in their first year of life. By 1930, that number had been lowered to 75 infants per 1,000, a 57 percent reduction. In 1870, 60 percent of all Philadelphians died from infectious disease (diphtheria, malaria, measles, scarlet fever, smallpox, tuberculosis, typhoid, and whooping cough). By 1930, less than 0.1 percent died from it. These gains were equally impressive in other cities such as New York and Milwaukee. These improvements resulted from progressives demanding better city services, such as filtered water supply, improved milk, and education on how to deal with diarrhea. Although other factors helped decrease these death rates (e.g., economic growth and general improvement in living standards), it is estimated that social reforms accounted for at least 33 percent of the decline in the death rate.[30]

Among progressive child-saving ideas, Julia Lathrop advocated implementing a nationwide infant and maternal health program. After four years of advocating for legislation, progressives convinced Congress to pass the Sheppard-Towner bill, which focused its efforts on prevention of health problems. The act provided money for new clinics that would conduct preventive health examinations for pregnant women and children at no charge. It also encouraged states to provide matching funds and to set up agencies that would coordinate state health programs with those of the Children's Bureau. Female doctors and nurses ran the health clinics, since women were often shut out of the hospitals and had difficulty setting up private practices because of sexism. This innovative and successful program operated for ten years but was shut down by Congress after male doctors strongly opposed the program. The male doctors argued that the clinics were offering "substandard" health care and were "socialistic" (when in reality, the clinics were providing economic competition). After the defeat of Sheppard-Towner, maternity and children's health care returned to the private sector and the domain of male doctors.[31]

The settlement house movement, as one part of the coalition involved in the larger progressive movement, played a major role in many of these victories. The settlement houses also had such local victories as cleaner neighborhoods, improved community services at public high schools, and appointments of residents to school boards and other public offices. At the same time, the residents helped neighborhoods by caring for the children, teaching English classes, and responding to the daily crises that affect poor people. Hull-House, with its belief in research-driven social reform, deeply influenced the "Chicago School" of urban sociology. Perhaps the greatest contribution of the settlement houses was to train a group of young individuals who would take their progressive ideals into the fields of public policy, education, research, and industry. For example, residents included Julia Lathrop and Grace Abbott, both of whom would go on to head the U.S. Children's Bureau; Harry Hopkins, designer of President Franklin Roosevelt's relief efforts; Florence Kelly, longtime director of the National Consumer's League; John Dewey, pioneering educator; Frances Perkins, first woman to serve in the U.S. Cabinet as Secretary of Labor; and Gerard Swope, president of General Electric and a leader of welfare capitalism. Not surprisingly, training future leaders as a strategy to improve society was one of the main goals of Henrietta and Samuel Barnett, the founders of the first settlement house, at Toynbee Hall.[32]

At the height of the settlement house movement in the 1910s, there were 400 settlement houses serving hundreds of thousands of working-class people across the United States. Although the settlement houses did not achieve the improvements they hoped for in working conditions, housing, or schools, they were never intended to be the final solution to poverty. They were too small, too decentralized, and had too little access to large-scale funds to address the root causes of poverty. They were also up against the power of capital and the urban political machines. Furthermore, the settlement houses were not flawless and sometimes failed to live up to their ideals. For example, at times they imposed their middle- and upper-class values on the poor, as happened when settlement house residents worked for temperance (bans on alcohol) despite the fact that many of the poor thought the saloons played an important social and cultural role in the community.[33]

Two of the major organizations focusing on poverty, the settlement house movement and Charity Organization Societies (COS), had bridged their differences. Openly opposed to settlement houses in the early 1890s, COS changed its philosophy to agree with settlement house advocates that poverty was the result of economic and social factors (e.g., unemployment, low pay, high living costs, unhealthy living conditions, overwork, child labor, etc.) rather than laziness, improvidence, bad morals, or drinking. The groups did not deny that personal inadequacies contributed to poverty, but they considered economic and social factors the primary cause. By the beginning of the twentieth century, COS and settlement houses were cooperating, and indeed merging, into the incipient field of social work. In 1905, the COS journal *Charities* and a settlement house journal, *The Commons,* merged into *Charity and the Commons.* In 1909, Jane Addams became the president of COS's National Conference on Charities and Corrections. In the years to come, the settlement house movement would lose its energy; however, the original vision of COS, which was to coordinate local poor relief, lives on, and can be seen today in the work of the United Way, an organization that has its roots in the late nineteenth-century COS movement.[34]

Although many progressive ideas changed the United States (e.g., the creation of a juvenile justice system that focused on rehabilitation, legislation to clean up corrupt political practices, suffrage for women, and grassroots participation in democracy), one other progressive idea played a major role in the reduction of poverty: William James's idea of "a moral equivalent to war." James, who is best known for his philosophy of pragmatism, which argued that "truth" was discovered through experience and not theory, was an admirer of Jane Addams and a supporter of progressive reforms. In the progressive tradition of urging more public responsibility, James proposed that young men be conscripted into national service as with the military, but rather than go to war, they would build roads, tunnels, buildings, or engage in whatever other challenging work the nation needed. James felt this service would inspire civic passion in a similar way to war, but the outcome would be constructive rather than destructive. It would also lead to a decrease in the gap between rich and poor and help young people develop compassion and critical thinking skills. This idea inspired youth programs aimed at fighting poverty, such as the Civilian Conservation Corps, Peace Corps, Volunteers in Service to America (VISTA), and AmeriCorps.[35]

Progressives also had an impact on national politics, as they influenced the Republican and Democratic Parties to move politically left, and eventually created the Progressive Party. In fact, the 1912 election was the first time that all major candidates claimed they were progressive.

The Radical Challenge of Labor

Another school of thought holds that the progressive movement blunted the radical challenge of labor and socialism since its reforms demonstrated that the worst parts of the system could be changed. Moreover, the business class reluctantly embraced some progressive ideas since they desired more stability in the social system, and class conflict was bad for business. Also, the success of the communist revolution in Russia in 1917 sent fear throughout the business class, and the capitalists did not want to see a repeat performance in the United States. Thus, in order to beat back labor unions and avoid fundamental change, it can be argued that capitalists allowed for some minor changes to occur to the system. Howard Zinn, the social historian, makes a case for this perspective. He states: "True, this was the 'Progressive Period,' the start of the Age of Reform; but it was a reluctant reform, aimed at quieting the popular risings, not making fundamental change.... Undoubtedly, ordinary people benefited to some extent from these changes. The system was rich, productive, complex; it could give enough of a share of its riches to enough of the working class to create a protective shield between the bottom and the top of the society."[36]

There is little doubt that the capitalist class wanted to stop the popular uprisings and not make fundamental change. For example, in the three labor strikes described earlier, the business class used deadly force to crush each of the uprisings. In Homestead, nine strikers were killed by Pinkerton private security agents (as well as seven Pinkertons); in the American Railway Union strike, thirty-four strikers were killed by federal troops and U.S. deputy marshals (who were paid by the railroads, and damage to railroad property was in the hundreds of thousands of dollars); and in Ludlow, the Colorado National Guard and deputies killed sixteen people, including twelve children. In the end, capital was victorious, but at a high cost in human lives.[37]

Business interests were also successful at beating back attempts from Coxey's army, the International Workers of the World, and the socialists. When Coxey and his followers arrived on May 1 in Washington, D.C., he was arrested while trying to deliver a speech on the Capitol steps. The district authorities charged Coxey with displaying a banner (i.e., a small lapel pin) on Capitol property and stepping on the Capitol's grass. Even though Coxey had walked on the paths instead of the grass, a hostile judge sentenced him to twenty days in prison and a $5 fine. After serving his jail time, Coxey did get the opportunity to speak to the House Labor Committee, which decided to hear testimony on the causes of the unemployment crisis. This was the single legislative victory won by the marchers. However, Congress was not interested in Coxey's proposal. It would take another forty years and the Great Depression for the U.S. government to enact a national public works program to reduce poverty.

Significantly, Coxey was the first to propose a national public works program; he was also the first to lead a march to the Capitol. Coxey's march to Washington was the beginning of a new type of social action in the United States, which entailed bringing masses of people to the source of U.S. political power and airing before the nation a set of grievances and a demand for action. In this way, Coxey's army was the precursor of the Woman Suffrage Procession of 1913, the Veterans' Bonus March of 1932, the March on Washington for Jobs and Freedom of 1963, the Vietnam antiwar protests of 1971, the Million Man March of 1995, and the March for Women's Lives in 2004.[38]

The Socialist Party and the IWW did not bring about the fundamental changes they desired, but they did have a profound impact on U.S. society. By 1910, the Socialist Party had recruited 100,000 members, had 1,200 officeholders in 337 towns and cities (including 73 socialist mayors), and ran a newspaper, *An Appeal to Reason,* with 500,000 subscriptions. Eugene Debs would run for U.S. president five times, garnering a high of 6 percent of the vote in 1912. The IWW, which had a membership of approximately 60,000, was involved in dozens of strikes, some of which brought about more pay and better working conditions, and some of which failed. And although the majority of American workers were not members of the IWW or the Socialist Party, the call for fundamental change had a radicalizing effect on the entire labor movement. Furthermore, the IWW's call to create an inclusive democratic union continues to motivate labor activists up to the present day.[39]

In light of capital's effort to defeat labor, welfare capitalism can be seen not as a benevolent reform, but as a way to avoid fundamental change. This perspective is supported by the fact that the leading businessmen who organized the National Civic Federation argued that progressive reforms such as "workmen's compensation" would allow big business to reach an accord with the conservative segment of labor and thus defuse the labor movement's efforts in politics and diminish the power of socialism. However, many in the business community opposed even these minor reforms. In practice, welfare capitalism helped only a small fraction of its workers. For example, in the companies guided by welfare capitalism, only 20 percent of all workers were provided pension plans and stock purchase plans. Also, the effort to build employment agencies was not effective and did little to reduce unemployment. Importantly, welfare capitalism did not win the workers' complete loyalty, and it did not stop the growth of unions. And during the Great Depression, most corporations dropped the benefit plans offered to workers under welfare capitalism.[40]

The Unprogressive Era

Although there are different schools of thought when it comes to determining the impact of the progressive era, there is general agreement that African American and Native American lives did not improve in this era. However, the ideas of Booker T. Washington and W. E. B. Du Bois had immense influence. After his Atlanta Exposition speech, which advocated black self-help and a temporary acceptance of segregation, Washington was catapulted into the national spotlight. Whites from all over the country embraced him as a nonthreatening and conservative black leader, and in the black community he was supported by the Baptist church, black newspapers, and a southern constituency of small businessmen, schoolteachers, and farmers. He was seen as the chief intermediary between the white and black communities, and when he died in 1915,

Washington was considered the most powerful black American leader. His ideological rival, W. E. B. Du Bois, continued to advocate, along with people such as Phillip Randolph and Ida B. Wells-Barnett, for the alternative vision of full political and social equality through protest and agitation. This vision reached its full expression in the civil rights movement of the 1950s and 1960s.[41]

Regrettably, Arthur Parker's "seven stolen rights" proposal to alleviate Native American poverty and suffering was not listened to at the time. It would take the next generation of U.S. leaders to embrace Parker's proposal for Indian self-determination and to recognize that Indian culture and values were worthwhile and deserving of respect.

A Civilian Conservation Corps member plants one of 3 billion trees

Chapter 5

The Great Depression and the New Deal Era

Prologue: Social Context and Overview of Solutions

During the Great Depression of the 1930s, citizen activists and politicians un-
leashed a variety of innovative social solutions to poverty. In order to solve the
problem of massive unemployment, they made such proposals as the "Share the
Wealth," the Townsend plan, and End Poverty in California (EPIC). President
Franklin Delano Roosevelt's New Deal programs would come to define this era,
but the alternative plans offered are critical to our understanding of historical
solutions to poverty.

159

1917–1929: The Red Scare and the Resurgence of Conservatism

The progressive spirit, which was so powerful a generation before, was still alive during this time period. For example, Robert La Follette ran as a Progressive Party candidate and received 17 percent of the vote for president in 1924. However, progressives were no longer shaping the national agenda. The progressive movement's desire for social justice had been stifled by the "red scare" that swept the United States after the communist victory in Russia. The retreat from radicalism was evident in the settlement house movement, which moved away from social reform and toward solving the individual problems of community members. Many of the settlement movement leaders as well as leaders from other progressive causes were stigmatized as being associated with socialism and therefore dangerous.[1]

The fear of communism also negatively affected the labor movement, as it suffered a series of setbacks in the late 1910s and 1920s. Throughout the period, leaders and supporters of the International Workers of the World (IWW), socialists, and other radical organizers were attacked, imprisoned, deported, and executed. One of the largest federal governmental sweeps took place in January 1920 with the arrest of 6,000 suspected radicals in thirty-three cities. Many of these people were held in custody without being formally charged of a crime, and they were not permitted to contact relatives or lawyers. Some of the arrested had no connection to radical activities, and others were coerced to sign confessions. Eventually, 600 people were deported. With constant antilabor intimidation by the business community and the business-friendly government, union membership declined from 5 million in 1920 to 3.6 million in 1923.

The 1920s started off with a short postwar depression as federal spending decreased rapidly after the end of World War I. This economic downturn led to the unemployment of millions of working-class people but had little effect on the middle class. In addition, 100,000 farmers lost their farms with the collapse of agricultural prices. By 1922, the economy recovered and a long period of economic growth occurred. National incomes for all social classes rose, with modest 15 percent growth for the working class over the next seven years. However, this prosperity was not shared evenly, as the amount of wealth held by the top 1 percent of the population increased from 31.6 percent in 1922 to 36.3 percent in 1929. Another way to look at this inequality is that in 1929, the top 5 percent took home 33 percent of all income. Amazingly, the richest one-tenth of 1 percent of families took home as much income as the 42 percent at the bottom (i.e., six million families). Concentration of power and wealth was now in the hands of the top 200 corporations, which controlled one-half of all corporate assets and had the capability to set prices and direct capital investments with huge consequences for the average American. With wealth and power concentrated at the top, it is estimated that 40 percent of the population lived in poverty.[2]

With the progressive and labor movements in retreat, two conservative Republican presidents were elected in the 1920s, Warren Harding and Calvin Coolidge. In 1928, a third business-friendly Republican, Herbert Hoover, was elected president. Hoover held a strong belief in American individualism, free enterprise, and decentralized government, but at the same time, he was not a supporter of laissez faire doctrine. He opposed an economic free-for-all since he believed it led to a concentration of power that stifled equality of opportunity and initiative. Rather, he believed in an individualism fused with public service. Hoover proposed that volunteerism within the community was the best antidote for poverty as well as for a myriad of other social problems. He called on individuals, local charity organizations, churches, and local governments to work cooperatively to alleviate suffering and distribute relief. Hoover claimed that voluntary cooperation was "self-government by the people outside of the Government."[3]

The Great Depression began in Hoover's first year in office. His strong belief in self-help and voluntary cooperation led him to oppose federal spending for relief to the unemployed. As the social conditions worsened, Hoover did approve a modest federal construction program and a federal loan program that initially supported business (e.g., banks, insurance companies, railroads, and agriculture associations), but eventually it was expanded to give loans to state governments to support local relief programs. However, in the face of mass poverty and unemployment, many Americans no longer believed that their economic destiny was determined by individual initiative, and the easy stereotypes about the poor did not seem to apply.[4]

In the weeks before Hoover announced his presidential reelection campaign in 1932, 20,000 World War I veterans, many of whom were unemployed, came to the capital to demand early payment of their promised military service "bonus" of roughly $1,000. The "Bonus Army" camped out in Washington, D.C. and over the next two months, they paraded and demonstrated in an attempt to pressure Congress to pass early payment legislation. However, on June 17, 1932, the U.S. Senate rejected this legislation by a vote of 62 to 18. Soon afterward, President Hoover decided to use the U.S. Army to evict the Bonus Marchers. Led by General Douglas MacArthur, the army attacked unarmed Bonus Marchers and violently drove them out of Washington. This was an inauspicious start to Hoover's presidential campaign, and Americans went on to reject his rugged individualism and self-help philosophy in the 1932 election.[5]

1929–1941: Social Suffering

The 1929 market crash, which initiated the Great Depression, was caused by wild stock speculation. The economy was not fundamentally sound as corporations were overproducing goods and the average person did not have enough money to buy these products because of unequal income and wealth distribution. Although the nation had experienced fifteen economic downturns in the past century, the depth and length of this economic downturn surpassed all others.[6]

The impact of the Great Depression on businesses was staggering. By 1933, more than 5,000 banks had gone bankrupt, and nine million people had lost their savings. In that same year, overall industrial production had decreased by 50 percent, auto production dropped by 75 percent, construction decreased by 78 percent, investment was down by 98 percent, and the steel factories operated at just 12 percent of capacity. These decreases in production and investment led to massive unemployment, with approximately fifteen million people, or 25 percent of the workforce, out of work. In addition, underemployment was a major problem, as the people with jobs had their hours and pay continually reduced.[7]

As desperation in the face of unemployment, underemployment, and poverty set in, bread lines were set up to feed the nation's hungry. Yet in 1933 in the city of New York—which at that time was one of the world's richest cities—139 people died of hunger and malnutrition. Evictions became commonplace as people no longer were able to pay the mortgage or rent. For example, in Philadelphia, 1,300 homes and apartment buildings were repossessed each month and sold off by the sheriff's office. The average person on relief in 1934 was a white male head of household, thirty-eight years old, with an elementary school education and ten years of experience in his profession.

At the same time, the Great Depression was particularly hard on the young and old. In Colorado, 50 percent of all children attending school were malnourished. One-quarter of a million youth under the age of twenty-one left their homes to look for work, food, and shelter. Workers under twenty and over sixty were twice as likely to be unemployed as middle-aged workers. Women—particularly married women—also suffered financially in the Great Depression, as some businesses fired all married women to make room for white men desperate to work.[8]

Also hard hit were people of color, many of whom were already poor before the Great Depression. African Americans, Mexican Americans, and Mexican nationals endured great hardship as native-born white workers demanded that they be given preference for jobs. Many African Americans worked in unskilled manufacturing, construction, lumber, and mining industries, and all of these industries experienced sharp declines in production. This downturn resulted in African Americans comprising 20 percent of the unemployment rolls, twice the rate in proportion to the overall population. In Los Angeles, there were two people for every job, and Mexican nationals and Mexican Americans suffered discrimination as thousands of whites moved to southern California as a result of the Dust Bowl drought in the plains states. In addition to discriminatory employment practices, state, federal and immigration authorities led police raids against Mexican nationals and Mexican Americans in California, Arizona, and Texas. The goal of the raids was to deport people in order to reduce the number of Mexican workers and thereby decrease the relief rolls.[9]

Yet, the depression wasn't bad for all. In 1933, although net incomes for the lower classes decreased sharply from the previous year, the number of millionaires doubled and corporate profits rose. In fact, for the affluent, life continued on throughout the Great Depression with little disruption.[10]

Social Solutions

With mass poverty and unemployment affecting much of the nation, a variety of social solutions were proposed. Dorothy Day, a Catholic layperson who co-founded the Catholic Worker movement in 1933 with Peter Maurin, developed a three-part strategy to reduce the suffering in New York and beyond. First, the Catholic Worker movement attempted to "clarify" people's thoughts by introducing a Catholic social philosophy based on compassion, social justice, community, nonviolence, and solidarity with workers. This activism took the shape of forums, lectures, and a newspaper, the *Catholic Worker*, edited by Dorothy Day. The newspaper critiqued the existing social system from a prophetic biblical tradition. Day and Maurin also developed "Houses of Hospitality" where the homeless and unemployed could live. The houses operated a bread line that fed hundreds of hungry people every day. Day felt that this work of mercy alleviated suffering and demonstrated Catholics' love for humanity and God. The Catholic Workers initiated farming communes as an alternative to industrial society. Catholic Workers felt that the agricultural life provided people with community, meaningful work, and the ability to control the fundamental activities influencing their lives.[11]

Ultimately, Day and Maurin wanted to create "a society where it is easier to be good." Day felt that this required both personal and institutional change. She called upon individuals to change their hearts in order to serve the poor. Day argued that "the greatest challenge of the day is: how to bring about a revolution of the heart, a revolution which has to start with each one of us." At the same time, she believed that institutional change was necessary. It was not enough for people with changed hearts to do good works for the poor; they needed to change the system that caused the oppression. When reflecting upon the lives of the saints, she wondered, "Why was so much done in remedying the evil instead of avoiding it in the first place? ... Where were the saints to try to change the social order, not just to minister to the slaves, but to do away with slavery?"[12]

In the same year that Day and Maurin cofounded the Catholic Worker movement, President Roosevelt, who had defeated Herbert Hoover in the 1932 election, initiated the New Deal to employ the unemployed. Breaking with tradition, the Roosevelt administration, with the support of Congress, initiated the Civil Works Administration (CWA) and the Civilian Conservation Corps (CCC). The CWA, led by Harry Hopkins, was an emergency and temporary response to avoid additional suffering—and possible disorder—during the upcoming winter. Its goal was to employ four million workers immediately in road building, school repair, sanitation work, and other construction work. In addition, the CWA hired unemployed teachers to teach adult education, literacy, and vocational courses, and unemployed artists to create murals and other public works of art. Likewise, the CCC provided the opportunity for 500,000 young men (ages eighteen to twenty-five) per year to work on environmental conservation projects at 2,600 camps in states throughout the union. The goal was to employ restless and discouraged young men, many of whom had previously roamed the nation looking for work. The CCC paid $30 per month, $25 of which had to be sent back to their families, and provided corps members educational assistance. Corps members signed up for six months, which could be extended up to two years. Although these federal programs as well as other New Deal initiatives involved the federal government in the economy, they did not break with the American principle of encouraging work and discouraging outdoor relief (or what was by then commonly called "the dole"). Roosevelt believed that the New Deal would not destroy the Protestant work ethic and capitalism; rather it would save them.[13]

As the depression continued into 1934 and 1935, some felt that Roosevelt's solutions were too conservative and that stronger action was necessary to solve poverty. Three of the most important plans came from Huey Long, Francis Townsend, and Upton Sinclair. Long, a Democratic senator from Louisiana and potential candidate for president, proposed the "Share the Wealth" plan. Long was highly critical of the New Deal, which he felt had exacerbated poverty and unemployment and had increased the wealth of the rich. Long wanted to limit the amount of income and wealth through progressive taxation and redistribute the money to the average citizen. Long's "Share the Wealth" plan proposed an initial redistribution of $5,000 to all citizens followed by a guaranteed income of $2,000–$2,500 each year, about double the wages of the average factory worker. With such a poverty level below which no one could fall, all Americans would have enough money for a comfortable home and modern conveniences such as an automobile and a radio.[14]

Francis Townsend, a citizen activist, proposed a flat federal pension for the elderly. The Townsend plan was much more generous than Roosevelt's social insurance plan, as it called upon the federal government to distribute $200 a month ($2,400 a year) to all seniors over sixty who had stopped working. The only limitation was that the seniors needed to spend the entire amount by the end of each month. Townsend argued that his pension plan would abolish old-age poverty, stimulate the economy by ending underconsumption, and remove a group of people from the employment pool who would normally be competing with others for jobs. The Townsend plan would be financed by a national sales tax of 2 percent on all business transactions. Significantly, both the Long and Townsend plans were uniquely American as they did not attempt to destroy the free-market system.[15]

Upton Sinclair, the writer and socialist, ran for governor of California on the Democratic ticket. His 1934 platform was entitled "End Poverty in California" (EPIC), and its goal was to turn over factories and agricultural land laying fallow to workers to be run as cooperatives. Sinclair argued that traditional relief operations financially benefited political machines rather than the poor. He felt that farm and industrial cooperatives—voluntary, democratic, and jointly owned enterprises created to meet economic and social needs—were the most effective way to employ more than 750,000 unemployed and underemployed Californians. Proponents of EPIC called for "public welfare against private greed" and hoped to build a new society that ended mass poverty through peaceful and orderly methods. Sinclair believed that his approach was not radical, but based in the American values of self-reliance, initiative, and equality.[16]

In response to the continuing depression, labor unrest (e.g., 1.5 million striking workers in 1934), and the need to respond forcefully to these alternative plans, Roosevelt put forward the Economic Security Act after his landslide victory in the 1936 election. This act included old-age pensions, unemployment insurance, workers' compensation, and aid to dependent children. Roosevelt's proposals were deeply influenced by the American experience. For example, several key components of the plan were to be operated by the states, which gave them the power to determine the amount and accessibility of the benefits. The old-age pension and unemployment insurance plans were to be funded in part by the workers themselves. Additionally, the unemployment plan was limited in the amount and length of the benefit, and farmworkers and domestic workers (mostly people of color) were entirely excluded from all the benefits plans.

Many industrialized nations had previously adopted old-age pensions, unemployment insurance, and workers' compensation, and implemented them in a way that blurred the distinction between public relief and social insurance. However, Roosevelt's Economic Security Act maintained a clear demarcation between social security, which Roosevelt believed Americans would feel they had "earned" because they paid into it, and public assistance, which he felt discouraged people from working and undercut their initiative. Secretary of Labor Frances Perkins, who was the first female cabinet minister and a key player in development of the act, observed that Roosevelt was adamant that the Economic Security Act not be a "dole."[17]

A competing social insurance bill sponsored by Congressmember Ernest Lundeen, a Democrat from Minnesota, had also garnered considerable support. This bill grew out of a series of Hunger Marches in 1931 and 1932 in Washington, D.C., and from the work of the Unemployed Councils, a communist-sponsored organization that had been very active in resisting house evictions of the destitute. The Lundeen bill (H.R. 2827) was a more comprehensive and progressive plan than Roosevelt's Economic Security Act since it (a) provided coverage for all workers; (b) offered a federal, rather than federal-state, system for unemployment insurance and aid to dependent children; (c) covered the workers who were then unemployed; (d) offered immediate compensation to workers at their average weekly wages, and guaranteed it until a job was found; (e) provided a sixteen-week paid maternity leave for women; (f) offered national criteria for unemployment and welfare; and (g) was funded by an inheritance tax on upper-middle-class and rich individuals and corporations. The Lundeen bill had the support of unemployed worker groups, feminist organizations, African American groups, ethnic and mutual aid societies, some labor unions, and the Communist Party USA.[18]

The Great Depression inspired some educators to get involved in the fight against poverty by making schools agencies of social change. This perspective became popular with the work of George Counts and Harold Rugg. Counts, a professor of education at Columbia University, argued that schools should work for the improvement of the general welfare and provide students with a "strong sense of social obligation." He urged teachers to develop curricula that focused on social and economic justice. Harold Rugg, a colleague of Counts at Columbia University, accepted the challenge and developed a series of K–12 textbooks for the curriculum examining issues of poverty, class conflict, racism, and civic action. Rugg's textbooks hit the market in the early 1930s, with titles like *The Conquest of America* and *Changing Governments and Changing Cultures: The World's March Toward Democracy.*[19]

A discussion of the New Deal and its attempt to reduce poverty is incomplete without mentioning two other important policy changes: the Wagner Act and the "Indian New Deal." After the Supreme Court ruled unconstitutional the 1933 National Industrial Recovery Act, which had included a provision to allow workers the right to organize and bargain collectively, Roosevelt decided to support the Wagner Act. The Wagner Act, which was signed into law in 1935, guaranteed the right of workers to choose their own unions, picket, boycott, and strike. The act made it illegal for employers to blacklist union leaders, to hire spies to infiltrate the union, and to operate company unions. The Wagner Act also established the National Labor Relations Board to ensure compliance. Roosevelt hoped that these new powers would allow the labor movement to increase worker wages in order to spark consumption.[20]

The Indian New Deal repudiated the Dawes Act and implemented some of the recommendations highlighted by Arthur Parker. Roosevelt's Native American policy, which had been developed by Commissioner of Indian Affairs John Collier, acknowledged the importance of tribal culture and encouraged its development. At last, the U. S. government recognized that tribal culture was deserving of respect. Furthermore, Native Americans were encouraged to hold their land collectively as they had previously done before U.S. intervention. Roosevelt's new Indian policy also led to the passage of the Indian Reorganization Act (IRA) of 1934, which recognized Native American tribal governments as sovereign.[21]

However, other minority groups did not benefit from the New Deal programs. The unremitting racist treatment throughout the New Deal era led a group of African Americans, headed by Phillip A. Randolph of the Brotherhood of Sleeping Car Porters, to call a march on Washington to end government discrimination. The march was to highlight federal discrimination in the military and war industries developing rapidly in 1940 as the United States prepared for war.[22]

The Importance of the Preservation of Self-Help and of the Responsibilities of Individual Generosity as Opposed to Deteriorating Effects of Government Appropriations (1931)

Herbert Hoover

President Hoover's comments were delivered to the press on February 3, 1931.
Certain senators have issued a public statement to the effect that unless the President and the House of Representatives agree to appropriations from the

Federal Treasury for charitable purposes they will force an extra session of Congress.

I do not wish to add acrimony to a discussion, but would rather state this case as I see its fundamentals.

This is not an issue as to whether people shall go hungry or cold in the United States. It is solely a question of the best method by which hunger and cold shall be prevented. It is a question as to whether the American people on one hand will maintain the spirit of charity and mutual self help through voluntary giving and the responsibility of local government as distinguished on the other hand from appropriations out of the Federal Treasury for such purposes. My own conviction is strongly that if we break down this sense of responsibility of individual generosity to individual and mutual self help in the country in times of national difficulty and if we start appropriations of this character we have not only impaired something infinitely valuable in the life of the American people but have struck at the roots of self-government. Once this has happened it is not the cost of a few score millions but we are faced with the abyss of reliance in future upon Government charity in some form or other. The money involved is indeed the least of the costs to American ideals and American institutions.

President Cleveland, in 1887, confronted with a similar issue stated in part:

> A prevalent tendency to disregard the limited mission of this power and duty should, I think, be steadfastly resisted, to the end that the lesson should be constantly enforced that though the people support the Government, the Government should not support the people.
>
> The friendliness and charity of our countrymen can always be relied upon to relieve their fellow-citizens in misfortune. This has been repeatedly and quite lately demonstrated. Federal aid in such cases encourages the expectation of paternal care on the part of the Government and weakens the sturdiness of our national character, while it prevents the indulgence among our people of that kindly sentiment and conduct which strengthens the bonds of a common brotherhood.

And there is a practical problem in all this. The help being daily extended by neighbors, by local and national agencies, by municipalities, by industry and a great multitude of organizations throughout the country today is many times any appropriation yet proposed. The opening of the doors of the Federal Treasury is likely to stifle this giving and thus destroy far more resources than the proposed charity from the Federal Government.

The basis of successful relief in national distress is to mobilize and organize the infinite number of agencies of self help in the community. That has been the American way of relieving distress among our own people and the country is successfully meeting its problem in the American way today....

But after and coincidently with voluntary relief, our American system requires that municipal, county and state governments shall use their own resources and credit before seeking such assistance from the Federal Treasury.

I have indeed spent much of my life in fighting hardship and starvation both abroad and in the southern states. I do not feel that I should be charged with lack of human sympathy for those who suffer but I recall that in all the organizations with which I have been connected over these many years, the foundation has been to summon the maximum of self help. I am proud to have sought the help of Congress in the past for nations who were so disorganized by war and anarchy that self help was impossible. But even these appropriations were but a tithe of that which was coincidently mobilized from the public charity of the United States and foreign countries. There is no such paralysis in the United States and I am confident that our people have the resources, the initiative, the courage, the stamina and kindliness of spirit to meet this situation in the way they have met their problems over generations.

I will accredit to those who advocate Federal charity a natural anxiety for the people of their states. I am willing to pledge myself that if the time should ever come that the voluntary agencies of the country together with the local and state governments are unable to find resources with which to prevent hunger and suffering in my country, I will ask the aid of every resource of the Federal Government because I would no more see starvation amongst our countrymen than would any senator or congressman. I have the faith in the American people that such a day will not come.

The American people are doing their job today. They should be given a chance to show whether they wish to preserve the principles of individual and local responsibility and mutual self help before they embark on what I believe is a disastrous system. I feel sure they will succeed if given the opportunity....

Houses of Hospitality (1938)

Dorothy Day

As editor of the Catholic Worker, *Day was also a prolific writer.*

In the Middle Ages when one out of every four was leprous, there were two thousand leper houses run by religious in France, alone. This is the startling and thought-provoking statement made in Farrow's book, "Damien, the Leper." That statement has not been contested. It may be horrifying to make such a comparison, but inasmuch as one out of every five workers today is unemployed or on work relief, the catastrophe which has visited us is comparable.

Unemployment is the gravest problem in the country today. It is immediate, so it is more pressing than the problem of war and peace. It means hunger and cold and sickness right now, so it is more immediate a problem than the unionizing of workers. In fact the unionizing of workers cannot get on while thirteen million men are unemployed and those employed are hanging on to their jobs like grim death and not willing to make any forward steps which would jeopardize those jobs. And we contend that the kind of shelter afforded these unattached unemployed is liable to make them leprous in soul and utterly incapable of working for sustenance or salvation.

There are thousands of men sheltered in the lodging houses of New York City, run by the city, and countless other thousands sitting up all night in missions and flop houses and roaming the streets. As the weather gets warmer you may see them sleeping in the shelter of buildings, in areaways, in subways, along the waterfront. They crawl into their holes by night, and by day come out to tramp from one end of the island to the other in search of food. Every other city—Pittsburgh, Boston, Detroit, Chicago, Milwaukee, St. Louis—has the same problem.

Peter Maurin, whose idea it was to start the *Catholic Worker,* began it with a simple program which called for round-table discussions, houses of hospitality and farming communes. Before the depression, he predicted it. During the depression he constantly stressed the problem of unemployment. He is still journeying from one end of the country to the other, speaking of a new social order wherein man is human to man and which can be built up on the foundation of the works of mercy and voluntary poverty.

He himself has been a transient worker and an unemployed worker. He spent twenty years traveling through the United States and Canada, doing the manual labor which built this country. And it is due to his constant indoctrinating, as he calls it, that groups in New York, Boston, Pittsburgh, Chicago, Detroit, Milwaukee, Troy, St. Louis, Houma, Louisiana, and Windsor, Ontario, have started what Peter himself called from the beginning houses of hospitality, where those in need can receive food, clothing and shelter, and hold round-table discussions, which point to the solution of problems. Peter is only doing what the great Saint Peter called for—working for a new heaven and a new earth, wherein justice dwelleth.

In New York, the unemployed come from all over, seeking work. They are not all single men. There are the married, as well as the sons of the family who leave home in order that they may not be a burden on those that remain. There are whole families migrating. There are young married couples. There are even lone women and girls.

Peter has always pointed out that according to canon law, all bishops should be running hospices, or houses of hospitality. But now, thinking in terms of state responsibility rather than personal responsibility, those in need are turned over to agencies, to the city or the state. There are isolated instances of hospices of the homeless of course. I have visited Father Dempsey's huge hospice in St. Louis, for instance. Father Dempsey was criticized for "bringing all the bums in the United States to St. Louis." But nevertheless his work was well supported and he was able to carry on his work for many, many years. There is a splendid hospice run by the St. Vincent de Paul Society in San Francisco, where a small charge of $.15 is made. There is a day shelter besides where men can remain during inclement weather. We believe of course that an absolutely free place is necessary for the wanderer not having any funds or not knowing the ropes. I have heard of a hospice in Philadelphia which I wish to visit, and doubtless there are many more. I hope readers of this article will let me know of others throughout the country, run under Catholic auspices.

I have visited all the hospices run by *Catholic Worker* groups, naturally, and they all have the same difficulties and the same problems and are all run on the same lines. They all started with no funds at all. A small group got together, decided they wanted a headquarters for propaganda and meetings, and rented a store for $10 or $15 a month. None of them ever knew where the next month's rent was coming from. Usually there was no money for paint or soap or mops or beds or stoves or cups. But little by little these things were contributed. Most of them began fearfully and are continuing fearfully. If any of them ever thought they were going to have to feed the numbers they are feeding, they would never have had the courage to start. (Oh, we of little faith!) Most of them hesitated along for several years before starting the endless task of feeding those who came. For as soon as the feeding began—as soon as the mood of hospitality began to make itself felt—lines formed at the door, and continued day after day.

In New York, our breakfast line, which began with a single friendly pot of coffee on the stove in the store where we hold our meetings, grew and grew until now we serve breakfast to approximately 1,000 men. They begin forming on the line at four-thirty in the morning. The door is not opened until six and then the work goes on until nine or nine thirty. During the day we have only sixty or so to the other two meals. We have to consider the work of the paper, letter writing, receiving visitors, taking care of those under our roof which number about fifty in the city and fifteen in the country. (In the summer there will be about fifty there too.)

In Boston they feed 250 men a day; in Pittsburgh, 200; in Detroit, 400; St. Louis, 200; and so on. The numbers are not so large, but if the reader will just contemplate saying to himself, "Two or three friends and I will undertake to feed 350 people a meal every day," not just for one day but indefinitely, stretching out month after month, year after year, he would be aghast. Just try it. He would not think it possible by himself of course, nor would he trust the Lord to fall in with his seemingly presumptuous plans.

Yet if we are thinking in terms of personal responsibility, to those who sit around and say, "Why don't the priests do this or that?" or "Why don't *they* [that indefinite *they*] do this or that?" we should reply, "Why don't we all?"

It is really the work of the lay apostolate. In this day of huge parishes, running into thousands of souls (sometimes even 10,000) it is hard to see how the priest can think of undertaking such a work. Bishops used to have personal knowledge and acquaintance with not only all their priests but many of their flock, whereas now the bishop of a large diocese has every moment taken with spiritual duties.

We not only believe that this is the work of the lay apostolate, but we believe that all over the country the faithful should gird up their loins, so to speak, and start two thousand houses. If France could start and continue for a few generations two thousand leper houses, until segregation, combined with the plague, wiped out leprosy, then surely we in the United States ought to be able to open and continue two thousand houses of hospitality and face the prospect of continuing them not only through this generation but until the social order has been reconstructed.

It is a grave emergency. The Holy Father says that the workers of the world are being lost to the Church. If we are all lay apostles and "other Christs" this is our responsibility.

Trade union leaders like John L. Lewis believe that through strong unions, labor leaders in politics, legislation, the thirty-hour week, insurance taxation, and public works financed through taxation of industrialists rather than of the poor through sales taxes, the unemployed can be reabsorbed and those not reabsorbed can be taken care of.

Perhaps a Christian state could do all these things. But since we are living under only a nominally Christian state, Christians will have to resort to those old-as-the-Church-itself methods of the works of mercy through houses of hospitality to care for immediate needs such as food, clothing and shelter.

These needs supplied under Christian auspices would make a startling change in the character of the unemployed. Hope, that most sinned-against of virtues would be restored. Hospices in the shadow of churches would mean a constant recognition of Christ the Worker, Christ our Brother. The priests living in close contact with the poorest of transients and ministering to them, holy Mass, missions, constant indoctrination through Catholic literature, Catholic surroundings—what a change this would make in the outlook of the poor!

As it is now, under the dubious hospitality of the city and state, it is as though God were unknown. There is no reminder to morning and evening prayer. Men have lost the sense of their own dignity, that dignity which they possess because Christ shared their humanity, their unemployment, their dire need.

Worse than that, men become drunken, drug-ridden, vicious and obscene in many cases. These are strong words but when one thinks what mobs are capable of, once their passions are aroused, it must be admitted that in our care for the poor we do nothing to give man the power to control his baser nature which through its black deeds most assuredly merits the hell which Christ died to save us from.

Who are most prominent in caring for transients and unemployed throughout the country? The Workers Alliance with its millions of members is strictly Marxist and materialist in its philosophy, however unformulated. There amongst those masses is the material for revolutionary mobs, and when we consider revolutions in the past, engineered by the few intellectual leaders with a theory of revolution as Lenin called it, when we consider the mass riots in New York in the last century which led to the building of our many armories, we can count on a well-directed mob throughout the country under the influence of whatever Marxist leaders or Fascist leaders that turn up in the future.

Unless—.

Civil Works (1936)

Harry Hopkins

These reflections are from the director of the Civil Works Administration one year after the program was terminated.

...Even without the pressure for work put upon us by groups of unemployed, the powerful logic of a work program had been clear to us from the first. The falling away of consumption which occurred within every family close upon the discharge of the breadwinner was not immediately visible, except in financial statements of business transacted. Outsiders had little knowledge of how much food was eaten, soap, coal, gas, electricity and telephone service consumed, or of how often garments were mended within the four secretive walls of a house. But the quick contraction of local public funds had had one result which could not be overlooked. School teachers lost their jobs right and left. Rural schools were closing their doors. The American people are great consumers of school services. They could not look lightly upon their stoppage. It might be all right to give groceries or cash relief to an unemployed textile worker, and let his former customer go without sheets. Sheets are private, and it is a matter of taste, and nobody's business whether you use them or not. School attendance, on the other hand, is widely advertised, even upheld by law. To feed the school teacher and dispense with his services was not enough. With more leisure, there was a greater demand for education, both to while away the boredom, and to acquire and improve skills for a constantly more critical labor market. New York with state relief money had initiated schools for the unemployed a year before the advent of FERA [i.e., Federal Employment Relief Administration], recognizing that food, shelter and clothing were not enough to keep body and soul together.

During 1932 and 1933 a growing number of unemployed teachers applied for relief after their resources had become exhausted. Shortly after the FERA was initiated we attempted to do something for this group of needy teachers. Obviously, it was hardly enough to give them direct relief. With thousands of teachers out of work there were, at the same time, hundreds of thousands of men and women in need of educational facilities. We decided to put these unemployed teachers to work teaching those unemployed who wanted instruction. The emergency education program of the latter part of 1933 was not designed to perform the normal educational functions of the public school systems—it was essentially a special type of work relief. The program included general adult education, literacy classes, vocational education, vocational rehabilitation, and nursery school work. Thus the emergency education program was essentially an adult education program, designed primarily to give employment to needy teachers and to provide educational opportunities to those who ordinarily could not obtain them. During the early part of 1934, the period when CWA [i.e., Civil Works Administration] was in operation, some 33,000 teachers, most of whom would otherwise have been on direct relief, were conducting adult education classes and nursery schools.

In other special fields, too, there had been a steady growth in work projects. Women were making garments for the use of families on relief. Some projects supervised by Federal bureaus were under way. Broadly speaking, however, aside from special programs looking toward the rehabilitation of certain well defined groups, their work was merely an alternative method of extending relief.

I should like to clarify here the difference between work relief and a job on a work program such as CWA and WPA [i.e., Works Progress Administration]. To the man on relief the difference is very real. On work relief, although he gets the disciplinary rewards of keeping fit, and of making a return for what he gets, his need is still determined by a social worker, and he feels himself to be something of a public ward, with small freedom of choice. When he gets a job on a work program, it is very different. He is paid wages and the social worker drops out of the picture. His wages may not cover much more ground than his former relief budget but they are his to spend as he likes. I am told that all over the country the response was the same when people went off work relief (and we had over 2,000,000 on work relief) and on to Works Progress. The wife of the WPA worker tossed her head and said, "We aren't on relief any more, my husband is working for the Government."

The project itself differs somewhat under these two systems. The work relief project, although it must offer useful work, and a maximum opportunity to the worker to use his special skill, is primarily judged on its merits as a labor absorber. On a long-term, well planned and integrated employment program such as WPA, where projects must be sponsored by local citizens, and scrutinized by state and Federal officials to see that they meet rigid procedural requirements, the projects are usually work that should be done even if there were no unemployed demanding jobs. It thus has a separate existence of its own. The consumer must want the product before the worker is put on the job.

Although the idea of the government putting men to work at day labor on force account rather than by contract was an old one, having been forwarded by John R. Commons in the *Federationist* as long ago as 1898, its application to the situation current in 1933 was as suddenly conceived as it was put into action and carried through. Re-employment in private industry was not occurring as fast as had been anticipated. The Public Works program which, it was hoped, would prove a considerable stimulus for industry, had of necessity been slow in getting started, and had not produced the expected effect of speedily reducing the relief load. Throughout the country, in all groups, the duration and inclusiveness of unemployment had convinced the public that in one way or another the unemployed must be put to work.

The very character of the workers who by now had been reduced to idleness, whether they were on relief or not, made it easily possible to imagine a stupendous and varied work program which could be prosecuted. Whereas it seems pretty generally accepted that the incidence of unemployment falls first on the least fit, by January, 1933, whole sections of American business had all but closed up shop, leaving brilliant, talented, and able men without a job. Ninety per cent of New York architects alone were unemployed.

The Civil Works Administration was, therefore, created November 9, 1933, by executive order of the President under authority of Title II of the National Industrial Recovery Act. From the first it was intended to be a very short program, carrying over the peak of a critical winter. Its chief, original aim was to put four million needy unemployed to work as speedily as possible and to keep them at work for the winter. The increase of purchasing power was a secondary objective.

One did not have to be on relief to take advantage of the new program. One half, or two million workers, were to be drawn from the needy unemployed who had so far stayed off relief, but whose morale was disintegrating through fear and the gradual inroads of destitution. With a spurt of wages they might catch up their family fortunes in mid-descent, and sufficiently revive their hope and morale so as to be eligible for re-employment at a private job.

As a matter of fact, the rush to get on the CWA payroll was so great that the arrangement of half relief to half non-relief was not strictly adhered to. Many unemployed workers, who had kept themselves off relief perhaps past the point where it was healthy for them to do so, enrolled now, fearing that they would lose out if they did not take the final step. As a consequence, during the period immediately preceding December 1st, relief lists were overloaded. Local offices took as many off the rolls as possible in order to cut down their relief expenditures. After December 1st the National Re-employment Service undertook the task of handling the applicants, and set up some eleven hundred additional offices throughout the country, CWA paying for their upkeep. The Service classified each applying worker according to his qualifications, so that there would be a maximum chance of his being put at the kind of work for which his skill and training fitted him.

Since an administrative set-up which would penetrate over 3,000 counties could follow only upon a large amount of precise planning at headquarters, it was clear from the first that we should have to reach the employment peak by gradual ascent. On the first pay day, November 23, 1933, 814,511 workers received CWA checks. Two weeks later 1,976,625 people were actually at work. By January 18, 1934, the peak was reached, and exceeded the original estimate of four million by 263,644 workers.

The President's executive order of November 9th had allocated $400,000,000 from Public Works Administration funds to the new CWA. An additional $88,960,000 was transferred to CWA from the Federal Emergency Relief appropriation. By Act of Congress, approved by the President on February 15, 1934, a further $345,000,000 was made available for carrying the program to its conclusion. In all, then, total Federal allocations for the program were $833,960,000.

This sum of money, like all the large figures with which we are accused of dealing so nonchalantly, has meaning only when it is converted into the object for which it was intended. In this instance it was wages.

The quotient we were after in CWA was wages. We also bought other things with our money. Our average ratio for labor to materials was 80–20. The purchase of materials we could also mark up as indirect stimulus to business. But wages were what we were after. Since the CWA received its original funds from appropriations made to the Federal Emergency Administration of Public Works under the NRA, the minimum wage rates and the maximum working hours stipulated by this act necessarily became the CWA schedule.

Under this act, the United States was divided into three zones for hourly rates of pay. For the southern states, the minimum rate for unskilled labor was forty cents an hour, and skilled labor a dollar. In the central states, unskilled labor got forty-five cents and skilled labor $1.10. In the northern states unskilled labor got sixty cents and skilled labor $1.20. If local rates were higher, these higher rates were accepted in lieu of the zone scale of PWA. Road work rates, however, were to follow those of the various State Highway Commissions. For clerical, office, statistical, survey and professional workers, the prevailing wage of the community was paid, but with minimum rates established. Rates for unskilled clerical workers in the South began with twelve dollars a week. Professional workers in the North ranged from twenty-four dollars to forty-five.

In certain rural districts where laborers rarely make enough to live on, this wage was unsettling, and many employers protested against it. We were told that workers were being spoiled. The assertion that workmen can be spoiled by a decent wage is always interesting, though never alarming. That the sum of money which has gone into the home of any family from the United States Treasury through the agencies of relief has ever been large enough to corrupt a man with luxury is hard to believe; although one should agree that the prolonged necessity of accepting it has almost unavoidably deteriorating effects upon its recipients....

Long after the workers of CWA are dead and gone and these hard times forgotten, their effort will be remembered by permanent useful works in every county of every state. People will ride over bridges they made, travel on their highways, attend schools they built, navigate waterways they improved, do their public business in courthouses and state capitols which workers from CWA rescued from disrepair. Constantly expanded and diversified to offer use for the special skills and training of different types of workers, the CWA program finally extended its scope to almost every kind of community activity. We had two hundred thousand CWA projects.

Roads constituted by far the greatest part of the work. Over $300,000,000 were spent chiefly on county secondary roads, to ease the pull of the farmer to market, or his children to school. This money bought approximately 250,000 miles of roads and streets improved or built. Work done on main highways consisted chiefly of straightening curves, putting in culverts, but above all in the repairing, reconditioning and building of bridges. Since the CWA program fell almost exclusively in winter, and a cold winter at that, the execution of much of this road work was very difficult.

Because taxes could not be collected or money borrowed with which to keep them up, most of the public buildings, town, city and state, were as run-down as the poorer private dwellings, whose lack of paint and loosening bricks and boards had made the landscape shabbier every year since 1929. The schools showed most plainly this lack of repair and modernization. Decent sanitary arrangements or water supply were often lacking. Wiring was defective or absent. Desks were rickety, walls blackened with dirt. Some buildings were too far gone for anything but demolition. We tore them down and put new ones in their places, sometimes made of the old materials, plus salvaged paving brick. The CWA workers put 40,000 schools into shape. University buildings and their laboratories were reconditioned.

Our sanitation program was composed of two types. Under the first, a campaign to reduce permanently the infection sources of endemic diseases in many rural districts, hundreds of thousands of acres of malarial land were drained and ditched, millions of rats destroyed, disease-bearing ticks were eradicated. Sewage disposal plants and reservoirs, some of considerable size, were built. More than 12,000,000 feet of sewer pipe were laid or repaired. Under the supervision of the U.S. Public Health Service 150,000 sanitary privies were built in a rural health campaign which had long been considered of extreme importance in the checking of typhoid and dysentery. This was probably the only type of work done on private property, but the owners supplied materials and part of the labor themselves. Rehabilitation and expansion of hospital facilities was a less dramatic part of this health work, yet much of it was done everywhere. In Arizona, CWA workers built a hospital to accommodate 1,000 tuberculosis patients.

We did some work for the publicly owned utilities. Detroit all but made a new street-car system, relaid tracks, painted and modernized cars. Telephone and telegraph lines were repaired and improved, old traffic light systems were improved, and new ones installed. Power and heating plants were built. Even a high tension line was moved while a road was being reconstructed, an important feat of engineering.

Thanks to CWA, also, during a severe depression year, the United States expanded its recreational resources to an unprecedented extent, adding some 200 swimming pools, over 3,700 playgrounds. After the program was shut down, many CWA workers, anxious to have their children benefit from these places to play, asked permission to finish their jobs without pay. Athletic stadiums, some of them spacious enough to accommodate thousands of spectators, were built, as well as bath-houses, boat-houses, camps, open-air fireplaces, trails and even lakes of considerable size. The forestry program, conducted primarily for another purpose, was closely allied to recreation. Hundreds of miles of firelines were cut, brush and dead trees removed. Erosion was partially checked. Old fish hatcheries were expanded, and new ones built; streams and preserves restocked with fish and wild game.

These were some of the tangible products of construction work in which the majority of CWA workers was engaged. We had, however, on our list of employees some 190,000 non-manual and professional workers. The Women's Division, the Emergency Educational Program and our Administration Offices had absorbed some of these before the advent of CWA. Now they began to work under a program known as Civil Works Service, which could profitably use technical people. These non-manual workers were also the ones who made possible many valuable surveys and researches, among them a real property inventory. Archeological and historical projects of excavation, indexing and research were conducted, supervised by highly trained technicians. About 3,000 artists, painters, sculptors, etchers, and mural painters were employed at Public Works of Art. By those well qualified to speak of the importance of their first venture of American government into the patronage of art, it was considered a major movement in the cultural history of the United States and one of which I shall speak later. This program, like almost all others conducted under CWA, was not dropped when the CWA period ended in the spring of 1934.

A true inventory of CWA would not group it into categories. Set up to cover local and unique situations, it had infinite variety. Minor details of the problems or of the inventiveness with which they were dealt adhere to the minds of those widely scattered persons who participated in that winter's program. The whole story of CWA can never be written. It touched actively between twenty and thirty million people who followed its ambitions, successes, failures and gossip with pride and anxiety.

The speed and volume of the work done that winter produced a momentum which jolted the community. I believe CWA will stand out, even when WPA has become past history, like a precocious child in a family of slower-going but more substantial children. For its special quality of having come and gone so quickly, yet having let loose great forces, both economic and spiritual, it shares certain of the memorable qualities of special events. A fraternity grew up among those who had worked in it, like the fraternity of a dramatic recruiting period. WPA exceeds CWA in scope, volume and efficiency. Without what we learned through our CWA experience of procedure, labor problems, supervision, planning and resources of the community, we could never have had WPA, and to that extent it can be looked upon as a preliminary, almost a probationary, period. Nevertheless, officers often recall those few months in which the people of the United States were galvanized to an unprecedented task and accomplished it.

American communities had had a taste of what could be accomplished under a government program for the unemployed. The logic was too simple to be overlooked. Once the cover was drawn away from the need, and we no longer talked about merely keeping the idle busy, that need revealed itself to be stupendous. The workers were there, imploring for both work and wages. Private money was standing still because it could not hope for profit, and by its apathy it was paralyzing consumption.

After CWA was over, many of those who denounced it as folly, and loudly complained about the chiselling, graft, and injustice which they saw or thought they saw in its performance, lamented its departure: CWA had brightened the retailers' tills. We had yet to learn that what we are leaving behind always looks good to those who oppose doing much for the man on relief; that upon which we are embarking looks extravagant, dangerous and all wrong. For a while it was a habit to ask about CWA, was it a success or wasn't it a success? In the relief business where our raw material is misery and our finished product nothing more than amelioration, effectiveness has to be measured in less ambitious terms than success. That word applies better to marginal profit, cash or otherwise. Relief deals with human insolvency.

Redistribution of Wealth (1935)

Huey Long

This speech was a radio address, which was later inserted by Senator Long into the Congressional Record.

Mr. LONG. Mr. President, I send to the desk a radio address and a letter by myself which I ask to have inserted in the RECORD.

There being no objection, the address and the letter were ordered to be printed in the RECORD, as follows:

Ladies and gentlemen, there is a verse which says that the

"Saddest words of tongue or pen

Are these: 'It might have been.'"

I must tell you good people of our beloved United States that the saddest words I have to say are:

"I told you so!"

In January 1932 I stood on the floor of the United States Senate and told what would happen in 1933. It all came to pass.

In March 1933, a few days after Mr. Roosevelt had become President and had made a few of his moves, I said what to expect in 1934. That came to pass.

As the Congress met in the early months of 1934 and I had a chance to see the course of events for that year, I again gave my belief on what would happen by the time we met again this January 1935. I am grieved to say to you that this week I had to say on the floor of the United States Senate, "I told you so!"

How I wish tonight that I might say to you that all my fears and beliefs of last year proved untrue! But here are the facts—

1. We have 1,000,000 more men out of work now than 1 year ago.

2. We have had to put 5,000,000 more families on the dole than we had there a year ago.

3. The newspapers report from the Government statistics that this past year we had an increase in the money made by the big men, but a decrease in the money made by the people of average and small means. In other words, still "the rich getting richer and the poor getting poorer."

4. The United States Government's Federal Deposit Insurance Corporation reports that it has investigated to see who owns the money in the banks, and they wind up by showing that two-thirds of 1 percent of the people own 67 percent of all the money in the banks, showing again that the average man and the poor man have less than ever of what we have left in this country and that the big man has more of it.

So, without going into more figures, the situation finally presents to us once more the fact that a million more people are out of work; 5,000,000 more are on the dole, and that many more are crying to get on it; the rich earn more, the common people earn less; more and more the rich get hold of what there is in the country, and, in general, America travels on toward its route to _____.

Now, what is there to comfort us on this situation? In other words, is there a silver lining? Let's see if there is. I read the following newspaper clipping on what our President of the United States is supposed to think about it. It reads as follows:

[From the New Orleans Morning Tribune, Dec. 18 1934]
PRESIDENT FORBIDS MORE TAXES ON RICH—TELLS CONGRESSMEN INCREASES MIGHT MAKE BUSINESS STAMPEDE
By the United Press
WASHINGTON, December 17.—The administration is determined to prevent any considerable increase in taxes on the very rich, many of whom pay no taxes at all, on the ground that such a plan would cause another "stampede" by business. Word has been sent up to Democratic congressional leaders that it is essential nothing be done to injure confidence. The less said about distribution of wealth, limitation of earned income, and taxes on capital, "new dealers" feel, the better.

Repeatedly since the Democrats won a two-thirds majority in both Houses in the congressional elections last month the administration has sought to assure the worker, the taxpayer, and the manufacturer that they had nothing to fear.

Meantime reports reached the Capital that fear of potential increases in inheritance taxes and gift levies at the coming Congress was in part responsible for the failure of private capital to take up a greater share of the recovery burden.

That ends the news article on what President Roosevelt has had to say.

President Roosevelt was elected on November 8, 1932. People look upon an elected President as the President. This is January 1935. We are in our third year of the Roosevelt depression, with the conditions growing worse. That says nothing about the state of our national finances. I do not even bring that in for important mention, except to give the figures:

Our national debt of today has risen to $28,500,000,000. When the World War ended we shuddered in our boots because the national debt had climbed to $26,000,000,000. But we consoled ourselves by saying that the foreign countries owed us $11,000,000,000 and that in reality the United States national debt was only $15,000,000,000. But say that it was all of the $26,000,000,000 today. Without a war our national debt under Mr. Roosevelt has climbed up to $28,500,000,000, or more than we owed when the World War ended by 2½ billions of dollars. And in the Budget message of the President he admits that next year the public debt of the United States will go up to $34,000,000,000, or 5½ billion dollars more than we now owe.

Now this big debt would not be so bad if we had something to show for it. If we had ended this depression once and for all we could say that it is worth it all, but at the end of this rainbow of the greatest national debt in all history that must get bigger and bigger, what do we find?

One million more unemployed; 5,000,000 more families on the dole, and another 5,000,000 trying to get there; the fortunes of the rich becoming bigger and the fortunes of the average and little men getting less and less; the money in the banks nearly all owned by a mere handful of people, and the President of the United States quoted as saying: "Don't touch the rich!"

I begged, I pleaded, and did everything else under the sun for over 2 years to try to get Mr. Roosevelt to keep his word that he gave to us; I hoped against hope that sooner or later he would see the light and come back to his promises on which he was made President. I warned what would happen last year and for this year if he did not keep these promises made to the people.

But going into this third year of Roosevelt's administration, I can hope for nothing further from the Roosevelt policies. And I call back to mind that whatever we have been able to do to try to hold the situation together during the past 3 years has been forced down the throat of the national administration. I held the floor in the Senate for days until they allowed the bank laws to be amended that permitted the banks in the small cities and towns to reopen. The bank deposit guaranty law and the Frazier-Lemke farm debt moratorium law had to be passed in spite of the Roosevelt administration. I helped to pass them both.

All the time we have pointed to the rising cloud of debt, the increases in unemployment, the gradual slipping away of what money the middle man and the poor man have into the hands of the big masters, all the time we have prayed and shouted, begged and pleaded, and now we hear the message once again from Roosevelt that he cannot touch the big fortunes.

Hope for more through Roosevelt? He has promised and promised, smiled and bowed; he has read fine speeches and told anyone in need to get in touch with him. What has it meant?

We must now become awakened! We must know the truth and speak the truth. There is no use to wait 3 more years. It is not Roosevelt or ruin; it is Roosevelt's ruin.

Now, my friends, it makes no difference who is President or who is Senator. America is for 125,000,000 people and the unborn to come. We ran Mr. Roosevelt for the Presidency of the United States because he promised to us by word of mouth and in writing:

1. That the size of the big man's fortune would be reduced so as to give the masses at the bottom enough to wipe out all poverty; and

2. That the hours of labor would be so reduced that all would share in the work to be done and in consuming the abundance mankind produced.

Hundreds of words were used by Mr. Roosevelt to make these promises to the people, but they were made over and over again. He reiterated these pledges even after he took his oath as President. Summed up, what these promises meant was: "Share our wealth."

When I saw him spending all his time of ease and recreation with the business partners of Mr. John D. Rockefeller, Jr., with such men as the Astors, etc., maybe I ought to have had better sense than to have believed he would ever break down their big fortunes to give enough to the masses to end poverty—maybe some will think me weak for ever believing it all, but millions of other people were fooled the same as myself. I was like a drowning man grabbing at a straw, I guess. The face and eyes, the hungry forms of mothers and children, the aching hearts of students denied education were before our eyes, and when Roosevelt promised, we jumped for that ray of hope.

So therefore I call upon the men and women of America to immediately join in our work and movement to share our wealth.

There are thousands of share-our-wealth societies organized in the United States now. We want a hundred thousand such societies formed for every nook and corner of this country—societies that will meet, talk, and work, all for the purpose that the great wealth and abundance of this great land that belongs to us may be shared and enjoyed by all of us.

We have nothing more for which we should ask the Lord. He has allowed this land to have too much of everything that humanity needs.

So in this land of God's abundance we propose laws, viz:

1. The fortunes of the multimillionaires and billionaires shall be reduced so that no one person shall own more than a few million dollars to the person. We would do this by a capital levy tax. On the first million that a man was worth we would not impose any tax. We would say, "All right for your first million dollars, but after you get that rich you will have to start helping the balance of us." So we would not levy any capital levy tax on the first million one owned. But on the second million a man owns we would tax that 1 per cent, so that every year the man owned the second million dollars he would be taxed $10,000. On the third million we would impose a tax of 2 percent. On the fourth million we would impose a tax of 4 percent. On the fifth million we would impose a tax of 8 percent. On the sixth million we would impose a tax of 16 percent. On the seventh million we would impose a tax of 32 percent. On the eighth million we would impose a tax of 64 percent; and on all over the eighth million we would impose a tax of 100 percent. What this would mean is that the annual

tax would bring the biggest fortune down to three or four million dollars to the person because no one could pay taxes very long in the higher brackets. But three to four million dollars is enough for any one person and his children and his children's children. We cannot allow one to have more than that because it would not leave enough for the balance to have something.

2. We propose to limit the amount any one man can earn in 1 year or inherit to $1,000,000 to the person.

3. Now, by limiting the size of the fortunes and incomes of the big men we will throw into the Government Treasury the money and property from which we will care for the millions of people who have nothing; and with this money we will provide a home and the comforts of home, with such common conveniences as radio and automobile, for every family in America, free of debt.

4. We guarantee food and clothing and employment for everyone who should work by shortening the hours of labor to 30 hours per week, maybe less, and to 11 months per year, maybe less. We would have the hours shortened just so much as would give work to everybody to produce enough for everybody; and if we were to get them down to where they were too short, then we would lengthen them again. As long as all the people working can produce enough of automobiles, radios, homes, schools, and theaters for everyone to have that kind of comfort and convenience, then let us all have work to do and have that much of heaven on earth.

5. We would provide education at the expense of the States and the United States for every child, not only through grammar school and high school but through to a college and vocational education. We would simply extend the Louisiana plan to apply to colleges and all people. Yes; we would have to build thousands of more colleges and employ a hundred thousand more teachers; but we have materials, men, and women who are ready and available for the work. Why have the right to a college education depend upon whether the father or mother is so well to do as to send a boy or girl to college? We would give every child the right to education and a living at birth.

6. We would give a pension to all persons above 60 years of age in an amount sufficient to support them in comfortable circumstances, excepting those who earn $1,000 per year or who are worth $10,000.

7. Until we could straighten things out—and we can straighten things out in 2 months under our program—we would grant a moratorium on all debts which people owe that they cannot pay.

And now you have our program, none too big, none too little, but every man a king.

We owe debts in America today, public and private, amounting to $252,000,000,000. That. means that every child is born with a $2,000 debt tied around his neck to hold him down before he gets started. Then, on top of that, the wealth is locked in a vice owned by a few people. We propose that children shall be born in a land of opportunity, guaranteed a home, food, clothes, and the other things that make for living, including the right to education.

Our plan would injure no one. It would not stop us from having million-aires—it would increase them tenfold, because so many more people could make a million dollars if they had the chance our plan gives them. Our plan would not break up big concerns. The only difference would be that maybe 10,000 people would own a concern instead of 10 people owning it.

But my friends, unless we do share our wealth, unless we limit the size of the big man so as to give something to the little man, we can never have a happy or free people. God said so! He ordered it.

We have everything our people need. Too much of food, clothes, and houses—why not let all have their fill, and lie down in the ease and comfort God has given us? Why not? Because a few own everything—the masses own nothing.

I wonder if any of you people who are listening to me were ever at a barbecue! We used to go there—sometimes a thousand people or more. If there were 1,000 people we would put enough meat and bread and everything else on the table for 1,000 people. Then everybody would be called and everyone would eat all they wanted. But suppose at one of these barbecues for 1,000 people that one man took 90 percent of the food and ran off with it and ate until he got sick and let the balance rot. Then 999 people would have only enough for 100 to eat and there would be many to starve because of the greed of just one person for something he couldn't eat himself.

Well, ladies and gentlemen. America, all the people of America, have been invited to a barbecue. God invited us all to come and eat and drink all we wanted. He smiled on our land and we grew crops of plenty to eat and wear. He showed us in the earth the iron and other things to make everything we wanted. He unfolded to us the secrets of science so that our work might be easy. God called: "Come to my feast."

Then what happened? Rockefeller, Morgan, and their crowd stepped up and took enough for 120,000,000 people and left only enough for 5,000,000 for all the other 125,000,000 to eat. And so many millions must go hungry and without these good things God gave us unless we call on them to put some of it back.

I call on you to organize share-our-wealth societies. Write to me in Washington if you will help.

Let us dry the eyes of those who suffer; let us lift the hearts of the sad. There is plenty. There is more. Why should we not secure laws to do justice—laws that were promised to us—never should we have quibbled over the soldiers' bonus.

We need that money circulating among our people. That is why I offered the amendment to pay it last year. I will do so again this year.

> Why weep or slumber, America?
> Land of brave and true,
> With castles, clothing, and food for all
> All belongs to you.
> Ev'ry man, a king, ev'ry man a king,
> For you can be a millionaire;
> But there's something belonging to others,
> There's enough for all people to share.
> When it's sunny June and December, too,
> Or in the wintertime or spring,
> There'll be peace without end.
> Ev'ry neighbor a friend,
> With ev'ry man a king.

Immediate EPIC (1934)

Upton Sinclair

This pamphlet was used during Upton Sinclair's gubernatorial campaign in California.

The purpose of this pamphlet is to discuss those steps of the Plan to End Poverty in California which have to be taken FIRST.

The EPIC Plan was prepared in August, 1933. There was neither time nor money for research work, so many of the propositions were stated in general terms. In the thirteen months which have since elapsed, the Plan has been widely discussed; more than a hundred audiences have been addressed, and thousands of questions answered. Naturally, our proposals have been revised in many details, and we know that the Plan is a sounder and wiser thing than it was a year ago.

We of the EPIC movement presume to tell the people of California that we know how to end poverty and will do it if elected. We are not professional politicians seeking office, but men of faith believing in the right and power of the people to manage their own affairs. We believe that democratic government confronts today the gravest crisis of its history. Our old and established industrial system is falling into ruins, and a new system has to be built in the midst of the collapse. Unless Democracy can find a way to do this, we shall have civil war, followed by Fascism and ultimately by Bolshevism. In the effort to avert these events, we present a plan to the people of California.

We expect to take power in January, 1935. We shall take over a state brought to the verge of bankruptcy by greedy and ignorant politicians. There will be a deficit of $35,000,000, plus an accumulating deficit of a million and a half per month; this without counting the expenses involved in the support of the unemployed and destitute. Despite the fact that we had nothing to do with the making of these conditions, the public will hold us responsible for them from the day we take power. That is an inescapable fact of political psychology. It would be difficult to find in American history a graver problem faced by the administration of a State.

Immediate action will be necessary, and the voters are entitled to know exactly what we propose to do. The purpose of this pamphlet is to answer the question, insofar as it can be answered, five months ahead of the beginning of the job.

… Now let us assume that our EPIC candidates are elected on November 6th, and take office January 3rd. It appears likely that we may have a majority of the Assembly pledged to the EPIC Plan. We cannot have a majority of the Senate, because only one-half of these senators come up for re-election; but if our electoral majority is sufficiently impressive, the hold-over senators may recognize the mandate of the people and the seriousness of the emergency, and consent that the EPIC Plan shall be given a trial….

What, precisely, will we do?

Our EPIC movement has a research group, composed of lawyers, statisticians, engineers, and technicians of both land and factory production. These men are now preparing a series of initiative measures, giving to the State administration the necessary authority to put the Plan into effect. These measures will be submitted to Government officials in Washington who have kindly promised their help, and thus perfected and made law-tight, the measures will be presented to the legislature. As a matter of precaution, they will also be filed as initiative petitions with the Secretary of State immediately after the November election—this will be done whether or not our EPIC candidates win.

The law requires that initiative petitions must be signed by a number of registered voters equal to 8 percent of the vote at the last election. That will mean that we must get some 160,000 signatures—a task which will not trouble our 1,000 EPIC clubs throughout the State. A quota will be assigned to each assembly district, and our secretaries will have the signed documents back in our hands within a week. The petitions will be filed, and if the Legislature fails to pass the laws promptly, a special election will be called and the people themselves will make the laws. The details of these procedures are, of course, matters for later study. Suffice it to say that we will act in the way which proves to be quickest and most certain.

The first measure will provide for a California State system of industry, including the three agencies described in the "I, Governor" book: the California Authority for Land (CAL), the California Authority for Production (CAP) and the California Authority for Money (CAM). These public enterprises will be conducted by a commission of experts appointed by the Governor. Their charters will be modeled upon the various Federal bodies which have received and are now exercising authority to do everything which the EPIC Plan calls for. Just now our opponents are desperately trying to frighten the people by telling them that our Plan is Marxian Socialism, or Communism, and that I am "an agent of Moscow," etc. Therefore I list here three of the thirty-odd governmental or quasi-governmental corporations which are now functioning with headquarters in our national capital, and which are engaged in doing all the things our EPIC Plan calls for.

First, the Commodity Credit Corporation "may produce, warehouse, ship, export, process, manufacture and market all farm products and related products; borrow money without limit for these purposes; buy or otherwise acquire any property in the United States or its territories which is necessary for its purposes; manage and maintain such properties."

Second, the Federal Subsistence Corporation "may build and operate factories, construct and own any subsistence homestead and all appurtenances; buy, construct and operate mines; buy, construct and operate industries, power plants, farms, commercial establishments, parks and forests."

Third, the Federal Civil Works Administration is "to construct, finance, or aid in constructing or financing of any public works project included in the civil works program and to acquire by purchase any real or personal property in connection with the accomplishment of any such project and to lease any such property with or without the privilege of purchase."

We shall establish a State Authority, with powers identical with the above, and provided with money enough for its immediate needs. How much will be required, and from what sources it will be obtained, is to be discussed later. For the moment, assume that we have the money. What will we do?

Factory Production First

We begin with factory production, because that is the part of our system capable of most rapid expansion, and in which EPIC will produce the most striking results.

There were in 1931 in California a total of 10,121 manufacturing establishments, with product valued at two billion. Using round figures, 22 percent of these factories had to do with food, 4 percent with textiles, 6 percent with forest products, 11 percent with printing and publishing, 5 percent with chemicals, 6 percent with petroleum and coal, 4 percent with iron and steel, 6 percent with machinery, etc. No official survey has been made as to the number of these factories which are idle or working on part time. According to figures, unofficial but dependable, one-sixth of our total manufacturing concerns in California are completely shut down and have been for a year or more. On a general average our plants are working at about 40 percent of capacity, employing two-thirds of their original personnel and paying 45 percent of the original pay rolls.

Now come our 425,000 able-bodied workers, desiring access to these factories in order to make shoes, clothing, bread, canned fruit, furniture, gasoline, cement, nails, etc., for themselves and their dependents, a total of 1,225,000 persons. These unemployed workers cannot now get access to the factories because they do not own them. It is the task of the State to obtain access for the workers—using, as we have said, means which are legal and constitutional. What percentage of the factories will be needed?

To determine how much of the various products could be used by 1,225,000 persons would be a complicated task. Many of these persons never had enough of anything in their lives. The safest way to proceed is to get some factories started at their maximum capacity, and see how rapidly their product is absorbed.

Assume that we acquire a factory for making women's dresses. This factory has been working at 40 percent of capacity. The unemployed dress workers come in and go to work, and by running full time we multiply production two-and-a-half times. By putting our workers on six-hour shifts and working the factory from six o'clock in the morning until midnight, we multiply that total by more than two. Experience proves that shorter work periods give a higher production per hour; so our one factory, on a system of production for use, becomes seven factories: which means that our State system will require only one-seventh as many factories per capita as our present anarchic system has built.

Assume that our large dress factory has been turning out a thousand dresses per day. We increase it to seven thousand per day; working three hundred days in a year, this totals 2,100,000 dresses per year, or about four dresses apiece for every woman in our EPIC set-up. In other words, one large dress factory, used to its full capacity, will suffice for our whole EPIC Plan.

I have to make sure the reader understands the basic point, that we shall be turning out goods FOR USE. At the present time the private owner of the factory cannot turn out dresses, because he cannot find anybody to buy them at a profit; therefore his factory stands idle. But if the State puts the unemployed at producing for themselves, the problem vanishes; because every woman in our EPIC set-up will proceed without hesitation to wear four new dresses per year. If we drive ahead too fast and make ten dresses a year, the sensible ones among the women will ask that we reduce the hours of the workers in the dress-factory, and let them have more time in which to show off the dresses already made.

The next point: How are we going to get this factory? At the outset, in the existing emergency, we shall rent it from the private owner. Many of our greatest manufacturing concerns have been running in the red for several years. They are still clinging to the hope that "prosperity is just around the corner," so they are keeping a skeleton staff, and paying their taxes, interest on bonds, etc., by money borrowed from the banks. But the end is close ahead; one gulp more and the bank has swallowed them down.

To the directors of such an enterprise the State system makes its approach, saying: "Gentlemen, we will consider renting your factory for three years, paying you a price sufficient to cover your overhead. We will be pleased if your executives will remain at their posts, receiving their present salaries and operating the factory under the supervision of the State. You may call in your old workers and put them at the machines. We ask and expect your loyal cooperation as citizens and patriots to help us over this emergency. If, as you expect, prosperity returns, you may have your factory back. If, on the other hand, your hope is disappointed, the State of California will enter into negotiations to purchase your factory at the end of the rental period."

A friend of mine put this proposition before a great California manufacturer the other day. "What would you answer?" my friend asked, and the manufacturer exclaimed: "My God, try me!"

The Method of Co-operation

Let us now examine another method of getting immediate production. Of the 10,121 factories in California, more than 1,600 are wholly out of use. Some of these have been dismantled and are out of repair. The owners are holding their property with difficulty, many being in arrears with their taxes. If the State should make an offer to rent these factories, giving certificates receivable for taxes, the owners would jump at the chance.

How can such factories be reconditioned and started up? The people have provided their answer in the form of co-operative, barter, and self-help groups all over California.

I visited one of these groups in Pomona. In an old garage they had set up half a dozen rickety oil stoves, each with a wash-boiler on top. With this primitive equipment they had stacked up half the garage with crates of canned peaches and tomatoes. When I offered to buy some of these goods, I was told that they were not permitted to be sold. It was fruit which otherwise would have rotted on the ground, and had been gathered on the agreement that it would not go upon the market.

In South Los Angeles I visited a co-operative bakery. The machinery was old and out of repair, but the workers had fixed it up and were turning out several thousand loaves of bread per day. They were exchanging this bread for vegetables grown by another group on a tract of land outside the city. The bakery interests objected to this practice and so did the produce merchants; therefore the relief officials cut off the gasoline supply of the truck used in this transaction.

I visited the UXA, a large barter group in Oakland, and listened for hours to curious tales of how they had managed to drum up business for themselves. They would find a crop of fruit which the farmer would let them have, in return for painting his barn; they would find a paint merchant who would take a cord of wood from a man who would take some of the fruit. Some of the deals were highly involved, with dozens of different services in a circle of transactions. I know an enthusiastic co-operator who discovered that debts could be exchanged. He would find a full circle of persons who owed money to one another, and for a small commission to the co-operative would constitute himself a clearing house and cancel the debts without a dollar changing hands.

For two generations or more, the American people have been victimized by a propaganda which identifies Americanism with capitalism. For my part, I assert that these self-help and barter groups represent Americanism more truly than any other phenomenon of our time. They embody all our true pioneer virtues—self-reliance, initiative, frugality, equality, neighborliness. They are the most precious products of the depression; and what have we done with them? The answer is that we have done everything to handicap them, to humiliate them, to buy their leaders away from them, to corrupt and finally to exterminate them.

Why have we done this? Partly because they are believed to threaten "big business," but mainly because they threaten the "relief racket," which has become the mainstay of the politicians in these difficult times.

Consider the achievement of the cooperative at Compton, which during the first seven months of this year has served 19,745 meals at a total money cost of less than half a cent a meal. Consider that the co-operatives of Los Angeles County, from August to December of 1932, maintained a hundred and fifty thousand members on a cash expenditure by the government of seventeen cents per family per month. Since a "family" is found to average 3.6 persons, this works out at less than one-sixth of a cent per person per day. Consider what that would have meant to the over-burdened taxpayers of California, who last year paid in one form or another forty-five cents per person for the same service, about two hundred and seventy times as much. You would have expected the taxpayers to hail the achievement of these co-operatives with loud cheers; but instead, the co-operatives have been crippled by every possible device.

When the Federal Government spends tens of millions of dollars for relief in California, a great part of this money goes for office rent and salaries of officials and relief workers, and serves to build up a political machine. Oddly enough, under the set-up in California, Federal funds portioned out by a Democratic administration went to building up the Republican machine of the late "Sunny Jim," and go now to the machine of his successor, Governor Merriam. When Los Angeles County votes bonds for unemployed relief, the money goes to build up the machine of Supervisor Quinn, who was one of Merriam's rivals for the Republican nomination. The survival of the politicians depends upon this relief, and the man who proposes to cut it off becomes Public Enemy Number One. That is why you see Republican candidates collecting campaign funds from special interests and spending the money for radio time to denounce Upton Sinclair as an atheist and agent of Moscow.

One of the declared purposes of EPIC is to put the credit power of the State behind the co-operatives and enable them to grow. All they ask is the use of the idle factories, with any old machinery they can find. They will put it into running order and start it up, and having got hold of one product, they will exchange it until they have all other products.

To the extent that the State puts money into the enterprises of the co-operatives, the State must have a voice in their management. The co-operatives will not object to this, provided that those appointed by the State know something about co-operation, and have as their purpose to foster it instead of breaking its back. I feel confident that if this were done, we should see every destitute man and woman in the State of California made independent and secure, by democratic and strictly American methods....

Social Security (1946)

Frances Perkins

These reflections are from Secretary of Labor Perkins one decade after the passage of the Economic Security Act.

Before his Inauguration in 1933 Roosevelt had agreed that we should explore at once methods for setting up unemployment and old-age insurance in the United States.

Therefore, early in 1933, the President encouraged Senator Wagner and Representative David J. Lewis, both deeply interested in the subject, to go ahead with their bill on unemployment insurance. The bill, a rough draft, was put in frankly for educational purposes. It was hoped that in the course of hearings the congressional committees and the introducers of the bill would work out a satisfactory and typically American measure.

The President urged me to discuss the matter in as many groups as possible. I began in the cabinet. I made a point of bringing it up, at the least, at every second meeting. Gradually the other cabinet members became sincerely and honestly interested.

Hearings were held before Congress. Effective people were invited to testify. I myself made over a hundred speeches in different parts of the country that year, always stressing social insurance as one of the methods for assisting the unemployed in times of depression and in preventing depressions. We stimulated others to talk and write about the subject.

The Wagner-Lewis bill in the Congress covered only unemployment insurance, but there was a great demand for old-age insurance also. It was easy to add this feature—and politically almost essential. One hardly realizes nowadays how strong was the sentiment in favor of the Townsend Plan and other exotic schemes for giving the aged a weekly income. In some districts the Townsend Plan was the chief political issue, and men supporting it were elected to Congress. The pressure from its advocates was intense. The President began telling people he was in favor of adding old-age insurance clauses to the bill and putting it through as one program....

It was evident to us that any system of social insurance would not relieve the accumulated poverty. Nor would it relieve the sufferings of the presently old and needy. Nevertheless, it was also evident that this was the time, above all times, to be foresighted about future problems of unemployment and unprotected old age. It was never, I think, suggested by any reasonable person that relief should be abandoned in favor of unemployment and old-age insurance, but it was thought that there could be a blend of the two.

I took pains to make certain that Roosevelt understood and pledged himself to support the program as we worked it out. It must be made clear that this technique of utilizing a cabinet committee to develop the program for him did not mean that he was evading the great issue. I had more than one concrete conference with him about the subjects we would have to consider in Committee.

I asked him if he thought it best for me to be chairman, since the public knew I favored the general idea. Perhaps it would be better, from the point of view of Congress and the public, if the Attorney General were chairman.

He was quick in his response. "No, no. You care about this thing. You believe in it. Therefore I know you will put your back to it more than anyone else, and you will drive it through. You will see that something comes out, and we must not delay. I am convinced. We must have a program by next winter and it must be in operation before many more months have passed."

I indicated to him that there were sound arguments, advanced by many thinkers, that since we were in the midst of deflation the collection of any money for reserves, no matter by what method, would be further deflationary.

"We can't help that," he replied. "We have to get it started or it never will start."

He was aware that 1936 was not too far away, that there might be a change of administration, and that this program, which, in his own mind, was his program, would never be accomplished, or at least not for many years, if it were not put through immediately....

By the time the study was fully launched the President's imaginative mind had begun to play over it. At cabinet meetings and when he talked privately with a group of us, he would say, "You want to make it simple—very simple. So simple that everybody will understand it. And what's more, there is no reason why everybody in the United States should not be covered. I see no reason why every child, from the day he is born, shouldn't be a member of the social security system. When he begins to grow up, he should know he will have old-age benefits direct from the insurance system to which he will belong all his life. If he is out of work, he gets a benefit. If he is sick or crippled, he gets a benefit.

"The system ought to be operated," this country gentleman would go on, "through the post offices. Just simple and natural—nothing elaborate or alarming about it. The rural free delivery carrier ought to bring papers to the door and pick them up after they are filled out. The rural free delivery carrier ought to give each child his social insurance number and his policy or whatever takes the place of a policy. The rural free delivery carrier ought to be the one who picks up the claim of the man who is unemployed, or of the old lady who wants old-age insurance benefits.

"And there is no reason why just the industrial workers should get the benefit of this. Everybody ought to be in on it—the farmer and his wife and his family.

"I don't see why not," he would say, as, across the table, I began to shake my head. "I don't see why not. Cradle to the grave—from the cradle to the grave they ought to be in a social insurance system."

It was not that I did not admire his bold conception of universal coverage, but I felt that it was impractical to try to develop and administer so broad a system before we had some experience and machinery for the preliminary and most pressing steps.

Moreover, I felt sure that the political climate was not right for such a universal approach. I may have been wrong. Having the administrative responsibility, I was more alarmed than he about how we were going to swing it. The question of financing was in the forefront of my mind, and Roosevelt, because he was looking at the broad picture, could skip over that difficult problem....

It was Harry Hopkins who recommended seriously that relief and social insurance be lumped together, that relief payments should be called unemployment and old-age insurance, and that payments should be made as a matter of right and not as a matter of need. This, of course, was a pretty extreme point of view for a country which had not had a social insurance system or a relief program before. When we took it to the President, only Hopkins and I went. Although Hopkins was eloquent, the President at once saw that this would be the very thing he had been saying he was against for years—the dole.

This prejudice served as a guidepost to warn him against unsystematic and unrelated distribution of funds from the Treasury. He insisted that the two systems, however much they might apply to the same people, should be kept separate because relief appropriations should be curtailed and canceled as soon as there was a revival of business and employment opportunities. The systems of unemployment and old-age insurance ought to continue as a permanent part of our economy.

Hopkins fought hard for his point of view. He pointed out that the unemployment insurance payments contemplated in any system then being discussed would not be adequate for the support of families whose breadwinners were long out of work.

This was admitted by all of us. It was pointed out to the President that all that was intended, or hoped for, was to establish a system of unemployment insurance to provide in the future some tide-over income during the early impact of unemployment. We always admitted that, if there should ever again be a major crisis, a cyclical depression, with accompanying unemployment, the unemployment insurance system would not be adequate for all the people. But we also pointed out that in the surveys we had made of the then unemployed, by far the largest number had had intermittent employment. If they had had unemployment insurance to draw upon, even in small weekly amounts, in the early part of the depression, their expenditures would have been sufficient to cushion the decline of business and to make a market for the continuing production and sale of goods and commodities—and thereby to reduce the total amount of unemployment.

Even if the allowance were small—and ten dollars a week for sixteen weeks might be a meager allowance for a family—nevertheless, if it came at the beginning of unemployment, it would sustain savings and credit, it would stave off evictions, it would serve to piece out the intermittent unemployment which members of a family might have during a depression. In short, it would be worth, in peace of mind, and in practical family budgeting, more than its cash value would indicate....

Roosevelt was determined to have a bona fide self-maintaining system—that is, the premiums paid in were to support the benefits paid out. Obviously an insurance program could not begin to pay benefits at once. Obviously it would be confined to those presently employed and paying premiums or having a portion of the premium paid on their behalf by their employers. But the suffering of those now out of work or aged or dependent or sick, for whom no such premiums ever could be paid, challenged our immediate attention.

We agreed that we must bring in a program for unemployment insurance and one for old-age insurance. Without too much debate we agreed that in addition to these two fundamental insurance programs we must recommend what we knew was not insurance but a relief program. It must include old-age assistance, assistance for dependent children, assistance for crippled and handicapped persons, and a continuation of emergency assistance to the unemployed then in operation.

With that much settled, the question was *how*. The Federal Government had unlimited taxing power, and out of the taxes so raised Congress could either make grants to the states on a matching basis or expend funds direct for the relief of old age, dependency, or the handicapped. Rather early in the considerations, we committed ourselves to support the recommendation of aid to dependent and indigent persons from federal appropriations made available to the states on a matching basis. That did not solve the "how" for unemployment and old-age insurance, which was the next big task....

One large school of thought held that unemployment insurance premiums should be assessed only against employers. Another, equally large and vigorous, felt that workers should pay their share of the costs. These were not illiberal or reactionary people either. Those who held, as I did, that only employers should make a contribution to the fund, believed that unemployment should be regarded as a natural risk of industry, just as workmen's compensation for accidental injuries is regarded as part of the cost of doing business. Debate on this point could easily kill the bill in Congress.

Another problem about which there was great divergence of feeling was the question of "merit rating." Should there be a flat contribution from all employers without regard to the particular industry? Or should there be, as had grown up under workmen's compensation procedure in many states, a merit rating, allowing a smaller contribution from firms with a low rate of unemployment and putting a larger tax upon those with a higher rate of unemployment? There was very vigorous feeling on both sides of this question, and again the debate in Congress would have been delaying....

Under the federal-state system the Federal Government collects the tax under its taxing powers. It holds the money for allotment to the states for their payment of benefits. The states, in turn, have the right and duty to determine other questions in their own way. Those states that want merit rating can have it. Those that want employee as well as employer contributions can have that. Out of a variety of systems we should get a mature American experience. So we argued.

There was one outstanding, and, in my mind, determining factor, at that time in favor of the federal-state system. Although we thought we were on the right track in using the taxing power of the Federal Government, we were never quite sure whether a federal system of unemployment insurance would be constitutional. The Federal Government could tax; that was clear. But could it distribute its funds on a basis of social benefit? The Attorney General's office, in fact, repeatedly advised us that it was a doubtful constitutional point and that we should be extremely careful.

If the federal aspects of the law were declared unconstitutional, in the federal-state system we would at least have state laws which could be upheld legally under the "police power" of the states. Though state laws might not be uniform, they would be giving unemployed persons some income during a period of unemployment, and that would be an advance. These were the arguments I had presented to the President before he made his November 1934 speech.

The truth is that the Committee could not keep its mind made up on this one point: should it be a federal-state system or a federal system? A few weeks after the President's speech somebody moved that we reconsider the whole matter. Most of us had been under a barrage of letters and opinions from people all over the country. We reconsidered. Henry Wallace argued firmly for a federal system. Josephine Roche, Assistant Secretary of the Treasury, who was sitting in for Morgenthau on this occasion, held with him.

After long discussion we agreed to recommend a federal system. We went back and informed colleagues in our own Departments. Within the day I had telephone calls from members of the Committee saying that perhaps we had better meet again.

There was grave doubt, our latest interviews with members of Congress had shown, that Congress would pass a law for a purely federal system. State jealousies and aspirations were involved. So we met again, and after three or four hours of debate we switched back to a federal-state system....

The President knew of only part of this confusion. He was always sympathetic, but he expected us to find the answer. If we were agreed on a method, then he was for it. The Committee must bear the responsibility for the pattern of unemployment insurance we have in this country today.

With old-age insurance we had an even more difficult time. It became obvious that old-age assistance on the pattern of a federal grant-in-aid for those now aged and needy must be adopted. That was easy to accept. We agreed readily that for old-age insurance the individual as well as the employer should make contributions.

There was greater debate on the size of the benefit to be paid to individuals upon old-age retirement. The easiest way would be to pay the same amount to everyone. But that is contrary to the typical American attitude that a man who works hard, becomes highly skilled, and earns high wages "deserves" more on retirement than one who had not become a skilled worker. As one looks back, one can see that there is much to be said for the flat rate.

We decided on the more complicated system where the benefit rate bears a percentage relationship to previous earnings.

Our next problem was concerned with those who were then forty-five or fifty years old. Probably they had worked since they were about nineteen. They were fifteen to twenty years short of retirement age. When they retired, they and their employers would have paid less than half the premium required to build them a decent, normal retirement allowance. The plan finally recommended contemplated paying such people at retirement a benefit larger than the value of their contributions, otherwise some would receive ridiculously small benefits. However, their benefits would not be so large as those of people retiring after forty years in the system.

Even with enlarged benefits to persons reaching retirement age in the next fifteen to twenty years, there would be ample funds to meet all immediate payments out of immediate income. But by any proper actuarial estimate, there would be, in the end, an accumulated deficit. The reserves would not suffice to pay benefits when those now twenty became sixty-five and eligible for retirement.

From an insurance company's point of view this was impossible; but underlying the whole government system was the credit of the United States. Perhaps in 1980 it would be necessary for the Congress to appropriate money to make up a deficit. After some hesitation and discussion, the Committee decided to recommend to the President this type of collection and payment, with accumulation of partial reserve and partial deficit against the future. This, of course, was along the line of what was later called a pay-as-you-go system. We thought we had agreement on this approach. A few days before the report was due, however, Secretary of the Treasury Morgenthau, though his substitute in the Committee had agreed, indicated his flat opposition to any system which would require a government contribution out of general revenues at any time.

The alternative appeared to be contributions in the early stages so large both from workers and employers as to be almost confiscatory.

It was characteristic of the President that when we took this proposal to him, he put his finger at once upon this difficult-to-explain procedure.

"Ah," he said, "but this is the same old dole under another name. It is almost dishonest to build up an accumulated deficit for the Congress of the United States to meet in 1980. We can't do that. We can't sell the United States short in 1980 any more than in 1935." And yet the President had told us that we must develop some kind of old-age insurance benefit.

"We have to have it," he said. "The Congress can't stand the pressure of the Townsend Plan unless we have a real old-age insurance system, nor can I face the country without having devised at this time, when we are studying social security, a solid plan which will give some assurance to old people of systematic assistance upon retirement." The President was in the midst of one of the minor conflicts of logic and feeling which so often beset him but kept him flexible and moving in a practical direction.

Altmeyer, Eliot, a few others, and I immediately went to work on a compromise. The contributions, instead of being so large at the beginning as to paralyze the system and frighten the people and Congress, would remain small for the first year but would be increased more rapidly and to a higher level in subsequent years than originally proposed. Altmeyer was very ingenious about this. He could not understand the President's intellectual conflict on this point, but he said, "You can trust Congress never to require enormous payments as contributions. They will think of some way out."

We finally reached an agreement with the Treasury on this intermediate position: while a full actuarial reserve would not be built up, it would be enough, with the interest added to current contributions, so that future revenues would cover future benefits provided the terms of the act were not changed.

But there was pressure from another direction also. The American Association for Old Age Security, of which Abraham Epstein was director and Bishop Francis McConnell, president, and which represented many intelligent social thinkers, was convinced that for stability, security, and permanence any old-age insurance schemes must have immediate government contributions. The plan of accumulating a future deficit and expecting that the government would meet it some time in the distant future did not satisfy the association. It set up considerable agitation for a plan requiring immediate annual government contributions in addition to payments by workers and employers.

A group in the Congress was also insistent on this point of view. We must remember, those were the days of the "share-the-wealth" schemes. There was a feeling that, unless the Government made a contribution out of general taxation, the rich who derived their income from investments rather than from business activity would not make a sufficient contribution to the fund. There would not be, these people argued, any sharing of the wealth....

At the first hearing before the House Ways and Means Committee we were startled to have Secretary Morgenthau make an appearance with a carefully prepared formal memorandum in which he apologized to his fellow members of the Committee on Economic Security. He said that the Treasury had decided, and he had concurred, that it would be unwise to give universal coverage under this act. He argued that it would be a difficult problem to collect payments from scattered farm and domestic workers, often one to a household or farm, and from the large numbers of employees working in establishments with only a few employees. He begged to recommend that farm laborers, domestic servants, and establishments employing less than ten people be omitted from the coverage of the act.

This was a blow. The matter had been discussed in the Committee on Economic Security, and universal coverage had been agreed upon almost from the outset. One could concede that it would be difficult for the Treasury to collect these taxes. But the whole administration of the act was going to be difficult.

The Ways and Means Committee members, impressed by the size of the project and the amount of money involved, nodded their heads to Secretary Morgenthau's proposal of limitation. There was nothing for me to do but accept, temporarily at least, though I continued to recommend universal coverage as the best and safest way for the United States.

The fact that in 1946 we still do not have universal coverage, though it had been "must" legislation for a number of years to extend the Social Security Act to all employed persons, is, I think, an indication that it would have been just as well to go ahead with the whole program at that time. But there were enough people afraid of the deflationary effects of this large money collection, enough people afraid of too large a system, and enough people confused about the desirability of social legislation by the Federal Government, to make it a foregone conclusion that if the Secretary of the Treasury recommended limitation, limitation there would be....

The House Committee and other members of Congress began to hear from their constituents in favor of the social security bill, and it was soon obvious it was going to be moved along. In August 1935 Republicans as well as Democrats voted for the bill, and there were only a very few who had the temerity to be counted against it....

Several years later a move got under way for a modification of the Social Security Act, particularly the old-age insurance system, to have what was euphemistically called the pay-as-you-go system. The President didn't like it, but he was interested in extending social security. He wanted it to protect more people. He wanted the benefits raised when the time came. The pay-as-you-go policy was a secondary consideration and all right if the Congress wanted it. I don't think he ever realized that that was the exact system which he had rejected in at least a modified form when the Committee on Economic Security had reported it to him in 1934.

He always regarded the Social Security Act as the cornerstone of his administration and, I think, took greater satisfaction from it than from anything else he achieved on the domestic front.

Workers' Unemployment, Old-Age, and Social Insurance Bill (1935)

Ernest Lundeen

This speech was given on the floor of the U.S. House of Representatives.

Provisions of the Lundeen Bill

The Lundeen unemployment, old-age, and social-insurance bill provides in section 1 that the—

Bill shall be known by the title "The workers' unemployment, old-age, and social-insurance act."

Section 2

The Secretary of Labor is hereby authorized and directed to provide for the immediate establishment of a system of unemployment insurance for the purpose of providing compensation for all workers and farmers above 18 years of age, unemployed through no fault of their own. Such compensation shall be equal to average local wages, but shall in no case be less than $10 per week plus $3 for each dependent. Workers willing and able to do full-time work but unable to secure full-time employment shall be entitled to receive the difference between their earnings and the average local wages for full-time employment. The minimum compensation guaranteed by this act shall be increased in conformity with rises in the cost of living. Such unemployment insurance shall be administered and controlled, and the minimum compensation shall be adjusted by workers and farmers under rules and regulations which shall be prescribed by the Secretary of Labor in conformity with the purposes and provisions of this act through unemployment-insurance commissions directly elected by members of workers' and farmers' organizations.

Section 3

The Secretary of Labor is hereby further authorized and directed to provide for the immediate establishment of other forms of social insurance for the purpose of providing compensation for all workers and farmers who are unable to work because of sickness, old age, maternity, industrial injury, or any other disability. Such compensation shall be the same as provided by section 2 of this act for unemployment insurance and shall be administered in like manner. Compensation for disability because of maternity shall be paid to women during the period of 8 weeks previous and 8 weeks following childbirth.

Section 4

All moneys necessary to pay compensation guaranteed by this act and the cost of establishing and maintaining the administration of this act shall be paid by the Government of the United States. All such moneys are hereby appropriated out of all funds in the Treasury of the United States not otherwise appropriated. Further taxation necessary to provide funds for the purposes of this act shall be levied on inheritances, gifts, and individual and corporation incomes of $5,000 a year and over. The benefits of this act shall be extended to workers, whether they be industrial, agricultural, domestic, office, or professional workers, and to farmers, without discrimination because of age, sex, race, color, religion, or political opinion or affiliation. No worker or farmer shall be disqualified from receiving the compensation guaranteed by this act because of past participation in strikes, or refusal to work in place of strikers, or at less than average local or trade-union wages, or under unsafe or unsanitary conditions, or where hours are longer than the prevailing union standards of a particular trade or locality, or at an unreasonable distance from home....

Epilogue: Outcomes

In 1933, when President Hoover left office, he was one of the most reviled politicians in U.S. history. His claim that Americans were not hungry was inaccurate. His belief in self-help and voluntary cooperation as a response to poverty had been discredited, and his modest construction projects and loans to state governments to support local relief programs fell far short of what was needed. However, this was not the end of the philosophy of limited self-government and individual and mutual self-help; Ronald Reagan would revive and champion it almost fifty years later.

Since Dorothy Day cofounded the Catholic Worker movement in 1933, thousands of people have been sheltered and millions of meals served. Currently, there are more than 185 Catholic Worker communities worldwide, which are committed to "nonviolence, voluntary poverty, prayer, and hospitality for the homeless, exiled, hungry, and forsaken." Today, the newspaper Day created, the *Catholic Worker*, has a circulation of 100,000, even though it has never been advertised. Yet Day believed that the measure of success was not in the number of people served or newspapers read; rather it was whether community was created through the opening of hearts and the extension of fellowship. In many ways, Day was ahead of her time, as her support of individual and social transformation through the application of the biblical prophetic tradition predated by thirty years the ideology of liberation theology that swept Latin America in the late 1960s and 1970s. In 2000, twenty years after her death, Cardinal John O'Connor began the process within the Catholic Church to canonize Dorothy Day as a saint.[23]

Harold Rugg's curriculum focusing on civic action to reduce poverty was initially well received and by 1939, 5.5 million of his textbooks were being used in more than 5,000 school districts. However, the curriculum came under increasing attack by conservative groups. In some communities, Rugg's curriculum was burned and in others it was blacklisted. By the mid-1940s, the curriculum had been forced out of most schools.[24]

Alternative Proposals to the New Deal

The alternative proposals offered in 1934 and 1935 played a crucial role in pushing Roosevelt to act. As noted in the Perkins document, Roosevelt was under tremendous pressure from citizens and from Congress to respond to the Townsend and Long plans. Groups supporting the Townsend plan developed all over the country, and candidates ran for Congress and won on a platform supporting the plan. However, critics argued that the plan was too expensive, claiming that the $200 payment to the 10 million people over sixty would cost $25 billion per year. In 1933, the federal budget was $4.5 billion, and tax revenues provided only $2 billion. However, this argument did not stop the Townsend movement. By 1936, there were more than 7,000 Townsend Clubs, with 2.2 million dues-paying members.[25]

Huey Long claimed that his "Share the Wealth" plan had 27,000 clubs, with a combined membership of 7.5 million. Although this was an overstatement, his plan did have many supporters. However, the Senate did not adopt Long's plan. On the Senate floor, Long did try to liberalize Roosevelt's Economic Security Act by replacing the payroll tax provision with a tax on wealth or property. Long's amendment was defeated by a voice vote. In this same period, the Lundeen bill was also defeated, this time in the House of Representatives by a vote of 204 to 52.[26]

Long was planning to challenge Roosevelt in the 1936 presidential election, and Roosevelt was concerned that Long had the political strength to make a viable run, but it did not come to pass, as Long was assassinated in September of 1935 in the Louisiana state capitol. After Long's assassination, there was an attempt to bring Townsend's and Long's supporters together, along with Father Charles Coughlin, a Catholic priest who used his radio show to criticize Roosevelt as a front man for the capitalist class, and to advocate for nationalization of banks and a guaranteed income. These groups formed the Unity Party in 1936. However, their candidate, William Lemke of South Dakota, received only 900,000 of the 45 million votes cast. When Roosevelt received 61 percent of the popular vote, the threat to the New Deal from alternative plans was over. Yet, Long's federal plan for a "guaranteed income" that would bring poor people into the middle class would be revived forty years later by Dr. Martin Luther King, Jr., and Johnnie Tillmon of the National Welfare Rights Organization.[27]

Upton Sinclair's EPIC plan made a strong showing in California. Sinclair surprised everyone when he won the California Democratic gubernatorial primary by 150,000 votes. His vote total was 100,000 more than that of Frank Merriam, who had won the Republican primary, raising the possibility of a Sinclair victory in the general election. With the likelihood of a socialist winning the governorship, the entire establishment, including the Democratic Party, turned against Sinclair. The media conducted a negative propaganda campaign, which was based mostly on lies. Even so, Sinclair most likely would have won the governorship had he not made two critical errors. First, he stated that he would defer the EPIC plan in favor of Roosevelt's national solutions, which included the Economic Security Act and a progressive national tax. This cost him votes since the EPIC plan was the main reason people supported him. Second, Sinclair opposed the Townsend plan since it was based on a regressive tax. This cost him votes with Townsend supporters, who had up to that point been EPIC supporters as well. On election day in 1934, Merriam received 48 percent to Sinclair's 37 percent. However, twenty-three EPIC supporters won seats in the California State Assembly, and the EPIC movement also helped to elect a U.S. senator from the state of Washington.[28]

New Deal Policies

President Roosevelt's policies led to a mixed record. On one level, Roosevelt's policies transformed U.S. policy on poverty. The federal government, which historically had not involved itself in relief efforts and public works projects because of a restricted view of liberty, now became instrumental in these efforts. During the first part of the New Deal, which took place from 1933 to 1935, the largest federal public works program in U.S. history was implemented. The Civil Works Administration (CWA)—which in many ways was Coxey's vision put into practice—provided meaningful work at real wages for more than 4.2 million people in 1934. The Civilian Conservation Corps (CCC) put another 400,000 youth to work. In addition, the Federal Emergency Relief Administration (FERA) was implemented to provide matching grants to the states to support relief efforts, ranging from $4.95 per person per month in Oklahoma to $45.12 in New York. By February 1934, more than eight million households, or 28 million people (22 percent of the population), were either working in the CWA and CCC, or receiving relief through FERA. The Roosevelt administration hoped that a large-scale public works program, in combination with a relief program, would put money in people's pockets and help stimulate the economy. In New York alone, 240,000 CWA workers received $41 million to spend. Although there was a drop in unemployment from a high of 25 percent in 1933 to 20 percent by 1935, there were not enough public works jobs offered to meet the need, and relief was sparse in many parts of the country, so the depression continued on.[29]

The second part of the New Deal, which began in the summer of 1935, included the passage of the Works Progress Administration (WPA), Economic Security Act, Wagner Act, and Fair Labor Standards Act. The WPA took over where the CWA had left off. Roosevelt had closed down the CWA after four months and the passing of winter, since he was worried that people were becoming too dependent on the federal government to provide jobs. However, with the nation still in a depression in 1935, Roosevelt resurrected the idea of massive public works. His new strategy was that the federal government would hire people who were unemployed, and return the responsibility of relief for the "unemployable" back to states and local governments. Within one year of its creation, the WPA had employed three million people, and by the end of the program in 1943, the WPA had employed a total of eight million. Its accomplishments were many: the WPA built or improved 5,900 schools, 2,500 hospitals, and 13,000 playgrounds. The WPA also hired artists for the Federal Art Project, Theater Project, Writing Project, and Music Project, all of which brought quality artistic expression to the general public. In fact, many poor and working-class people attended live concerts for the first time because of the WPA's 110 concert orchestras, 48 symphony orchestras, and 80 bands.[30]

The CCC continued into the second part of the New Deal, providing about 500,000 jobs per year to young men. Before Congress defunded the CCC in 1942, it provided a total of three million jobs to the economy and achieved many feats; for example, it planted three billion trees, built 97,000 miles of fire roads, arrested twenty million acres from soil erosion, built 800 state parks, stocked 1 billion fish, and provided more than 7 million person-days worth of work on improving streams, conserving water, and protecting wildlife habitats.[31]

The Economic Security Act provided for old-age assistance and insurance, unemployment insurance, workers' compensation, and aid to dependent children. Roosevelt's original proposal included national health insurance, but the doctors opposed it and it was removed from the act. Importantly, the Economic Security Act introduced the notion of entitlement into the U.S. social system. People saw old-age pensions and unemployment insurance as entitlements given to all citizens rather than as relief to only the poor. These two programs were defined as social insurance, so the middle class felt no stigma in receiving them. There was no means test for these two programs, and payment went to people regardless of their income level or wealth, so once again, the middle class was comfortable with them.

Not surprisingly, old-age assistance and unemployment insurance were the most popular parts of the act. Old-age assistance provided immediate help to seniors, with payments to the elderly of $15 to $30 a month. Unemployment insurance paid benefits of 50 percent of a person's wages with a cap of $15 per week. In California, people received between $6 and $15 per week for sixteen weeks. Although there was less demand for old-age insurance, Roosevelt was committed to providing this benefit as he felt that it would lessen the need for old-age relief. However, old-age insurance did not start until 1942, seven years after the passage of the act. Today, Social Security provides 47 million Americans—retirees and their dependents, the disabled, and youth whose parents have died—a monthly check. In 2005, the average check for a sixty-five-year-old retiree was $1,184 a month, or $14,208 a year. For seven million seniors, or the poorest 20 percent, this is the only income they receive. Without this monthly check, 48 percent of the seniors would live below the poverty line; with it, 8 percent live below it.[32]

Surprisingly, aid to dependent children, which initially was conceived to be a small program to help widows, was expanded greatly in the latter part of the twentieth century as the number of single women with children grew. This program would become known as Aid to Families with Dependent Children (AFDC)—and later as Temporary Assistance to Needy Families (TANF)—and would undergo intense criticism by conservatives. Most likely, Roosevelt would have agreed with the critiques of AFDC, since he had always opposed the federal government's involvement in "the dole" as a way to alleviate poverty.[33]

In the second part of the New Deal, the Roosevelt administration supported and the Democratic Congress passed legislation creating the minimum wage and the forty-hour maximum workweek, as well as prohibiting child labor. Although all of these policies have had an effect on improving the conditions and wages of the working class, the Wagner Act (the right to bargain collectively) may have done the most to reduce poverty, for it changed the operating rules of capitalism. Union membership grew from 3.7 million in 1935 to 7.3 million in 1940 and to 15 million by 1950. With these larger memberships, and with the knowledge that the government was supporting rather than opposing labor, the unions won a series of major victories. One of the most notable was the General Motors (GM) strike in the winter of 1936–1937, when the largest corporation in the world was forced to recognize the United Auto Workers as the sole arbitrator on behalf of the workers after a series of dramatic sit-down strikes. This victory led to many more labor victories as workers came to believe that if the union could defeat GM, they could do the same in other industries—and they did.[34]

The New Deal also had a profound effect on Native Americans. Under the leadership of John Collier, the U.S. government purchased 2.5 million acres for American Indians, finally reversing the loss of native land under the Dawes Act. In addition, Native American self-government was recognized by the federal government for the first time, which proved to be controversial on some reservations since it mandated that Indians use voting and elections to choose their leaders rather than traditional ways such as consensus. Additionally, the public works programs benefited American Indians, with the CCC providing approximately 15,000 jobs per year to Native Americans.[35]

Unfortunately, not all people of color benefited from the New Deal. As mentioned earlier, Mexican Americans and Mexican nationals were rounded up by police and deported. In addition to these deportations, punitive measures included barring noncitizens from civic works projects and providing relief to Mexican nationals only if they agreed to leave the country. These policies led to the repatriation of 400,000 people during the 1930s, reducing by one-third the number of Mexican Americans and Mexican nationals in California and Texas. Clearly, these policies violated Mexican Americans' civil rights, as they were forced to leave the country and not compensated for their loss of possessions.[36]

African Americans were both helped and harmed by New Deal policies. They benefited when they received federal jobs from the WPA. For example, federal jobs in Cleveland reduced black unemployment from 50 percent to 30 percent, and New Deal projects built over 3,000 housing units for black residents. At the same time, New Deal agricultural policies harmed blacks as they lost jobs when land was forced out of production in order to boost prices. Also, more than 200,000 African Americans did participate in the CCC, but did so in mostly segregated camps. Agricultural workers and domestic servants were not included in the unemployment insurance and old-age pensions, as well as minimum wage laws and the forty-hour maximum workweek, which excluded two-thirds of all blacks from participating in these programs. In addition, the New Deal allowed the states to control many parts of the Economic Security Act, since racist legislators demanded that the system be state-based or they would not support it. The "separate and unequal" system that operated in the United States, particularly in the South, allowed the states to limit the amount of assistance to blacks. This inequitable state-based system is still in place today for unemployment benefits, workers' compensation, and aid to dependent children. The state-based policy sets apart the United States as the only industrialized country that lacks a national insurance system.[37]

As a result of racist practices in government and business, a group of African Americans began organizing a march on Washington, D.C., for jobs and racial justice. With the prospect of tens of thousands of people marching on the nation's Capitol, Roosevelt relented and issued executive order 8802, which banned racial discrimination in the nation's defense industries. For the first time, the threat of a march on Washington had produced immediate action by the federal government. With their goal reached, the committee sponsoring the march called it off. However, twenty-two years later, Phillip A. Randolph, a key leader of the committee, once again called for a march for jobs and racial justice. This time, 200,000 people participated in the march, and Dr. Martin Luther King, Jr., electrified the nation with his dramatic appeal for justice.[38]

The New Deal policies had a profound impact on the nation, as they fundamentally changed the relationship between the federal government and its citizens. The federal government had adopted the sociological perspective that one's destiny is not solely determined by one's effort, but that social factors beyond one's control play an important, if not decisive, role. Since these social factors were national in scope, the federal government had a responsibility to intervene and help solve the problem. Of course, this required the government to become deeply involved in the economy and the lives of its citizens, which led to an expansion in the size and scope of the federal government. This also led to an enormous increase in the resources spent on public assistance. For example, in 1913 and 1923, the federal government spent only 1 percent of the budget on public aid; in 1933, it had increased to 7 percent and by 1939, it spent 27 percent.[39]

Yet, with such a transformation, the New Deal was not successful in ending the depression. In 1939, six years into the New Deal, unemployment was still at 17 percent. Although the WPA employed three million people a year, there were another ten million people who needed jobs. The Economic Security Act, as highlighted by the earlier analysis of the Lundeen bill, revealed the deficiencies of the New Deal. Roosevelt's "cradle to grave" security system had developed into a patchwork of programs that left many people in need without the necessary support. Public assistance was not based on need, but rather was dependent on which state the individual lived in, how long she had lived in that state, how much he had made in his previous job, or a particular characteristic, such as age or race. At the same time, it maintained the belief that there were the deserving and undeserving poor, who warranted different treatment and benefits.[40]

Sadly, it was war that brought about the end of the depression. By 1943, a year after the United States entered World War II, unemployment had dropped to 2 percent, and it would stay that way throughout the conflict. In order to appease big business, which was producing the defense weapons needed to fight the war, Roosevelt decided to hold back on any new social reforms.[41]

Martin Luther King, Jr., and Malcolm X in 1964

Chapter 6

The War on Poverty

Prologue: Social Context and Overview of Solutions

As the end of World War II neared, and President Roosevelt's attention returned to domestic issues, he put forth a bold vision for a second Bill of Rights focusing on the abolition of poverty. Soon afterward, ordinary citizens rose up against Jim Crow segregation in the streets and in the courts, and destroyed the legal foundation for segregation and racial discrimination. However, civil rights activists soon realized that ending Jim Crow laws and getting the right to vote did not end poverty and that new ideas were needed to eradicate it. Black leaders such as Malcolm X and Dr. Martin Luther King, Jr., argued for a change of strategy from civil rights to human rights, and the federal government launched its own "War on Poverty."

1941–1950: The Economic Bill of Rights

In his 1941 State of the Union speech, President Roosevelt had articulated four essential human freedoms that the United States supported at home and abroad. These essential human freedoms were freedom from want, freedom from fear, freedom of speech and expression, and freedom of religion. By including freedom from want as an essential human freedom, Roosevelt reinterpreted freedom so as to reduce the tension that has existed historically between rugged individualism and social equity.[1]

As Roosevelt refocused his efforts on domestic issues, he called on the United States to develop an "economic bill of rights." Building on his four freedoms speech, he argued that the original Bill of Rights (e.g., the First Amendment rights of free speech, free press, and free worship) had provided Americans with the "life and liberty" Jefferson had set out in the Declaration of Independence. However, as industrial capitalism developed, "these political rights proved inadequate to assure us equality in the pursuit of happiness." Roosevelt noted, as Paine did before him, that "necessitous men are not free men" since "true individual freedom cannot exist without economic security and independence." In order to secure these economic rights, Roosevelt proposed a second bill of rights, which should cover the following areas:

> The right to a useful and remunerative job in the industries or shops or farms or mines of the nation; The right to earn enough to provide adequate food and clothing and recreation; The right of every farmer to raise and sell his products at a return which will give him and his family a decent living; The right of every businessman, large and small, to trade in an atmosphere of freedom from unfair competition and domination by monopolies at home or abroad; The right of every family to a decent home; The right to adequate medical care and the opportunity to achieve and enjoy good health; The right to adequate protection from the economic fears of old age, sickness, accident, and unemployment; The right to a good education.[2]

After Roosevelt's death in 1945, President Harry Truman spent the next five years attempting to enact the key elements of Roosevelt's plan: health insurance, a living wage, and affordable housing. However, after a four-year fight with Congress, national health insurance was once again defeated with the assistance of the American Medical Association (AMA), which argued that it would damage the quality of health care and take away the professional autonomy of doctors. The AMA played down the fact that many Americans didn't have access to adequate medical care or the money to pay for it.[3]

At the same time, the Democrats worked on passing legislation on the right to work. The original bill, which was entitled the Full Employment Act of 1945, declared that all Americans were "entitled to an opportunity for useful and remunerative, regular, and full time employment" and that the government was to provide the investment and expenditures to achieve full employment. However, conservative critics charged that the bill was socialistic, and its major provisions were eliminated. By the time it passed, the title of the bill had been changed to the Employment Act of 1946, and the text had been weakened so that the federal government's commitment was to "promote maximum employment, production, and purchasing power." A similar fate occurred with the housing bill, which had originally proposed federal construction of hundreds of thousands of homes, many of which were targeted for low-income people. Truman felt that the free market would not build enough homes for poor people, and that the federal government needed to become directly involved in order to ensure a decent home to all Americans. However, by the time the 1946 Housing Act was passed, it too was greatly weakened by Congress.[4]

1954–1965: The End of Legalized Racial Discrimination

From 1954, when the Supreme Court struck down segregation in public schools in *Brown v. Board of Education,* to 1968, when Dr. Martin Luther King, Jr., and Robert Kennedy were murdered, the civil rights movement dominated the attention of the nation. But there was another movement that overlapped and was interconnected with the civil rights movement, and that was the War on Poverty. Clearly, the fight for racial justice was deeply connected to the fight to end poverty. It is difficult to imagine an end to poverty when a group of people is denied jobs, houses, education, and the right to vote because of skin color. However, as many civil rights leaders recognized at the time, even the great achievements of the civil rights movement were not enough to end poverty. It would take a full-scale attack on poverty itself, and the civil rights leaders focused their attention on this after the landmark passage of the Civil Rights Act of 1964 and the Voting Rights Act of 1965.

Civil Rights on New Level

Ten years after the 1955–1956 Montgomery Bus Boycott, King had concluded that black equality with whites could not be achieved without fundamental changes to U.S. society. King called the changes achieved between 1955 and 1966 "surface changes" and he called on the movement to undergo a major transformation, from civil rights to human rights, and from reform to revolution. He felt that the civil rights movement had done little to address the economic inequality between blacks and whites. Although King recognized that civil rights victories made it possible for blacks to sit down at a restaurant, it did little good if they could not afford the meal.[5]

King noted that there was still a "strange formula" that defined the unequal relationship between whites and blacks. He said that this formula dated back to the writing of the U.S. Constitution, when a black person was considered 60 percent of a human being in order to determine taxation and representation. King was fond of saying that there was another "curious formula" that existed in the 1960s that implied African Americans were 50 percent of a person. King observed that blacks had half the income of whites, but twice the rate of unemployment and infant mortality as whites. King maintained that this formula also applied to those who fought and died in war, as there was twice the proportion of blacks in comparison to whites in combat in Vietnam, and twice the number of blacks killed in proportion to their numbers in the military.[6]

To change this formula, King declared that American capitalism would have to change. Privately, King confided that he now supported a democratic form of socialism to solve the nation's poverty. In public, King's language kept within American tradition as he borrowed from Roosevelt the idea of an economic bill of rights. He argued that the richest nation in the world had the financial means to provide full employment for those who were able to work and to guarantee an income for those who were not able to work. King argued that with a public works program ensuring full employment and a guaranteed income tied to middle-class income levels, poor whites, blacks, and other people of color would have the money to pay for adequate housing, food, clothing, and health care. King acknowledged that an economic bill of rights would cost the United States money, but as he declared: "It didn't cost the nation one penny to integrate lunch counters. It didn't cost the nation one penny to guarantee the right to vote. But now we are dealing with issues that cannot be solved without the nation spending billions of dollars and undergoing a radical redistribution of economic power."[7]

In 1964, Malcolm X offered black Americans a different vision for ending poverty. By this time, Malcolm was no longer associated with the Nation of Islam and had created his own organization entitled the Muslim Mosque, which was open to both blacks and whites. Malcolm X's solution to poverty was black nationalism. Since white liberals could not be counted on to end oppression of the black community, he felt that the way to uplift the community was to have blacks control the local economy and politics. This involved owning and supporting black businesses as well as electing black politicians who promoted black interests. Malcolm also believed that the civil rights movement needed to be taken to the level of human rights, since he argued that so long as Americans called it civil rights, it was confined to the jurisdiction of the United States, whereas human rights made it an international issue. Malcolm wanted to take the case of black oppression to the General Assembly of the United Nations and charge the United States with violating the human rights of black Americans.[8]

Building on Malcolm X's vision of black nationalism, Huey Newton of the Black Panther Party advocated for "complete control of the institutions in the community." Newton—who was named for Huey Long—concluded that although this strategy had worked for the Irish and Italians, the black community would also need to develop cooperatives (democratic and jointly owned enterprises) since there were not enough jobs in the black community to achieve full employment. He was also attracted to cooperatives since they did not exploit the workers. In addition, Newton and Bobby Seale cowrote the Black Panther Party's ten-point program, which included reparations for slavery, decent housing, education that teaches the true history of the United States, free health care, an end to police brutality, an end to all wars of aggression, and freeing all black men and poor people in prison.[9]

The War on Poverty

Early in the 1960s, the U.S. public rediscovered the issues of poverty and hunger. Using the newly created poverty line, which was developed by Mollie Orshansky, the federal government calculated that 36.4 million Americans (or 19 percent of the population) were living in poverty in 1963. There was a general feeling among social policy experts and practitioners that the current efforts to assist the poor were not working. There were not enough living-wage jobs, welfare benefits were inadequate and varied from state to state, governmental regulations broke up families, and the welfare bureaucracy seemed uncaring and insensitive to its clients. In response, President John Kennedy had decided to propose a major initiative to reduce poverty. However, with the assassination of Kennedy, it was up to Lyndon Johnson to push this agenda forward.[10]

President Johnson decided early to make poverty one of his top priorities. Just six weeks into his presidency, Johnson declared in his 1964 State of the Union address an "unconditional war on poverty in America." Later in the spring, Johnson returned to the University of Michigan, where Kennedy had three years before unveiled the Peace Corps, and announced his goal to build a "Great Society." In this speech, the president framed his vision of ending poverty in the larger context of what it meant to be a great nation. Johnson asserted that while the United States was a rich and powerful country, it was destined for a higher calling:

> The Great Society rests on abundance and liberty for all. It demands an end to poverty and racial injustice, to which we are totally committed in our time. But that is just the beginning. The Great Society is a place where every child can find knowledge to enrich his mind and to enlarge his talents. It is a place where leisure is a welcome chance to build and reflect, not a feared cause of boredom and restlessness. It is a place where the city of man serves not only the needs of the body and the demands of commerce but the desire for beauty and the hunger for community. It is a place where man can renew contact with nature. It is a place which honors creation for its own sake and for what it adds to the understanding of the race. It is a place where men are more concerned with the quality of their goals than the quantity of their goods.[11]

In the summer of 1964, Johnson led the effort to pass the Economic Opportunity Act, which served as the official charter of the War on Poverty. The act created the Office of Economic Opportunity (OEO), which was responsible for the development and oversight of the War on Poverty programs. According to Sargent Shriver, the first director of OEO, the goal of the War on Poverty was "to offer the poor a job, an education, a little better place to live. The basic idea was to give an incentive." Consequently, the War on Poverty focused attention on opportunity rather than on inequality. The advocates of the War on Poverty argued that material want was not caused by a defect in the U.S. economy; rather it was caused by barriers that blocked opportunity. The Johnson administration attempted to remove some of these barriers through the elimination of institutionalized racism. Johnson realized there was a strong relationship between race and poverty, stating that "many Americans live on the outskirts of hope—some because of their poverty, and some because of their color, and all too many because of both. Our task is to help replace their despair with opportunity." Johnson pushed for the passage of the Civil Rights and Voting Rights Acts, with the hope that by demonstrating that the federal government supported civil rights, opportunity for African Americans would greatly increase.[12]

War on Poverty supporters also promoted education as a main strategy to end poverty. This came out of the belief that poor people were culturally deprived. These advocates argued that poor people had developed a "culture of poverty" as a response to their deprived condition. In order to overcome this alleged lack of cultural skills as well as a weak family support structure, the Johnson administration supported the rapid expansion of new educational opportunities such as Project Head Start, Follow Through, Upward Bound, Job Corps, and Volunteers in Service to America (VISTA). Head Start was a comprehensive preschool program that included intellectual stimulation, nutrition, and health care services. Follow Through built on the work of Head Start by providing a continuation of Head Start services through the first three years of schooling. Upward Bound was a program designed to prepare teenagers for college. The Job Corps was a vocational training program for unskilled young adults who had not completed high school. VISTA was a domestic version of the Peace Corps for people with a college education. The War on Poverty supporters argued that with the racist barriers removed and the necessary educational skills obtained, all could compete for the rewards of society in an equal fashion. They realized that this would not guarantee equality of results, but they argued that it allowed for equality of opportunity.[13]

In addition to these new educational programs, the Johnson administration and the Democratic-controlled Congress pushed for the expansion of new services to assist the poor. Most importantly, Johnson worked to create Medicaid, a low-income health care assistance plan; Medicare, a health insurance program for seniors; and the Department of Housing and Urban Development, which committed itself to building six million subsidized low-income housing units over a ten-year period. Other programs created included neighborhood health centers and legal aid services to the poor. Johnson also pushed for the increase of direct income support to the poor, such as Aid to Families with Dependent Children (AFDC), food stamps, and rent assistance.

The most controversial and radical idea that came out of the War on Poverty was the Community Action Program (CAP). This program, which was slipped into the War on Poverty legislation with very little discussion, was designed to engage the poor in solving poverty. The goal of the federal government was to encourage "maximum feasible participation" of the people living in impoverished communities. To accomplish this goal, the federal government, working through the OEO, directly subsidized local community groups to work on education, welfare, health, and housing issues. For the first time in the nation's history, poor people were funded to organize their own communities to fight poverty. Just as labor was given a voice and influence through the New Deal's Wagner Act, OEO hoped that CAP would empower the poor and thereby lead to poverty solutions and to a more democratic society as the poor became active citizens rather than passive recipients of aid.[14]

Protest and Resistance Spread

The black freedom struggle, along with the Great Society programs, provided legitimacy to the protests of the poor, as well as those of Mexican Americans and Native Americans. One of the poverty groups that took advantage of this supportive environment was the National Welfare Rights Organization (NWRO), founded in 1966. The NWRO's focus was on engaging unemployed women to fight for a welfare system that provided a sufficient level of income, food, and housing for their families. Since the creation of AFDC during the New Deal, relief had been provided, particularly to women of color, in a condescending fashion. Many times, welfare authorities arbitrarily denied benefits to women, and turned away approximately 50 percent of them. Furthermore, AFDC paid only 33 percent of the federal poverty income level in the early 1960s, which was $3,000 a year for a family of four.[15]

The NWRO founders believed women's poverty resulted from a capitalist economy that provided too few opportunities for poor women in general and for black women in particular. Thus, they declared welfare a right that all unemployed women deserved. To ensure this right, the NWRO protested at welfare offices when mothers were arbitrarily denied benefits, did not receive checks, did not receive their full amount, were wrongly terminated, or were treated in a demeaning manner. They also protested when mothers did not receive grants of clothing and household furnishings that were available to them by law, but were denied them by welfare relief workers who did not inform the women about the benefits. These protests were significant since it was the first time that poor women, many of whom were previously disempowered and stigmatized, had collectively fought for increased welfare benefits.

In 1971, Johnnie Tillmon was hired as associate director of the NWRO, becoming the first black woman and welfare mother to be hired for a high-level staff position; in 1972, she became the director. Tillmon knew from firsthand experience that women preferred a living-wage job to welfare. She had conducted a survey of poor women in her Watts housing project and found that out of the 600 women who participated in the study, all but one preferred work. However, poor women had little access to living-wage jobs. In order to solve this dilemma, she called on the federal government to create a guaranteed income. Although she and King came to a similar conclusion, that a guaranteed income was the key to solving poverty, Tillmon's focus was on poor women. By calling for dignity and liberation for all women, including people who were seen as the "undeserving poor," Tillmon incorporated poor and black women into the second wave of the feminist movement. As she stated, "For a lot of middle-class women in this country, Women's Liberation is a matter of concern. For women on welfare it's a matter of survival."[16]

Mexican Americans also were engaged in social protest against poverty. In New Mexico, Reis López Tijerina and several hundred followers were fighting for individual and communal land that had been stolen from the Hispanos, who had first settled in New Mexico in the sixteenth century. In Denver, Rudolfo "Corky" González led the Crusade for Justice's call for better education, housing, labor rights, and an end to police brutality. In California, Cesar Chavez, Dolores Huerta, and other Mexican and Filipino farmworkers formed the United Farm Workers (UFW) to end the unjust conditions in the fields.[17]

Historically, farmworkers had been excluded from the New Deal labor laws that protected workers' rights. Farmworkers were not guaranteed the right to organize, receive a minimum wage, or obtain unemployment insurance and Social Security. Without regulation, farmers paid the workers extremely low wages and treated them in an oppressive manner. In 1964, the average farmworker made $9 a day and worked only seasonal or part-time for large-scale agricultural farms; in that same year, these large-scale farms grossed $42 billion. Farmworkers lacked adequate housing, education, health care, and nutrition. As Chavez stated, "We are men and women who have suffered and endured much, and not only because of our abject poverty but because we have been kept poor."[18]

The conditions for organizing changed in 1964, when the *bracero* program was ended after twenty-two years. Originally designed to help with the labor shortage brought about by World War II, the program had allowed millions of Mexicans to come to the United States as guest workers. With the end of the *bracero* program, farmers could no longer turn to this source of labor to be used as strikebreakers. Chavez and the UFW used this opportunity to launch a series of boycotts, strikes, pickets, and marches to force the farm owners to recognize the union and to increase wages.[19]

Although Chavez saw collective bargaining as the key to ending poverty for farmworkers, he also viewed the UFW as more than just a union involved in negotiations with the growers. He called the UFW a community union, which meant that the union worked on both farmworker issues and community issues. For example, with the farmworkers spending much of their income on maintaining and operating their cars, the UFW decided to develop car and gas co-ops so the workers could buy auto parts and gasoline at cheap prices. Chavez also believed that a community union needed to transcend economic needs and become involved in limiting the use of pesticides in the fields. As Chavez stated, "What good does it do to achieve the blessings of collective bargaining and make economic progress for people when their health is destroyed in the process?" This concern for the health of the workers as well as for the general public led Chavez and the UFW to become leaders in the battle to ban highly toxic pesticides.[20]

Native Americans were also engaged in protest against poverty and racism in the 1960s. Reservations had the highest unemployment rates in the nation, lacked adequate housing, and had health conditions resembling those in the poorest countries in the Southern Hemisphere. Urban Indians, many of whom had been encouraged to move off the reservations as part of the federal government's attempt to terminate all reservations in the 1950s, also experienced high levels of poverty and racism.[21]

Inspired by the activism of blacks in the civil rights movement, several new organizations formed to make change. The National Indian Youth Council (NIYC) was organized by college students, and they led a series of "fish-ins" to assert control of fishing rights they believed were owned by the Makah and other tribes in the state of Washington. The American Indian Movement (AIM) began in St. Paul, Minnesota, as a response to discrimination by the police. AIM used the same strategy as the Black Panthers and began to follow the police in Indian areas of the city to ensure they did not harass community members. As AIM grew to more than sixty-seven chapters in the United States, it began to tackle issues of poverty, housing, and employment.

In California, a group entitled Indians of All Nations led a takeover of Alcatraz Island, which was an abandoned federal prison, to focus the nation's attention on the state of Native America. A young Mohawk Indian by the name of Richard Oakes was one of the key leaders who planned the occupation and reclamation. Oakes explained the meaning of the occupation in this way:

> Ironically, Alcatraz was a fitting place for us to take... [and] in many ways it was like a reservation—barren, isolated, devoid of water. When we landed, the place felt full of despair, very hopeless, very uncompromising. It wouldn't yield any kind of harvest at all. The white man has taken all of the productive land, the real Mother Earth. In a sense, the invasion represented the end of the era of the white man's harshness to Mother Earth. All the white man does is spread concrete over the land. There are no vibrations. There's no breath. Nothing can come from our Mother. She has been smothered.[22]

After landing on Alcatraz, Oakes read a proclamation to the media that called for the development of a variety of Indian institutions to be built on Alcatraz, including centers for Native American studies, spirituality, and ecology as well as a training school that would focus on ending hunger and unemployment.[23]

Where Do We Go from Here? (1967)

Martin Luther King, Jr.

This speech was Dr. King's last as president of the Southern Christian Leadership Conference (SCLC), and was delivered at its tenth anniversary convention in Atlanta.

Now, in order to answer the question, "Where do we go from here?" which is our theme, we must first honestly recognize where we are now. When the Constitution was written, a strange formula to determine taxes and representation declared that the Negro was 60 percent of a person. Today another curious formula seems to declare that he is 50 percent of a person. Of the good things in life, the Negro has approximately one half those of whites. Of the bad things of life, he has twice those of whites. Thus half of all Negroes live in substandard housing. And Negroes have half the income of whites. When we view the negative experiences of life, the Negro has a double share. There are twice as many unemployed. The rate of infant mortality among Negroes is double that of whites and there are twice as many Negroes dying in Vietnam as whites in proportion to their size in the population.

In other spheres, the figures are equally alarming. In elementary schools, Negroes lag one to three years behind whites, and their segregated schools receive substantially less money per student than the white schools. One-twentieth as many Negroes as whites attend college. Of employed Negroes, 75 percent hold menial jobs.

This is where we are. Where do we go from here? First, we must massively assert our dignity and worth. We must stand up amidst a system that still oppresses us and develop an unassailable and majestic sense of values. We must no longer be ashamed of being black. The job of arousing manhood within a people that have been taught for so many centuries that they are nobody is not easy.

Even semantics have conspired to make that which is black seem ugly and degrading. In Roget's *Thesaurus* there are 120 synonyms for blackness and at least sixty of them are offensive, as for example, blot, soot, grim, devil and foul. And there are some 134 synonyms for whiteness and all are favorable, expressed in such words as purity, cleanliness, chastity and innocence. A white lie is better than a black lie. The most degenerate member of a family is a "black sheep." Ossie Davis has suggested that maybe the English language should be reconstructed so that teachers will not be forced to teach the Negro child sixty ways to despise himself, and thereby perpetuate his false sense of inferiority, and the white child 134 ways to adore himself, and thereby perpetuate his false sense of superiority.

The tendency to ignore the Negro's contribution to American life and to strip him of his personhood is as old as the earliest history books and as contemporary as the morning's newspaper. To upset this cultural homicide, the Negro must rise up with an affirmation of his own Olympian manhood. Any movement for the Negro's freedom that overlooks this necessity is only waiting to be buried. As long as the mind is enslaved, the body can never be free. Psychological freedom, a firm sense of self-esteem, is the most powerful weapon against the long night of physical slavery. No Lincolnian emancipation proclamation or Johnsonian civil rights bill can totally bring this kind of freedom. The Negro will only be free when he reaches down to the inner depths of his own being and signs with the pen and ink of assertive manhood his own emancipation proclamation. And, with a spirit straining toward true self-esteem, the Negro must boldly throw off the manacles of self-abnegation and say to himself and to the world, "I am somebody. I am a person. I am a man with dignity and honor. I have a rich and noble history. How painful and exploited that history has been. Yes, I was a slave through my foreparents and I am not ashamed of that. I'm ashamed of the people who were so sinful to make me a slave." Yes, we must stand up and say, "I'm black and I'm beautiful," and this self-affirmation is the black man's need, made compelling by the white man's crimes against him.

Another basic challenge is to discover how to organize our strength in terms of economic and political power. No one can deny that the Negro is in dire need of this kind of legitimate power. Indeed, one of the great problems that the Negro confronts is lack of power. From old plantations of the South to newer ghettos of the North, the Negro has been confined to a life of voicelessness and powerlessness. Stripped of the right to make decisions concerning his life and destiny he has been subject to the authoritarian and sometimes whimsical decisions of this white power structure. The plantation and ghetto were created by those who had power, both to confine those who had no power and to perpetuate their powerlessness. The problem of transforming the ghetto, therefore, is a problem of power—confrontation of the forces of power demanding change and the forces of power dedicated to the preserving of the status quo. Now power properly understood is nothing but the ability to achieve purpose. It is the strength required to bring about social, political and economic change. Walter Reuther defined power one day. He said, "Power is the ability of a labor union like the UAW to make the most powerful corporation in the world, General Motors, say, 'Yes' when it wants to say 'No.' That's power."

Now a lot of us are preachers, and all of us have our moral convictions and concerns, and so often have problems with power. There is nothing wrong with power if power is used correctly. You see, what happened is that some of our philosophers got off base. And one of the great problems of history is that the concepts of love and power have usually been contrasted as opposites—polar opposites—so that love is identified with a resignation of power, and power with a denial of love.

It was this misinterpretation that caused Nietzsche, who was a philosopher of the will to power, to reject the Christian concept of love. It was this same misinterpretation which induced Christian theologians to reject the Nietzschean philosophy of the will to power in the name of the Christian idea of love. Now, we've got to get this thing right. What is needed is a realization that power without love is reckless and abusive, and love without power is sentimental and anemic. Power at its best is love implementing the demands of justice, and justice at its best is power correcting everything that stands against love. And this is what we must see as we move on. What has happened is that we have had it wrong and confused in our own country, and this has led Negro Americans in the past to seek their goals through power devoid of love and conscience.

This is leading a few extremists today to advocate for Negroes the same destructive and conscienceless power that they have justly abhorred in whites. It is precisely this collision of immoral power with powerless morality which constitutes the major crisis of our times.

We must develop a program that will drive the nation to a guaranteed annual income. Now, early in this century this proposal would have been greeted with ridicule and denunciation, as destructive of initiative and responsibility. At that time economic status was considered the measure of the individual's ability and talents. And, in the thinking of that day, the absence of worldly goods indicated a want of industrious habits and moral fiber. We've come a long way in our understanding of human motivation and of the blind operation of our economic system. Now we realize that dislocations in the market operations of our economy and the prevalence of discrimination thrust people into idleness and bind them in constant or frequent unemployment against their will. Today the poor are less often dismissed, I hope, from our consciences by being branded as inferior or incompetent. We also know that no matter how dynamically the economy develops and expands, it does not eliminate all poverty.

The problem indicates that our emphasis must be twofold. We must create full employment or we must create incomes. People must be made consumers by one method or the other. Once they are placed in this position we need to be concerned that the potential of the individual is not wasted. New forms of work that enhance the social good will have to be devised for those for whom traditional jobs are not available. In 1879 Henry George anticipated this state of affairs when he wrote in *Progress and Poverty:* "The fact is that the work which improves the condition of mankind, the work which extends knowledge and increases power and enriches literature and elevates thought, is not done to secure a living. It is not the work of slaves driven to their tasks either by the task, by the taskmaster, or by animal necessity. It is the work of men who somehow find a form of work that brings a security for its own sake and a state of society where want is abolished."

Work of this sort could be enormously increased, and we are likely to find that the problems of housing and education, instead of preceding the elimination of poverty, will themselves be affected if poverty is first abolished. The poor transformed into purchasers will do a great deal on their own to alter housing decay. Negroes who have a double disability will have a greater effect on discrimination when they have the additional weapon of cash to use in their struggle.

Beyond these advantages, a host of positive psychological changes inevitably will result from widespread economic security. The dignity of the individual will flourish when the decisions concerning his life are in his own hands, when he has the means to seek self-improvement. Personal conflicts among husbands, wives and children will diminish when the unjust measurement of human worth on the scale of dollars is eliminated.

Now our country can do this. John Kenneth Galbraith said that a guaranteed annual income could be done for about twenty billion dollars a year. And I say to you today, that if our nation can spend thirty-five billion dollars a year to fight an unjust, evil war in Vietnam, and twenty billion dollars to put a man on the moon, it can spend billions of dollars to put God's children on their own two feet right here on earth.

Now, let me say briefly that we must reaffirm our commitment to nonviolence. I want to stress this. The futility of violence in the struggle for racial justice has been tragically etched in all the recent Negro riots. Yesterday, I tried to analyze the riots and deal with their causes. Today I want to give the other side. There is certainly something painfully sad about a riot. One sees screaming youngsters and angry adults fighting hopelessly and aimlessly against impossible odds. And deep down within them, you can see a desire for self-destruction, a kind of suicidal longing.

Occasionally Negroes contend that the 1965 Watts riot and the other riots in various cities represented effective civil rights action. But those who express this view always end up with stumbling words when asked what concrete gains have been won as a result. At best, the riots have produced a little additional antipoverty money allotted by frightened government officials, and a few water-sprinklers to cool the children of the ghettos. It is something like improving the food in the prison while the people remain securely incarcerated behind bars. Nowhere have the riots won any concrete improvement such as have the organized protest demonstrations. When one tries to pin down advocates of violence as to what acts would be effective, the answers are blatantly illogical. Sometimes they talk of overthrowing racist state and local governments and they talk about guerrilla warfare. They fail to see that no internal revolution has ever succeeded in overthrowing a government by violence unless the government had already lost the allegiance and effective control of its armed forces. Anyone in his right mind knows that this will not happen in the United States. In a violent racial situation, the power structure has the local police, the state troopers, the National Guard and, finally, the army to call on—all of which are predominantly white. Furthermore, few if any violent revolutions have been successful unless the violent had the sympathy and support of the nonresistant majority. Castro may have had only a few Cubans actually fighting with him up in the hills, but he could never have overthrown the Batista regime unless he had the sympathy of the vast majority of Cuban people.

It is perfectly clear that a violent revolution on the part of American blacks would find no sympathy and support from the white population and very little from the majority of the Negroes themselves. This is no time for romantic illusions and empty philosophical debates about freedom. This is a time for action. What is needed is a strategy for change, a tactical program that will bring the Negro into the mainstream of American life as quickly as possible. So far, this has only been offered by the nonviolent movement. Without recognizing this we will end up with solutions that don't solve, answers that don't answer and explanations that don't explain.

And so I say to you today that I still stand by nonviolence. And I am still convinced that it is the most potent weapon available to the Negro in his struggle for justice in this country. And the other thing is that I am concerned about a better world. I'm concerned about justice. I'm concerned about brotherhood. I'm concerned about truth. And when one is concerned about these, he can never advocate violence. For through violence you may murder a murderer but you can't murder murder. Through violence you may murder a liar but you can't establish truth. Through violence you may murder a hater, but you can't murder hate. Darkness cannot put out darkness. Only light can do that....

I want to say to you as I move to my conclusion, as we talk about "Where do we go from here," that we honestly face the fact that the movement must address itself to the question of restructuring the whole American society. There are forty million poor people here. And one day we must ask the question, "Why are there forty million poor people in America?" And when you begin to ask that question, you are raising questions about the economic system, about a broader distribution of wealth. When you ask that question, you begin to question the capitalistic economy. And I'm simply saying that more and more, we've got to begin to ask questions about the whole society. We are called upon to help the discouraged beggars in life's marketplace. But one day we must come to see that an edifice which produces beggars needs restructuring. It means that questions must be raised. You see, my friends, when you deal with this you begin to ask the question, "Who owns the oil?" You begin to ask the question, "Who owns the iron ore?" You begin to ask the question, "Why is it that people have to pay water bills in a world that is two-thirds water?" These are questions that must be asked.

Now, don't think that you have me in a "bind" today. I'm not talking about communism. What I'm saying to you this morning is that communism forgets that life is individual. Capitalism forgets that life is social, and the kingdom of brotherhood is found neither in the thesis of communism nor the antithesis of capitalism but in a higher synthesis. It is found in a higher synthesis that combines the truths of both. Now, when I say question the whole society, it means ultimately coming to see that the problem of racism, the problem of economic exploitation, and the problem of war are all tied together. These are the triple evils that are interrelated.

If you will let me be a preacher just a little bit—One night, a juror came to Jesus and he wanted to know what he could do to be saved. Jesus didn't get bogged down in the kind of isolated approach of what he shouldn't do. Jesus didn't say, "Now Nicodemus, you must stop lying." He didn't say, "Nicodemus, you must stop cheating if you are doing that." He didn't say, "Nicodemus, you must not commit adultery." He didn't say, "Nicodemus, now you must stop drinking liquor if you are doing that excessively." He said something altogether different, because Jesus realized something basic—that if a man will lie, he will steal. And if a man will steal, he will kill. So instead of just getting bogged down in one thing, Jesus looked at him and said, "Nicodemus, you must be born again."

He said, in other words, "Your whole structure must be changed." A nation that will keep people in slavery for 244 years will "thingify" them—make them things. Therefore they will exploit them, and poor people generally, economically. And a nation that will exploit economically will have to have foreign investments and everything else, and will have to use its military might to protect them. All of these problems are tied together. What I am saying today is that we must go from this convention and say, "America, you must be born again!" ...

The Ballot or the Bullet (1964)

Malcolm X

This speech was given in Cleveland at the Cory Methodist Church and was part of a symposium on "The Negro Revolt—What Comes Next?" sponsored by the local chapter of the Congress of Racial Equality (CORE).

... So, where do we go from here? First, we need some friends. We need some new allies. The entire civil-rights struggle needs a new interpretation, a broader interpretation. We need to look at this civil-rights thing from another angle—from the inside as well as from the outside. To those of us whose philosophy is black nationalism, the only way you can get involved in the civil-rights struggle is give it a new interpretation. That old interpretation excluded us. It kept us out. So, we're giving a new interpretation to the civil-rights struggle, an interpretation that will enable us to come into it, take part in it. And these handkerchief-heads who have been dillydallying and pussyfooting and compromising—we don't intend to let them pussyfoot and dillydally and compromise any longer.

How can you thank a man for giving you what's already yours? How then can you thank him for giving you only part of what's already yours? You haven't even made progress, if what's being given to you, you should have had already. That's not progress. And I love my Brother Lomax, the way he pointed out we're right back where we were in 1954. We're not even as far up as we were in 1954. We're behind where we were in 1954. There's more segregation now than there was in 1954. There's more racial animosity, more racial hatred, more racial violence today in 1964, than there was in 1954. Where is the progress?

And now you're facing a situation where the young Negro's coming up. They don't want to hear that "turn-the-other-cheek" stuff, no. In Jacksonville, those were teenagers, they were throwing Molotov cocktails. Negroes have never done that before. But it shows you there's a new deal coming in. There's new thinking coming in. There's new strategy coming in. It'll be Molotov cocktails this month, hand grenades next month, and something else next month. It'll be ballots, or it'll be bullets. It'll be liberty, or it will be death. The only difference about this kind of death—it'll be reciprocal. You know what is meant by "reciprocal"? That's one of Brother Lomax's words, I stole it from him. I don't usually deal with those big words because I don't usually deal with big people. I deal with small people. I find you can get a whole lot of small people and whip hell out of a whole lot of big people. They haven't got anything to lose, and they've got everything to gain. And they'll let you know in a minute: "It takes two to tango; when I go, you go."

The black nationalists, those whose philosophy is black nationalism, in bringing about this new interpretation of the entire meaning of civil rights, look upon it as meaning, as Brother Lomax has pointed out, equality of opportunity. Well, we're justified in seeking civil rights, if it means equality of opportunity, because all we're doing there is trying to collect for our investment. Our mothers and fathers invested sweat and blood. Three hundred and ten years we worked in this country without a dime in return—I mean without a dime in return. You let the white man walk around here talking about how rich this country is, but you never stop to think how it got rich so quick. It got rich because you made it rich.

You take the people who are in this audience right now. They're poor, we're all poor as individuals. Our weekly salary individually amounts to hardly anything. But if you take the salary of everyone in here collectively it'll fill up a whole lot of baskets. It's a lot of wealth. If you can collect the wages of just these people right here for a year, you'll be rich—richer than rich. When you look at it like that, think how rich Uncle Sam had to become, not with this handful, but millions of black people. Your and my mother and father, who didn't work an eight-hour shift, but worked from "can't see" in the morning until "can't see" at night, and worked for nothing, making the white man rich, making Uncle Sam rich.

This is our investment. This is our contribution—our blood. Not only did we give of our free labor, we gave of our blood. Every time he had a call to arms, we were the first ones in uniform. We died on every battlefield the white man had. We have made a greater sacrifice than anybody who's standing up in America today. We have made a greater contribution and have collected less. Civil rights, for those of us whose philosophy is black nationalism, means: "Give it to us now. Don't wait for next year. Give it to us yesterday, and that's not fast enough."

I might stop right here to point out one thing. Whenever you're going after something that belongs to you, anyone who's depriving you of the right to have it is a criminal. Understand that. Whenever you are going after something that is yours, you are within your legal rights to lay claim to it. And anyone who puts forth any effort to deprive you of that which is yours, is breaking the law, is a criminal. And this was pointed out by the Supreme Court decision. It outlawed segregation. Which means segregation is against the law. Which means a segregationist is breaking the law. A segregationist is a criminal. You can't label him as anything other than that. And when you demonstrate against segregation, the law is on your side. The Supreme Court is on your side....

When we begin to get in this area, we need new friends, we need new allies. We need to expand the civil-rights struggle to a higher level—to the level of human rights. Whenever you are in a civil-rights struggle, whether you know it or not, you are confining yourself to the jurisdiction of Uncle Sam. No one from the outside world can speak out in your behalf as long as your struggle is a civil-rights struggle. Civil rights comes within the domestic affairs of this country. All of our African brothers and our Asian brothers and our Latin-American brothers cannot open their mouths and interfere in the domestic affairs of the United States. And as long as it's civil rights, this comes under the jurisdiction of Uncle Sam.

But the United Nations has what's known as the charter of human rights. It has a committee that deals in human rights. You may wonder why all of the atrocities that have been committed in Africa and in Hungary and in Asia and in Latin America are brought before the UN, and the Negro problem is never brought before the UN. This is part of the conspiracy. This old, tricky, blue-eyed liberal who is supposed to be your and my friend, supposed to be in our corner, supposed to be subsidizing our struggle, and supposed to be acting in the capacity of an adviser, never tells you anything about human rights. They keep you wrapped up in civil rights. And you spend so much time barking up the civil-rights tree, you don't even know there's a human-rights tree on the same floor.

When you expand the civil-rights struggle to the level of human rights, you can then take the case of the black man in this country before the nations in the UN. You can take it before the General Assembly. You can take Uncle Sam before a world court. But the only level you can do it on is the level of human rights. Civil rights keeps you under his restrictions, under his jurisdiction. Civil rights keeps you in his pocket. Civil rights means you're asking Uncle Sam to treat you right. Human rights are something you were born with. Human rights are your God-given rights. Human rights are the rights that are recognized by all nations of this earth. And any time any one violates your human rights, you can take them to the world court. Uncle Sam's hands are dripping with blood, dripping with the blood of the black man in this country. He's the earth's number-one hypocrite. He has the audacity—yes, he has—imagine him posing as the leader of the free world. The free world!—and you over here singing "We Shall Overcome." Expand the civil-rights struggle to the level of human rights, take it into the United Nations, where our African brothers can throw their weight on our side, where our Asian brothers can throw their weight on our side, where our Latin-American brothers can throw their weight on our side, and where 800 million Chinamen are sitting there waiting to throw their weight on our side.

Let the world know how bloody his hands are. Let the world know the hypocrisy that's practiced over here. Let it be the ballot or the bullet. Let him know that it must be the ballot or the bullet.

When you take your case to Washington, D.C., you're taking it to the criminal who's responsible; it's like running from the wolf to the fox. They're all in cahoots together. They all work political chicanery and make you look like a chump before the eyes of the world. Here you are walking around in America, getting ready to be drafted and sent abroad, like a tin soldier, and when you get over there, people ask you what are you fighting for, and you have to stick your tongue in your cheek. No, take Uncle Sam to court, take him before the world.

By ballot I only mean freedom. Don't you know—I disagree with Lomax on this issue—that the ballot is more important than the dollar? Can I prove it? Yes. Look in the UN. There are poor nations in the UN; yet those poor nations can get together with their voting power and keep the rich nations from making a move. They have one nation—one vote, everyone has an equal vote. And when those brothers from Asia, and Africa and the darker parts of this earth get together, their voting power is sufficient to hold Sam in check. Or Russia in check. Or some other section of the earth in check. So, the ballot is most important....

I would like to say, in closing, a few things concerning the Muslim Mosque, Inc., which we established recently in New York City. It's true we're Muslims and our religion is Islam, but we don't mix our religion with our politics and our economics and our social and civil activities—not any more. We keep our religion in our mosque. After our religious services are over, then as Muslims we become involved in political action, economic action and social and civic action. We become involved with anybody, anywhere, any time and in any manner that's designed to eliminate the evils, the political, economic and social evils that are afflicting the people of our community.

The political philosophy of black nationalism means that the black man should control the politics and the politicians in his own community; no more. The black man in the black community has to be re-educated into the science of politics so he will know what politics is supposed to bring him in return. Don't be throwing out any ballots. A ballot is like a bullet. You don't throw your ballots until you see a target, and if that target is not within your reach, keep your ballot in your pocket. The political philosophy of black nationalism is being taught in the Christian church. It's being taught in the NAACP. It's being taught in CORE meetings. It's being taught in SNCC [Student Nonviolent Coordinating Committee] meetings. It's being taught in Muslim meetings. It's being taught where nothing but atheists and agnostics come together. It's being taught everywhere. Black people are fed up with the dillydallying, pussyfooting, compromising approach that we've been using toward getting our freedom. We want freedom *now*, but we're not going to get it saying "We Shall Overcome." We've got to fight until we overcome.

The economic philosophy of black nationalism is pure and simple. It only means that we should control the economy of our community. Why should white people be running all the stores in our community? Why should white people be running the banks of our community? Why should the economy of our community be in the hands of the white man? Why? If a black man can't move his store into a white community, you tell me why a white man should move his store into a black community. The philosophy of black nationalism involves a re-education program in the black community in regards to economics. Our people have to be made to see that any time you take your dollar out of your community and spend it in a community where you don't live, the community where you live will get poorer and poorer, and the community where you spend your money will get richer and richer. Then you wonder why where you live is always a ghetto or a slum area. And where you and I are concerned, not only do we lose it when we spend it out of the community, but the white man has got all our stores in the community tied up; so that though we spend it in the community, at sundown the man who runs the store takes it over across town somewhere. He's got us in a vise.

So the economic philosophy of black nationalism means in every church, in every civic organization, in every fraternal order, it's time now for our people to become conscious of the importance of controlling the economy of our community. If we own the stores, if we operate the businesses, if we try and establish some industry in our own community, then we're developing to the position where we are creating employment for our own kind. Once you gain control of the economy of your own community, then you don't have to picket and boycott and beg some cracker downtown for a job in his business.

The social philosophy of black nationalism only means that we have to get together and remove the evils, the vices, alcoholism, drug addiction, and other evils that are destroying the moral fiber of our community. We ourselves have to lift the level of our community, the standard of our community to a higher level, make our own society beautiful so that we will be satisfied in our own social circles and won't be running around here trying to knock our way into a social circle where we're not wanted.

So I say, in spreading a gospel such as black nationalism, it is not designed to make the black man re-evaluate the white man—you know him already—but to make the black man re-evaluate himself. Don't change the white man's mind—you can't change his mind, and that whole thing about appealing to the moral conscience of America—America's conscience is bankrupt. She lost all conscience a long time ago. Uncle Sam has no conscience. They don't know what morals are. They don't try and eliminate an evil because it's evil, or because it's illegal, or because it's immoral; they eliminate it only when it threatens their existence. So you're wasting your time appealing to the moral conscience of a bankrupt man like Uncle Sam. If he had a conscience, he'd straighten this thing out with no more pressure being put upon him. So it is not necessary to change the white man's mind. We have to change our own mind. You can't change his mind about us. We've got to change our own minds about each other. We have to see each other with new eyes. We have to see each other as brothers and sisters. We have to come together with warmth so we can develop unity and harmony that's necessary to get this problem solved ourselves....

We Give You a Hand Up, Not a Handout (1979)

Sargent Shriver

The Origins of Head Start

This is a transcription of an interview of Sargent Shriver that was conducted by Jeanette Valentine. Shriver edited the transcribed interview.

When we started the War on Poverty, there was nationwide ignorance about poor people: who they were, where they were, what their problems were, and so on. There was a fantastic lack of fundamental knowledge. We at the Office of Economic Opportunity (OEO) started out, however, believing that there were some groups that really needed help. We had programs for young people out of work, like the Job Corps or the Neighborhood Youth Corps. We had been in business for a number of months before we were able to make a statistical analysis of the poor that revealed to me (I stress *me*, others may have known it) that 50 percent of all people who are poor are children sixteen and under. Consequently, I came to the conclusion that if we were conducting what was then called a war—an all-out war—against poverty, we couldn't really think we were doing very well if we didn't have special programs to help 50 percent of the target population, namely children. The question then arose, "Well, what can you do about children?" And nobody had any particularly good ideas.

At the same time that I was running the Peace Corps and the War on Poverty, I was also fully involved with my wife in the Joseph P. Kennedy, Jr., Foundation's activities. That foundation worked with mentally retarded persons, trying to find cures for mental retardation and to alleviate the problems of the retarded. In this work we had funded a research project in Tennessee, run by a brilliant psychologist, Susan Gray, at the George Peabody Teachers' College. We had financed her research with mentally retarded children living in underprivileged areas in and around Nashville. Those studies, which were conducted for the purpose of finding out what to do about mental retardation, revealed that if you intervene effectively and intelligently at, let's say, three, four, or five years of age, you can actually change the IQ of mentally retarded children.

When I first heard about this, I was dumbfounded. Like many or perhaps most Americans, I thought that at birth one was born with a certain IQ, as one might be born with black or red hair, and that in fact it was impossible to change the genetic make-up that determined IQ. But these studies by Susan Gray, for the first time, showed that the right kind of intervention can raise a child's IQ that is as low as 60. They also demonstrated that the proper kind of continuing intervention can really affect a person's social as well as intellectual development.

Well, that bit of information just sort of rolled around in the back of my skull. Then, at one point, when I was trying to think of what to do about poor children, the thought clicked in the back of my mind that if we, through the Kennedy Foundation, could effectively change the IQ of retarded children by early-childhood intervention, could early intervention have a beneficial effect on the children of poor people? I do not mean to say the purpose was to raise the IQs of these children. It was not primarily an IQ idea. It was the idea of intervening early in their lives to modify or help them become more capable of going to school, which is normally the first hurdle outside the home a person faces.

In addition to studies which showed that the IQ of children could be modified, the Kennedy Foundation had financed a research project on nutrition and its effect on mental development. The study—which showed that malnutrition does, in fact, affect a person's intellectual development—was done in the late fifties or early sixties by Dr. Philip Dodge, chairman now of the Department of Pediatrics at the Washington University Medical School in St. Louis. One doesn't have to be at all smart to realize that if malnutrition affects intellectual development, it can affect other aspects of development as well.

I knew about Susan Gray's and Phil Dodge's studies because of my involvement in the field of mental retardation, and not from within the government. It was nothing from within the War on Poverty that put these ideas into my head. So when we were trying to think of something to do about poor children, it occurred to me that if we could actually help retarded children by giving them better nutritional programs in early life, we probably could produce similar beneficial results for poor kids.

I started talking about this idea with people at the Kennedy Foundation, for example with Dr. Robert Cooke, who was then chairman of its Scientific

Advisory Committee and also chairman of the department of pediatrics at Johns Hopkins medical school. I got some rather good responses from people like Dr. Cooke. I tried out these ideas on a good friend of mine, Dr. Joseph English. He is a child psychiatrist, and was the medical officer for the Peace Corps. We put together a little group. We came to the conclusion that a lot of poor kids arrive at the first grade beaten or at least handicapped before they start. To use an analogy from sports, they stand ten, twenty, and thirty feet back from the starting line; other people are way ahead of them. They don't get a fair, equal start with everybody else when they come to school at age six. So we said, "What can we do to help these youngsters? How can we help them to arrive at the starting line even with other children?"

We didn't know anything about theoretical models; none of us was a scientist, least of all me. True, I had been president of the Board of Education in Chicago for five years, and I had seen how the cards are stacked against kids in the slums in a huge number of ways. There are just so many ways in which they don't have a chance: no books, no parental guidance, nobody in the family who reads, nobody who ever went to school, not to mention malnutrition, bad classrooms, dilapidated housing, narcotics, and so on. Since it was clear that a large proportion of our poor people were coming from these slums and since a large proportion of them were children, it was just transparent to me that we had to do something to give them a fair chance. So we assumed that if we could intervene very early—at three, four, and five years of age—we could perhaps have a substantial deterring effect on ultimate poverty. I might also emphasize that we were not interested in giving anybody what some might call a "handout." We were interested in trying to change the poor so that they could become independent human beings, so they would not be dependent on welfare, dependent on charity, or dependent on anything. And the only way we could do that was by giving them the resources, the personal resources, to become independent. This was part of the philosophy of the whole War on Poverty.

I began talking to a number of other people, and I remember one day having lunch with my wife and Joseph Alsop, the well-known Washington newspaper correspondent, in the Hay-Adams Hotel. I said to him, "Joe, what do you think about this?" It was about November or December of the first year of the War on Poverty. I raised this with him specifically because I figured that if anybody would be skeptical and caustic about it, perhaps even cynical, it would be Joe Alsop. From Joe I would find out immediately what kind of negative reaction we could expect if we came out with the idea of doing something for children in the War on Poverty. But, to my pleasure, and also a little bit to my surprise, Joe was extremely supportive. He thought it was a great idea. I suddenly realized then that there was another advantage to doing something about children—particularly from the racial point of view. The advantage was this: In our society there is a bias against helping adults. The prevalent idea is: "By God, there's plenty of work to be done, and if poor people had any get-up-and-go they'd go out and get jobs for themselves." But there's a contrary bias in favor of helping children. Even in the black belt of the deepest South, there's always been a prejudice in favor of little black children. The old-time term "pickaninny" was one of endearment. It wasn't until blacks grew up that white people began to feel animosity or show actual violence toward them. I hoped that we could overcome a lot of hostility in our society against the poor in general, and specifically against black people who are poor, by aiming for the children. Well, Joe thought that was a great idea. And I said to myself, "If *he* isn't knocking it, it's not likely to be knocked."

So I went back to the office and said, "Look, we've got to get a program going, and this is the theory behind it. The theory is that we'll intervene early; we'll help IQ problems and the malnutrition problem; we'll get these kids ready for school and into the environment of a school. Many children (I knew this from being president of the Board of Education) came to school at age six never having been in a school building before. Even middle-class children are a little bit frightened when they go into a new building and leave their mothers and fathers, maybe for the first time. They have the trauma of going to class for the first time and seeing a whole lot of strange kids there. Well, if that's true for the normal child, it's often a lot worse for the poor child. Maybe the child doesn't have the right clothes, the right books, the right haircut, or whatever. There are a huge number of psychological problems. And I said, "Let's get these youngsters *ahead* of time, bring them into school and 'culturally' prepare them for school: for the buildings and teachers, desks, pencils and chalk, discipline, food, etc. At the same time, we'll give them the books ahead of time, show them what they are like, and what you do with books. We'll find out where they stand in reading, and find out if they need 'shots' (most of these poor youngsters don't get the right kinds of vaccinations)." Some of them have eye problems, but their parents are so poor they've never taken them to a doctor, so they don't know they've got eye problems. Often the kid can't see the blackboard. I remembered that from Chicago—a kid might get slapped in class for not reading what was on the blackboard, but he was sitting in the back of the class and couldn't read because he couldn't see. Or perhaps he had dyslexia, and nobody had ever given him a test.

So we figured, we'll get these kids into school ahead of time; we'll give them food; we'll give them medical exams; we'll give them the shots or the glasses they need; we'll give them some acculturation to academic work—we'll give them (this is where the name came in) a *head start....*

Another thing I'd like to discuss about planning Project Head Start is the size of the program. When we initiated this project, I had extensive talks with Dr. Cooke. Then I learned there are "experts" in child development, and I started talking to some of them. One was Dr. Jerome Bruner at Harvard. At that time he had a project going on in Cambridge, and he was supposed to be, and obviously is, one of the world's great theorists in child development. I asked him whether or not we should do Head Start, and he said he thought it would be very beneficial to try. I asked him some rather simple questions, and then I said to him, "How many children do you think we could put into a program like this in the first year?" He said he thought if we enrolled 2,500 it would be a tremendous effort, and it was questionable in his mind as to whether there were enough qualified teachers to handle any more than 2,500. It would be difficult to find qualified teachers even for 2,500; and it would be difficult to find the right places. I think I said to him, and I know I said to myself, that it would be stupid for us to try to reach only 2,500 children, considering the size of the population we were dealing with. We were talking about a million children nationwide who were living in poverty. To do something about only 2,500 would be absurd. We had to devise programs that could have mass application, mass effectiveness. They could not be just particularized, individualized projects. I remember being very discouraged after talking to Dr. Bruner.

But then, I got the idea that if we could move fast enough—this was in December of 1964—we *could* get the program off the ground on a massive scale if we could use the summertime for the preschool program, when school buildings are usually empty and many teachers are not busy. From my experience on the Board of Education in Chicago, I knew the teachers only had a contract for nine months. In the remaining three months they usually took vacations, studied, or did other things. So despite Dr. Bruner's gloomy forecast, we went charging ahead. I felt that we had to reach somewhere around 10,000 to 25,000 kids the first summer alone....

I used to say that what happened next happened naturally, in the best sense of the word. We designed the program, announced it, and made it available to the American people according to specific criteria. But it was the American people who assured Head Start's success because of their fantastic nationwide response. No one—Dr. Cooke, myself, Dr. Bruner, or anyone else—really sensed how good the response was going to be. It was like wildcatting for oil in your own backyard and suddenly hitting a gusher. I can remember it very well because I had thought that the program, at least initially, would be small. I said to Dr. Cooke at the committee meeting, "Well, let's set aside, say, $10 million for this program." But then the applications began pouring in. I invited Dr. Julius

Richmond to Washington to run Head Start. He organized it, and I detailed one of our Washington bureaucrats—a very good one, Jule Sugarman—to work with him. Every two or three weeks, it seemed to me, they'd come back and say, "Look, Sarge, this thing is just exploding, and we certainly can't begin to finance it with $10 million or $20 million or even $30 million." By the time July came around, I had committed almost $70 million to the program!

That illustrates one of the fantastic aspects of OEO. I increased the funding by myself! I didn't have to go to Congress; I didn't have to go to the president; I didn't have to go to the Bureau of the Budget. Congress had appropriated money, and if I wanted to spend it on Head Start, I could spend it on Head Start. If I wanted to spend it on the Job Corps, I could spend it on the Job Corps. There are very few occasions in government history where any administrator of a program ever had the kind of freedom and power I had at OEO....

Because of the five years I had spent as president of the Board of Education in Chicago, I had a bias in favor of education, and originally I had thought of Head Start as an educational program. But Head Start was not alone among OEO programs in its educational emphasis. We established what we called Parent and Child Centers for younger children and we initiated a program called Upward Bound for adolescent children. We also initiated programs called Follow Through, the Job Corps, and the Work-Study Program. All those approaches were educational. The Work-Study Program is a good example. Very few people even today know that OEO started the first federally supported work-study program.

During my stay in Chicago, I recall driving through depressed communities in the city and seeing groups of youngsters standing on street corners. One can do the same today. It's a national tragedy. Going through any similar urban area such as the South Bronx or Watts one can see on most corners four, five, six, sometimes ten or a dozen young men, who look to be somewhere between fifteen and twenty, just standing there doing nothing. That's a national calamity. As an educator I asked myself, "Couldn't we start boarding high schools rather than just day high schools, take these kids out of that environment, and put them into a controlled environment where we could teach proper work habits, perseverance on a job, what a job is, etc." When they attend day school, they go right back into an environment that often is anti-work and anti-job. Nobody in the community has a job. For many of these kids, nobody in their family has had a job for *three* generations!

The surrounding environment of peers, neighborhood, and community has a much stronger impact than the family itself as the child gets older, especially for adolescents. For this reason, it seemed to make sense that for older children growing up in poverty we needed to develop a strategy that competed with the social environments from which these children were coming. We were trying to "break the cycle of poverty." Head Start was a beginning link in the chain aimed at interrupting what some people felt was the inevitable cycle, or culture of poverty. Prior to my OEO days, then, as an administrator in the public school system, I had tried to establish a boarding school program for children from communities in Chicago that were severely depressed economically. When I became director of OEO, I thought, "Here's my chance. We'll start Job Corps centers, and we'll take kids out of that environment of poverty and put them into a place for two years, and we'll really break the cycle." People said at the time, "Why don't you just send them there for six months, teach them the skills?" But that's not enough. They say in the army and navy that it takes four years at West Point or the Naval Academy to make an army or navy officer. And they're starting with the best kids in the country! Well, how can anybody think that it's possible to take a poor person who's caught in a cycle or culture of poverty and who has been there for two generations, maybe three, and turn him into an upstanding, hard-working fellow in two weeks, or even two months? It's impossible. That's why we started the Job Corps. The Job Corps is an educational program. As a matter of fact, at one point someone attacked OEO, saying that we were trying to set up a complete parallel educational system in the United States, starting with three-year-old children, going to Head Start, from Head Start to Follow Through, from Follow Through into Upward Bound, to the Job Corps, and so on up the line....

Head Start and the Community Action Program

The development of the Head Start program had its roots in the events and issues just described. Once the program was implemented, however, Head Start came to play a significant role in the overall OEO effort, in particular as part of the Community Action Program (CAP). Head Start was a "National Emphasis program" of the Office of Economic Opportunity. National Emphasis programs were federal programs originating from Washington but actually administered at the local level, usually through the Community Action agencies (local CAPs).

In reconstructing the history of Head Start and of OEO it must always be remembered that there was widespread opposition to OEO as soon as the legislation passed. Within ninety days after OEO's start, the House of Representatives authorized a special Investigations Committee to determine what OEO was doing wrong! This happened even before OEO had had time to do much, if anything at all. Local opposition also appeared.

Faced with local and congressional hostility, I felt that National Emphasis programs, one of them being Head Start, could ameliorate some of this hostility to OEO's CAP efforts by establishing certain national programs that many communities would consider desirable. In other words, the hostility to Community Action could be ameliorated by the community itself, if it was the conduit for certain desirable programs like Head Start, legal aid, or health programs. Otherwise, the Community Action Program would be looked upon exclusively as an effort to empower the poor politically and economically. We knew that endowing a particular group in a community with money and political power would generate hostility toward that effort from others in that community. If local CAPs were seen as nothing more than "Saul Alinsky–type" revolutionary centers financed by Washington to upset local government and social structure (which is what some people thought they were), the opposition they would meet would negate all their positive qualities. We also supported the administration of National Emphasis programs by local CAPs because these agencies were in touch with the poor and could inform us of their reactions to these programs. Through CAP agencies we felt we could establish very good "consumer panels," so to speak. The Community Action agencies served a number of other purposes, of course, and so did the National Emphasis programs. But when I saw how much pressure the CAPs were taking a year or two later, I was more insistent than ever that we retain Head Start, Upward Bound, and other National Emphasis programs, and use Community Action agencies so that they would have other things to offer besides just "community action."

The interesting fact is, however, that a number of Community Action agencies were not interested in Head Start. Some of the philosophers or theorists of community action did not believe in what they called "services." They believed that OEO should not give services to poor people. Rather, we should *empower* poor people politically and economically. The idea that these "experts" had of community action was: "We are going to give power, economic and political, to the poor people. Then they themselves will pull themselves up by their own bootstraps." Services were looked upon as being paternalistic, old-style. And Head Start, or legal services, or neighborhood health services, were service programs. Instead of transferring power, these programs were just offering services.

I was sitting in the middle of that fight, and I would say, "We have to have both—we have to provide services, and we have to help poor people regain power." But some Community Action agencies were dominated by power groups. For example, Saul Alinsky, a theoretician of community action, started out by being a very good friend of mine for fifteen years and ended up attacking us and OEO relentlessly. He called our whole effort at OEO "political pornography."

What he meant was that we were not really giving poor people the power to change their own conditions, economically or otherwise; that OEO was therefore a palliative, and all we were doing was spoon-feeding the poor with programs like Head Start. Consequently, some Community Action agencies did not want the Head Start program.

When I became involved with the War on Poverty, I started out with a bias that the American people would work together, that there was not and need not be a profound antipathy between local politicians, local businessmen, the local philanthropic sector, and the poor. I felt that we should try to develop a sense of community responsibility through community action rather than an action by one group in the community against other groups. Community action could lead to joint responsibility for the poor, and for the community as a whole. Some people think that community action is designed to empower poor people to "grab their share." I have always thought of community action as community development, which is what we did in the Peace Corps all over the world. We tried to develop a sense of community responsibility; we tried to develop a sense of community health, of community justice. And so, even though there were people on both sides who were against programs like Head Start, as well as the CAPs, I fought like fury for both the National Emphasis programs and for local CAPs. I believed that some programs could be run more efficiently and economically on a national basis. And, even though these were "service" programs, many of them were very popular at the grassroots level—especially, as the record shows, Project Head Start....

Head Start Today

... I have always thought, however, that all the poverty programs, including Head Start, were grossly, savagely underfinanced. It is ludicrous to me that this country, with all the wealth we have, can so short-change its own people. For example, I met a man from Tel Aviv. He laid out in front of me the program they have in Tel Aviv for children before they are in school—for maternal and child assistance, clinics, and so on. And I said to him, "You've come over here to find out from us what to do about this? Programs such as you have in Israel are what we ought to have in our country, but sadly do not." He had studied at an American university. We teach people in our universities to go out and organize programs for mothers and children, something like Head Start, and they are able to do it in Tel Aviv, but can't do it in the United States. The reason is that our society does not put a high enough priority on that kind of public expenditure. All of the OEO programs (Head Start, neighborhood health centers, legal aid, Job Corps, and Community Action) were and are tragically underfinanced by this society....

Head Start was not and is not the final answer to poverty. OEO started many programs that covered health, justice, education, jobs. It is hard to say which effort contributed most to alleviating poverty. The reality is that deficiencies in all these areas handicap the poor. A poor person in this society is a person who is suffering from multiple bruises and lacerations. And those bruises and lacerations are medical, psychological, and intellectual. From the time of conception onward, the poor suffer from multiple wounds to their egos, brains, and bodies. It is impossible to turn such victims into independent persons capable of earning their own way, of becoming fully participating members of a highly industrialized society, solely by giving them a job, a visit to a hospital, or a house, or an opportunity for an education. In fact, we've got to provide *all* those things. And nobody in this society likes that. Americans resent such efforts because we all share the obsolete notion that "I got to where I am by myself. I worked to get there. Why don't those other guys just work as hard as I do?" But the truth is that no one does it alone.

Of course every individual has to make an effort as well. The slogan of the War on Poverty was: "We give you a hand up, not a handout." No matter what anybody does for an individual, ultimately he or she has to do something for himself or herself. Everything in the War on Poverty was designed to offer the poor a chance. We were continually trying to maneuver things to induce people to lift themselves out of poverty. We would offer a job, an education, a little better place to live. The basic idea was to give an incentive. But it's true, however, that no matter how many incentives you offer people, a certain proportion of them, poor and rich alike, will do nothing.

In the final analysis one could ask, "Was Head Start enough?" The answer is obviously "No." Was it, is it as good as it could be? Again, the answer is "No." But Head Start still was a miracle. It has been and continues to be a terrific thing for families and children.

Welfare Is a Women's Issue (1972)

Johnnie Tillmon

The Liberation News Service first carried Tillmon's statement. It later appeared in Ms. Magazine *that same year.*

I'm a woman. I'm a black woman. I'm a poor woman. I'm a fat woman. I'm a middle-aged woman. And I'm on welfare.

In this country, if you're any one of those things—poor, black, fat, female, middle-aged, on welfare—you count less as a human being. If you're all those things, you don't count at all. Except as a statistic.

I am a statistic.

I am 45 years old. I have raised six children.

I grew up in Arkansas, and I worked there for fifteen years in a laundry, making about $20 or $30 a week, picking cotton on the side for carfare. I moved to California in 1959 and worked in a laundry there for nearly four years. In 1963 I got too sick to work anymore. Friends helped me to go on welfare.

They didn't call it welfare. They called it A.F.D.C.—Aid to Families with Dependent Children. Each month I got $363 for my kids and me. I pay $128 a month rent; $30 for utilities, which include gas, electricity, and water; $120 for food and nonedible household essentials; $50 for school lunches for the three children in junior and senior high school who are not eligible for reduced-cost meal programs.

There are millions of statistics like me. Some on welfare. Some not. And some, really poor, who don't even know they're entitled to welfare. Not all of them are black. Not at all. In fact, the majority—about two-thirds—of all the poor families in the country are white.

Welfare's like a traffic accident. It can happen to anybody, but especially it happens to women.

And that is why welfare is a women's issue. For a lot of middle-class women in this country, Women's Liberation is a matter of concern. For women on welfare it's a matter of survival.

Forty-four percent of all poor families are headed by women. That's bad enough. But the *families* on A.F.D.C. aren't really families. Because 99 percent of them are headed by women. That means there is no man around. In half the states there really can't be men around because A.F.D.C. says if there is an "able-bodied" man around, then you can't be on welfare. If the kids are going to eat, and the man can't get a job, then he's got to go. So his kids can eat.

The truth is that A.F.D.C. is like a supersexist marriage. You trade in *a* man for *the* man. But you can't divorce him if he treats you bad. He can divorce you, of course, cut you off anytime he wants. But in that case, *he* keeps the kids, not you.

The man runs everything. In ordinary marriage, sex is supposed to be for your husband. On A.F.D.C., you're not supposed to have any sex at all. You give up control of your own body. It's a condition of aid. You may even have to agree to get your tubes tied so you can never have more children just to avoid being cut off welfare.

The man, the welfare system, controls your money. He tells you what to buy, what not to buy, where to buy it, and how much things cost. If things—rent, for instance—really cost more than he says they do, it's just too bad for you.

There are other welfare programs, other kinds of people on welfare—the blind, the disabled, the aged. (Many of them are women too, especially the aged.) Those others make up just over a third of all the welfare caseloads. We A.F.D.C.s are two-thirds.

But when the politicians talk about the "welfare cancer eating at our vitals," they're not talking about the aged, blind, and disabled. Nobody minds them. They're the "deserving poor." Politicians are talking about A.F.D.C. Politicians are talking about us—the women who head up 99 percent of the A.F.D.C. families—and our kids. We're the "cancer," the "undeserving poor." Mothers and children.

In this country we believe in something called the "work ethic." That means that your work is what gives you human worth. But the work ethic itself is a double standard. It applies to men and to women on welfare. It doesn't apply to all women. If you're a society lady from Scarsdale and you spend all your time sitting on your prosperity paring your nails, well, that's okay.

The truth is a job doesn't necessarily mean an adequate income. A woman with three kids—not twelve kids, mind you, just three kids—that woman earning the full federal minimum wage of $2.00 an hour, is still stuck in poverty. She is below the Government's own official poverty line. There are some ten million jobs that now pay less than the minimum wage, and if you're a woman, you've got the best chance of getting one.

The President keeps repeating the "dignity of work" idea. What dignity? Wages are the measure of dignity that society puts on a job. Wages and nothing else. There is no dignity in starvation. Nobody denies, least of all poor women, that there is dignity and satisfaction in being able to support your kids through honest labor.

We wish we could do it.

The problem is that our country's economic policies deny the dignity and satisfaction of self-sufficiency to millions of people—the millions who suffer every day in underpaid dirty jobs—and still don't have enough to survive.

People still believe that old lie that A.F.D.C. mothers keep on having kids just to get a bigger welfare check. On the average, another baby means another $35 a month—barely enough for food and clothing. Having babies for profit is a lie that only men could make up, and only men could believe. Men, who never have to bear the babies or have to raise them and maybe send them to war.

There are a lot of other lies that male society tells about welfare mothers; that A.F.D.C. mothers are immoral, that A.F.D.C. mothers are lazy, misuse their welfare checks, spend it all on booze and are stupid and incompetent.

If people are willing to believe these lies, it's partly because they're just special versions of the lies that society tells about *all* women....

On TV, a woman learns that human worth means beauty and that beauty means being thin, white, young and rich.

She learns that her body is really disgusting the way it is, and that she needs all kinds of expensive cosmetics to cover it up.

She learns that a "real woman" spends her time worrying about how her bathroom bowl smells; that being important means being middle class, having two cars, a house in the suburbs, and a minidress under your maxicoat. In other words, an A.F.D.C. mother learns that being a "real woman" means being all the things she isn't and having all the things she can't have.

Either it breaks you, and you start hating yourself, or you break it.

There's one good thing about welfare. It kills your illusions about yourself, and about where this society is really at. It's laid out for you straight. You have to learn to fight, to be aggressive, or you just don't make it. If you can survive being on welfare, you can survive anything. It gives you a kind of freedom, a sense of your own power and togetherness with other women.

Maybe it is we poor welfare women who will really liberate women in this country. We've already started on our own welfare plan.

Along with other welfare recipients, we have organized together so we can have some voice. Our group is called the National Welfare Rights Organization (N.W.R.O.). We put together our own welfare plan, called Guaranteed Adequate Income (G.A.I.), which would eliminate sexism from welfare.

There would be no "categories"—men, women, children, single, married, kids, no kids—just poor people who need aid. You'd get paid according to need and family size only—$6,500 for a family of four (which is the Department of Labor's estimate of what's adequate), and that would be upped as the cost of living goes up.

If I were president, I would solve this so-called welfare crisis in a minute and go a long way toward liberating every woman. I'd just issue a proclamation that "women's" work is *real* work.

In other words, I'd start paying women a living wage for doing the work we are already doing—childraising and house-keeping. And the welfare crisis would be over, just like that. Housewives would be getting wages, too—a legally determined percentage of their husband's salary—instead of having to ask for and account for money they've already earned.

For me, Women's Liberation is simple. No woman in this country can feel dignified, no woman can be liberated, until all women get off their knees. That's what N.W.R.O. is all about—women standing together, on their feet.

The Poorest of the Poor and the Weakest of the Weak (1968)

Cesar Chavez

This speech was given at an interfaith luncheon of clergy and labor people at Calvary Episcopal Church in Manhattan.
We are not in the age of miracles, and yet it is surprising that we can attract, and keep, and increase the type of support that is needed to keep our economic struggle going for 33 months. It is a struggle in which the poorest of the poor and weakest of the weak are pitted against the strongest of the strong. We are fighting not against the family farm, not against agriculture, but against agribusiness.

When we think of powerful interests, we think of General Motors and other great corporations. But we must turn our minds to the power of the land. It is hard to think that agribusiness could have such tremendous power as it has in California—it is worth five billion dollars in our state alone. We must see it as it is, a similar situation to Latin America. The interests can control not only the land but everything that moves, everyone that walks in the land. They control even the actions of the Congress of the United States, even some church groups. Right up to today, some groups in the churches think we are a bunch of communists. I can take the credit for one of the first ecumenical actions of the churches in the Delano area. Some ministers and priests got together to make a statement denouncing us as outside agitators.

You must have some of the background of agriculture in California to understand what we have been doing. The three basic elements: people, poor people, to provide the cheap labor.

We know how the land was acquired. The railroads, the Union Pacific and the Southern Pacific, got large tracts of land, and so did the Bank of America. Who would think that the Bank of America is a grower, but it is.

When the land was reclaimed, water had to be brought in from great distances, even six-hundred to seven-hundred miles. Your taxes are paying for this water supply today. Ours are not, right now, because we are on strike. Back in the early part of this century, legislators began to see that the family farm should be helped. So water was to be supplied to 160-acre farms. This was never enforced. The water went to the larger tracts.

One thing was necessary to the success of the exploitation of California land: workers. The whole cry to get poor people to do the work of the land is a story in itself. When the Southern Pacific and Union Pacific railroads were completed, the Chinese were left without work to do. They went to the cities. The growers who needed workers dealt with contractors who supplied the Chinese. The contractors, who were Chinese themselves, began to sell their brothers for profit. When the Chinese wanted to own their own land, we had the Chinese Exclusion Act. The Chinese land workers could not own land nor could they marry Caucasian women, so they left agriculture for the cities.

The growers went to Congress for special legislation. Tailor-made immigration laws made it possible for them to recruit labor from Japan. When the Japanese used the slow-down (they had no unions and could not strike) to get better conditions, the growers began to get rid of them. The Japanese could not own land, either, but began to rent it. In time they began to exploit the laborers.

The growers even went to India for labor, and in the early twenties they were recruiting in the Philippines. When they saw that many Mexicans were leaving their country because of the Revolution, they saw an opportunity. One grower explained that Mexicans were good for California land work because they were short and close to the ground. The growers went further than they ever went before. During World War II, our own government became the recruiter for laborers, "braceros." Even today, as I stand here talking to you, we cannot choke off production on the great farms for one simple reason. The regulations on immigration are not being enforced. Our own government is the biggest strike-breaker against the union. The biggest weapon in the hands of the growers is the "green card" commuter.

You can live in Mexico and come in to work for a season and then go back home. This is not like the regulations covering immigrants from Europe. Hundreds of thousands of people are recruited and put into employers' camps. We cannot reach them there. They are like concentration camps. If the laws were enforced, we would not have to boycott. Employers are not supposed to recruit workers while labor disputes are in progress.

We have to play the game without any rules or procedures. In New York, the rights of unions are enforced, but in our case, 95 percent of the workers were signed up with the union but the producer of table grapes, Giumarra, refused to sit down with us for representation procedures. We were willing to abide by the results of the election. The employers would not talk to us. The only approach left to us is the strike and the boycott.

Now that the growers are hurting, they want an election. Their strikebreakers are inside. Who can win an election this way? This is the predicament we are in. We say to Giumarra, you are not going to get two bites at the same apple. You will have to sign an agreement under pressure. With Edison, we called off the strike and the boycott and we had a contract. Then the land was sold to another grower and we are out of a contract. The day the contract is concluded with Giumarra, that day we take off the pressure.

Even if you have an election—without rules or procedures or protection—what do you have but the law of the jungle? The Board says we have no protection, but when we institute a boycott, the growers go to the Board and get protection.

People raise the question: Is this a strike or is it a civil-rights fight?

In California, in Texas, or in the South, any time you strike, it becomes a civil-rights movement. It becomes a civil-rights fight.

The local courts say we have no right to use an amplifier to reach strikebreakers who are a quarter of a mile away. In every case, the growers get an injunction against us immediately. Then we go up to the Appellate Court and up to the Supreme Court. Justice is very expensive sometimes.

We go further. We take advantage of modern technology. I even went up in a plane with two priests to broadcast to the strikebreakers from seven hundred feet up. As soon as we came down, the growers were there to protest.

We have had priests with us before, during and after the strike. The priests of the California Migrant Ministry, Chris Hartmeier and Jim Drake, have been with us from the beginning. They took losses in their church because of the Migrant Ministry and the suffering they accepted was for the migrants and for justice. It was from them that we learned the importance of the support of the church in our struggle. The church is the one group that gives help and never qualifies it or asks for favors.

The priests and ministers do everything from sweeping floors to giving out leaflets. They developed a true worker-priest movement. In the field and in the center, a minister and a worker joined together. The importance of Christian teachings to the worker and to his struggle for dignity becomes clear. Now we have a Franciscan priest working full time with us.

The three most important issues at this time are these.

First, union recognition by the employers. We have certain rights as human beings. Every law is for this recognition—except when it comes to farm workers. Recognizing the union is recognizing us as human beings. Second, an increase in wages is important. Third, in my opinion and in the opinion of the workers, is safety. The whole question of pesticides and insecticides must be met. The men who work to apply these poisons should have protection. Two or three weeks after working with pesticides a man begins to have trouble with his sight. In some cases, he begins to lose his fingernails. It does not happen immediately. Someday our government will have to undertake real research to determine the effects of these poisons, not only on the workers who are in direct contact with them, but on the consumers. Millions of dollars are spent in the research on the effectiveness of the poisons in destroying pests and insects on plants. This is from the business angle. Millions must also be spent on the effects of the same poisons on human beings.

There is a fine dust that nature puts on grapes. It is called bloom. The contamination from the insecticides remains in this fine dust.

I don't eat grapes because I know about these pesticides. You can stop eating grapes for your safety as well as for the boycott. Even our strongest supporters are afraid of the boycott of table grapes. The key to the success of this boycott is right here in New York. Action is necessary. If you don't do anything, you are permitting the evil. I would suggest that labor take a page in the largest newspaper and make the issue clear to all, and I would suggest that the clergy also take a page. The message of the clergy should be different, bringing out the morality of our struggle, the struggle of good people who are migrants, and therefore the poorest of the poor and the weakest of the weak.

The Alcatraz Proclamation to the Great White Father and His People (1969)

Indians of All Nations

This proclamation was read aloud by Richard Oakes upon the taking of Alcatraz.

Fellow citizens, we are asking you to join with us in our attempt to better the lives of all Indian people.

We are on Alcatraz Island to make known to the world that we have a right to use our land for our own benefit.

In a proclamation of November 20, 1969, we told the government of the United States that we are here "to create a meaningful use for our Great Spirit's Land."

We, the native Americans, reclaim the land known as Alcatraz Island in the name of all American Indians by right of discovery.

We wish to be fair and honorable in our dealings with the Caucasian inhabitants of this land, and hereby offer the following treaty:

We will purchase said Alcatraz Island for twenty-four dollars in glass beads and red cloth, a precedent set by the white man's purchase of a similar island about 300 years ago. We know that $24 in trade goods for these 16 acres is more than was paid when Manhattan Island was sold, but we know that land values have risen over the years. Our offer of $1.24 per acre is greater than the $0.47 per acre the white men are now paying the California Indians for their lands.

We will give to the inhabitants of this island a portion of the land for their own to be held in trust ... by the Bureau of Caucasian Affairs ... in perpetuity—for as long as the sun shall rise and the rivers go down to the sea. We will further guide the inhabitants in the proper way of living. We will offer them our religion, our education, our life-ways in order to help them achieve our level of civilization and thus raise them and all their white brothers up from their savage and unhappy state. We offer this treaty in good faith and wish to be fair and honorable in our dealings with all white men.

We feel that this so-called Alcatraz Island is more than suitable for an Indian reservation, as determined by the white man's own standards. By this, we mean that this place resembles most Indian reservations in that:

1. It is isolated from modern facilities, and without adequate means of transportation.
2. It has no fresh running water.
3. It has inadequate sanitation facilities.
4. There are no oil or mineral rights.
5. There is no industry and so unemployment is very great.
6. There are no health-care facilities.
7. The soil is rocky and non-productive, and the land does not support game.
8. There are no educational facilities.
9. The population has always exceeded the land base.
10. The population has always been held as prisoners and kept dependent upon others.

Further, it would be fitting and symbolic that ships from all over the world, entering the Golden Gate, would first see Indian land, and thus be reminded of the true history of this nation. This tiny island would be a symbol of the great lands once ruled by free and noble Indians.

What use will we make of this land? Since the San Francisco Indian Center burned down, there is no place for Indians to assemble and carry on tribal life here in the white man's city. Therefore, we plan to develop on this island several Indian institutions:

1. A Center for Native American Studies will be developed which will educate them to the skills and knowledge relevant to improve the lives and spirits

of all Indian peoples. Attached to this center will be traveling universities, managed by Indians, which will go to the Indian Reservations, learning those necessary and relevant materials now about.

2. An American Indian Spiritual Center, which will practice our ancient tribal religious and sacred healing ceremonies. Our cultural arts will be featured and our young people trained in music, dance, and healing rituals.

3. An Indian Center of Ecology, which will train and support our young people in scientific research and practice to restore our lands and waters to their pure and natural state. We will work to de-pollute the air and waters of the Bay Area. We will seek to restore fish and animal life to the area and to revitalize sea-life which has been threatened by the white man's way. We will set up facilities to desalt sea water for human benefit.

4. A Great Indian Training School will be developed to teach our people how to make a living in the world, improve our standard of living, and end hunger and unemployment among all our people. This training school will include a center for Indian arts and crafts, and an Indian restaurant serving native foods, which will restore Indian culinary arts. This center will display Indian arts and offer Indian foods to the public, so that all may know of the beauty and spirit of the traditional Indian ways.

Some of the present buildings will be taken over to develop an American Indian Museum which will depict our native food and other cultural contributions we have given to the world. Another part of the museum will present some of the things the white man has given to the Indians in return for the land and life he took:

> disease, alcohol, poverty, and cultural decimation (as symbolized by old tin cans, barbed wire, rubber tires, plastic containers, etc.). Part of the museum will remain a dungeon to symbolize both those Indian captives who were incarcerated for challenging white authority and those who were imprisoned on reservations. The museum will show the noble and tragic events of Indian history, including the broken treaties, the documentary of the Trail of Tears, the Massacre of Wounded Knee, as well as the victory over Yellow-Hair Custer and his army.

In the name of all Indians, therefore, we reclaim this island for our Indian nations, for all these reasons. We feel this claim is just and proper, and that this land should rightfully be granted to us for as long as the rivers run and the sun shall shine.

We hold the rock!

Epilogue: Outcomes

The great movements to end poverty ultimately were not successful. Neither King's economic bill of rights nor the NWRO's guaranteed income was implemented. Malcolm X's vision of taking economic control of local communities did not occur, and the Alcatraz Training Center was not built. Yet, all was not lost. African Americans did gain more control over their immediate neighborhoods. The War on Poverty did help cut the percentage of people in poverty by 50 percent. The UFW was finally recognized by the growers and signed collective bargaining contracts with them.

Economic Bill of Rights and Guaranteed Income

In order to compel the United States to implement an economic bill of rights, King planned to bring several thousand multiracial poor people to Washington, D.C., for massive nonviolent civil disobedience. The goal of the "Poor People's Campaign" was to occupy the city by blocking transportation, boycotting the schools, filling up the hospitals, and sitting in at governmental agencies until the Johnson administration and Congress acceded to their demands of $30 billion for full employment, a guaranteed annual income, and the construction of 500,000 low-cost housing units per year. As King stated, "We ought to come in mule carts, in old trucks, any kind of transportation people can get their hands on. People ought to come to Washington, sit down if necessary in the middle of the street and say, 'We are here; we are poor; we don't have any money; you have made us this way; you keep us down this way; and we've come to stay until you do something about it.'" As King was planning this campaign, he went to Memphis to support striking garbage collectors, where he was murdered. The campaign proceeded, but with inadequate planning and without King's charismatic leadership, it broke down into squabbling among the various protestors and collapsed.[24]

President Richard Nixon surprised supporters of these efforts by calling for the implementation of a Family Assistance Plan (FAP). The FAP would ensure that a poor family of four would receive no less than $1,600 a year in income (i.e., a maximum of $500 per adult and $300 per child); the family would also receive $800 in food stamps per year. Participants would be required to sign up for work, except for women with children under the age of six. Nixon's plan was basically a guaranteed income plan, but he refused to use this language for political reasons. Stating that the present welfare system was a failure, Nixon argued that FAP would end "welfare dependency" and encourage work by allowing poor individuals the right to keep the first $60 per month of income with no loss of government assistance. Tillmon and the NWRO agreed with Nixon that the welfare system was a failure, but they disagreed strongly with the amount proposed, since $1,600 was too low. The NWRO used governmental records to show that $1,600 was the cost of a family's food budget alone, and in turn argued that the cash benefit base should be set at $5,500. Thus, if a family made $4,000, which was a bit more than the poverty line in 1970, the family would receive $1,500 from the federal government. Furthermore, the NWRO opposed the FAP work requirement, since it didn't allow women to stay home and raise their children after the age of six. With the NWRO working to defeat the proposal from the left, and the right wing arguing that the government shouldn't financially assist the supposedly able-bodied poor, Nixon's Family Assistance Plan was defeated in Congress.[25]

The War on Poverty

President Lyndon Johnson's "unconditional War on Poverty" did not end material want: although its rhetoric implies that all means necessary would be used to accomplish the mission, not enough money was dedicated toward the social uplift programs, and the focus on education was not the most effective short-term strategy. However, this is not to say that the administration's focus on poverty reduction had no effect at all; it did cut poverty by almost one-half from 1960 to 1970.

At no time did Johnson and the Congress dedicate more than 1 percent of the federal budget to the War on Poverty programs. According to conservative estimates, Johnson's program needed at least 90 percent more funding in order to reach its goals. As King commented, "the war on poverty is not even a battle, it is scarcely a skirmish." King and others blamed the administration for directing the necessary resources to the war in Vietnam instead of fighting poverty. The historical record bears out this charge, for when Sargent Shriver had put together a long-range budget for the War on Poverty and went to talk to the president about it, Johnson rebuffed him. In the meeting, Shriver recalled that Johnson claimed that because of the cost of the Vietnam War, there was not enough money to fulfill Shriver's request.[26]

The OEO, the federal agency in charge of the War on Poverty, focused on education, rather than on the creation of public jobs or a guaranteed income. The program also did not attempt to structurally change American-style capitalism or deal with unequal distribution of wealth, which would have been even more costly and controversial than the underfunded Great Society programs. Some of the lasting War on Poverty education programs such as Head Start are generally viewed in a favorable light by today's politicians and parents with children in the program. In 2004, there were 905,851 preschool children enrolled in Head Start programs, which is about 40 percent of the children eligible. Not surprisingly, there is little evidence that demonstrates that Head Start reduces poverty. The research behind the program has been focused at the individual level and does not take into account such structural issues as the capitalist system, the family structure, or institutional racism. The majority of Head Start research has focused on quantifiable gains on IQ tests. This research has shown that Head Start supports initial test gains, but after the children leave Head Start, the improvement fades, becoming insignificant by the third grade. At the same time, Head Start programs that have been well funded and had intensive intervention produced students more likely to complete high school, who have lower crime rates, and who suffer fewer teenage pregnancies.[27]

Some War on Poverty programs provided new services. Two of these successful programs were Neighborhood Health Centers, which improved comprehensive health care services to the poor, and Legal Services, which provided several thousand lawyers to pursue class action lawsuits relating to welfare, medical aid, and landlord-tenant relations. Importantly, both of these innovative programs included poor people in the planning and operating of the services. However, in 1972, the Nixon administration abolished the Neighborhood Health Centers. By 1974, the issue of providing legal representation to the poor had become too politically controversial. The Nixon administration and Congress decided to remove the program from the executive branch and to create instead an independent nonpartisan board to oversee it. Today, the Legal Services Corporation, the successor to Legal Services, continues the work of providing legal representation to poor communities.[28]

The most controversial of the War on Poverty programs was the Community Action Program (CAP). More than 1,000 CAP agencies were funded in the first year to organize and mobilize poor people to influence city hall, school boards, welfare agencies, and housing departments. Soon, both liberal and conservative local officials opposed the program. CAP activities caused embarrassment for big-city liberal mayors as poverty groups publicly agitated for change. At the same time, conservative and racist politicians did not like CAP as it threatened the racial hierarchy. CAP was seen as a direct challenge to the local officials, as money and control were directed straight to the poverty organizations in an end-run around the local and state agencies. However, for the poor themselves, CAP was a cause for hope and excitement.[29]

Under pressure from local officials, OEO was changed in 1967 so that the federal government could fund only agencies that had the tacit approval of the state governor. In addition, the federal government reduced the ability of OEO to fund local CAP agencies. The result was that OEO lost control of more than 60 percent of its $846 million budget. With Congress deciding which antipoverty programs to fund, more OEO money was directed to Head Start, Upward Bound, and Legal Services. In 1973, the Nixon administration did not include CAP funding in its 1974 budget, but Congress appropriated the money for it anyway. Nixon then ordered his appointee for the OEO executive, Howard Phillips, not to spend any CAP money. Nixon was sued in federal court, with the judge ruling that the president did not have the right to control money that was appropriated by Congress. After Nixon was forced to resign because of the Watergate cover-up, President Ford dismantled the OEO. CAP was replaced by the Community Services Administration (CSA), which was supposed to continue funding the various local community action agencies. The remaining OEO programs were transferred to other governmental departments.[30]

In 1970, more than twenty-five million Americans still lived in poverty. But clearly, poverty was reduced by the War on Poverty. In 1964, 19 percent of the total population, or 36.1 million people, lived in poverty; by 1969, it had been cut to 12 percent, or 24 million people. This is one of the greatest decreases in poverty in the shortest amount of time in the history of the nation. Interestingly, the most successful poverty-reducing program came from the expansion of AFDC and Social Security. Both of the programs provided cash assistance that helped to lift poor people out of poverty. Economic growth was also strong during this period, but it was not responsible for lifting seniors and single women with children out of poverty; the existing public assistance and social insurance programs created by the New Deal accomplished this. During the 1960s and early 1970s, many more women with children gained access to welfare. From 1960 to 1969, the number of AFDC recipients increased from 3 million to 6.2 million and then to 11 million by 1974. This growth in income transfer payments to women occurred because welfare regulations were loosened, and because CAP agencies and the NWRO educated poor people about their rights to receive public benefits. Yet economic conditions for African Americans were declining as southern agriculture became mechanized, and female-headed households living in poverty were increasing, with divorce rates on the rise.[31]

Along with AFDC, the food stamp program increased sixfold from $36 million to almost $1.9 billion between 1965 and 1972. This dramatic increase in availability of food stamps, along with school lunch programs and nutritional supplements for women and young children, nearly eliminated hunger and malnutrition. In addition, infant mortality went down 33 percent with the assistance of the Neighborhood Health Centers, nutrition programs, and Medicaid. Seniors also benefited from 1963 to 1973, as the minimum Social Security payment increased by 135 percent and the maximum payment increased by 270 percent, while inflation rose by 45 percent. Although the majority of this expanded benefit did not go to the poor, enough went to the poor to reduce elderly poverty rates from approximately 32 percent to 16 percent.[32]

The 1964 Civil Rights Act and 1965 Voting Rights Act signed into law by President Johnson increased economic opportunity for African Americans. From 1960 to 1970, the number of black Americans in white-collar jobs doubled from 11 percent to 28 percent, and the median income of black men in comparison to white men increased from 59 to 69 percent. These civil rights changes, along with the changes to welfare and insurance programs, led to a decrease in African American poverty from approximately 54 percent of the population in 1960 to 30 percent in 1974.[33] Interestingly, on the night that the Voting Rights Act passed, Johnson predicted that the Democratic support of this landmark legislation would lead white southerners to switch to the Republican Party; in fact, this is exactly what happened.

One cautionary note to this analysis is that the rates of poverty discussed above are based on the U.S. definition of poverty, which tends to underestimate the number of poor people. Mollie Orshansky, a social scientist working for the government in the early 1960s, developed what became the government's official statistical definition for poverty. Poverty is calculated by multiplying by three the amount of a low-cost food budget that provides a nutritionally adequate diet, since food is estimated to consume one-third of a family budget. This figure varies by size of family, and each year it is adjusted using the consumer price index. Unfortunately, this poverty standard has many flaws. From the beginning, the poverty threshold has been set unrealistically low. People who live at the poverty line have a very difficult time surviving. The poverty threshold fails to keep pace with inflation, ignores geographic location, overlooks the fact that people have different medical needs, and leaves out poor people who have no permanent home, because it is based on the U.S. Census. Thus, people such as the homeless, farmworkers who move with the harvest, and people who live in rural areas that are not easily accessible are sometimes overlooked.[34]

More recently, some have claimed that Orshansky's assumption that poor people also spend one-third of their budget on housing costs is no longer accurate. For instance, the "severely poor" are those who live at one-half the poverty level or below; they comprise 39 percent of the poor population today and spend 50 percent of their income on housing. Lastly, the definition does not include the "near poor," some 12 million people whose income is above the poverty line, but below 125 percent of the threshold.[35]

Black Nationalism

Malcolm X never had the opportunity to bring the United States before the UN General Assembly or implement his philosophy of black nationalism, as he was murdered in 1965 by black rivals. Also, the Federal Bureau of Investigation (FBI) and local police agencies systematically targeted many of the leading black nationalists, with tactics including eavesdropping, infiltration, disinformation, provocation, jailing, and lethal force. In a 1967 memo, FBI Director J. Edgar Hoover wrote that he was ordering his national counterintelligence program, COINTELPRO, to "expose, disrupt, misdirect, discredit, or otherwise neutralize the activities of black nationalist hate-type organizations and groupings, their leadership, spokesmen, members, and supporters." Although under attack, the Black Panther Party started a free breakfast program for children, an elementary school entitled Liberation, food giveaways to community members, an escort service for seniors, and a free health clinic. However, U.S. government repression and internal divisions led to the demise of the Black Panther Party.[36]

The black nationalist vision of controlling the economic institutions in the community did not materialize, but African Americans have gained through their struggle some political control over their immediate surroundings as a result of the success of the Voting Rights Act. In 1960, there were fewer than 200 black elected officials in the United States (in municipal, county, state, federal, education, judicial, and law enforcement offices). By 1970, the number of black public officials grew to 1,469, and by 2001, the number had risen to 9,061. Close to 70 percent of these officials are located in the South, the region that has the largest black population. Black nationalists continue to influence public policy. In the late twentieth century, black nationalists played an instrumental role in the development of the reparations movement.[37]

The Occupation of Alcatraz

Native Americans occupied Alcatraz Island for nineteen months. Although eighty people comprised the original "invasion" force, this number varied throughout the occupation as people came and went. In June of 1971, federal marshals removed the fifteen remaining occupiers from Alcatraz. Although the training center and other institutions were not built on Alcatraz, the occupation had a powerful impact. Foremost, it provided Native Americans a model for social protest, inspiring more than fifty additional federal land or building seizures over the next five years. By reclaiming federal land, it focused national and international attention on the relationship between land and Indian poverty as well as the pending land claims of many Indian nations. Indian activism in the late 1960s and early 1970s led to the passage of the 1975 Indian Self-Determination and Education Assistance Act, which repudiated the termination policy of the previous twenty years and committed the federal government to Indian tribal self-government.[38]

United Farm Workers

After a five-year strike, the UFW, which by then had become a Mexican American operation, had signed contracts with most of the table-grape growers. These victories, which were won using militant nonviolent methods, doubled the wages of farmworkers and provided them with rest breaks and drinking water. The UFW contracts also provided clothing to limit exposure from pesticides and banned the spraying of these toxic chemicals when farmworkers were in the fields. In fact, the UFW was responsible for banning the use of DDT in grape fields under union contract six years before the Environmental Protection Agency (EPA) banned it in the rest of the United States. In 1975, California granted farmworkers the right to organize.[39]

Yet, in the 1980s, the gains that farmworkers had fought so hard to achieve were undermined by conservative policies. For example, Governor George Deukmejian of California stopped enforcing the state's farm labor law, which made it difficult for farmworkers to bargain collectively. After Chavez's death in 1993, the UFW began a new organizing drive. The farmworkers responded by voting for the UFW in eighteen straight union elections. By 2000, the UFW had signed twenty-four new agreements with the growers, and its membership grew from 20,000 to 27,000. The vision for a new social order based on human dignity, respect, and the end of poverty and toxic pesticides in the fields was flourishing once again. However, the struggle is far from over as most farmworkers in the United States still do not have the legal right to organize and bargain collectively.[40]

Protestors march for a living wage

Chapter 7

Dismantling the New Deal and War on Poverty: Contemporary Solutions

Prologue: Social Context and Overview of Solutions

With the assassinations of Martin Luther King, Jr., and Robert Kennedy, as well as the decision of President Johnson not to run for reelection in 1968, three of the most important national leaders who had championed the cause of the poor were eliminated. The vision to end poverty through government involvement, which was put forth in President Roosevelt's economic bill of rights and carried forward by President Johnson's War on Poverty, was on its way out and a resurgent conservative movement replaced it. Today, President George W. Bush's "compassionate conservatism" is the federal government's solution to poverty. However, this has not deterred progressives from developing solutions, from

William Julius Wilson's universal program of reform to Randall Robinson's proposal for reparations for the enslavement of African Americans.

The Reemergence of Conservatism

The resurrection of conservatism, with its enduring belief in rugged individualism and small government, began with the election and reelection of President Richard Nixon in 1968 and 1972, and was solidified with the election and reelection of President Ronald Reagan in 1980 and 1984. With the election of President George Bush in 1988, and his more conservative son, George W. Bush, in 1996 and 2000, conservative ideology has been the dominant thinking in the White House and in many parts of the country for the past thirty-eight years.

This change in public opinion has complex roots, but reflects core agreement from white, middle-class America with the explanations conservatives offer for the social problems of the day. Whether it be the rise in poverty rates, which increased from 11 percent (25 million) to 15 percent (35 million) from 1978 to 1983; the growing inequality between rich and poor that took place from 1980 to 1989 (the bottom 20 percent of the population suffered a 5 percent loss in real income while the wealthiest 1 percent experienced a 63 percent increase); the U.S. economy moving from "permanent economic growth" between 1960 and 1973 to a post-1973 "world of scarcity"; or myriad other social problems, the conservative response is the same: lower taxes, reduce government (i.e., decrease social programs to the poor), create a "color-blind" society (i.e., no additional assistance for people of color), and build a stronger military. As Reagan said, "government is not the solution to our problem; government is the problem." Josiah Quincy, S. Humphrey Gurteen, and Herbert Hoover would have been pleased.[1]

Reagan's Public Policy Changes: 1981–1989

In effect, conservatives have been dismantling the New Deal and War on Poverty programs. As discuss previously, Nixon attempted to eliminate the Community Action Programs (CAP). Soon afterward, Ford dismantled the Office of Economic Opportunity (OEO), which was the centerpiece of the War on Poverty. After a brief setback because of the Watergate scandal, the conservatives regained the White House in 1980 with Ronald Reagan, and targeted more New Deal and Great Society programs and ideas.

The Reagan administration was inspired by Charles Murray, who in his book *Losing Ground* had argued that the increase in poverty of the late 1970s and early 1980s was because expanding social welfare programs had discouraged work. The budget for Aid to Families with Dependent Children (AFDC) had increased from $2.5 billion in 1970 to $8.3 billion by 1984, and Social Security had increased from $30 billion to $181 billion during the same time period. Early in his presidency, Reagan wanted to cut Social Security. In comparison to public assistance, Social Security was costing much more money, but there was just too much support from the middle and upper-middle classes to change this social insurance program.[2]

The same cannot be said for public assistance. Murray, Reagan, and the conservative movement saw AFDC as detrimental to an individual's work ethic, and this program was politically vulnerable as it primarily supported poor women with children, two groups without much political power. Although many on the left did not like various aspects of AFDC, they recognized that this income transfer program was responsible for helping people escape poverty and were reluctant to cut it. In the early 1980s, the Reagan administration was adamant about reducing public assistance, and through legislation and regulation changes it forced 299,000 people to lose their AFDC benefits and another 408,000 people to lose their AFDC eligibility. These cuts decreased the percentage of all poor families receiving AFDC from 88 percent in 1979 to 63 percent by 1984. Between 1982 and 1985, AFDC and food stamps were cut by 13 percent, child nutrition by 28 percent, and unemployment insurance by 7 percent. AFDC payments, which had already been decreasing in the mid-1970s because of inflation, dropped 22 percent for a mother with three children (in 1984 dollars), from a high of $8,894 in 1972 to $7,486 in 1980 and to $6,955 by 1984, which was only a few hundred dollars higher than in 1960. One of the biggest reductions was in federal support for subsidized housing, which was cut 81 percent, from $32 billion to $6 billion, between 1981 and 1989.[3]

Two other policy changes are noteworthy. First, one of the early actions of the Reagan administration was to change the 1970 regulation that allowed the near poor (those who lived just above the poverty rate) to receive food stamps at a reduced price. This seemingly small change had large implications, as it was the only program that crossed the boundary between social insurance and public assistance to the poor. Throughout the 1970s, the working poor and welfare recipients were both eligible for food stamps, and this was in stark contrast to all other social welfare programs. This blurring of lines between the working poor and welfare recipients had the potential to destigmatize public assistance. With Reagan's regulation change, the wall between the deserving and undeserving poor was once again clearly defined. Second, Reagan abolished the

Community Services Administration (CSA), which housed the Community Action Agencies (CAAs), the remnant of the CAPs, the most radical of the War on Poverty programs. More than 1,000 CSA staff members were fired and the CAAs were weakened severely.[4]

Hunger and malnutrition had almost been eliminated by 1977 because of the large increase in funding for food stamps, school lunch programs, and nutritional supplements for women and young children between 1969 and 1974. However, with subsequent cuts in foods stamps and nutrition programs as well as AFDC regulation changes, malnutrition and hunger once again returned to the nation. In response, a group of prominent medical doctors, health experts, and academic and religious leaders formed the Physician Task Force on Hunger in America to examine the problem. In 1985, the task force reported that hunger was at "epidemic proportions," estimating that some 20 million Americans experience hunger at some point each month, and one-half million children experience malnutrition. The task force claimed that America was becoming a "soup kitchen society" and argued that this crisis was the result of federal government policies. They called on Congress to end hunger, which they believed could be accomplished in six months by strengthening the food stamp program and by strengthening meal programs for schoolchildren and seniors.[5]

Transformation of the Economy

Generally speaking, white middle-class America has accepted the conservative assertion that individuals are responsible for their economic success, that welfare is detrimental to the work ethic, and that a limited and decentralized government is the answer to our myriad social problems. But this perspective does not take into account the variety of structural changes that occurred to capitalism, the family structure, and urban spatial structure in the last half of the twentieth century. In the 1970s, a fundamental shift in capitalism began to occur. Markets became increasingly globalized as improved communication and transportation made it possible to manufacture and move products around the world. To lower labor costs and increase profits, multinational corporations took advantage of these improvements and moved their factories and plants to the developing world and nonunionized developing countries. The result of deindustrialization, with its "offshoring" of jobs, has been devastating to the working class, as their living-wage union jobs have nearly disappeared. For example, in the manufacturing sector, the overall percentage of jobs decreased from 26 percent of the economy in 1969 to 19 percent in 1984 and to 15 percent by 1998. In one five-year stretch from 1983 to 1988, almost ten million manufacturing jobs were lost to plant closings and layoffs. What replaced these living-wage jobs were low-skilled poverty-wage jobs. In the 1980s, one-half of all new jobs were unskilled jobs paying wages below the poverty line. These repositioned workers are "the new poor."[6]

To make matters worse, the minimum wage has declined in real value from what it was in the 1960s. In 1965, the national minimum wage in real dollars (adjusted for inflation) was $7.50 per hour. By 2005, the minimum wage had lost almost one-half its value. That means for the ten million workers earning the minimum wage, 70 percent of whom are adults, full-time employment does not lift many of them out of poverty, since it takes $9.25 an hour to earn more than the poverty level for a family of four.[7]

These policy and economic changes, as well as the economic recession in the early 1980s, created the current homeless crisis. In the 1970s, homelessness was not a major social issue, as there were 6.4 million low-income housing units for 7.3 million poor renters; by 1989, the stock of low-income units dropped to 5.5 million, but the number of low-income renters increased to 9.6 million. The resulting increase in homelessness to approximately 300,000, according to the Reagan administration—or 3 to 4 million as estimated by the National Coalition for the Homeless—brought dramatic attention to the nation's most poor. The general response by the government and nonprofits to this crisis has been to house people in temporary shelters. Douglas Timmer, Stanley Eitzen, and Kathryn Talley argue that this is the wrong approach and that what is needed is a massive infusion of money to build houses since, ultimately, the homeless problem is a housing problem.[8]

People have also begun to organize at the local level against the inequitable economy and the diminished minimum wage. Unions, faith communities, and community-based organizations have joined together to build a new movement for a living wage. According to Robert Pollin, a professor of economics and an advocate for the living wage, the basic principle of the movement is that people who work should not have to raise their families in poverty. Consequently, the initial goal of the living-wage movement has been to pass municipal ordinances that mandate that companies have service contracts with the city to pay a living wage to their workers. This issue has taken on new importance as cities, in order to cut costs, have privatized services.

In order to fight the unjust economy, unions have also attempted to change the overall rules governing labor in the United States. Clearly, the labor movement has been weakened over the past forty years because of mechanization and globalization, which have led to a significant drop in numbers of unionized workers from 35 percent of the overall workforce in the 1950s to 13 percent in

2004. Disagreement over how to reverse this drop in union membership has led two major unions—the Service Employees International Union (SEIU) and the International Brotherhood of Teamsters (which together represent three million workers)—to break off from the main labor federation, the AFL-CIO. These dissident unions, calling themselves the "Change to Win Coalition," plan to focus their resources on increasing union membership through recruitment and organizing rather than on political lobbying and central office staff.[9]

At the same time, some in the labor movement believe that the rules governing labor relations have to be changed if unions are to become strong again. Specifically, they want to repeal the 1947 Taft-Hartley Act, which dealt a crippling blow to labor unions when it outlawed secondary boycotts, allowed management to work against a union-organizing drive, and allowed the president to force strikers back to work for up to eighty days when the nation's "safety and health" were at stake, along with a series of other policies that fundamentally altered the balance of power in favor of business. Cesar Chavez noted that when the Taft-Hartley bill passed over the veto of President Truman, labor leaders called it the "slave labor act." Reflecting on how Taft-Hartley affected the United Farm Workers (UFW), Chavez stated: "it seems to me that the capitalists are at least twenty-five years ahead of most of the unions in this country. Coming from a background of not knowing anything about injunctions and Taft-Hartley and so forth, it seems to me very difficult to understand. For instance, if I am on strike here, how come my brother, who belongs to this other union, cannot do something in direct action to help me or vice versa.... For instance, why do we have so many laws to control the activities of unions?"[10]

The labor movement has also begun to work to change the rules that govern global capitalism. Labor unions have banded together with environmentalists and community organizations to support "fair trade" rather than free trade. When members of the World Trade Organization (WTO), the body that regulates global capitalism, met in Seattle in 1999 to discuss its expansion, they were greeted by approximately 50,000 protestors who paralyzed the city for several days. Protestors were upset at a system whereby the benefits of global economic growth have gone to the rich countries over the poor and to the U.S. upper class over the working class. Protestors were also frustrated at the antidemocratic nature of the WTO, since the judicial body is appointed and not elected, and upset that the WTO can enforce its policies and decisions against the will of individual nation-states (e.g., regarding environmental regulations). At the protest, Brian McWilliams of the International Longshore and Warehouse Union (ILWU) called for a world trade policy that offered just treatment for all workers and a form of capitalism in which the benefits are shared equally.[11]

Transformation of U.S. Cities

Over the past fifty years U.S. cities have also been transformed. Since the late nineteenth century, cities have been composed of people of various European ethnic heritages, who might not have originally been seen as white when they arrived (e.g., Irish and Italians) but became so as the second and third generations became Americanized. Today, metropolitan areas have been transformed, as Cornel West says, into chocolate cities and vanilla suburbs. From 1945 to 1960, 33 percent of the southern black population moved, many to northern cities, as the mechanization of agriculture greatly reduced the need for farm labor. During the 1970s, African Americans as well as Latinos continued moving to urban areas. For example, from 1970 to 1980, 102,000 African Americans moved to Detroit, and 176,000 African Americans and 204,000 Latinos moved to New York. At the same time, there was a mass exodus of whites to the suburbs, with 418,000 whites leaving Detroit and 1.4 million whites exiting New York.[12]

The movement of Latinos to U.S. cities was part of a larger movement of people because of changes in immigration policy. In 1965, Congress passed a law abolishing the 1924 quota system that had favored northern European immigrants. This liberalization of U.S. immigration policy led to an increase in people entering from Latin America, Asia, and Africa as people fled war and poverty. As a result, immigration jumped from 1 million during 1951 to 1960 to 7.3 million during 1981 to 1990, with 47 percent coming from Latin America and 37 percent from Asia. There has also been an increase in undocumented immigrants, with an estimated 11 million people without documents living in the United States in 2006.[13]

The mass movement of whites to the suburbs coincided with changes in the demography of jobs. As manufacturing companies outsourced jobs to other countries for cheap labor, and as the United States moved toward a high-tech and service economy (e.g., real estate, finance, and insurance), the managerial class no longer needed to work near the plant and their jobs were moved closer to the "business parks" near the suburbs. Although the desire for more living space and access to jobs drove this "white flight," racism was also a major factor. By the late twentieth century, 86 percent of U.S. suburbs were less than 1 percent black. A side effect of this exodus has been a sharp reduction of the cities' tax base.[14]

These factors have made it difficult for the urban working class and poor—particularly African Americans—to access the available new jobs. William Julius Wilson's research demonstrates that many African Americans have become spatially isolated in urban areas where jobs have disappeared. Blacks who have been left behind by the loss of jobs and the resulting deterioration of the community (e.g., increased crime, divorce, welfare, and drug addiction) have found themselves part of a ghetto underclass that is "truly disadvantaged." For example, Wilson's research shows that the labor-force participation rate of white men dropped from 82 percent in 1940 to 76 percent in 1980, but the black male labor-force participation rate fell from 84 percent to 67 percent. At the same time, labor-force participation for white men twenty-four and under increased, but decreased for young black men of the same age. More recently, research conducted in New York City found that only 52 percent of African American men age sixteen through sixty-four were employed between 2000 and 2003.[15]

In order to solve the problem of joblessness, Wilson argues for a universal program that would provide the unemployed with jobs. This public and private job creation program would be open to all Americans, but its impact, of course, would most greatly benefit the truly disadvantaged. In the short term, the focus of the universal program would be on temporary WPA-like public works projects, but in the long term it would be on training programs for young adults and retraining programs that would help them adapt to private-sector labor needs. At the macro level, Wilson advocates an economic policy that promotes a tight labor market and economic growth. At the regional level, Wilson proposes the development of privately subsidized carpool and vanpool networks to help the urban poor to get to suburban jobs, as well as relocation assistance in order to move there. Although Wilson agrees that some race-based programs, such as affirmative action, are necessary, he believes that a race-neutral strategy that generates a tight labor market will not only be the most effective at reducing poverty among the urban poor but is also the most politically viable solution.[16]

As Wilson argued for universal job creation programs, some in the 1990s began promoting the idea of reparations to African Americans for the damage that has been done to the black community. The heritage of 246 years of enslavement, 100 years of Jim Crow, and current racial discrimination has made Martin Luther King, Jr.'s "curious formula" applicable today. The poverty rate for African Americans is 24 percent compared to 9 percent for whites; the black child poverty rate is 34 percent compared to 12 percent for whites; the black unemployment rate is 10 percent compared to 5 percent among whites; and the black infant mortality rate is 14 percent compared to 7 percent for whites.

In order to fundamentally change the "curious formula," Randall Robinson and others have demanded that the U.S. government pay reparations. Robinson states, "No nation can enslave a race of people for hundreds of years, set them free bedraggled and penniless, pit them, without assistance in a hostile environment, against privileged victimizers, and then reasonably expect the gap between the heirs of the two groups to narrow."[17]

Robinson's reparation plan does not mention a specific amount of compensation, as he feels that it is first necessary to conduct a comprehensive assessment to determine the cost to repair the damage to black society. However, he does suggest that the money for reparations be put in a trust fund to supplement K–12 offerings in advanced math, sciences, English, and foreign languages; develop residential K–12 schools for black children living in unhealthy families or neighborhoods; and provide free college tuition for any academically qualified student. Reparations might also fund economic empowerment as well as the civil rights advocacy work necessary to combat institutional racism.[18]

Transformation of Family Structure

In addition to large-scale changes in public policy and the economy, the American family structure has been fundamentally altered. In 1950, 60 percent of all U.S. households fit the nuclear family mold, with husband as breadwinner, wife as stay-at-home mom, and kids. At the beginning of the twenty-first century, the nuclear family is no longer the norm, with less than 10 percent of households fitting this pattern. At the same time, households headed by women increased from 10 percent of all families in 1960 to 18 percent in 2003. There are several reasons for this change in family structure. First, as public opinion moved away from the idea that divorce was a "moral violation," and divorce laws were loosened, the divorce rate increased. From 1950 to 2000, the percentage of people divorced at age twenty-five to thirty-four increased from 2 to 6 percent for men and 3 to 9 percent for women, and for people aged thirty-five to fifty-nine, the percentage of people divorced increased from 3 to 13 percent for men and 3 to 16 percent for women. Another way to report the data is to say that 50 percent of all marriages today end in divorce, as there were 7.5 marriages per 1,000 and 3.8 divorces per 1,000 in 2003.[19]

The change in family structure has also been affected by the transformation of the economy. As manufacturing jobs, many of which were dominated by men, were outsourced, families experienced downward mobility. This economic dislocation has led to stress, marital tension, and divorce. An additional strain on marriages has been the change in women's work roles. As men experienced unemployment and underemployment, women entered the job market and obtained employment in the expanding service and high-tech fields. Service and high-tech fields have "dual escalators," with one group moving up (with high-paying managerial jobs) and one going down (with low-paying and non-unionized jobs). Unfortunately, many women were on the escalator going down. Nonetheless, these women were no longer full-time homemakers, and new roles in the family had to be negotiated. The couples unable to negotiate these new roles have experienced increased marital tension and divorce.[20]

The increase in divorce rates has affected all social classes, but working-class and poor women have been hit extremely hard. In 2003, the poverty rate for families headed by women with children under eighteen years of age was 36 percent, in comparison with 7 percent for married couples. Additionally, the number of families headed by women as a percentage of all poor families nearly doubled, from 24 percent in 1960 to 51 percent by 2003. This large increase in the number of families headed by women can be explained by the doubling of the divorce rate, the fact that children generally live with mothers after divorce, the gender gap in income, and the conservative changes in public assistance. As a result of these changes—which have been labeled the "feminization of poverty"—18 percent of all children, or 13 million, live in poverty today. When analyzed by race, the children living in poverty are 33 percent African American, 29 percent Latino, 10 percent Asian, and 9 percent white. The number of children living in poverty is down from 27 percent in 1960 (pre–Great Society), but up from 14 percent in 1969. The largest increases in child poverty were from 16 to 22 percent between 1979 and 1983 (the end of the Carter era and beginning of the Reagan era) and from 19 percent to 23 percent between 1989 and 1993 (the first Bush era).[21]

To deal with the increasing numbers of poor children, the Children's Defense Fund (CDF), which was founded by civil rights activist Marian Wright Edelman, has called for the elimination of child poverty by 2010. Reminiscent of the child-saving movement and other earlier liberal and progressive ideas, CDF demands that all children and their parents have health insurance, that all children have decent and affordable housing, and that all children have enough to eat through expanded food programs. CDF also calls for full funding of Head Start and new investments in quality childcare and universal preschool.

In counterpoint to CDF's liberal agenda, President George W. Bush initiated his agenda of "compassionate conservatism" after his election victory in 2000. At the core of this agenda is Bush's faith-based program, which in many ways is a return to the moral language of the early nineteenth century. Social problems are generally seen as individual "problems of the heart" and faith in God is a major part of the solution. Compassionate conservatism also harkens back to the late nineteenth century when private philanthropy at the local level was seen as the most effective approach to poverty. Stating that "traditional social programs are often too bureaucratic, inflexible, and impersonal to meet the acute and complex needs of the poor," Bush has called for a partnership between the federal government and faith-based organizations to solve poverty at the community level. Bush highlights his $300 million pilot program to promote "healthy marriages" as a way to deal with the rise in divorce rate and the feminization of poverty. The Bush administration proposes to offer welfare recipients premarital counseling for nonmarried couples and skills training for married couples. Bush argues that if a couple is married, the chances of the family living in poverty will be reduced.[22]

The End of Welfare and Social Security as We Know It?

With the ascendancy of conservatism in the late twentieth century, two of the New Deal's social welfare programs—AFDC and Social Security—have been under attack. In the 1992 presidential election, Bill Clinton pledged to "end welfare as we know it." Four years later, President Clinton followed through on his word and signed into law the Personal Responsibility and Work Opportunity Act. The act, which was passed primarily with the support of conservative congressmembers, ended the entitlement to aid for all poor families with children. The major components of the act were: (a) needy families are restricted to a lifetime maximum of five years' worth of aid, and states were able to lower this maximum; (b) welfare recipients are required to work within two years of receiving cash assistance or they will be cut off; (c) a $54.5 billion cut in federal programs for the poor over six years, including $24 billion from food stamps, and $3 billion from child nutrition; and (d) a $16.4 billion annual cap on federal money going to states.[23]

Although poverty reduction was not part of President Clinton's rhetoric, with the assistance of First Lady Hillary Clinton he did attempt to pass a universal health insurance program in 1993 that would have been extremely beneficial to the poor. Clinton also promoted and signed a 1993 law that significantly increased the Earned Income Tax Credit (EITC), a 1975 federal tax relief program designed to assist hard-pressed working families. However, as poverty reduction was not a Clinton priority, the poor benefited only slightly throughout one of the greatest economic expansions in U.S. history. Only at the end of the seven-year economic boom did the poverty rate begin to fall as full employment was almost reached, and people who were seen as unemployable just a few years before were now seen as employable. This modest reduction in poverty was from

35.6 million people (or 13 percent of the population) in 1997 to 31.6 million people (11 percent) in 2000.[24]

After President George W. Bush's reelection in 2004, his administration set out to change the other major New Deal program. Social Security has been one of America's most successful poverty reduction plans, as it was instrumental in reducing poverty for seniors from 35 percent in 1959 to 10 percent in 2003. The strength of this insurance program has been that (a) it is government protected; (b) it distributes risk across society; (c) it guarantees the amount of benefits; (d) it guarantees growth over time, with indexed increases; (e) it guarantees disability payments and death benefits to spouses and children; and (f) it guarantees retirement benefits no matter how long a person lives. Bush's plan would allow all workers to put 4 percent of their payroll tax into a personal retirement account, radically altering Social Security since none of the current benefits are included in his privatization plan. Bush feels that this change is necessary to financially fix the Social Security program.[25]

This proposed change to Social Security is part of Bush's larger vision of an "ownership society." In describing its benefits, Bush states, "if you own something, you have a vital stake in the future of our country. The more ownership there is in America, the more vitality there is in America, and the more people have a vital stake in the future of this country." However, Michael Sherraden and other contemporary egalitarian thinkers have been exploring since the early 1990s how to take this idea of individual property stakeholding and use it as a poverty reduction strategy. Several recent studies indicate that 30 percent of American adults possess zero or negative net financial assets. These asset-poor people lack savings, stocks, bonds, and retirement funds, all of which increase in value over time. In order to change this unequal distribution, Sherraden has called on the United States to develop a new social welfare model based on asset building. The basic idea is to have the government match an individual's contribution to personal savings plans (e.g., education and homeownership) in order to build wealth. Although Sherraden still believes in Social Security and an income-based welfare when necessary, he wants to see more emphasis put on the assets-based approach. He argues that this strategy is more effective in reducing poverty and is more in line with America's capitalist tradition of accumulation and economic self-sufficiency.[26]

Recently, some supporters of an assets-based model have directly challenged Bush's notion of an ownership society. They claim that instead of a privatized ownership society in which individuals rely more on themselves to build assets and less on the government, the goal should be to build a progressive ownership society that looks to government to help expand assets. These assets would include (a) human capital assets (free K–12 education, access to college, and retraining and skills programs); (b) income-related assets (adequate pay, collective bargaining, access to employment, ability to advance, and unemployment insurance); and (c) financial assets (homeownership, saving accounts, individual retirement accounts, and death, disability, and retirement protection under Social Security).

This idea for an egalitarian ownership society is in many ways groundbreaking. Sherraden and others have taken an idea normally associated with conservatism—wealth creation through accumulation and investment—and used it to rethink social welfare policy for progressive ends. This innovation has its roots in the work of other American thinkers who advocated providing people with assets so they could achieve social mobility, from Thomas Paine's idea for a capital fund to provide grants to ensure a good start in life, to the Homestead Act, which gave land to white Americans; and from the GI Bill, which provides financial assistance to veterans for college and a home, to the home mortgage deduction, which allows homeowners to receive a significant tax break by subtracting mortgage interest payments from total taxable income.[27]

The First Americans

We end the book where we started, with a discussion of the First Americans. On the positive side, the population of Native Americans increased tenfold in the twentieth century, up from a nadir of 250,000 in 1900 to 2.5 million by 2000. This increase in the American Indian population bodes well for the future. Negatively, Native Americans are at or near the bottom on all economic, social, and health indicators. Currently, 23 percent of American Indians live in poverty, with the rate climbing to 40 percent on the reservation, where 50 percent of Indians live. The unemployment rate is 12 percent for Native Americans, and on reservations it is 14 percent. Housing is a major problem, with 90,000 Indian families homeless or living with another family. The percentage of high school dropouts (ages sixteen to nineteen) is 16 percent. Since all of these Native American economic and social indicators are twice the rate or more than that of whites, it appears King's "curious formula" also applies to Native Americans as well. Clearly, these statistics are a direct result of the U.S. government's policies of manifest destiny and confiscation of Indian land, lack of commitment to its treaty obligations, attempted destruction of Indian cultural identity through assimilation, educational practices that have historically stigmatized traditional life, and overall lack of resource investment.[28]

The solution to Indian poverty often highlighted in the media is the development of casinos. Since most reservation land is barren and isolated, Native Americans have had to develop alternative development strategies to survive, and casinos provide one of these approaches. However, an approach that receives almost no attention from the media but is extremely important to the future of the indigenous people is the "traditionalist" perspective, which attempts to apply the time-honored ways of the ancestors to today's issues. Two of these traditionalists are Mary and Carrie Dann, Western Shoshone (Newe) elders who have for forty years led the resistance to the U.S. government's attempt to purchase 24 million acres (two-thirds of Nevada and parts of California, Utah, and Wyoming), which was never legally ceded. The government has offered a onetime payment of $20,000 to each of the 6,000 Western Shoshone, using the 1872 rate of 15 cents an acre to calculate the settlement. The Dann sisters and the Western Shoshone leadership have refused the money, arguing that they want a land base to practice traditional cultural and spiritual practices, and to be economically self-sustaining. Describing the struggle, Carrie Dann states, "This has always been about the land, our rights to continue to use and occupy our lands for the benefit of our families and the future generations." Not surprisingly, the cultural and spiritual practices of the Western Shoshone are egalitarian.[29]

Eliminating Hunger in America (1985)

Physician Task Force on Hunger in America

The Physician Task Force report awoke the nation to the once-defeated problem of hunger.

As a body of doctors and health care professionals, we believe it is time to end hunger in America.

It is our judgment that hunger and related ill-health have no place in a democratic society, especially one with the resources of the United States.

This nation has the resources and ability to end hunger. We have heard no one deny that this is true. America is not a poverty-stricken Third World nation caught between the pincers of a poor economy and inadequate food supply. To the contrary, we produce enough food to feed our people probably several times over. Our nation's warehouses bulge with food, so much food that each year thousands of tons are wasted or destroyed. Clearly lack of food is not the cause of hunger in America.

Neither do we lack the financial resources to end hunger in this land. Ours is perhaps the strongest economy in the world. We cannot maintain that we lack the resources to end hunger when numerous other industrialized nations have done so. That is illogical. In fact, by increasing annual federal food programs just by the amount we spend on two CVN Nuclear Attack Carriers, we could probably eliminate hunger in the nation. No, lack of money is not the cause of hunger in America.

Neither do we have hunger because we don't know how to end it. Through very recent experience, we are certain that we can end hunger if we wish to do so. Hunger and malnutrition were serious problems in this country in 1968. Then as today, national organizations, church groups, and universities investigated and found hunger. Government agencies, as today, found hunger. And as today, doctors went into regions of the country and reported that it was a widespread and serious problem.

The nation responded to that problem. In the decade between 1970 and 1980 we extended the food stamp program from the 2 million poor Americans which it covered at the time to some 20 million people. While this did not cover all Americans living in poverty, other nutrition programs provided assistance. We expanded the free school lunch and breakfast programs. We established elderly feeding programs (congregate meal sites and Meals-on-Wheels for shut-ins) to insure that our senior citizens did not go hungry. And we established the Women, Infants, and Children (WIC) program to insure adequate nourishment for low-income pregnant women and their infants.

These programs were established in response to hunger among American people, and they worked. Teams of doctors in 1977 retraced the routes they had covered the previous decade when they found serious hunger and malnutrition. Summarizing their findings, the medical teams stated:

> Our first and overwhelming impression is that there are far fewer grossly mal-nourished people in this country today than there were ten years ago ... many poor people now have food and look better off. This does not appear to be due to an overall improvement in living standards. In fact, the facts of life for Americans living in poverty remain as dark or darker than they were ten years ago.
>
> But in the area of food there is a difference. The food stamp program, the nutritional component of Head Start, school lunch and breakfast programs, and to a lesser extent the Women, Infants, and Children (WIC) program have made the difference.

In a few years this nation basically eliminated hunger as a problem. The success was relatively swift and not difficult to see. So, clearly, we do not lack the experience or the knowhow to end hunger in America. We have enough food to end hunger in this land. We have enough wealth to end hunger. And we have recent experience upon which to rely. All that remains is the political will.

Immediate Steps to End Hunger

Today we have a public health crisis which threatens a significant segment of our population. We must respond to it as we would any other problem of epidemic proportions.

We would not permit other health crises to become so widespread before acting. Yet hunger afflicts more of our citizens than does AIDS or Legionnaires Disease. In fact it constitutes one of the more serious problems imperiling the health and well-being of our people today.

But while hunger is a health epidemic, it cannot be ended by those in the medical profession. Like most public health problems it must be addressed in the political and public policy arena. In short, our political leaders must be responsible for ending hunger. The essence of political leadership is to lead—to respond to problems. That, in part, is why we have government. Today, we need leadership from our political leaders. It is time to end the contrived befuddlement of some who wring their hands wondering what to do about hunger.

It is time to stop responding to hunger by cutting children's school lunches. It is time to show more compassion for hungry families than by reducing their food stamps even as they become poorer. And it is time to set aside compassionate platitudes and political rhetoric about how loving a people we are.

Let us feed the hungry of our nation.

We call upon Republicans and Democrats in the United States Congress to take immediate action to feed the hungry.

We ask that the leadership of the House and Senate, on a bipartisan basis, announce that it will prepare an emergency legislative package to respond to the hunger crisis. The components of the plan should include:

• *Strengthening the food stamp program*

Increase food stamp benefits to American families and individuals by a minimum of 25 percent, to the level of the USDA low-cost food plan.

Remove restrictive food stamp measures which eliminated the "new poor" and working poor from the program; families with gross incomes of up to 150 percent of poverty, but whose disposable income is below poverty, should be assisted.

Alter asset restrictions so families experiencing temporary economic hardship are not driven further into poverty as a condition for getting food stamps.

Alter restrictive deductions such as those for shelter, child care, and residency requirements in the food stamp program.

Take immediate legislative action (similar to that enacted recently for Social Security Disability Insurance) to terminate administrative policies which harass and otherwise prevent food stamp assistance.

* *Strengthening school and other meals programs for children*

Restore eligibility for free and reduced-price meals for children recently removed from the programs.

Increase the federal subsidy for free and reduced-price meals to enable more children from families living on the economic margins to participate in the program.

Restore the child care, milk, and summer feeding programs for children whose family incomes previously permitted them to participate.

* *Utilizing the WIC and Medicaid programs more fully to protect high-risk children*

Expand the WIC (Women, Infants, and Children Supplemental Feeding Program) to cover all currently eligible mothers who wish to participate.

Extend Medicaid benefits to all pregnant women and children under 18 living below the federal poverty level, to insure better health care and birth outcomes.

* *Expanding elderly meals programs to be certain that all low-income elderly have access to congregate meals or the Meals-on-Wheels program*
* *Protecting families by strengthening income support programs*

Expand unemployment benefits for unemployed families left without work so that the two-thirds of the unemployed now with no benefits are covered by the program.

Expand AFDC assistance by federal legislation to bring children above the poverty level; this should include coverage for the unborn child to insure adequate nutrition, and should include mandatory coverage in all states for fathers in the home so that federal and state policy no longer forces families to break apart to become eligible for help.

Congress should pass legislation to create a permanent and independent body to monitor the nutritional status of the population.

Our nation should have on-going access to current data on the nutritional status of its people, particularly high-risk populations such as children, pregnant women, and the elderly. This proposal was made by the 1969 White House Conference on Food, Nutrition, and Health convened by President Nixon. It should be established without further delay.

We ask that appropriate Congressional committees direct responsible administrative agencies to report on a quarterly basis progress made in eliminating hunger, until such time as it has been ended in America.

We believe that, based on past experience and the fact that we have the programmatic vehicles still in place, our nation can eliminate hunger within six months. Such a time frame, however, will require continuing oversight by appropriate Congressional committees to be certain that administrative departments and agencies are carrying out the will of the Congress.

Longer-Term Steps to Prevent the Return of Hunger

If the Congress agrees to undertake the above plan of action, it will end the present hunger crisis. But the proposed plan alone may be insufficient to end poverty in America.

The fact that hunger, once nearly ended in the nation, returned as such a serious problem clearly points to the need to undertake more serious and far-reaching policies to eliminate the poverty which underlies hunger. We would do well to address this more fundamental problem.

We ask the United States Congress to establish a Bipartisan Study Commission to recommend legislative changes to protect all our citizens from the ravages of poverty and its attendant ills in the future.

As a body of physicians and other health professionals, we believe it is unwise to permit hunger and malnutrition to exist in this nation. We believe not only that these problems must be eradicated, but that our country can and should address the underlying poverty which victimizes so many of our citizens.

We would not tell sick patients that they might improve without medical treatment if we have the means to treat them and limit their present pain and discomfort. Neither should our political leaders hope that hungry Americans will one day be less hungry when our nation now has the means to respond to their suffering and its underlying cause.

Making Homelessness Go Away: Politics and Policy (1994)

Douglas A. Timmer, D. Stanley Eitzen, and Kathryn D. Talley

Timmer, Eitzen, and Talley are leading authorities on homelessness, poverty, and inequality in America, and they have authored numerous books on these topics.

Urban Housing Crisis

Low-income and affordable housing is dwindling, particularly in U.S. cities. The urban housing market has been transformed by gentrification, investments in middle-class and luxury housing, the destruction of SROs (single-room occupancy hotels), slumlording, and rising rents. The shrinking supply of low-income and affordable housing has been exacerbated by failed federal housing policies, including urban renewal and rollbacks in public housing. Subsidizing the private sector to provide low-income housing has proven to be inefficient, ineffective, and costly. Blacks and other racial minorities in our cities have suffered disproportionately from these negative housing trends.

Policy Recommendations

What can be done to counter these trends in the urban housing market? How can government assist, rather than hinder, its citizens' search for affordable housing? If subsidies to private developers do not work, what will?

Rent control is not the answer. There is no consistent evidence that cities with or without rent control develop more affordable or low-income housing or that average rental costs decline. At least potentially, strong rent control does preserve the existent stock of affordable housing and should be supported. However, in many cities with weak ordinances, there are numerous schemes by which rent control is circumvented. As Gilderbloom and Appelbaum write in *Rethinking Rental Housing,* "Rent control has had a more political than economic impact."

Voucher programs are not the answer. Vouchers, intended to fill the gap between what a poor family can afford and the cost of housing in the private market, fall into the same trap as subsidy programs in general—they try to solve a problem caused by the market with a market-based solution. The Reagan administration allocated 1 million housing vouchers for 1988, substituting this program for the scandal-ridden HUD developer loan programs of the early and mid-1980s. The need for vouchers in that year is estimated at minimally six times the 1 million vouchers distributed. Even if vouchers were given to all who need them, however, the program still would not work, as it fails to expand the supply of affordable housing. Vacancy rates for this housing are so low in many cities that one-half or more of all voucher holders would not be able to use their certificates. Using Dreier and Atlas's analogy, "It is similar to giving out food stamps when the supermarket shelves are empty." The only way voucher programs can work is if the grants are so generous that certificate holders compete for middle-class or upper-middle-class housing. This size voucher is certainly not what its advocates intend, and it is not politically feasible in the United States.

Selling off public housing to tenants is not the answer. Even if these properties were sold for $1, this response is unworkable. Given the extremely low household income of persons currently residing in public housing without significant subsidies, the poor cannot afford the utility costs, maintenance and taxes associated with home ownership. And once again, this response does nothing to increase the stock of affordable housing.

So what is the answer? The answer is a massive infusion of federal funds into low-income and affordable housing, part of a "Marshall Plan" to rebuild American cities. This initiative would include sums for the construction of new public housing, maintenance and rehabilitation of existing public housing, and encouragement of not-for-profit, community-based housing production, ownership, and management.

Nonprofit organizations build new or renovate existing housing, rent out the units, and manage the development. Without the necessity of making a profit, rents can be set at considerably lower levels than in the private sector. Publicly funded nonprofit housing banks could provide construction or rehabilitation loans to the nonprofit organizations at very low rates of interest, further reducing the costs of building and maintaining these developments. This solution to the housing crisis increases the supply of units and keeps them permanently affordable. Housing is removed from the private market, remaining in the control of local communities.

This is not a new idea. Nonprofit developers in the United States, including groups representing churches, unions, and community development corporations, have increased tenfold over the past decade, numbering about 2,000 today. Their emergence coincides with the federal government's withdrawal of support and funding for affordable housing through the 1980s. Most of the affordable housing constructed or rehabilitated through that period and into the present results from the efforts of these nonprofit groups.

In addition to the nonprofits in our own country, we can look to Canada for examples of innovative, small-scale, low-income housing built, restored, or rehabilitated by nonprofit groups. In short, both from our own and from other societies' experience, we know how to build and run affordable housing. The issue now: Are we willing to fund it? Nonprofits have been able to scrape together necessary funds on a local level, but the housing needs of this country are far beyond their limited scope.

Only the federal government has the power and resources to forcefully confront the nation's massive housing needs, and it must be dedicated to that end. Sorely needed is a federal housing initiative, which would funnel significant sums of money into nonprofit organizations for the express purpose of providing low-income and affordable housing. This program must also address new construction and maintenance and rehabilitation of current public housing stock. Legislation outlining such a comprehensive housing program has been drafted by Congressman Ron Dellums of California. The passage of this or similar legislation, with an estimated price tag of more than $50 billion, would signal a genuine commitment to the housing needs of all American citizens.

The Shelterization Response

The overriding societal response to the problem of homelessness has been the provision of emergency shelters and shelter services, including job training, health care, education, and substance abuse counseling. These programs have been funded primarily through the Stewart B. McKinney Homeless Assistance Act, passed by Congress in 1987. Once shelters and their services are assumed to be the answer to homelessness, social service professionals operating these institutions are defined as the experts who know best how to proceed. But do they? Are shelters and their services necessary stopgaps (if not perfect, at least benign) or debilitating, dependency-creating institutions? We often ask what shelters do *for* the homeless; perhaps we should ask, what do shelters do *to* the homeless?

Shelterization as a solution to homelessness is at best a temporary necessity—emergency food and a bed when there is no other alternative. At its worst, the shelter contributes to the further victimization of the homeless by labeling these persons as deviants. Shelters may in fact harm those they intend to serve....

The Politics of Compassion

Hoch and Slayton offer another approach from which to view the harmful effects of the shelterization response. They point out how in the mid-1980s social service providers succeeded in formulating the language of the homeless debate so as to emphasize the physical and social vulnerabilities of homeless persons rather than the right of all citizens to housing. Homelessness was thus defined as a social problem requiring professional caregivers and their skills. A population of "clients" whose "needs" warranted professional intervention was created. This ideological position portrayed and treated the homeless as passive, needy victims.

The Rejection of Shelterization by the Homeless

The "politics of compassion" results in the provision of shelters and shelter services. But these "refuges" have been rejected by the homeless themselves, who resent the numerous rules and regulations common to the shelter experience. The overt control exerted over every aspect of life, including the scheduling of waking, sleeping, eating, and showering, restrictions on personal habits, and demands to be enrolled in required programs to continue to receive shelter, is compared by many shelter residents to that of correctional facilities. Perceiving shelters as places lacking in autonomy and privacy, most homeless persons avoid them. They use shelter facilities only when absolutely necessary, as when winter cold becomes life-threatening.

The rejection of the shelter must be placed in historical context. As Hoch and Slayton's work highlights, the economically marginal in America's cities have not always had such limited choices. Earlier in this century, a variety of housing options, from the SRO, to the lodging house, to the working-class cage hotel, to the "flop" hotel, gave the poorest of the poor housing alternatives. Even though this housing may have been physically deteriorated, it provided residents what they most cherished: personal freedom and a lock on the door.

Suspicion and resentment of the shelter and its services are evident in reports of a growing "shelter rebellion" among homeless people. In New York, for example, homeless persons set up a tent city in Tompkins Square rather than enter the city's shelter system. Similar protests have occurred in Los Angeles, where a short-lived tent city was constructed in 1984, and Chicago, where homeless squatters broke into vacant Chicago Housing Authority units in 1988. This rejection of shelters is also evident in occupancy rates. In Chicago, for example, the average shelter occupancy rate in 1987 hovered around 84 percent, and the 4,250 available beds were filled to capacity less than half the time. These vacancies exist even as the City of Chicago Department of Human Services estimates the number of homeless at 40,000 to 49,000 over a year's time.

Those homeless persons who do enter shelters recognize them as dismal places of last resort, not welcomed "treatment centers." In the words of Kitty, a shelter resident in Tampa, "It's like a correctional institution and I'm not a criminal.... I haven't done anything wrong." Other first-person accounts speak of the hope of "escaping the shelters" and existing "on the verge of madness, so hungry for a little privacy and peace that I was afraid I'd start screaming in my sleep." "No one should have to live like that." Interviewing homeless persons in Chicago, researchers from the National Opinion Research Center found that most who had used shelters agreed that they offered a clean and decent place to sleep, but almost half complained about a lack of security and privacy and resented the restrictions on their personal freedom. Shelters are perceived by the homeless not only as demoralizing but also as dangerous. Fear, both of losing one's meager possessions and suffering personal injury, is often cited by those who have experienced shelter life.

Increasing numbers of homeless people are organizing, speaking out for themselves and against shelterization. One group, the National Union for the Homeless, consists of fourteen local chapters representing 30,000 homeless individuals. This organization's underlying principle, and the basis for its collective protest, is that citizens have a right to housing. In the words of Alicia Christian, a union member, "Homeless people are saying they don't want any more stopgaps. They don't want shelters, they want houses. They don't want welfare, they want jobs. That's a profound threat to people who say they want to enable but really want to control." Christian's statement also indicates a class difference between the homeless and their "advocates." Many homeless advocacy groups are dominated by middle-class and upper-middle-class persons, including professional service providers and shelter operators. These professionals and the homeless they "serve" have quite distinct, if not opposing, agendas and ideologies. This supports McKnight's critique of social service caregivers as creating dependency rather than self-sufficiency and gives credence to the National Union for the Homeless in its claim that the homeless must speak for themselves....

Living Wage, Live Action (1998)

Robert Pollin

Robert Pollin is a professor of economics at the University of Massachusetts, and is coauthor, along with Stephanie Luce, of The Living Wage: Building a Fair Economy.

This past summer, security workers at LAX airport in Los Angeles began their first-ever union organizing drive. They were motivated, labor activists say, by the city's foot-dragging in implementing a living-wage ordinance that had passed the previous year and guaranteed a minimum of $7.25 an hour (rising with inflation every July 1), plus health benefits and twelve paid days off. Workers unaccustomed to challenging income and power inequities suddenly felt emboldened by the experience of that earlier drive, which, like similar efforts taking off elsewhere in the country, began with the simple premise that no one who works for a living should have to struggle in poverty.

As of 1997, 7.3 million American families were officially poor, and in 66 percent of them at least one person had a job. At the current minimum wage of $5.15 an hour, someone who works full time for fifty weeks earns only $10,300 a year—below the national poverty threshold for a family of two. A "traditional" family of four with one wage-earner falls nearly 40 percent below the line. True, this family is eligible to receive an earned-income tax credit, food stamps and Medicaid, but the need for such programs to support a full-time worker's household only underscores the fact that $5.15 an hour is not close to being a living wage.

In opposition to this state of affairs the living-wage movement was initiated four years ago by unions, community groups and religious organizations. It has succeeded in passing living-wage ordinances—higher minimum-wage standards for workers affected by the measures—in seventeen cities. Now organizing campaigns are pressing forward in twenty-four other municipalities.

There are a number of lessons from these campaigns, not least that even in an expansion, real wages will not rise without strong, creative organizing efforts. The real value of the minimum wage is 30 percent below what it was in 1968, even though the economy is 50 percent more productive than it was thirty years ago, and even after the seven-year "Clinton boom." Now it looks as if we're coming to the end of that boom. Given the September 22 defeat of Senator Kennedy's bill to raise the minimum wage by a dollar over two years, it's clear that, in a weakening economy, workers can win higher wages and better conditions only if they fight effectively.

The living-wage movement has been strategically astute since its inception. It has emerged primarily at the level of municipal politics because organizers correctly assessed that their efforts have a greater chance of success when they attempt to change municipal laws rather than those of states or the federal government, where business has a great capacity to use its money and lobbying clout. Various local campaigns are gaining strength through building national connections. This past May, the first National Living Wage Campaign Training Conference, sponsored by labor groups and ACORN, drew organizers from thirty-four cities to discuss strategy and consider ways to coordinate their work. But a local focus is still central to building grassroots support.

Organizing at the municipal level is also the most effective tactic for fighting the trend toward outsourcing—contracting out government services to private firms. Because private contractors pay lower wages and offer fewer benefits, outsourcing saves cities money by driving down the living standards of workers. In Chicago the outsourcing of public sector jobs from 1989 to 1995 meant income losses of between 25 and 49 percent for watchmen, elevator operators, cashiers, parking attendants, security guards and custodians whose jobs were privatized. Forcing private firms with city contracts to pay living wages at least weakens the incentive for cities to achieve budget cuts on the backs of their workers....

Living-wage laws targeting city contractors will, however, affect only a small proportion of low-wage workers. Some organizers have thus taken a more ambitious approach, pushing for laws that would apply to all workers in a municipality, regardless of who their employer is, just as national or statewide minimum-wage laws apply to virtually all workers within a geographic area. Recently, organizers in Denver and Houston advanced these more ambitious proposals but were soundly defeated at the polls. At least in part, they lost because of their ambitious scope, which invited an even more determined opposition. So how are living-wage organizers and supporters to assess the range of possibilities before them? And how are they to answer their critics?

Will Living-Wage Laws Backfire?

Opponents of *minimum-wage* laws—of which the municipal living-wage ordinances are one variant—have long argued that such laws actually hurt their intended beneficiaries, pricing unskilled workers out of the job market and so causing unemployment among the poor. Against municipal living-wage laws in particular, opponents make two other arguments: that these will place severe strains on the already overstretched budgets of cities, perhaps forcing painful cuts in other benefits to low-income families; and that they will discourage firms from locating in municipalities, thus increasing unemployment and poverty in these areas.

Blustering politicians are usually the most visible mouthpieces for such views. In Los Angeles, then—deputy mayor for economic development Gary Mendoza said a living-wage law there would mean "entire industries could be wiped out or move overseas." Such fulminations can be easily dismissed. But can we be confident that the critics are completely wrong?

The answer depends, first, on the specifics of any given ordinance. The LA law, for example, affects employees of three types of private businesses: those holding city service contracts of more than $25,000, such as accounting or janitorial companies; concessionaires on city property, such as LAX; and firms receiving city subsidies of more than $1 million. This law, applying as it does only to city contractors and subsidy recipients, resembles those passed in Baltimore, Boston, Portland and Chicago.

My colleague Stephanie Luce and I have estimated that, at the outside, this ordinance will raise the pay of 7,600 full- and part-time workers in LA. Over a year, the income of a full-time living-wage worker will rise by $3,600. These increases will be spread among the roughly 1,000 firms that are obligated to comply with the law, making the cost per firm about $24,000. But since these 1,000 firms produce about $4.4 billion in goods and services in a year, the extra $24 million in their combined wage bill amounts to only about 0.5 percent of their annual budgets.

The health benefits to workers and the paid days off provided under the ordinance will together amount to another $28 million. A final likely, though not mandated, effect of the law is pressure for wage increases for workers in the affected firms who now earn more than the $7.25 minimum. This ripple effect of wage increases is likely to pertain to workers earning perhaps as much as $9.25 once their lower-paid co-workers get a raise.

When we add these additional costs to the basic mandated wage increases, the sum still comes to only about 1.5 percent of the total annual budget of the average affected firm. Indeed, for about 85 percent of the firms involved, the total annual increase in costs will be less than 1 percent of their budgets.

City Budgets Won't Go Bust

Most companies faced with a cost increase of 1 percent or less would be willing to absorb the cost if it were the only condition on which they could keep winning city contracts. Some may refuse to absorb these increases, but competitors seeking the same contracts would likely step into the breach. This means that, through intelligent bargaining, a city government can purchase essentially the same quality of services from most private firms after the passage of a living-wage ordinance with virtually no impact on its budget.

For the roughly 15 percent of firms that will experience cost increases over 1 percent, a city should expect to absorb some of these increased costs if it wants to maintain at least a stable level of services. Here too the impact should be negligible. If, for example, LA's city government allowed companies to pass on all increases above 3 percent of their total budgets, the new costs to the city would amount to less than 0.5 percent of its $3.4 billion budget.

Will firms simply exit the city rather than face the higher costs? In fact, there is nothing in the Los Angeles ordinance or its equivalents elsewhere that encourages relocation. That's because these ordinances apply to all firms with city contracts, regardless of where they are located. The same rules for city contracting, including adherence to the living-wage ordinance, apply to companies whether they are in LA, an adjacent city like Santa Monica, or anywhere inside or outside the United States....

Would a Citywide Living-Wage Law Work?

The very features that make the LA proposal and its equivalents so manageable are also their limitations. Getting raises for 7,000 low-wage workers in a city is a major accomplishment. But 2.4 million other low-wage workers in the LA area are still not covered by the ordinance. What would be the impact of a more sweeping municipalitywide law, such as those that were proposed but defeated in Denver and Houston and the one that is now getting off the ground in New York? Peter Phillips, an organizer in Sonoma County, California, told me at a recent conference that this sort of proposal was the only one that made sense for his area. With either proposal, he argued, the organizers would have to launch an ambitious educational campaign. But only a few hundred workers would get raises through a contractors-only proposal, while several thousand would benefit through the municipalitywide approach.

In LA a countywide minimum wage of $7.25 would bring raises to some 2.4 million workers. At the same time, the impact per firm, on average, would not be significantly different from that of the contractors-only law now in place in the city. In terms of creating incentives for firms to relocate, however, a countywide ordinance could be substantially different. This is because, under such a proposal, affected firms could avoid paying higher wages by moving outside the municipal boundaries. The question, therefore, is: How many firms would actually leave rather than pay a living wage, and what would be the effect of their departure?

In fact, even here, fears of a mass exodus are unfounded. Most companies facing significant cost increases under a countywide ordinance would not relocate. A high proportion of these are restaurants, hotels or retail outlets, and are tied to their existing locations. Indeed, only one type of firm would have a strong incentive to relocate. These are manufacturers that are not tied to their locations and that employ a high percentage of low-wage workers. Some of these may choose simply to raise wages rather than incur the costs of relocation. But even if we assume that all such manufacturers did relocate just outside the county limits, the main loss for the Los Angeles County government would be the loss of tax revenues. Stephanie Luce and I estimate that the number of firms likely to leave would generate a loss in county tax revenue of between $50 million and $60 million. This is no small amount, but it is still less than 1 percent of the total wage increases that workers would enjoy with a $7.25 minimum wage. The county would likely experience some additional losses, such as a decline in property values due to firms leaving their existing locations. But all those costs would also total less than an additional 1 percent of the wage increases received by workers. Meanwhile, the workers would have more money to spend, would pay more in taxes and would rely less on government subsidies. The negative effects would be more severe if firms moved completely outside the region, since workers would also have to move to keep their jobs. But here again, nothing in a municipalitywide living wage would encourage firms to leave the region altogether, as opposed to getting themselves just beyond the county line.

Why Not a National Living Wage?

The viability of the living-wage proposals, whether applied to government contractors alone or to all companies in a region, invites consideration of an even more ambitious proposal: a national living wage of $7.25. If that sounds outlandish, it is only because the presumptions of greed have so dominated US economic policy discussions for a generation. After all, in today's dollars, the minimum wage was $7.37 thirty years ago when the economy was 50 percent less productive. If the minimum wage had just kept pace with productivity over the intervening years, it would today be $11.07. If nothing else were to change in the economy, bringing all workers up to at least $7.25 would require only small adjustments in income distribution. Just to illustrate the degree of redistribution necessary, the wage increases needed to bring all minimum-wage workers up to $7.25 would be equal to a reduction of only 6.6 percent in the incomes of the richest 20 percent of households, from roughly $106,600 to $100,000....

The living-wage proposals gaining ground will directly contribute only modestly toward eliminating poverty. But their importance far exceeds their immediate measurable impact. As more cities gain experience with these laws over the next few years, their limitations as well as strengths will become evident. The process of political and economic education will then provide a platform from which to launch more ambitious egalitarian wage and employment programs and to deepen the movement for economic justice in this country.

Labor Leaders and Allies Call for Repeal of the Taft-Hartley Act (2002)

Tony Mazzocchi, Bruce J. Klipple, Kay McVay,
Ralph Nader, and Thomas Geoghegan

Tony Mazzocchi is the national organizer for the Labor Party; Bruce J. Klipple is the secretary-treasurer for the United Electrical, Radio, and Machine Workers of America; Kay McVay, RN, is the president of the California Nurses Association; Ralph Nader is a consumer rights advocate; and Thomas Geoghegan is the author of Which Side Are You On?

This year marks the 55th anniversary of the passage of the Taft-Hartley Act, one of the great blows to American democracy.

The Act, which was drafted by employers, fundamentally infringed on workers' human rights. Legally, it impeded employees' right to join together in labor unions, it undermined the power of unions to represent workers' interests effectively, and it authorized an array of anti-union activities by employers.

Taft-Hartley undermined many of the gains achieved with passage of the National Labor Relations Act, which had been enacted [in 1935] to narrow the gap between employer and employee power and introduce a measure of democracy into the workplace, and to stimulate wages and the national economy.

Among its key provisions, Taft-Hartley:

- Established the "right" of management to campaign against a union organizing drive.
- Required that election hearings on matters of dispute be held before a union recognition election, thus delaying the election. Delay virtually always benefits management, giving the employer time to threaten and coerce workers into rejecting the union.
- Authorized states to enact so-called right-to-work laws. These laws undermine the ability to build effective unions by restricting union security clauses and creating a free-rider problem—workers can enjoy the benefits of union membership without actually joining the union or paying union dues. Right-to-work laws increase employer leverage to resist unions and vastly decrease union membership, thus dramatically diminishing unions' bargaining power.
- Defined "employee" for purposes of the Act as excluding supervisors and independent contractors. This diminished the pool of workers eligible to be unionized. The exclusion of supervisors meant they would be used as management's "front line" in anti-organizing efforts.

- Permitted employers to petition for a union certification election, thus undermining the ability of workers and unions to control the timing of an election.
- Prohibited secondary boycotts—boycotts directed to encourage neutral employers to pressure the employer with which the union has a dispute. Secondary boycotts had been one of organized labor's most potent tools for organizing, negotiating and dispute settlement.

The political damage of Taft-Hartley was just as severe. The Act sent a message to employers: It was OK to bust unions and deny workers their rights to collectively bargain.

In short, Taft-Hartley solidified employer control in the workplace, with ramifications that are more severe today than ever. Union membership is at historic lows, employer violations of labor rights are routine, and illegal firings of union supporters in labor organizing drives are at epidemic levels. The reduction in the ranks of organized labor has both diminished living standards for the vast majority of working people and denied them the experience of participating in vibrant democratic institutions, with damaging effects for our broader civic culture.

We join together to call for the repeal of Taft-Hartley, as one important step in restoring workers' right to organize into unions and in revitalizing American democracy.

We Demand Fair Trade—Not Free Trade (1999)

Brian McWilliams

McWilliams, president of the International Longshore and Warehouse Union (ILWU) gave this speech at the protests against the World Trade Organization in Seattle, Washington.

The free trade advocates of the WTO have come to Seattle to further their strategic takeover of the global economy. We in the ILWU want to give them the welcome they deserve and let them know what we think of their plans. So we've closed the Port of Seattle and other ports on the West Coast. There will be no business as usual today.

In closing these ports the ILWU is demonstrating to the corporate CEOs and their agents here in Seattle that the global economy will not run without the consent of the workers. And we don't just mean longshore workers, but workers everywhere in this country and around the world. When the ILWU boycotted cargo from El Salvador and apartheid South Africa, when we would not work scab grapes from the California valley or cross picket lines in support of the fired Liverpool dockers, these were concrete expressions of our understanding that the interests of working people transcend national and local boundaries, and that labor solidarity truly means that when necessary we will engage in concrete action.

That is why the ILWU is here today, with all of you—to tell the agents of global capital that we, the workers, those who care about social justice and protecting our rights and our planet, will not sit quietly by while they meet behind closed doors to carve up our world. We know that what they have in mind for us is a race to the bottom, dismantling our protective laws wherever they find us weak, that they want to pit workers of one country against the workers of another, to erase our protections and standards in an international corporate feeding frenzy in which workers are not just on the menu—we are the main course. We will not cooperate! We know our history, our legacy and our ongoing responsibility. No one can make this statement stronger than longshore workers who make their living moving international cargo. And what do we want? We demand fair trade—not free trade—not the policies of the WTO that are devastating workers everywhere and the planet that sustains us.

And let us be clear. Let's not allow the free traders to paint us as isolationist anti-traders. We are for trade. Don't ever forget—it is the labor of working people that produces all the wealth. When we say we demand fair trade policies we mean we demand a world in which trade brings dignity and fair treatment to all workers, with its benefits shared fairly and equally, a world in which the interconnectedness of trade promotes peace and encourages healthy and environmentally sound and sustainable development, a world which promotes economic justice and social justice and environmental sanity. The free traders promote economic injustice, social injustice and environmental insanity.

We are sending the WTO this message loud and clear. We will not sit idly by while you corporate puppets of the WTO plot this economic coup.

You will not seize control of our world without a fight.

Are you ready for the fight? Damn right!

The Hidden Agenda: From Group-Specific to Universal Programs of Reform (1987)

William Julius Wilson

This article, which is taken from Wilson's classic work, outlines his call for a universal approach to solving poverty, and away from race-specific solutions.

... Comprehensive economic policies aimed at the general population but that would also enhance employment opportunities among the truly disadvantaged—both men and women—are needed. The research presented in this study suggests that improving the job prospects of men will strengthen low-income black families. Moreover, underclass absent fathers with more stable employment are in a better position to contribute financial support for their families. Furthermore, since the majority of female householders are in the labor force, improved job prospects would very likely draw in others.

I have in mind the creation of a macroeconomic policy designed to promote both economic growth and a tight labor market. The latter affects the supply-and-demand ratio and wages tend to rise. It would be necessary, however, to combine this policy with fiscal and monetary policies to stimulate noninflationary growth and thereby move away from the policy of controlling inflation by allowing unemployment to rise. Furthermore, it would be important to develop policy to increase the competitiveness of American goods on the international market by, among other things, reducing the budget deficit to adjust the value of the American dollar.

In addition, measures such as on-the-job training and apprenticeships to elevate the skill levels of the truly disadvantaged are needed. I will soon discuss in another context why such problems have to be part of a more universal package of reform. For now, let me simply say that improved manpower policies are needed in the short run to help lift the truly disadvantaged from the lowest rungs of the job market. In other words, it would be necessary to devise a national labor-market strategy to increase "the adaptability of the labor force to changing employment opportunities." In this connection, instead of focusing on remedial programs in the public sector for the poor and the unemployed, emphasis would be placed on relating these programs more closely to opportunities in the private sector to facilitate the movement of recipients (including relocation assistance) into more secure jobs. Of course there would be a need to create public transitional programs for those who have difficulty finding immediate employment in the private sector, but such programs would aim toward eventually getting individuals into the private sector economy. Although public employment programs continue to draw popular support, as Weir, Orloff, and Skocpol point out, "they must be designed and administered in close conjunction with a nationally oriented labor market strategy" to avoid both becoming "enmeshed in congressionally reinforced local political patronage" and being attacked as costly, inefficient, or "corrupt."

Since national opinion polls consistently reveal strong public support for efforts to enhance work in America, political support for a program of economic reform (macroeconomic employment policies and labor-market strategies including training efforts) could be considerably stronger than many people presently assume. However, in order to draw sustained public support for such a program, it is necessary that training or retraining, transitional employment benefits, and relocation assistance be available to all members of society who choose to use them, not just to poor minorities.

It would be ideal if problems of the ghetto underclass could be adequately addressed by the combination of macroeconomic policy, labor-market strategies, and manpower training programs. However, in the foreseeable future employment alone will not necessarily lift a family out of poverty. Many families would still require income support and/or social services such as child care. A program of welfare reform is needed, therefore, to address the current problems of public assistance, including lack of provisions for poor two-parent families, inadequate levels of support, inequities between different states, and work disincentives. A national AFDC benefit standard adjusted yearly for inflation is the most minimal required change. We might also give serious consideration to programs such as the Child Support Assurance Program developed by Irwin Garfinkel and colleagues at the Institute for Research on Poverty at the University of Wisconsin, Madison. This program, currently in operation as a demonstration project in the state of Wisconsin, provides a guaranteed minimum benefit per child to single-parent families regardless of the income of the custodial parent. The state collects from the absent parent through wage withholding a sum of money at a fixed rate and then makes regular payments to the custodial parent. If the absent parent is jobless or if his or her payment from withholdings is less than the minimum, the state makes up the difference. Since all absent parents regardless of income are required to participate in this program, it is far less stigmatizing than, say, public assistance. Moreover, preliminary evidence from Wisconsin suggests that this program carries little or no additional cost to the state.

Many western European countries have programs of family or child allowances to support families. These programs provide families with an annual benefit per child regardless of the family's income, and regardless of whether the parents are living together or whether either or both are employed. Unlike public assistance, therefore, a family allowance program carries no social stigma and has no built-in work disincentives. In this connection, Daniel Patrick Moynihan has recently observed that a form of family allowance is already available to American families with the standard deduction and the Earned Income Tax Credit, although the latter can only be obtained by low-income families. Even though both have been significantly eroded by inflation, they could represent the basis for a more comprehensive family allowance program that approximates the European model.

Neither the Child Support Assurance Program under demonstration in Wisconsin nor the European family allowances program is means tested; that is, they are not targeted at a particular income group and therefore do not suffer the degree of stigmatization that plagues public assistance programs such as AFDC. More important, such universal programs would tend to draw more political support from the general public because the programs would be available not only to the poor but to the working- and middle-class segments as well. And such programs would not be readily associated with specific minority groups. Nonetheless, truly disadvantaged groups would reap disproportionate benefits from such programs because of the groups' limited alternative economic resources. For example, low-income single mothers could combine work with adequate guaranteed child support and/or child allowance benefits and therefore escape poverty and avoid public assistance.

Finally, the question of child care has to be addressed in any program designed to improve the employment prospects of women and men. Because of the growing participation of women in the labor market, adequate child care has been a topic receiving increasing attention in public policy discussions. For the overwhelmingly female-headed ghetto underclass families, access to quality child care becomes a critical issue if steps are taken to move single mothers into education and training programs and/or full- or part-time employment. However, I am not recommending government-operated child care centers. Rather it would be better to avoid additional federal bureaucracy by seeking alternative and decentralized forms of child care such as expanding the child care tax credit, including three- and four-year-olds in preschool enrollment, and providing child care subsidies to the working-poor parents....

By emphasizing universal programs as an effective way to address problems in the inner city created by historic racial subjugation, I am recommending a fundamental shift from the traditional race-specific approach of addressing such problems. It is true that problems of joblessness and related woes such as poverty, teenage pregnancies, out-of-wedlock births, female-headed families, and welfare dependency are, for reasons of historic racial oppression, disproportionately concentrated in the black community. And it is important to recognize the racial differences in rates of social dislocation so as not to obscure problems currently gripping the ghetto underclass. However, as discussed above, race-specific policies are often not designed to address fundamental problems of the truly disadvantaged. Moreover, as also discussed above, both race-specific and targeted programs based on the principle of equality of life chances (often identified with a minority constituency) have difficulty sustaining widespread public support.

Does this mean that targeted programs of any kind would necessarily be excluded from a package highlighting universal programs of reform? On the contrary, as long as a racial division of labor exists and racial minorities are disproportionately concentrated in low-paying positions, antidiscrimination and affirmative action programs will be needed even though they tend to benefit the more advantaged minority members. Moreover, as long as certain groups lack the training, skills, and education to compete effectively on the job market or move into newly created jobs, manpower training and education programs targeted at these groups will also be needed, even under a tight-labor-market situation. For example, a program of adult education and training may be necessary for some ghetto underclass males before they can either become oriented to or move into an expanded labor market. Finally, as long as some poor families are unable to work because of physical or other disabilities, public assistance would be needed even if the government adopted a program of welfare reform that included child support enforcement and family allowance provisions.

For all these reasons, a comprehensive program of economic and social reform (highlighting macroeconomic policies to promote balanced economic growth and create a tight-labor-market situation, a nationally oriented labor-market strategy, a child support assurance program, a child care strategy, and a family allowances program) would have to include targeted programs, both means tested and race-specific. However, the latter would be considered an offshoot of and indeed secondary to the universal programs. The important goal is to construct an economic-social reform program in such a way that the universal programs are seen as the dominant and most visible aspects by the general public. As the universal programs draw support from a wider population, the targeted programs included in the comprehensive reform package would be indirectly supported and protected. Accordingly, *the hidden agenda for liberal policymakers is to improve the life chances of truly disadvantaged groups such as the ghetto underclass by emphasizing programs to which the more advantaged groups of all races and class backgrounds can positively relate.*

America's Debt to Blacks (2000)

Randall Robinson

Randall Robinson is the founder and president of TransAfrica, and is the author of The Debt: What America Owes to Blacks.

Well before the birth of our country, Europe and the eventual United States perpetrated a heinous wrong against the peoples of Africa and sustained and benefited from the wrong through the continuing exploitation of Africa's human and material resources. America followed slavery with more than a hundred years of legal racial segregation and discrimination of one variety or another. It was only in 1965, after nearly 350 years of legal racial suppression, that the United States enacted the Voting Rights Act. Virtually simultaneously, however, it began to walk away from the social wreckage that centuries of white hegemony had wrought. Our country then began to rub itself with the memory-emptying salve of contemporaneousness. (If the wrong did not *just* occur, then it did not occur in a way that would render the living responsible.)

But when the black living suffer real and current consequences as a result of wrongs committed by a younger America, then contemporary America must shoulder responsibility for those wrongs until such wrongs have been adequately righted. The life and responsibilities of a nation are not limited to the life spans of its mortal constituents. Federal and state governments were active participants not only in slavery but also in the exclusion and dehumanization of blacks that continued legally up until the passage of key civil rights legislation in the sixties. Black calls for reparations began almost from the moment that slavery officially ended in 1865. However, although our calls far predate those of either the Japanese or the Jews, only the latter two communities have been responded to in a spirit of sober compassion and thoughtful humanity.

In response to our call, individual Americans need not feel defensive or under attack. No one holds any living person responsible for slavery or the later century-plus of legal relegation of blacks to substandard education, exclusion from home ownership via restrictive covenants and redlining, or any of the myriad mechanisms for pushing blacks to the back of the line. Nonetheless, we must all, as a nation, ponder the repercussions of those acts.

There are many ways to begin righting America's massive wrong. But resolving economic and social disparities so long in the making will require great resources (in the form of public initiatives, not personal checks) and decades of national fortitude. Habit is the enemy. Whites and blacks see each other the only way they can remember seeing each other—in a relationship of economic and social inequality. The system, which starts each child where its parents left off, is not fair. This is particularly the case for African-Americans, whose general economic starting points have been rearmost because of slavery and its aftermath. Slaves for two and a half centuries saw not just their freedom taken from them but their labor as well. Were it a line item in today's gross national product report, that value would undoubtedly run into billions of dollars.

America has made an art form by now of grinding its past deeds, no matter how despicable, into mere ephemera. And African-Americans, unfortunately, have accommodated this amnesia all too well. It would behoove African-Americans to remember that history forgets first those who forget themselves. To do what is necessary to accomplish anything approaching psychic and economic parity in the next half-century will require a fundamental shift in America's thinking. Before the country in general can be made to understand, African-Americans themselves must come to understand that this demand is not for charity. It is simply for what they are owed on a debt that is old but compellingly obvious and valid still. (Do not be fooled by individual examples of conspicuous black success. They have closed neither the economic nor the psychic gaps between blacks and whites, and are statistically insignificant.)

The blacks of Rosewood, Florida, and Greenwood, Oklahoma, have successfully brought their case for reparations to national attention. Indeed, in Oklahoma a biracial commission has just concluded that justice demands that reparations be paid to the victims of Oklahoma's Greenwood massacre. Congressman John Conyers has introduced HR 40, a bill "to examine the institution of slavery," subsequent "de jure and de facto discrimination against freed slaves and their descendants," the impact of these forces "on living African-Americans" and to make recommendations to Congress on "appropriate remedies." Passage of this bill is crucial; even the making of a well-reasoned case for broader national restitution will do wonders for the spirits of blacks.

This is a struggle that African-Americans cannot lose, for in the very making of it we will discover, if nothing else, ourselves. And it is a struggle that all Americans must support, as the important first step toward America's having any chance for a new beginning in which all its inhabitants are true co-owners of America's democratic ideals.

Faith-Based Charities Work Daily Miracles (2002)

George W. Bush

President Bush gave this speech in Philadelphia, Pennsylvania, at a White House Conference on Faith-Based and Community Initiatives.

... We have work to do. We must be honest about it. We have got a lot of work to do in this country, because there are pockets of despair in America. There are men and women who doubt the American Dream is meant for them. There are people who face the struggles of illness and old age with no one to help them or pray with them. There are men and women who fight every minute of the day against terrible addictions. There are boys with no family but a gang, and teenage moms who are abandoned and alone. And then there are the children who wonder if anybody loves them.

We've reformed welfare in America to help many, yet welfare policy will not solve the deepest problems of the spirit. Our economy is growing, yet there are some needs that prosperity can never fill. We arrest and convict dangerous criminals; yet building more prisons is no substitute for responsibility and order in our souls.

No government policy can put hope in people's hearts or a sense of purpose in people's lives. That is done when someone, some good soul puts an arm around a neighbor and says, God loves you, and I love, and you can count on us both.

And we find that powerful spirit of compassion in faith-based and community groups across our nation: people giving shelter to the homeless; providing safety for battered women; giving care and comfort to AIDS victims; bringing companionship to lonely seniors.

I saw that spirit of compassion earlier today when I visited adults and children involved in a program called Amachi at the Bright Hope Baptist Church right here in Philadelphia. In the Amachi program, good people from more than 50 churches in this area serve as mentors to the children of prisoners. They share their time and attention. They just serve as a friend.

Most of us find it difficult to imagine the life of a child who has to go through a prison gate to be hugged by their mom or dad. Yet this is the reality for almost a million-and-a-half American boys and girls. They face terrible challenges that no child deserves to face. Without guidance, they have a higher risk of failing in school and committing crimes themselves. The volunteers of Amachi, who are with us here today with the children they are loving, are such wonderful givers of guidance and love.

I'm told that "amachi" is a Western African word that means, "Who knows what God has brought us through this child." That attitude is the inspiration of a good mentoring program. No child is a problem or a burden; every child is a priority and a blessing. That is the message of the almighty God who cares for these, and that is the message carried to the city by the volunteers of Amachi. And I want to thank them for being here today. And I want to thank them for their love. And I want to thank them for their example for other Americans to follow.

Faith-based charities work daily miracles because they have idealistic volunteers. They're guided by moral principles. They know the problems of their own communities, and above all, they recognize the dignity of every citizen and the possibilities of every life. These groups and many good charities that are specifically religious have the heart to serve others. Yet many lack the resources they need to meet the needs around them.

They deserve the support of the rest of us. They deserve the support of foundations. They deserve the support of corporate America. They deserve the support of individual donors, of church congregations, of synagogues and mosques. And then deserve, when appropriate, the support of the federal government.

Faith-based groups will never replace government when it comes to helping those in need. Yet government must recognize the power and unique contribution of faith-based groups in every part of our country. And when the federal government gives contracts to private groups to provide social services, religious groups should have an equal chance to compete. When decisions are made on public funding, we should not focus on the religion you practice; we should focus on the results you deliver.

The Amachi program receives 38 percent of its funding from the federal government. My administration has been working for nearly two years to encourage this kind of support to good faith-based programs. And we're making some progress. The Department of Housing and Urban Development, run by Mel, we've changed regulations in eight programs which cover over $8 billion in grants to encourage competition that includes faith-based groups. We've opened up more than $1 billion in after-school programs to competition, including faith-based groups. We're reaching out to grassroots community groups and helping them learn the complicated process of grant-making. I see a lot of heads nodding when it comes to complicated process.

Yet there's a lot to do. In government, we're still fighting old attitudes, habits and rules that discriminate against religious groups for no good purpose. In Iowa, for example, the Victory Center Rescue Mission was told to return grant money to the government because the mission's board of directors was not secular enough. The St. Francis House Homeless Shelter in South Dakota was denied a grant because voluntary prayers were offered before meals. A few years ago in New York, the Metropolitan Council on Jewish Poverty was discouraged from even applying for federal funds because it had the word "Jewish" in its name.

These are examples of a larger pattern, a pattern of discrimination. And this discrimination shows a fundamental misunderstanding of the law. I recognize that government has no business endorsing a religious creed, or directly funding religious worship or religious teaching. That is not the business of the government. Yet government can and should support social services provided by religious people, as long as those services go to anyone in need, regardless of their faith. And when government gives that support, charities and faith-based programs should not be forced to change their character or compromise their mission.

And I don't intend to compromise either. I have worked for a faith-based initiative to rally and encourage the armies of compassion. I will continue to work with Congress on this agenda. But the needs of our country are urgent and, as President, I have an authority I intend to use. Many acts of discrimination—many acts of discrimination against faith-based groups are committed by Executive Branch agencies. And, as the leader of the Executive Branch, I'm going to make some changes, effective today.

First, in a few minutes—you'll be happy to hear—I am going to sign an executive order directing all federal agencies to follow the principle of equal treatment in rewarding social service grants.

Every person in every government agency will know where the President stands. And every person will have the responsibility to ensure a level playing field for faith-based organizations in federal programs. No funds will be used to directly support inherently religious activities; yet no organization that qualifies for funds will ever be forced to change its identity.

And secondly, I have directed specific action in several federal agencies with a history of discrimination against faith-based groups. FEMA will revise its policy on emergency relief so that religious nonprofit groups can qualify for assistance after disasters like hurricanes and earthquakes. HUD and HHS, who provide so much grant money to communities across America, will revise their regulations to reflect the principle of nondiscrimination.

In addition, we're issuing a guidebook which you've received. The book explains in plain English how faith-based groups can qualify for government grants. It gives guidance on what you can and cannot do with taxpayers' money. We're going to distribute this guidebook widely. We will continue to hold regional conferences like this one all around the United States of America. The rules for dealing with the government are clear, and we want more and more faith-based charities to become partners in our efforts, our unyielding efforts to change America one heart, one conscience, one soul at a time.

Through all these actions, I hope that every faith-based group in America, the social entrepreneurs of America, understand that this government respects your work and we respect the motivation behind your work. We do not want you to become carbon copies of public programs. We want you to follow your heart. We want you to follow the word. We want you to do the works of kindness and mercy you are called upon to do. Thank you.

For too long, for too long, some in government believed there was no room for faith in the public square.

AUDIENCE MEMBER: Preach on, brother!

THE PRESIDENT: I guess they've forgotten the history of this great country. People of faith led the struggle against slavery. People of faith fought against child labor. People of faith worked for women's equality and civil rights. Every expansion of justice in American history received inspiration from men and women of moral conviction and religious belief. And in America today, people of faith are waging a determined campaign against need and suffering.

When government discriminates against religious groups, it is not the groups that suffer most. The loss comes to the hungry who don't get fed, to the addicts who don't get help, to the children who drift toward self-destruction. For the sake of so many brothers and sisters in need, we must and we will support the armies of compassion in America.

The steps we take today will help clear away a legacy of discrimination against faith-based charities. In the new year, I will announce further initiatives to help community groups that serve their neighbors.

Our nation needs more mentors. Particularly, mentors for children whose mom or dad is in prison. Our nation needs more centers to treat addiction. Our nation must recognize that if we can change a heart, we're more than likely to change someone's habits, and addiction on drugs and alcohol. Instead of building towering bureaucracies, government should be finding new and creative ways to support local efforts.

I call this approach compassionate conservatism. And in my State of the Union message, I will ask members of both political parties to move forward with me on this vision. By promoting the compassion of our people, by promoting the great strength of America, we will bring new hope to neighborhoods all across this land.

You know something about America? We meet every challenge that faces our country. That's why I'm so optimistic about our future. And we will answer the call of our times. We will defend our freedoms, and we will lead the world toward peace. And we will unite America behind the great goals of justice and compassion.

In the work of compassion, it is not the people in government who are the experts; the people in this room are the experts. The people in this room are helping lead America to a better day. You just need to know that. And you need to know that I am incredibly grateful for what you do. There is a saying, nobody can teach you how to be a good servant of God, you have to learn it on the job. And you are doing that job so incredibly well.

AUDIENCE MEMBER: And you are, too!

THE PRESIDENT: I appreciate your commitment—I appreciate your commitment. I appreciate your service. I appreciate your love. And now I'm proud to sign this executive order providing equal treatment for faith-based charities all across the greatest land on the face of the Earth, the United States of America. May God bless you all.

Building Assets to Fight Poverty (2000)

Michael Sherraden

Professor Sherraden is one of the leading thinkers on individual development accounts.

A shift toward asset-based policy seems to be under way in the United States. This can be seen in the introduction and growth of 401(k)s, 403(b)s, IRAs, Roth IRAs, the Federal Thrift Savings Plan, Educational Savings Accounts, Medical Savings Accounts, Individual Training Accounts, College Savings Plans in the states, and proposed individual accounts in Social Security. Some of these are public and some are "private," but it is important to bear in mind that even the "private" plans are typically defined by public policies and receive substantial tax subsidies. All these asset-building accounts have been introduced in the United States since 1970; they are the most rapidly growing form of domestic policy. Asset accounts may become a primary form of domestic policy during the 21st century.

Asset-based policy, however, is considerably more regressive than the social insurances and means-tested transfers that were the mainstays of social policy in the 20th century. The reasons are twofold: first, the poor often do not participate in asset-building programs; and second, asset-building policies operate primarily through highly regressive tax expenditures that benefit the poor little, if at all. Sixty-seven percent of retirement tax benefits go to households with incomes over $100,000; 93 percent go to households with incomes over $50,000.

Homeownership policy, a central way of encouraging asset accumulation, is almost as regressive. Homeowners can receive interest deductions on mortgages up to a million dollars and on mortgages for second homes. These deductions can exceed $25,000 per year for a single individual. Fifty-four percent of home mortgage interest tax benefits go to households with incomes over $100,000; 91 percent go to households with incomes over $50,000.

Asset Building for the Poor

Extending asset building to the poor makes sense for two reasons. First, fairness. The extraordinarily regressive federal tax expenditures to individuals are estimated at over $500 billion in 2000. If these massive benefits were distributed equally among the population, each adult in the country could receive over $2,000 per year, enough for a fully funded IRA. If the benefits were distributed progressively (more for the poor), they could provide every low-income person in the country with a decent home and health insurance coverage, plus a fully funded IRA.

Second, assets are a key to family and community development based on capacity rather than maintenance. Welfare policy for the poor has focused on income-for-consumption, which is essential but not enough. In order to develop capacity, families and communities must accumulate assets and invest for long-term goals. Public policy should focus on both income support and asset building.

Unfortunately, means-tested transfer policies for the poor, with "asset limits," have done just the opposite; they have discouraged saving and asset accumulation among the poor. This double standard in public policy—large asset subsidies for the wealthy, but discouraging asset accumulation by the poor—is misguided. The goal should be to bring everyone into asset-building policy, with adequate resources for social protections and household development.

Toward Progressive Asset-Based Policy

Individual development accounts (IDAs) were created as a step in this direction. IDAs are matched savings accounts for the poor, to be used for homeownership, education, small business, or other development purposes. IDAs first began in community organizations in the early 1990s, including housing organizations, community action agencies, microenterprise programs, social service agencies, and community development financial institutions. Today at least 200 IDA programs exist, and hundreds more are being planned.

Several prominent organizations have established IDA networks. AmeriCorps VISTA has IDA volunteers working at community development credit unions and other community organizations. The Eagle Staff Fund of the First Nations Development Institute has begun IDAs on several Native American reservations. United Ways in Atlanta and St. Louis have funded multi-site IDA programs, and the Neighborhood Reinvestment Corporation has started its own IDA program.

At least 27 states have passed IDA legislation for welfare recipients and/or other low-income residents. Five states have passed legislation for other asset-building initiatives for education or job training, and almost all states have raised asset limits for welfare. Altogether, there is some type of IDA policy or initiative in 44 states, typically with broad bipartisan support.

At the federal level, IDA legislation also has bipartisan support. Two important IDA provisions were included as state options in the federal "welfare reform" act of 1996. First, states can use Temporary Assistance to Needy Families (TANF) funds to match savings in IDAs. Second, assets accumulated in an IDA are exempt from asset limits for all federal means-tested programs—in other words, in IDAs the welfare poor can save without penalty. Another federal IDA initiative, the Assets for Independence Act of 1998, provides $125 million for IDA demonstrations over five years. At this writing, the Savings for Working Families Act of 2000 has been introduced in the House and Senate; it would create over one billion dollars in tax credits to financial institutions and others who support IDAs.

This legislative interest in IDAs appears to be warranted. A large demonstration project on IDAs, funded by eleven foundations, finds that participants are saving an average of $33 per month, matched at an average of 2:1 for accumulations of about $100 per month. Interestingly, very low-income households are saving almost as much as households who are not as poor, and saving a larger proportion of their incomes.

IDAs have demonstrated that low-income, low-wealth households can save and accumulate assets if they have similar opportunities and incentives to the non-poor. This can lay the groundwork for inclusive, progressive asset-based policies now emerging.

Emerging Policy Directions

Senator Bob Kerrey (D-NE) has proposed Children's Savings Accounts (CSAs), with federal deposits for all children from birth through age 18, to be used for education and later retirement security. Every economically advanced nation except the United States has some form of monthly payment to families with children, designed for consumption support. Western European countries spend an average of 1.8 percent of GDP on child allowances. That much of the United States' GDP would be more than enough to deposit $2,000 per year into CSAs.

Michael Stegman, former Assistant Secretary for Policy Development and Research at HUD and currently public policy professor at University of North Carolina at Chapel Hill, has proposed incorporating IDAs in Electronic Funds Transfer (EFT). At present, a large portion of the poverty population is "unbanked," i.e., they have no mainstream financial services. Instead, they pay high prices for financial services in check cashing outlets, pawn shops, and the like. The transition to EFT presents an unusual opportunity to provide a full range of financial services, not merely transaction accounts, for nearly all Americans. As Stegman proposes, this could include matched saving in the form of IDAs.

In his 1999 State of the Union Address, President Clinton proposed using 11–12 percent of the budget surplus—an estimated $38 billion per year at the outset—to create progressive Universal Savings Accounts (USAs) for retirement. The federal government would make annual deposits plus matching deposits into low- and middle-income workers' accounts—covering most of the working population—on a progressive basis, i.e., the largest subsidies would be at the bottom. Some have described this as a 401(k) available to all workers.

In the 2000 State of the Union Address, Clinton proposed Retirement Savings Accounts (RSAs), a scaled-down version of USAs, estimated at $5.4 billion per year. RSAs could also be used for homeownership, education, and other goals. In making these proposals, Clinton mentioned the early success of IDAs in showing that the poor can save.

Homeownership for the Poor

In America, homeownership is a high priority for most families, including many low-income families. Fifty-five percent of participants in the "American Dream Demonstration" prefer to use their IDAs for homeownership.

Interest in homeownership for low-income households has grown markedly over the past decade. Current policy initiatives include the Section 8 Homeownership Program, Fannie Mae's homeownership initiatives, and the Community Reinvestment Act's regulatory provisions. Indeed, home mortgage lending to low-income households has increased substantially in recent years.

However, there is a long way to go, and housing advocates should not be satisfied with tinkering at the edges of homeownership policy. The federal government is passing out a great deal of money for homeownership, and poor people are not getting much of it. A better policy would promote homeownership across a broader population with progressive, or at least equal, benefits to enable more low-income, low-wealth families to become homeowners.

The popular wisdom is that tax benefits for homeownership are an almost untouchable political issue. But current housing policy is so regressive that it is unjust to the majority of U.S. households. When the majority's interests are at stake, it should be possible to mobilize support for policy change. A good first step would be to cap the home mortgage interest tax deduction to loan amounts no higher than $200,000 (why should the government support above-average housing?) and use the additional resources to subsidize homeownership among the poor.

As asset-building policy continues to expand, inclusion of the poor is the greatest challenge. Homeownership, as the fundamental American Dream, should be at the center of asset-building policy and community development.

We Know the Creation Stories of Our People (2003)

Carrie Dann

Dann gave this speech at an awards ceremony in honor of her work on Western Shoshone rights.

Good evening. My name is Carrie Dann. I am Western Shoshone. It is an honor to be a part of this group and I accept this award on behalf of my sister Mary, and myself. It is good that an organization like this recognizes two old women like ourselves. I don't know that we deserve any award, but we do try to live our lives in a good way and keep our understanding of freedom in our hearts and in our minds and in our soul.

I am indigenous to this Turtle Island, what is now called the United States. What that means is that my parents, and grandparents and all of my ancestors before me were born and raised and died on these lands—lands in what is known now as the State of Nevada.

Our teachings tell us that the Creator placed us here as caretakers of the lands, the animals, all the living things. We were placed here with a responsibility. I, and my sister Mary, as traditional Shoshone, live that responsibility every day of our lives. In indigenous society, there are four things that are sacred above all. Those things are the land, the air, the water and the Sun.

We see the earth as our mother, that which gives us all life. The water is like the blood in our veins, the air, that which nourishes the cycle of life and the sun, that which encourages growth, warmth and replenishment. This is our religion. That which is sacred and defines who we are as a people.

We know the creation stories of our people and our land and now, in today's times, the powers of the United States government and the corporations want to rip us from this belief system by paying us in crumbs through a legislative measure called the Western Shoshone Distribution Bill, in the House it is bill number 884, sponsored by Congressman Gibbons.

Not only do they want to rip us from our lands, but the activities the government is allowing to happen in the name of the almighty dollar are destroying our earth, contaminating our water and contaminating our air. One example is the gold mining. The process being used is open pit cyanide leach mining. In that process, the gold companies—large multinationals such as Kennecott, Placer Dome, Barrick and Newmont and others—take the water out of the water table at a rate of 30–70 thousand gallons of water per minute.

Do you know what happens to the earth when that happens? Do we know what the earth mother is saying when they are draining her vital liquids? Is she crying out in pain? Do we know? And what are the future generations saying to us as we do these things? Are they saying to us stop! Wake up! What are you doing to our world? And this is not just limited to humans, but to all life. As everyone watches Iraq, and world politics and who's killing who—all the while, our earth mother, that which provides us with ALL life is being raped and mutilated, over and over and over again.

Let me tell you quickly—very briefly—what my sister and I have been fighting for. We fight in a battle we were born into as indigenous people in the United States. We did not ask to be in this struggle, we did not look for struggle and controversy—it was forced upon us.

In 1973, the Department of Interior served my sister with a notice of trespass for our animals grazing on lands where they had always grazed. My sister asked what the notice was. The man told her our cattle were in trespass. My sister responded that they couldn't be in trespass because they were on Shoshone lands. The only time we would be trespassing, she told him, would be if we were on Paiute land—over to the west. The Department of Interior sued us anyway.

Our problem is that the lands we were placed upon have now been seen as valuable to the gold corporations, the energy industry and the nuclear industry. Currently, our lands produce the third largest production of gold in the world. We went through the United States Court systems, all the way to the Supreme Court, we went to the United Nations, the Organization of American States. Instead of respecting our rights, the United States set up what is called the Indian Claims Commission—an agency to pay us for something we never sold or want to sell—our land which to us is our culture and our identity.

In the United States, the courts shut us out without a hearing on land title— why? Because we are native people. Because this country is founded on racism and oppression. This is not just an historic truth, it is the truth of the situation today. Genocide may no longer be taking place against our people in a physical way, but spiritually, we are under full attack—and we're fighting like hell.

My sister, Mary always talks about how she thought this country was founded on freedom and justice. But all we have seen from the courts and the commissions is injustice. Our rights guaranteed under the Constitution of the United States have been denied to the indigenous peoples and we have never been given a hearing on our land title. A year ago in December, the Organization of American States, the Inter-American Commission on Human Rights ruled in our favor and found the United States in violation of international law and our rights to property, to due process and to equality under the law.

Instead of sitting down and talking with our people in good faith, the United States instead has been using armed military force on our lands to steal cattle and horses and to conduct ongoing surveillance as a way to intimidate us into just accepting the crumbs they are throwing out to us. Now, in the halls of Congress, with the Western Shoshone Distribution Bill, members of Congress seem to hold our fate in their hands.

Economically we were a self-sustaining people. With these recent actions stealing our livelihood we are now facing economic starvation designed to remove us from our lands. To me, that is terrorism. Domestic terrorism. This behavior is designed to steal our dignity, our honor and to make us feel that we are less than or lower than human—we are treated like animals. We are being dehumanized.

Many Western Shoshone continue to press these issues on an international level because to allow the United States to treat indigenous peoples in this way sets an example to the rest of the world that it is ok to treat people in this manner. Hopefully, our actions will help to move the United States into doing what is right in the name of dignity and human rights. Here, in the United States, we have just filed another lawsuit—this one challenges the United States directly on the unconstitutional nature of the Indian Claims Commission and the unlawful manner in which the United States is trying to force us off our lands. Only time will tell if we will be successful, but history will reflect our struggle and the fact that we have never agreed to sell our birth rights. Our land is not for sale—the United States thinks it can do whatever it wants, but we know and our children and grandchildren will know that we never sold our land.

Thank you for your time this evening and again, thank you for this honor.

Epilogue: Outcomes

The changes to capitalism, American cities, family structures, and public policy (i.e., the reemergence of conservatism) have all played a role in the growing gap between the haves and have-nots. For example, from 1979 to 2000, the bottom 80 percent of the population experienced a small increase in after-tax income. Specifically, the average after-tax-income for the lowest fifth of the population ($13,700) increased 9 percent ($1,100), the second fifth ($29,000) increased 13 percent ($3,400), the middle fifth ($41,900) increased 15 percent ($5,500), and the fourth fifth ($59,200) increased 24 percent ($11,500). However, the modest increase that occurred for the bottom 80 percent of the population was in stark contrast to the highest fifth, where the average after-tax income for the 81st to the 95th percentile ($88,700) increased 36 percent ($23,400), the 96th to the 99th percentile increased 53 percent ($55,000), and the top 1 percent ($862,700) increased 201 percent ($576,400).[30]

This growing inequality can also be seen in the amount of wealth held by the rich and the poor. For example, the percentage of total wealth held by the top 1 percent of the population reached 39 percent in 1995, which is almost double the level of 20 percent in 1969. Additionally, the top 10 percent controlled 72 percent of the wealth and the top fifth controlled 85 percent. At the same time, the bottom 80 percent of the population experienced a decline in their total wealth. With this staggering increase in inequality, the poor experienced hunger once again.

Eliminating Hunger and Homelessness in America

In the late twentieth century, plans to eliminate hunger and homelessness were presented. The Physician Task Force on Hunger announced the results of their study to a roomful of sixty reporters. The task force reported that in 1985, there were approximately 20 million Americans experiencing hunger. This revelation generated over 1,200 newspaper articles as well as a statement from the Reagan administration that the number was grossly exaggerated. As a result of the publicity surrounding the study and the political pressure brought to bear on Congress, most of the Reagan cuts in food stamps and nutrition programs were restored by the early 1990s. However, these gains were lost with the passage of the 1996 Personal Responsibility and Work Opportunity Act, which cut $27 billion from food stamps and child nutrition programs over the next years.[31]

Larry Brown, director of the Physician Task Force on Hunger in America, reports that in 2005, "the hunger situation in the U.S. today is strikingly similar to what we described in 1985." Currently, 12.6 million households, or approximately 36 million Americans, experience food insecurity, which means that at some point during the year, they are not certain or unable to acquire food. In addition, 3.9 million households, or 9.6 million people, experience hunger at some point during the year. This information is known because in 1995, the U.S. government initiated an annual questionnaire as part of the Current Population Survey (CPS) administered by the Census Bureau to estimate the number of households experiencing hunger and food insecurity. Although this survey does not constitute an independent and permanent body to monitor the nutritional status of all Americans as recommended by the Physician Task Force, at least it provides some information about the nature of the crisis. Clearly, things would have been different if the task force recommendations had been implemented, but there was no action on (a) a bipartisan emergency legislative package to respond to the hunger crisis; (b) unemployment benefits, which have actually become more restrictive; (c) elderly meal programs; and (d) the quarterly progress report.[32]

There have been some attempts to deal with the 13 million (18 percent) children that experience food insecurity. On the positive side, the number of schools participating in child nutrition programs has gone up each year, and Congress is considering a "Universal Free Breakfast Program." During the 2003–2004 school year, 16.5 million children received free or reduced-price lunches, but only 6.9 million children participated in free or reduced-price breakfasts. One of the main reasons for this difference is that Congress spends more than three times the amount on school lunch programs than it does on breakfast programs. A recent pilot study reported a large increase in participation when the breakfast program became universal rather than based on income (i.e., 130 percent below the poverty rate). If Congress passes a universal free breakfast program, child hunger will be reduced.[33]

A 2005 survey the federal government asked all cities and counties to conduct found that there were 727,304 homeless people in the United States. In order to solve homelessness, Timmer, Eitzen, and Talley called for a huge infusion of federal funds for low-income and affordable housing. Although nothing like a "Marshall Plan" for low-income housing has yet been implemented, there is a grassroots movement advocating the development of a national housing trust fund. The goal of a trust fund is to produce and rehabilitate 1.5 million affordable housing units for low-income people during the next ten years. This ongoing and dedicated source of money would come from a 5 percent surcharge on after-tax profits on Fannie Mae and Freddie Mac. A bill to create the trust fund, entitled the Federal Housing Finance Reform Act, is currently being debated by Congress.[34]

Labor Solutions

Three labor-related solutions to poverty were offered: the living wage, the repeal of Taft-Hartley, and the repeal or amendment of the WTO. The living wage has had a series of successes. In 1994, the living wage movement had its first victory.

Baltimore became the first city to pass an ordinance stipulating that companies that contract with the city had to pay $6.10 per hour in 1996 and $7.70 per hour in 1998, with the wage subsequently adjusted for inflation. Although this was hardly a living-wage, it was a breakthrough. By 1998, twelve cities had passed living-wage laws and campaigns were ongoing in many other cities. Although the proposal varies from city to city, the gist of it is the same: if a company wants a city contract, it must pay more than the minimum wage. The next stage for the living-wage campaign is to pass citywide proposals. In the fall of 2003, San Francisco voters did just this when they approved an increase of the minimum wage to $8.50 per hour until December 31, 2004, with the wage subsequently adjusted for inflation. After more citywide and countywide proposals are passed, the living-wage coalition is considering plans for a national campaign.[35]

Both the WTO and Taft-Hartley are still in place, but there is pressure mounting, particularly against the WTO. In Seattle, 50,000 protestors shut down the city for several days and forced the international talks to end in failure. Mass protests have continued to be held whenever WTO meetings take place as well as World Bank and International Monetary Fund meetings (i.e., the two other major international capitalist institutions). It should be noted that in 2004, Congressman Dennis Kucinich ran for president in the Democratic primary on a platform of repealing Taft-Hartley and the WTO. Kucinich did not win the nomination, finishing near the bottom of states that voted; however, he did win 31 percent of the caucus participants in Hawaii and 25 percent in Maine.[36]

Universal and Race-Specific Proposals

With the rise of conservatism, which has led to right-wing control of all branches of the federal government, there has been little effort to implement Wilson's proposal of a WPA-like public works project or of a substantial training and retraining program. However, Wilson's idea for allowing residents from segregated inner cities to move closer to jobs in the suburban areas has had some positive effects on income, employment, and education. A recent study examined the Gautreaux program in Chicago, which has funded the relocation of 7,000 black families to the six-county metropolitan area as part of a discrimination lawsuit against the city's public housing office. The result of this relocation has been that families that moved to suburban areas saw a 24 percent increase in income, while families that remained in isolated communities experienced only an 11 percent increase. However, the Moving to Opportunity Program, a federal program initiated in 1994 that provided $234 million to help 4,600 families move from spatially isolated communities in five U.S. cities to more affluent ones, has not had a strong impact on their income. Nevertheless, children who moved to more affluent areas have had higher rates of school success, college attendance, and employment, demonstrating that there may be more long-term benefits to such programs.[37]

It could be argued that Wilson's vision of a tight labor market and noninflationary growth was attained during the Clinton administration, which led to the expected decline in unemployment and poverty. In the African American community, unemployment dropped by almost 50 percent, from a decade high of 15 percent in 1992 to 8 percent by 1999. However, with a stagnant minimum wage and an hourglass economy, which produces large numbers of low-wage jobs, poverty was only modestly reduced by 2 percent. As the economy moved into a recession in 2000, black unemployment once again began to rise, reaching almost 12 percent by mid-2003.[38]

The assets-based approach to welfare has gathered momentum as grassroots organizations have been at the forefront of promoting and creating individual development accounts (IDAs). The movement has also brought together foundations, local nonprofits, and states to work out the various policy details. IDA supporters were successful in including language in the 1996 welfare reform act that allowed states to use IDAs as an option and in persuading Congress in 1998 to authorize $125 million for "account matching" as part of a five-year IDA pilot project. Today, there are twenty-four states with some form of state-funded IDA program. In addition, it is estimated that 10,000 low-income people now possess an IDA. Research on the effect of IDAs is still in its early phase, but it appears that the small pilot IDA programs have had a positive effect on savings, homeownership, health, and marriage.[39]

One asset program that has been in place since 1975, and was expanded in 1993, is the Earned Income Tax Credit (EITC). During the Clinton years and even today, this tax credit has become one of the nation's most effective poverty reduction programs. In 2004, 21 million low- and moderate-income working families claimed the EITC on their tax forms, which generated $36 billion in benefits, and moved almost 5 million people out of poverty. The average EITC refund is approximately $1,500.[40]

Reparations

The reparations movement is still working to pass House Resolution 40, which has been introduced in Congress every year since 1989 by Representative John Conyers (D-MI). The bill would set up a national commission to study the damage caused by enslavement of African Americans in the past and present, and to make recommendations for suitable remedies in the form of an apology and compensation.

This issue has gained some support in the past several years as several important books have come out in support of reparations. At the grassroots level, organizations like the National Coalition of Blacks for Reparations in America (N'COBRA) continue to mobilize and organize to pass HR 40. In the courts, lawyers have begun to bring high-profile lawsuits against private companies (e.g., Aetna, CSX Rail Company, and FleetBoston) that had a role in providing insurance policies to owners for their slaves or benefited from the work of the enslaved.[41]

Traditionalist Solutions

On July 7, 2004, President Bush signed into law a bill that will distribute $145 million (i.e., the original 1979 award of $27 million plus interest) to the Western Shoshone as well as set up an education fund. This distribution will take place over the objection of eight resolutions by Western Shoshone governing bodies. Many Western Shoshone leaders vowed continued resistance, arguing that they will not take the money and give up the right to their land, since they believe the U.S. government has stolen the land based on a fraudulent claim. Soon after the passage of the bill, Carrie Dann wrote:

> This bill does not change the fact that title of the land still exists with the Western Shoshone. Fraud is fraud, and no matter what the U.S. does to us we will never give up our struggle to protect our Sacred Earth Mother.... I have said this a thousand times, I am not taking money for this land. This land has no value, there is no price for it. In Western Shoshone culture, the earth is our mother. We can not sell it. Taking our land is not only a cultural genocide, it is also a spiritual genocide. The United States is attempting to steal our religion and our culture.[42]

As of spring 2006, no money was distributed to the Western Shoshone people. It should be noted that the Western Shoshone land dispute is one of many current land disputes between American Indian nations and the U.S. government. Ever since the "discovery" of America, the struggle for land has been a struggle against poverty as well as cultural and spiritual genocide.

Where We Are Today

In 2004, the nation's poverty threshold for a family of four with two children was $19,157 or less. A family of two with no children is considered to live in poverty if they make $12,649 or less, and a single person sixty-five or older lives in poverty if she makes $9,060 or less. Using this poverty measurement, 37 million people, or almost 13 percent of the population, currently live below the poverty line. If a more realistic formula for counting the poor were used, without the flaws of the current poverty threshold, the number of poor would rise to at least 50 million. These figures put the United States in the dishonorable position of having the highest poverty rates in the industrialized world.[43]

When analyzed by race, the 2004 U.S. poverty rates are 9 percent for whites, 10 percent for Asian and Pacific Islanders, 22 percent for Latinos, 24 percent for American Indian and Alaska natives, and 25 percent for African Americans. However, statistics can sometimes hide as much as they reveal. By examining poverty rates from the perspective of ethnicity, one can gain a more accurate picture. For example, in the 2000 census, when Asian and Pacific Islanders are broken down by ethnicity, there is a wide range of poverty rates, varying from 6 percent for Filipinos to 38 percent for Hmong. In the middle, there are other Asian groups, with Japanese at 10 percent, Chinese at 14 percent, Vietnamese at 16 percent, and Cambodians at 29 percent. The same can be said for Latinos, whose poverty rates vary from 15 percent for Cubans to 26 percent for Puerto Ricans, with Central Americans (20 percent) and Mexicans (24 percent) in the middle. Some of the factors affecting these numbers are the education and social class levels of each group upon immigration or conquest, shade of skin color, citizenship status, English-language ability, and the length of time in the country.[44]

If poverty levels were broken down by age, nearly all would agree that child poverty in the United States is an outrage. Today, 18 percent (13 million) of American children under the age of eighteen live in poverty, and the number rises to 29 percent for Latino and 33 percent for African American kids. These figures rank the United States number one in child poverty in the industrialized world. At the same time, the overall poverty rate for seniors is 10 percent. This overall senior poverty rate is significantly lower than for the youth as a direct result of government-supported programs. However, the senior poverty rates for blacks and Latinos are 24 percent and 19 percent respectively. When gender is combined with race, the economic condition continues to worsen, as the rate for elderly black women over seventy-five increases to 29 percent and for elderly Latinas to 27 percent. In comparison, the poverty rate for elderly white women is 12 percent.[45]

As stated earlier, approximately 36 million Americans experience food insecurity and 9.6 million people experience hunger; in addition, there are more than 700,000 people without homes. Furthermore, the United States is the only industrialized nation that does not provide national health insurance to all of its people. Today, 45 million, or 16 percent of Americans, do not have health insurance.[46]

President Bush's signature programs, faith-based initiatives, have not decreased the number of people living in poverty. In fact, poverty has gone up for four consecutive years under Bush, increasing by four million people since 2001. Middle-class incomes remain stagnant. Bush's Social Security plan seems to be stalled, but with conservatives holding all three branches of government, it is still possible for some type of privatization plan to be enacted. The other great change the conservative Congress and the moderate Clinton brought about was the elimination of a guaranteed safety net, replacing it with Temporary Assistance to Needy Families (TANF). Politicians have been delighted by the over 60 percent drop in welfare rolls, from 5 million cases (14.2 million people) in 1994 to 1.9 million cases (4.5 million people) by the middle of 2005, but there is little evidence that former AFDC recipients are economically better off.[47] Additionally, we don't know what will happen when there is a long-term recession or depression, since benefits are capped at a total of five years and expenditures at $16.4 billion.

As stated above, not all Americans are doing poorly. Over the past twenty-five years, the rich have done extremely well, and that continues to be the case today. For example, the top 1 percent has received one-third of all tax cuts enacted under President George W. Bush, which amounts to an average tax cut of $78,460 for people making $1 million annually. However, the households in the middle fifth have received an average tax cut of $1,090, and the bottom fifth have received a tax cut of $250.[48]

I believe this is the way it will be until poor people, in coalition with other groups, rise up to change the direction of the country, as was previously done by the working class, the unemployed, women, African Americans, farmworkers, and Native Americans. As this book has shown, it is possible for America to reduce poverty as it did in the 1960s and with seniors. Quite possibly, the time may be right for social change after Hurricane Katrina demonstrated to all that the United States is a nation divided between the haves and the have-nots. It is now up to you to decide what to do with the plans and proposals that have been highlighted in this book. My advice is to choose a solution that you believe is the most effective and try to implement it.

Notes

Chapter 1

1. Bruce E. Johansen, *Forgotten Founders: Benjamin Franklin, the Iroquois, and the Rationale for the American Revolution* (Ofipswich, MA: Gambit, 1982); Henry Steele Commager, *The Empire of Reason: How Europe Imagined and America Realized the Enlightenment* (Garden City, NY: Anchor, 1978), 154.

2. Jack M. Weatherford, *Indian Givers: How the Indians of the Americas Transformed the World* (New York: Crown, 1988).

3. Michel de Montaigne, "On Cannibals," in George B. Ives, trans., *The Essays of Montaigne*, vol. 1 (Cambridge, MA: Harvard University Press, 1925); William Brandon, *New Worlds for Old: Reports from the New World and Their Effect on the Development of Social Thought in Europe, 1500–1800* (Athens: Ohio University Press, 1986); William Shakespeare, *The Tempest* (New York: Penguin, 1987); Meredith A. Skura, "Discourse and the Individual: The Case of Colonialism in *The Tempest*," in Virginia M. Vaughan and Alden T. Vaughan, eds., *Critical Essays on Shakespeare's* The Tempest (New York: G. K. Hall, 1998).

4. Weatherford, *Indian Givers*.

5. James C. Adair, *History of the American Indians* (London: E. and C. Dilly, 1775); Matthew Wheelock, *Reflections, Moral and Political on Great Britain and Her Colonies* (London: T. Becket, 1770), 177; Gilbert L. Wilson, "Diaries, Notebooks, and Reports, Undated and 1905–1929, vol. 22," in Karen Kilcup, ed., *Native American Women's Writing 1800–1924: An Anthology* (Malden, MA: Blackwell Publishers, 2000), 128.

6. Cadwallder Colden, *The History of the Five Indian Nations of Canada, Which Are Dependent on the Province of New York and Are a Barrier Between the English and the French in That Part of the World* (New York: A. S. Barnes, 1904); John D. Hunter, *Memoirs of a Captivity Among the Indians of North America, from Childhood to the Age of Nineteen: With Anecdotes Descriptive of Their Manners and Customs; to Which Is Added, Some Account of the Soil, Climate, and Vegetable Productions of the Territory Westward of the Mississippi* (1823; reprint New York: Johnson, 1970), 317.

7. Brandon, *New Worlds for Old.*

8. Julia Averkiva, "The Tlingit Indians," in Eleanor B. Leacock and Nancy O. Lurie, eds., *North American Indians in Historical Perspective* (Prospect Heights, IL: Waveland Press, 1971), 317–342; Bruce E. Johansen, "Native American Self-Government and Its Impact on Democracy's Development," in Donald A. Grinde, Jr., ed., *Native Americans* (Washington, DC: Congressional Quarterly Press, 2002), 22; Harold E. Driver, *Indians of North America* (Chicago: University of Chicago Press, 1969).

9. Thomas Paine, "Agrarian Justice," in Harry Clarke, ed., *The Pioneers of Land Reform: Thomas Spence, William Ogilvie, and Thomas Paine, with an Introduction by M. Beer* (London: G. Bell and Sons, 1920), 179–203.

10. Reginald Horsman, "United States Indian Policies, 1776–1815," in William C. Sturtevant and Wilcomb E. Washburn, eds., *History of Indian-White Relations*, vol. 4 (Washington, DC: Smithsonian Institution, 1988), 29–39.

11. Russell Thornton, *American Indian Holocaust and Survival: A Population History Since 1492* (Norman: University of Oklahoma Press, 1987).

12. Walter O'Meara, *In the Country of the Walking Dead* (New York: Award Books, 1976).

Chapter 2

1. Seth E. Rockman, *Welfare Reform in the Early Republic: A Brief History with Documents* (Boston: Bedford/St. Martin's, 2003); Gary B. Nash, "Poverty and Poor Relief in Pre-Revolutionary Philadelphia," *William and Mary Quarterly* 33 (January 1976): 28; Raymond A. Mohl, "Poverty in Early America, a Reappraisal: The Case of Eighteenth Century New York City," *New York History* 50 (January 1969): 5–27.

2. Rockman, *Welfare Reform in the Early Republic;* Nash, "Poverty and Poor Relief in Pre-Revolutionary Philadelphia," 28; Charles Burroughs, "A Discourse Delivered in the Chapel of the New Almshouse" (1834), reprinted in David J. Rothman, ed., *The Jacksonians on the Poor: Collected Pamphlets* (New York: Arno Press, 1971), 5–108; Mohl, "Poverty in Early America, a Reappraisal"; Charles Redenius, *The American Ideal of Equality: From Jefferson's Declaration to the Burger Court* (Port Washington, NY: Kennikat Press, 1981).

3. Rockman, *Welfare Reform in the Early Republic.*

4. "Report of the Committee on the Pauper Laws of This Commonwealth" (1821), reprinted in David J. Rothman, ed., *The Almshouse Experience: Collected Pamphlets* (New York: Arno Press, 1971), 1–36; Katz, *In the Shadow of the Poorhouse: A Social History of Welfare in America* (New York: Basic Books, 1986); Mohl, "Poverty in Early America, a Reappraisal."

5. John V. Yates, "Report of the Secretary of State in 1824 on the Relief and Settlement of the Poor" (1824), reprinted in Rothman, ed., *The Almshouse Experience: Collected Pamphlets*, 939–1145; Katz, *In the Shadow of the Poorhouse;* Burroughs, "A Discourse Delivered in the Chapel of the New Almshouse," 9.

6. Rockman, *Welfare Reform in the Early Republic;* Matthew Carey, "A Plea for the Poor, Particularly Females. An Inquiry How Far the Charges Alleged Against Them of Improvidence, Idleness, and Dissipation, Are Founded on Truth" (1837), reprinted in David

J. Rothman, ed., *The Jacksonians on the Poor: Collected Pamphlets*; Matthew Carey, "Address to New York Ladies," in *Miscellaneous Essays* (New York: Burt Franklin, 1830), 282.

7. Wilson Pierson and George R. McFarland, "Address of the Association of Working People of New-Castle County," *Free Enquirer*, October 7, 1829, 393; Thomas Skidmore, *The Rights of Man to Property! Being a Proposition to Make It Equal Among the Adults of the Present Generation: And to Provide for Its Equal Transmission to Every Individual of Each Succeeding Generation, on Arriving at the Age of Maturity* (New York: A. Ming, Jr., 1829), 3–4.

8. Christopher B. Doob, *Racism: An American Cauldron* (New York: Longman, 1999); Rockman, *Welfare Reform in the Early Republic*.

9. Katz, *In the Shadow of the Poorhouse*.

10. Female Missionary Society for the Poor of the City of New York and Its Vicinity, *Second Anniversary Report* (New York: E. B. Gould, 1818), 7; Society for the Prevention of Pauperism in the City of New York, *Documents Relative to Savings Banks, Intemperance, and Lotteries* (New York: E. Conrad, 1818), 21; Rockman, *Welfare Reform in the Early Republic*.

11. Rockman, *Welfare Reform in the Early Republic*; Katz, *In the Shadow of the Poorhouse*.

12. Heman Humphrey, *On Doing Good to the Poor: A Sermon, Preached at Pittsfield, on the Day of the Annual Fast, April 4, 1818* (Pittsfield, MA: Phinehas Allen, 1818); Yates, "Report of the Secretary of State in 1824," 951; Quincy, "Report of the Committee on the Pauper Laws of the Commonwealth," 4.

13. Rockman, *Welfare Reform in the Early Republic*, 104.

14. Katz, *In the Shadow of the Poorhouse*.

15. Pierson and McFarland, "Address of the Association of Working People of New-Castle County," 393; Frances Wright, "Lecture on the Existing Evils and Their Remedy," *Free Enquirer*, December 12, 1829, 49–53.

16. Katz, *In the Shadow of the Poorhouse*, 66.

17. New York State Senate, Select Committee, *Report of Select Committee Appointed to Visit Charitable Institutions Supported by the State and City and County Poor and Work Houses and Jails*, no. 8, January 9, 1857, 5.

18. Katz, *In the Shadow of the Poorhouse*.

19. Amos G. Warner, *American Charities* (New York: Crowell, 1908); Katz, *In the Shadow of the Poorhouse*.

20. W. C. Vanderwerth, *Indian Oratory: Famous Speeches by Noted Indian Chieftains* (Norman: University of Oklahoma Press, 1971); Francis P. Prucha, "United States Indian Policies, 1815–1860," in Sturtevant and Washburn, eds., *History of Indian-White Relations*, vol. 4, 40–50.

21. Rockman, *Welfare Reform in the Early Republic*.

Chapter 3

1. W. E. B. Du Bois, "The Freedmen's Bureau," *Atlantic Monthly* 87 (1901): 354–365; Katz, *In the Shadow of the Poorhouse*; Nelson Lichtenstein, Susan Strasser, and Roy Rosenzweig, *Who Built America? Working People and the Nation's Economy, Politics, and Society: 1877 to the Present*, vol. 2 (New York: Worth Publishers, 2000).

2. Du Bois, "The Freedmen's Bureau."

3. International Indian Treaty Council, "Response to the United States of America's First Periodic Report, Dated September 30, 2000, to the United Nations Committee on the Elimination of Racial Discrimination," http://www.treatycouncil.org/section_211415. htm (accessed January 23, 2005); William T. Hogan, "United States Indian Policies, 1860–1900," in Sturtevant and Washburn, eds., *History of Indian-White Relations,* vol. 4, 51–65.

4. Henry Dawes, quoted in Angie Debo, *And Still the Waters Run* (Princeton, NJ: Princeton University Press, 1940), 21–22.

5. Matthew C. Snipp, "The First Americans: American Indians," in Silvia Pedraza and Rubén G. Rumbaut, eds., *Origins and Destinies: Immigration, Race, and Ethnicity in America* (Belmont, CA: Wadsworth, 1996); International Indian Treaty Council, "Response to the United States of America's First Periodic Report."

6. Lichtenstein, Strasser, and Rosenzweig, *Who Built America,* 27; Redenius, *The American Ideal of Equality.*

7. Paul S. Boyer, *Urban Masses and Moral Order in America: 1820–1920* (Cambridge, MA: Harvard University Press, 1978); Charles and Mary Beard, quoted in Walter I. Trattner, *From Poor Law to Welfare State: A History of Social Welfare in America* (New York: Free Press, 1979), 71; Lichtenstein, Strasser, and Rosenzweig, *Who Built America.*

8. Katz, *In the Shadow of the Poorhouse;* Lichtenstein, Strasser, and Rosenzweig, *Who Built America,* 25; Judith F. Clark, *America's Gilded Age: An Eyewitness History* (New York: Facts on File, 1992), Howard Zinn, *A People's History of the United States: 1492–Present* (New York: HarperPerennial, 1995).

9. Trattner, *From Poor Law to Welfare State;* Lichtenstein, Strasser, and Rosenzweig, *Who Built America.*

10. Zinn, *A People's History of the United States;* Clark, *America's Gilded Age.*

11. Trattner, *From Poor Law to Welfare State;* Clark, *America's Gilded Age;* Lichtenstein, Strasser, and Rosenzweig, *Who Built America,* 91.

12. Terrency V. Powderly, *Thirty Years of Labor: 1859–1889* (Columbus, OH: Excelsior, 1889), 243.

13. Powderly, *Thirty Years of Labor;* Susan B. Anthony, "Woman Wants Bread, Not the Ballot," in Ida H. Harper, *Life and Work of Susan B. Anthony: Including Public Addresses, Her Own Letters, and Many from Her Contemporaries During Fifty Years,* vol. 2 (Indianapolis: Bowen-Merrill, 1898), 1002.

14. Lucy E. Parsons, *Twenty-Fifth Anniversary Eleventh of November Memorial Edition: Souvenir Edition of the Famous Speeches of Our Martyrs, Delivered in Court When Asked If They Had Anything to Say Why Sentence of Death Should Not Be Passed upon Them, October 7, 8, and 9, 1886* (Chicago, IL: Lucy E. Parsons, 1912).

15. Edward Bellamy, *Looking Backward: 2000–1887* (Boston: Houghton Mifflin, 1917), 42.

16. Henry George, *Progress and Poverty: An Inquiry into the Cause of Industrial Depressions and of Increase of Want with Increase of Wealth; the Remedy* (New York: Robert Schalkenbach Foundation, 1987); Henry George, "The Single Tax—What It Is, and Why We Urge It," in *The Christian Advocate* (New York: T. Carlton and J. Porter, July 24, 1890), 481.

17. Katz, *In the Shadow of the Poorhouse.*

18. Katz, *In the Shadow of the Poorhouse*; Cynthia Rose, ed., *American Decades Primary Sources, 1930–1939* (Detroit, MI: Thompson/Gale, 2004).

19. Josephine S. Lowell, *Public Relief and Private Charity* (New York: Arno Press, 1971), 110–111; Katz, *In the Shadow of the Poorhouse.*

20. S. Humphreys Gurteen, *A Handbook of Charity Organization* (Buffalo, NY: author, 1882).

21. W. E. B. Du Bois, *Black Reconstruction* (Millwood, NY: Kraus-Thomson, 1976).

22. Thomas Hall, quoted in Zinn, *A People's History of the United States,* 193; Du Bois, *Black Reconstruction*; Trattner, *From Poor Law to Welfare State*; Stewart E. Tolnay and E. M. Beck, *A Festival of Violence: An Analysis of Southern Lynchings, 1882–1930* (Urbana: University of Illinois Press, 1995); Robert L. Zangrando, *The NAACP Crusade Against Lynching, 1909–1950* (Philadelphia, PA: Temple University Press, 1980).

23. Lichtenstein, Strasser, and Rosenzweig, *Who Built America.*

24. Sandra Baxter and Marjorie Lansing, *Women and Politics: The Visible Majority* (Ann Arbor: University of Michigan Press, 1983); Lichtenstein, Strasser, and Rosenzweig, *Who Built America.* The numbers reported by Baxter and Lansing were registered voters; thus, the number of actual voters would have been even smaller. Also, the number of registered voters was restricted due to discrimination against women of color.

25. Clark, *America's Gilded Age*; Zinn, *A People's History of the United States.*

26. Katz, *In the Shadow of the Poorhouse.*

Chapter 4

1. Katz, *In the Shadow of the Poorhouse.*

2. Esther Ngan-Ling Chow, "Family, Economy, and the State: A Legacy of Struggle for Chinese American Women," in Pedraza and Rumbaut, eds., *Origins and Destinies,* 110–124.

3. Silvia Pedraza, "Origins and Destinies: Immigration, Race, and Ethnicity in American History," in Pedraza and Rumbaut, eds., *Origins and Destinies,* 1–20; Ricardo Romo, "Mexican Americans: Their Civic and Political Incorporation," in Pedraza and Rumbaut, eds., *Origins and Destinies,* 84–97.

4. Pedraza, *Origins and Destinies*; Katz, *In the Shadow of the Poorhouse*; Lichtenstein, Strasser, and Rosenzweig, *Who Built America.*

5. Jacob A. Riis, *How the Other Half Lives: Studies Among the Tenements of New York* (Cambridge: MA: Harvard University Press, 1970), 32–33.

6. Katz, *In the Shadow of the Poorhouse.*

7. Zinn, *A People's History of the United States.*

8. Lichtenstein, Strasser, and Rosenzweig, *Who Built America.*

9. Katz, *In the Shadow of the Poorhouse.*

10. Allen F. Davis, *Spearheads for Reform: The Social Settlements and the Progressive Movement, 1890–1914* (New York: Oxford University Press, 1967); Trattner, *From Poor Law to Welfare State.*

11. Addams, *Twenty Years at Hull-House* (New York: Macmillan, 1910), 92; Davis, *Spearheads for Reform*; Lichtenstein, Strasser, and Rosenzweig, *Who Built America*.

12. Julia C. Lathrop, "Child Welfare Standards: A Test of Democracy," in *Proceedings of the National Conference of Social Work at the Forty-Sixth Annual Session Held in Atlantic City, New Jersey, June 1–8, 1919* (Chicago, IL: University of Chicago Press, 1920), 5–9.

13. Katz, *In the Shadow of the Poorhouse*.

14. Davis, *Spearheads of Reform*; Trattner, *From Poor Law to Welfare State*.

15. Lichtenstein, Strasser, and Rosenzweig, *Who Built America*; Booker T. Washington, *Up from Slavery* (New York: Penguin Books, 1986 [1901]).

16. W. E. B. Du Bois, *The Souls of Black Folk* (Chicago, IL: A. C. McClurg, 1953 [1903]), 57–58.

17. Russell Thornton, "North American Indians and the Demography of Contact," in Pedraza and Rumbaut, eds., *Origins and Destinies*, 43–59.

18. Thornton, "North American Indians and the Demography of Contact"; Luther Standing Bear, *Land of the Spotted Eagle* (Lincoln: University of Nebraska Press, 1978).

19. Elizabeth V. Burt, *The Progressive Era: Primary Documents on Events from 1890–1914* (Westport, CT: Greenwood Press, 2004); Zinn, *A People's History of the United States*.

20. Burt, *The Progressive Era*; Lichtenstein, Strasser, and Rosenzweig, *Who Built America*.

21. Burt, *The Progressive Era*; Lichtenstein, Strasser, and Rosenzweig, *Who Built America*.

22. Burt, *The Progressive Era*; Lichtenstein, Strasser, and Rosenzweig, *Who Built America*.

23. Lucy G. Barber, *Marching on Washington: The Forging of an American Political Tradition* (Berkeley: University of California Press, 2002); Carlos A. Schwantes, *Coxey's Army: An American Odyssey* (Lincoln: University of Nebraska Press, 1985).

24. William D. Haywood, *The Autobiography of William D. Haywood* (New York: International Publishers, 1958); Joyce L. Kornbluh, *Rebel Voices: An IWW Anthology* (Ann Arbor: University of Michigan Press, 1964).

25. Haywood, *The Autobiography of William D. Haywood*; Kornbluh, *Rebel Voices*.

26. Jean Y. Tussey, ed., *Eugene V. Debs Speaks* (New York: Pathfinder Press, 1972).

27. Zinn, *A People's History of the United States*; Ralph M. Easley, "Social, Industrial, and Civic Progress," *Bankers' Magazine* (November 1912): 484.

28. Zinn, *A People's History of the United States*.

29. Lichtenstein, Strasser, and Rosenzweig, *Who Built America*.

30. Katz, *In the Shadow of the Poorhouse*.

31. Katz, *In the Shadow of the Poorhouse*.

32. Katz, *In the Shadow of the Poorhouse*.

33. Lichtenstein, Strasser, and Rosenzweig, *Who Built America*.

34. Katz, *In the Shadow of the Poorhouse*; United Way of America, "Our History," http://national.unitedway.org/about/history.cfm (accessed December 18, 2005).

35. William James, "The Moral Equivalent to War," in Norman Foerster, Frederick A. Manchester, and Karl Young, eds., *Essays for College Men* (New York: Henry Holt, 1915), 365–387.

36. Zinn, *A People's History of the United States,* 341.

37. Zinn, *A People's History of the United States;* Lichtenstein, Strasser, and Rosen-zweig, *Who Built America.*

38. Henry Vincent, *The Story of the Commonweal: Complete and Graphic Narrative of the Origin and Growth of the Movement* (Chicago: W. K. Conkey, 1894); Barber, *Marching on Washington.*

39. Zinn, *A People's History of the United States;* Vincent St. John, *The IWW: Its History, Structure, and Methods* (Chicago, IL: Industrial Workers of the World, 1919).

40. Katz, *In the Shadow of the Poorhouse;* Lichtenstein, Strasser, and Rosenzweig, *Who Built America.*

41. Washington, *Up from Slavery.*

Chapter 5

1. Katz, *In the Shadow of the Poorhouse.*

2. Robert F. Himmelberg, *The Great Depression and the New Deal* (Westport, CT: Greenwood, 2001); Harold R. Kerbo, *Social Stratification and Inequality: Class Conflict in Historical, Comparative, and Global Perspective* (New York: McGraw-Hill, 2003); Zinn, *A People's History of the United States;* Lichtenstein, Strasser, and Rosenzweig, *Who Built America.*

3. Herbert Hoover, "Campaign Speech at Madison Square Garden, New York City, October 31, 1932," in William S. Myers, ed., *The State Papers and Other Public Writings of Herbert Hoover,* vol. 2 (reprint New York: Kraus, 1970), 410.

4. Himmelberg, *The Great Depression and the New Deal;* Herbert Hoover, "The Importance of the Preservation of Self-Help and of the Responsibilities of Individual Generosity as Opposed to Deteriorating Effects of Government Appropriations," in William S. Myers, ed., *The State Papers and Other Public Writings of Herbert Hoover,* vol. 1 (New York: Doubleday, Doran, 1934), 496–499; Katz, *In the Shadow of the Poorhouse.*

5. Barber, *Marching on Washington;* Himmelberg, *The Great Depression and the New Deal.*

6. Zinn, *A People's History of the United States;* Himmelberg, *The Great Depression and the New Deal;* Hoover, "Campaign Speech at Madison Square Garden."

7. Lichtenstein, Strasser, and Rosenzweig, *Who Built America.*

8. Grace Hutchins, *What Every Working Woman Wants* (New York: Workers Library, 1935); Robert S. McElvaine, ed., *Encyclopedia of the Great Depression,* vol. 1 (New York: Macmillan, 2004); Lichtenstein, Strasser, and Rosenzweig, *Who Built America.*

9. McElvaine, *Encyclopedia of the Great Depression;* Lichtenstein, Strasser, and Rosenzweig, *Who Built America;* Ricardo Romo, "Mexican Americans: Their Civic and Political Incorporation," in Pedraza and Rumbaut, eds., *Origins and Destinies,* 84–97.

10. Lichtenstein, Strasser, and Rosenzweig, *Who Built America;* Hutchins, *What Every Working Woman Wants;* Himmelberg, *The Great Depression and the New Deal.*

11. Robert Ellsberg, ed., *Dorothy Day: Selected Writings* (Maryknoll, NY: Orbis, 1997).

12. Ellsberg, *Dorothy Day: Selected Writings*, 47; Dorothy Day, *Loaves and Fishes* (San Francisco: Harper and Row, 1963), 215; Dorothy Day, *Union Square to Rome* (New York: Arno Press, 1978 [1938]), 47.

13. Nels Anderson, *The Right to Work* (New York: Modern Age, 1938); Harry Hopkins, *Spending to Save: The Complete Story of Relief* (New York: W. W. Norton, 1936); National Association of Civilian Conservation Corps Alumni, "Roosevelt's Tree Army," available at http://www.ccc.alumni.org/history1.html (accessed March 24, 2006); Katz, *In the Shadow of the Poorhouse*; Himmelberg, *The Great Depression and the New Deal*.

14. Huey Long, "Redistribution of Wealth," January 14, 1935, 74th Congress, *Congressional Record* 79, pt. 1: 410–412.

15. Francis E. Townsend, *New Horizons: An Autobiography* (Chicago, IL: J. L. Stewart, 1943); Rose, *American Decades Primary Sources, 1930–1939*.

16. Upton Sinclair, *I, Governor of California, and How I Ended Poverty* (Los Angeles: author, 1934), 22.

17. Franklin Folsom, *Impatient Armies of the Poor: The Story of Collective Action of the Unemployed 1808–1942* (Niwot: University Press of Colorado, 1991); Frances Perkins, *The Roosevelt I Knew* (New York: Viking Press, 1946); Katz, *In the Shadow of the Poorhouse*.

18. Hutchins, *What Every Working Woman Wants*; Folsom, *Impatient Armies of the Poor*.

19. Kathleen P. Bennett and Margaret D. LeCompte, *The Way Schools Work: A Sociological Analysis of Education* (New York: Longman, 1990); Peter F. Carborne, Jr., *The Social and Educational Thought of Harold Rugg* (Durham, NC: Duke University Press, 1977); George S. Counts, *The Social Foundations of Education* (New York: Charles Scribner's Sons, 1934), 542.

20. Leon H. Keyserling, "Why the Wagner Act?" in Louis G. Silverberg, ed., *The Wagner Act: After Ten Years* (Washington, DC: Bureau of National Affairs, 1945); Rose, *American Decades Primary Sources, 1930–1939*; Lichtenstein, Strasser, and Rosenzweig, *Who Built America*.

21. Snipp, "The First Americans: American Indians"; Himmelberg, *The Great Depression and the New Deal*.

22. Negroes' Committee to March on Washington for Equal Participation in National Defense, "Call to Negro America," *The Black Worker*, vol. 7, no. 5 (New York: Brotherhood of Sleeping Car Porters, May 1941), 4.

23. Robert Ellsberg, *Dorothy Day: Selected Writings*; The Catholic Worker Movement, http://www.catholicworker.org (accessed May 24, 2005).

24. Bennett and LeCompte, *The Way Schools Work*; Carborne, Jr., *The Social and Educational Thought of Harold Rugg*.

25. Rose, *American Decades Primary Sources, 1930–1939*.

26. Rose, *American Decades Primary Sources, 1930–1939*; Carmen D. Solomon, *Major Decisions in the House and Senate on Social Security: 1935–1985* (Washington, DC: Congressional Research Service, 1986).

27. Rose, *American Decades Primary Sources, 1930–1939*; Solomon, *Major Decisions in the House and Senate on Social Security: 1935–1985*.

28. "Upton Sinclair," in *The History of Social Security*, http://www.ssa.gov/history/sinclair.html (accessed May 25, 2005); Lichtenstein, Strasser, and Rosenzweig, *Who Built America*.

29. Herbert Benjamin, *Shall It Be Hunger Doles or Unemployment Insurance?* (New York: Workers Library, 1934); Bonnie F. Schwartz, *Civil Works Administration, 1933–1934: The Business of Emergency Employment in the New Deal* (Princeton, NJ: Princeton University Press, 1984); Katz, *In the Shadow of the Poorhouse;* Lichtenstein, Strasser, and Rosenzweig, *Who Built America;* Himmelberg, *The Great Depression and the New Deal.*

30. Anderson, *The Right to Work;* Lichtenstein, Strasser, and Rosenzweig, *Who Built America;* Katz, *In the Shadow of the Poorhouse.*

31. National Association of Civilian Conservation Corps Alumni, "Roosevelt's Tree Army."

32. Katz, *In the Shadow of the Poorhouse;* Gerald D. Nash, Noel H. Pugasch, and Richard F. Tomasson, "An Overview of American Social Security 1935–1985," in Gerald D. Nash, Noel H. Pugasch, and Richard F. Tomasson, eds., *Social Security: The First Half-Century* (Albuquerque: University of New Mexico Press, 1988).

33. Katz, *In the Shadow of the Poorhouse;* Nash, Pugasch, and Tomasson, "An Overview of American Social Security 1935–1985"; Rose, *American Decades Primary Sources, 1930–1939;* Roger Lowenstein, "A Question of Numbers," *New York Times Magazine* (January 16, 2005): 40–47, 72, 76, 78.

34. Katz, *In the Shadow of the Poorhouse.*

35. Katz, *In the Shadow of the Poorhouse;* McElvaine, *Encyclopedia of the Great Depression;* Lichtenstein, Strasser, and Rosenzweig, *Who Built America.*

36. John Collier, Annual Report of the Secretary of the Interior (Washington, DC: U.S. Government Printing Office, 1938); Josephine C. Brown, *Public Relief: 1929–1939* (New York: Henry Holt, 1940).

37. McElvaine, *Encyclopedia of the Great Depression;* Romo, "Mexican Americans: Their Civic and Political Incorporation"; Steven Mintz, "Mexican Americans," Digital History, http://www.digitalhistory.uh.edu/database/article_display.cfm?HHID=469 (accessed May 24, 2005).

38. National Association of Civilian Conservation Corps Alumni, "Roosevelt's Tree Army"; Katz, *In the Shadow of the Poorhouse.*

39. Barber, *Marching on Washington.*

40. Katz, *In the Shadow of the Poorhouse.*

41. Katz, *In the Shadow of the Poorhouse.*

42. Beth Stevens, "Blurring the Boundaries: How the Federal Government Has Influenced Welfare Benefits in the Private Sector," in Margaret Weir, Ann S. Orloff, and Theda Skocpol, eds., *The Politics of Social Policy in the United States* (Princeton, NJ: Princeton University Press, 1988), 123–148; Lichtenstein, Strasser, and Rosenzweig, *Who Built America.*

Chapter 6

1. Franklin D. Roosevelt, "The Four Freedoms," in Cynthia Rose, ed., *American Decades Primary Sources, 1930–1939* (Detroit, MI: Thompson/Gale, 2004).

2. Franklin D. Roosevelt, State of the Union Address, in Samuel Rosenman, ed., *The Public Papers and Addresses of Franklin D. Roosevelt,* vol. 13 (New York: Harper, 1950), 40–42.

3. Harry Truman, "Text of Truman Plea for Public Health Program," in Cynthia Rose, ed., *American Decades Primary Sources, 1940–1949.*

4. G. J. Santoni, "The Employment Act of 1946: Some Historical Notes," in *Review* (St. Louis, MO: Federal Reserve Bank of St. Louis, 1986), 12; Truman, "Text of Truman Plea for Public Health Program."

5. David J. Garrow, *Bearing the Cross: Martin Luther King, Jr., and the Southern Christian Leadership Conference* (New York: Vintage, 1986).

6. Martin Luther King, Jr., *Where Do We Go from Here: Chaos or Community?* (New York: Harper and Row, 1967).

7. Martin Luther King, Jr., "Showdown for Nonviolence," in James M. Washington, ed., *A Testament of Hope: The Essential Writings of Martin Luther King, Jr.* (San Francisco: Harper and Row, 1986), 64–72; King, *Where Do We Go from Here*; Martin Luther King, Jr., transcription of a speech from video, "The Promised Land, 1967–1968," in *Eyes on the Prize II* (Boston, MA: Blackside, 1990).

8. Malcolm X, *February 1965: The Final Speeches* (New York: Pathfinder, 1992).

9. Huey P. Newton, with the assistance of J. Herman Blake, *Revolutionary Suicide* (New York: Harcourt Brace Jovanovich, 1973), 167; Jim Haskins, *Power to the People: The Rise and Fall of the Black Panther Party* (New York: Simon and Schuster, 1997).

10. D. Stanley Eitzen and Kelly E. Smith, *Experiencing Poverty: Voices from the Bottom* (New York: Thomson and Wadsworth, 2003); Harrell R. Rodgers, Jr., *Poverty amid Plenty: A Political and Economic Analysis* (Reading, MA: Addison-Wesley, 1979); Katz, *In the Shadow of the Poorhouse.*

11. Lyndon B. Johnson, "Annual Message to the Congress on the State of the Union," *Public Papers of the Presidents of the United States: Lyndon B. Johnson; Containing the Public Messages, Speeches, and Statements of the President, 1963–1964,* vol. 1 (Washington, DC: Government Printing Office, 1965), 114; Johnson, "Remarks at the University of Michigan," *Public Papers of the Presidents of the United States,* vol. 1, 704.

12. Edward Zigler and Karen Anderson, "An Idea Whose Time Had Come: The Intellectual and Political Climate," in Edward Zigler and Jeanette Valentine, eds., *Project Head Start: A Legacy of the War on Poverty* (New York: Free Press, 1979), 67; Katz, *In the Shadow of the Poorhouse;* Johnson, "Annual Message to the Congress on the State of the Union," 113.

13. Zigler and Anderson, "An Idea Whose Time Had Come: The Intellectual and Political Climate"; Katz, *In the Shadow of the Poorhouse.*

14. Lichtenstein, Strasser, and Rosenzweig, *Who Built America.*

15. Guida West, *The National Welfare Rights Movement: The Social Protest of Poor Women* (New York: Praeger, 1981); Lichtenstein, Strasser, and Rosenzweig, *Who Built America.*

16. West, *The National Welfare Rights Movement;* Johnnie Tillmon, "Welfare as a Women's Issue," *Liberation News Service,* February 26, 1972.

17. James D. Vigil, "Que Viva la Raza: The Many Faces of the Chicano Movement, 1963–1971," in Pedraza and Rumbaut, eds., *Origins and Destinies,* 225–237.

18. Cesar Chavez, "Testimony Before the Subcommittee of Labor of the Senate Committee on Labor and Public Welfare," in Richard J. Jensen and John C. Hammerback, eds., *The Words of Cesar Chavez* (College Station: Texas A&M University Press, 2002), 37–45; Vigil, "Que Viva la Raza"; Cesar Chavez, "Letter from Delano," in Richard J. Jensen and John C. Hammerback, eds., *The Words of Cesar Chavez,* 142.

19. Vigil, "Que Viva la Raza," in Pedraza and Rumbaut, eds., *Origins and Destinies,* 225–237.

20. Cesar Chavez, "La Causa and La Huelga," in Joan L. Ecklein and Armand Lauffer, eds., *Community Organizers and Social Planners: A Volume of Case and Illustrated Materials* (New York: Wiley and Sons, 1972); Cesar Chavez, "Speech at Pacific Lutheran University, March 1989," in Richard J. Jensen and John C. Hammerback, eds., *The Words of Cesar Chavez,* 142.

21. Stephen Cornell, "American Indians and Political Protest: The 'Red Power Years,'" in Pedraza and Rumbaut, eds., *Origins and Destinies,* 238–249.

22. Richard Oakes, "Alcatraz Is Not an Island," *Earth Treaty,* http://www.earth-treaty.com/ts_roakesalcatraz.html (accessed July 6, 2005).

23. Hazel W. Hertzberg, "Indian Rights Movement, 1887–1973," in Sturtevant and Washburn, eds., *History of Indian-White Relations,* 305–323; Cornell, "American Indians and Political Protest."

24. Martin Luther King, Jr., quoted in Garrow, *Bearing the Cross,* 535; Barber, *March on Washington.*

25. West, *The National Welfare Rights Movement;* Katz, *In the Shadow of the Poorhouse.*

26. Martin Luther King, Jr., quoted in Garrow, *Bearing the Cross,* 539; Michael Harrington, *The New American Poverty* (New York: Holt, Rinehart, and Winston, 1984).

27. Jeanne Ellsworth and Lynda J. Ames, "Hope and Challenge: Head Start Past, Present, Future," in Jeanne Ellsworth and Lynda J. Ames, *Critical Perspectives on Project Head Start: Revisioning the Hope and Challenge* (New York: State University of New York Press, 1998); Janet Currie and Duncan Thomas, "Does Head Start Make a Difference?" *American Economic Review* (American Economic Association, 1995), 341–364; "Head Start Statistical Fact Sheet," U.S. Department of Health and Human Resources: Head Start Bureau, http://www.acf.hhs.gov/programs/hsb/about/index.htm (accessed July 5, 2005).

28. Katz, *In the Shadow of the Poorhouse;* "History of Civil Legal Aid," *National League Aid and Defender Association,* http://www.atjsupport.org/About/About_HistoryCivil (accessed July 5, 2005).

29. Leslie Farrell, "My Brother's Keeper" [videorecording], *America's War on Poverty* (Boston, MA: Blackside, 1995).

30. Katz, *In the Shadow of the Poorhouse;* Jim Masters, "History of Community Action Agencies," Iowa Community Action Association, http://www.iowacommunityaction.com/CAAHistory.htm (accessed July 6, 2005).

31. Rodgers, *Poverty amid Plenty;* Joseph Dalaker, *Poverty in the United States, 2000* (Washington, DC: U.S. Census Bureau, 2001); Katz, *In the Shadow of the Poorhouse.*

32. Katz, *In the Shadow of the Poorhouse.*

33. Katz, *In the Shadow of the Poorhouse;* Dalaker, *Poverty in the United States, 2000;* David Halberstam, *The Children* (New York: Random House, 1998). Note that food stamps and Medicaid are excluded from the definition of income and are not represented in poverty levels.

34. Eitzen and Smith, *Experiencing Poverty.*

35. Eitzen and Smith, *Experiencing Poverty.*

36. Garrow, *Bearing the Cross;* Herbert Hoover, quoted in Ward Churchill and Jim V. Wall, *Agents of Repression: The FBI's Secret Wars Against the Black Panther Party and the American Indian Movement* (Boston, MA: South End, 1988), 58; Haskins, *Power to the People.*

37. "Statistical Abstract of the United States: 2004–2005," U.S. Census Bureau, Tables 405 and 440, 1998, http://www.census.gov/prod/www/statistical-abstract-04.html

(accessed July 23, 2005); Theodore Caplow, Louis Hicks, and Ben J. Wattenberg, *The First Measured Century: An Illustrated Guide to Trends in America, 1900–2000* (Washington, DC: AEI Press, 2001); Deborah Kong, "Coming of Age: Number of Black Elected Officials Rising," *Detroit Free Press*; March 28, 2002, http://www.freep.com/news/nw/pols28_20020328.htm (accessed July 23, 2005); Adjoa A. Aiyetoro, "The National Coalition of Blacks for Reparations in America (N'COBRA): Its Creation and Contribution to the Reparations Movement," in Raymond A. Winbush, ed., *Should America Pay? Slavery and the Raging Debate on Reparations* (New York: Amistad, 2003), 209–225.

38. Hertzberg, "Indian Rights Movement, 1887–1973," Cornell, "American Indians and Political Protest"; Paul C. Smith and Robert A. Warrior, *Like a Hurricane: The Indian Movement from Alcatraz to Wounded Knee* (New York: New Press, 1996).

39. Vigil, "Que Viva la Raza"; Cesar Chavez, "Speech in Coachella, 1973," in Richard J. Jensen and John C. Hammerback, eds., *The Words of Cesar Chavez*, 78–79; "Cesar Chavez Chronology," United Farm Workers, http://www.ufw.org (accessed June 29, 2005); Cesar Chavez, "Speech at Pacific Lutheran University, March 1989," in Richard J. Jensen and John C. Hammerback, eds., *The Words of Cesar Chavez*, 140–150.

40. "Cesar Chavez Chronology," United Farm Workers.

Chapter 7

1. Michael Katz, *The Undeserving Poor: From the War on Poverty to the War on Welfare* (New York: Pantheon Books, 1989); Harold R. Kerbo, *Social Stratification and Inequality: Class Conflict in Historical, Comparative, and Global Perspective* (Boston: McGraw Hill, 2003); Ronald Reagan, "First Inaugural Address," *Ronald Reagan Presidential Foundation*, January 20, 1981, http://www.reagan.utexas.edu/archives/speeches/1981/12081a.htm (accessed August 2, 2005).

2. Charles Murray, *Losing Ground: American Social Policy, 1950–1980* (New York: Basic Books, 1984); Katz, *In the Shadow of the Poorhouse*.

3. Katz, *In the Shadow of the Poorhouse*; Physician Task Force on Hunger in America, *Hunger in America: The Growing Epidemic* (Middletown, CT: Wesleyan University Press, 1985); Doug A. Timmer, D. Stanley Eitzen, and Kathryn D. Talley, *Paths to Homelessness: Extreme Poverty and the Urban Housing Crisis* (Boulder, CO: Westview Press, 1994).

4. Masters, "History of Community Action Agencies."

5. Physician Task Force on Hunger in America, *Hunger in America*.

6. Katz, *The Undeserving Poor*; Kerbo, *Social Stratification and Inequality*; D. Stanley Eitzen and Maxine B. Zinn, *Social Problems* (New York: Allyn and Bacon, 2006).

7. D. Stanley Eitzen and Kelly E. Smith, *Experiencing Poverty*; U.S. Census Bureau, "Value of the Federal Minimum Wage, 1938–1997," http://www.dol.gov/dol/esa/public/minwage/chart2.htm (accessed January 16, 2001); AFL-CIO, "Working Families Deserve a Real Minimum Wage," http://www.aflcio.org/yourjobeconomy/minimumwage (accessed July 14, 2005). Thirteen states pay more than the federal minimum wage, and it ranges between $5.70 in Wisconsin and $7.35 in Washington.

8. Timmer, Eitzen, and Talley, *Paths to Homelessness*.

9. Steven Greenhouse, "Among Dissident Union Leaders, the Backgrounds May Vary but the Vision Is the Same," *New York Times,* July 22, 2005, A15; Steven Greenhouse, "Membership in Unions Drops Again," *New York Times,* January 28, 2005, A20.

10. Cesar Chavez, "Chávez Speech at Solidarity House, April 1, 1967," in Richard J. Jensen and John C. Hammerback, eds., *The Words of Cesar Chavez,* 30.

11. Brian McWilliams, "We Demand Fair Trade—Not Free Trade," *Labornet Newsline,* November 30, 1999, http://www.labornet.org/news/121599/06.html (accessed July 18, 2005).

12. Cornel West, "Readings and Conversation," *Frontpage Magazine* (June 25, 2003), http://www.frontpagemag.com/Articles/Printable.asp?ID=11419 (accessed July 14, 2005); Katz, *The Undeserving Poor.*

13. Pedraza, "Origins and Destinies," in Pedraza and Rumbaut, eds., *Origins and Destinies,* 1–20; Associated Press, "Illegals in U.S. Double," *CBS News,* January 23, 2003, http://www.cbsnews.com/stories/2002/01/23/national/main325300.shtml (accessed July 29, 2005); Rachel L. Swarns, "Bill to Broaden Immigration Law Gains in Senate," *New York Times,* March 28, 2006, A1.

14. Katz, *The Undeserving Poor.*

15. William J. Wilson, *The Truly Disadvantaged: The Inner City, the Underclass, and Public Policy* (Chicago, IL: University of Chicago Press, 1987); Salim Muwakkil, "The Best and Worst of Times," *In These Times* (August 5, 2004): 18–19.

16. Wilson, *The Truly Disadvantaged;* William J. Wilson, *When Work Disappears: The World of the New Urban Poor* (New York: Vintage, 1987).

17. Carmen DeNavas-Walt, Bernadette D. Proctor, and Robert J. Mills, "Income, Poverty, and Health Insurance Coverage in the United States: 2004" (Washington, DC: U.S. Census Bureau, 2004), http://www.census.gov/hhes/www/poverty/poverty.html (accessed November 26, 2005); Kenneth D. Kochanek, Sherry L. Murphy, Robert N. Anderson, and Chester Scott, "Deaths: Final Data for 2002," *National Vital Statistics Reports* 53, no. 5 (October 12, 2004): 1–116, http://www.cdc.gov/nchs/fastats/infmort.htm (accessed July 21, 2005).

18. Randall Robinson, *The Debt: What America Owes Blacks* (New York: Dutton, 2000).

19. Eitzen and Zinn, *Social Problems;* Rose M. Kreider and Tavia Simmons, *Marital Status: 2000* (Washington, DC: U.S. Census Bureau, October 2003); Martha L. Munson and Paul D. Sutton, *Birth, Marriages, Divorces, and Deaths: Provisional Data for 2003,* National Vital Statistics Reports; vol 52, no. 22 (Hyattsville: MD: National Center for Health Statistics, 2004).

20. Judith Stacey, *Brave New Families: Stories of Domestic Upheaval in Late Twentieth-Century America* (New York: Basic Books, 1990); Katherine S. Newman, *Falling from Grace: The Experience of Downward Mobility in the American Middle Class* (New York: Free Press, 1988); Timmer, Eitzen, and Talley, *Paths to Homelessness.*

21. DeNavas-Walt, Proctor, and Mills, "Income, Poverty, and Health Insurance Coverage in the United States: 2004."

22. Children's Defense Fund, *The State of America's Children, 2004* (Washington, DC: Children's Defense Fund, 2004); George W. Bush, "Rallying the Armies of Compassion," White House, http://www.whitehouse.gov/news/reports/faithbased.html (accessed July 26, 2005); Robert E. Rector and Melissa G. Pardue, "Understanding the President's Healthy Marriage Initiative," Heritage Foundation, March, 26, 2004, http://www.heritage.org/Research/Family/bg1741.cfm (accessed July 27, 2005).

23. Eitzen and Smith, *Experiencing Poverty.*

24. Carmen DeNavas-Walt, Bernadette D. Proctor, and Robert J. Mills, "Income, Poverty, and Health Insurance Coverage in the United States: 2003" (Washington, DC: U.S. Census Bureau, 2003), www.census.gov/prod/2004pubs/p60-226.pdf (accessed July 27, 2005).

25. George W. Bush, "State of the Union," http://www.whitehouse.gov/ stateoftheunion/2005/index.html#2 (accessed July 21, 2005); J. Larry Brown, Robert Kuttner, and Thomas M. Shapiro, *Building a Real Ownership Society* (New York: Century Foundation, 2005).

26. Michael Sherraden, *Assets and the Poor: A New American Welfare Policy* (Armonk, NY: M. E. Sharpe, 1991). Ray Boshara, ed., *Building Assets: A Report on the Asset-Development and IDA Field,* December 2001, http://www.cfed.org/think.m?id=169&clusterid=1 (accessed August 2, 2005).

27. White House, "President George W. Bush, Fact Sheet: America's Ownership Society: Expanding Opportunities," http://www.whitehouse.gov/news/releases/ 2004/08/20040809-9.html (accessed July 21, 2005); Brown, Kuttner, and Shapiro, *Building a Real Ownership Society.*

28. Kelly Moore, "Health Status of American Indian and Alaska Native Children," paper given at American Academy of Pediatrics Seventeenth Annual Indian Health Service Research Conference, April 29, 2004, www.aap.org/nach/MoorePlenary.pdf (accessed July 21, 2005); Tribal Court Clearinghouse, "Housing Resources," http://www. tribal-institute.org/lists/housing.htm (accessed July 21, 2005).

29. Charlie LeDuff, "Range War in Nevada Pits U.S. Against Two Shoshone Sisters," *New York Times,* October 31, 2002, A16; Carrie Dann, quoted in International Indian Treaty Council, "Federal Government Seizes Shoshone Livestock, Violating Treaty of Peace and Friendship," May 25, 2002, http://www.treatycouncil.org/new_page_57111. htm (accessed August 2, 2005).

30. Robert Greenstein and Isaac Shapiro, "The New, Definitive CBO Data on Income and Tax Trends," Center on Budget and Policy Priorities, http://www.cbpp.org/9-23-03tax.htm (accessed December 9, 2005). These figures are adjusted for inflation and are expressed in 2000 dollars.

31. Larry Brown, e-mail message to the author, February 2, 2005. In a telephone conversation with the author on July 15, 2005, Larry Brown described the situation surrounding the release of the Physician Task Force report.

32. Mark Nord, Margaret Andrews, and Steven Carlson, *Household Food Security in the United States, 2003* (Washington, DC: Economic Research Service, U.S. Department of Agriculture, 2004).

33. Economic Research Service, "Food Security in the United States: History of the Food Security Measurement Project," http://www.ers.usda.gov/Briefing/FoodSecurity/ history (accessed July 26, 2005).

34. Martin Kasindork, "Nation Taking a New Look at Homelessness, Solutions," *USA Today,* October 11, 2005, http://www.usatoday.com/news/nation/2005-10-11-homeless-cover_x.htm (accessed October 12, 2005); National Housing Trust Fund, "The Campaign's Policy Proposal," http://www.nhtf.org/about/proposal.asp (accessed July 27, 2005).

35. David Reynolds and Jen Kern, "An Activist's Guide to Building the Movement for Economic Justice" (Detroit, MI: Wayne State University Labor Studies

Center, 2003), www.laborstudies.wayne.edu/Resources/guide2002.pdf (accessed May 1, 2005).

36. Associated Press, "Kucinich Gets Extra Boost in Final Caucus Numbers," March 8, 2004, http://www.kpua.net/news.php?id=1538 (accessed July 28, 2005); Muslims for Kucinich, "Kucinich Increases National Delegate Count by More Than 62 Percent This Week," May 22, 2004, http://www.muhajabah.com/muslims4kucinich/archives/2004/05/kucinich_increa.php (accessed July 28, 2005).

37. Wilson, *When Work Disappears*; Micere Keels, Greg J. Duncan, Stefanie Deluca, Ruby Mendenhall, and James Rosenbaum, "Fifteen Years Later: Can Residential Mobility Programs Provide a Long-Term Escape from Neighborhood Segregation, Crime, and Poverty?" *Demography* 42 (2005): 51–73; John Goering, Judith D. Feins, and Todd M. Richardson, "What Have We Learned About Housing Mobility and Poverty Deconcentration?" in John Goering and Judith D. Fein, eds., *Choosing a Better Life? Evaluating the "Moving to Opportunity" Social Experiment* (Washington, DC: Urban Institute Press, 2003).

38. U.S. Department of Labor, "Employment Situation Summary," June 2005, http://www.bls.gov/news.release/empsit.nr0.htm (accessed July 28, 2005); Randall Mikkelsen, "Bush Vows More Jobs," *Forbes,* http://www.forbes.com/home_asia/newswire/2003/07/28/rtr1040038.html (accessed July 28, 2005); Center for Social Development, "Why Asset Building, Children's Accounts and a Universal Model?" http://gwbweb.wustl.edu/csd/asset/seed_about.htm (accessed July 29, 2005).

39. Karen Edwards and Lisa M. Mason, "State Policy Trends for Individual Development Accounts in the United States, 1993–2003," *Social Development Issues* 25, no. 1 (2003): 118–129.

40. Internal Revenue Service, "Earned Income Tax Credit (EITC) Can Lower Federal Tax," http://www.irs.gov/individuals/article/0,,id=96406,00.html (accessed July 29, 2005); Jonathan B. Foreman, "Earned Income Tax Credit," in Joseph J. Cordes, Robert D. Ebel, and Jane G. Gravelle, eds., *The Encyclopedia of Taxation and Tax Policy* (Washington, DC: Urban Institute Press, 1999), 83–85.

41. Aiyetoro, "The National Coalition of Blacks for Reparations in America (N'COBRA)" in Winbush, ed., *Should America Pay?*, 209–225; Jon M. Van Dyke, "Reparations for the Descendents of American Slaves Under International Law," in Winbush, ed., *Should America Pay?*, 57–78.

42. Carrie Dann, "George W. Bush Signs Shoshone Land Claim Bill," *News from Indian Country,* July 7, 2004, http://www.indiancountrynews.com/fullstory.cfm?ID=63 (accessed July 28, 2005); Jerry Reynolds, "Bush Signs Western Shoshone Legislation; Tribal Leaders View Bills as Massive Fraud," *News from Indian Country,* July 9, 2004, http://msnbc.msn.com/id/5404691 (accessed July 28, 2005).

43. U.S. Department of Health and Human Services, "The 2005 HHS Poverty Guidelines," http://aspe.hhs.gov/poverty/05poverty.shtml (accessed July 29, 2005); Eitzen and Smit, *Experiencing Poverty;* Lawrence Mishel, Jared Bernstein, and Sylvia Allegretto, *State of Working America 2004–2005* (Ithaca, NY: Cornell University Press, 2005).

44. DeNavas-Walt, Proctor, and Mills, "Income, Poverty, and Health Insurance Coverage in the United States: 2004"; Terrance J. Reeves and Claudette E. Bennett, *We the People: Asians in the United States* (Washington, DC: U.S. Census Bureau, 2004), www.census.gov/prod/2004pubs/censr-17.pdf (accessed July 27, 2005); Roberto R. Ramirez,

We the People: Hispanics in the United States (Washington, DC: U.S. Census Bureau, 2004), www.census.gov/prod/2004pubs/censr-18.pdf (accessed July 27, 2005).

45. DeNavas-Walt, Proctor, and Mills, "Income, Poverty, and Health Insurance Coverage in the United States: 2004"; Eitzen and Smith, *Experiencing Poverty.*

46. DeNavas-Walt, Proctor, and Mills, "Income, Poverty, and Health Insurance Coverage in the United States: 2004."

47. U.S. Department of Helath and Human Services: Administration for Children and Families, "AFDC Total Caseload" http://www.acf.hhs.gov/programs/ofa/caseload/afdc/1994/fycytotal94.htm (accessed May 12, 2006); U.S. Department of Health and Human Services: Administration for Children and Families, "TANF; Total Number of Recipients," http://www.acf.dhhs.gov/programs/ofa/caseload/2005/recipient05tanf.htm (accessed May 12, 2006); U.S. Department of Health and Human Services: Administration for Children and Families, "TANF: Total Number of Families," http://www.acf.hhs.gov/programs/ofa/caseload/2005/family05tanf.htm (accessed May 12, 2006).

48. Edmund L. Andrews, "Report Finds Tax Cuts Heavily Favor the Wealthy," *New York Times,* August 13, 2004, http://www.nytimes.com/2004/08/13/politics/campaign/13tax.html?ex=1250136000&en=6f84660636ae70cd&ei=5090&partner=rssuserland (accessed December 9, 2005).

Credits

Chapter 1

Illustration: Courtesy of the City of Montreal, Records Management and Archives (Phileas Gagnon collection). Artist unknown.

Michel de Montaigne, "On Cannibals," in George B. Ives, trans., *The Essays of Montaigne*, vol. 1 (Cambridge, MA: Harvard University Press, 1925), 270–271, 273–278, 285–286.

Louis Armand de Lom d'Arce Lahontan, "Curious Dialogues," in Reuben Thwaites, ed., *Lahontan's Voyages to North America*, vol. 2 (Chicago, IL: A. C. McClurg, 1905), 551–556, 558–561, 568–572, 578–579, 582–587.

J. Hector St. Crèvecoeur, "Distresses of a Frontier Man," in *Letters from an American Farmer* (New York: Albert and Charles Boni, 1925), 300–301, 304–308, 312–313.

Thomas Paine, "Agrarian Justice," in Harry Clarke, ed., *The Pioneers of Land Reform: Thomas Spence, William Ogilvie, and Thomas Paine, with an Introduction by M. Beer* (London: G. Bell and Sons, 1920), 179–188, 194–197, 200–203.

The General Council of Indians at Miami Rapids, "Message from the Western Indians to the Commissioners of the United States," in Ernest A. Cruikshank, ed., *The Correspondence of Lt. Governor John Graves Simcoe, with Allied Documents Relating to this Administration of the Government of Upper Canada*, vol. 2 (Toronto: Ontario Historical Society, 1924), 19–20.

Chapter 2

Illustration: Courtesy of the Huntington Library.

Boston Society for the Moral and Religious Instruction of the Poor, *Third Annual Report* (Boston: U. Crocker, 1819), 22–23.

Josiah Quincy, *Report of the Committee on the Pauper Laws of This Commonwealth* (Boston: Massachusetts General Court Committee on Pauper Laws, 1821), 2–10.

Wilson Pierson and George R. McFarland, "Address of the Association of Working People of New-Castle County," *Free Enquirer,* October 7, 1829, 393.

Frances Wright, "Lecture on the Existing Evils and Their Remedy," *Free Enquirer,* December 12, 1829, 49–53.

Thomas Skidmore, *The Rights of Man to Property! Being a Proposition to Make It Equal Among the Adults of the Present Generation: And to Provide for Its Equal Transmission to Every Individual of Each Succeeding Generation, on Arriving at the Age of Maturity* (New York: A. Ming, Jr., 1829), 137–138, 284–285, 355–358, 385–388.

Tecumseh, "Sleep Not Longer, O Choctaws and Chickasaws," in H. B. Cushman, *History of the Choctaw, Chickasaw, and Natchez Indians* (Greenville, TX: Headlight, 1899), 310–314.

Chapter 3

Photo: Courtesy of Cook Collection, Valentine Richmond History Center.

W. E. B. Du Bois, "The Freedmen's Bureau," *Atlantic Monthly* 87 (1901): 354–365.

Senate Select Committee to Examine the Conditions of the Sioux and Crow Indians, *Conditions of Indian Tribes in Montana and Idaho,* 48th Congress, 1st session, 1884, Report no. 283, 71–72, 79–81.

Terrence V. Powderly, *Thirty Years of Labor: 1859–1889* (Columbus, OH: Excelsior, 1890), 484–486, 488–492.

Susan B. Anthony, "Woman Wants Bread, Not the Ballot," in Ida Harper, ed., *Life and Work of Susan B. Anthony: Including Public Addresses, Her Own Letters, and Many from Her Contemporaries During Fifty Years,* vol. 2 (Indianapolis: Bowen-Merrill, 1898), 996, 999–1002.

Lucy E. Parsons, *Souvenir Edition of the Famous Speeches of Our Martyrs, Delivered in Court When Asked If They Had Anything to Say Why Sentence of Death Should Not Be Passed upon Them, October 7, 8, and 9, 1886* (Chicago, IL: author, 1912); 66–72, 101–102, 106, 115.

S. Humphreys Gurteen, *A Handbook of Charity Organization* (Buffalo, NY: author, 1882), 118–126.

Chapter 4

Photo: Courtesy of http://www.picturehistory.com.

Jane Addams, *Twenty Years at Hull-House: With Autobiographical Notes* (New York: Macmillan, 1911), 281–292, 295–303, 306–309.

Julia C. Lathrop, "Child Welfare Standards: A Test of Democracy," in *Proceedings of the National Conference of Social Work at the Forty-Sixth Annual Session Held in Atlantic City, New Jersey, June 1–8, 1919* (Chicago, IL: University of Chicago Press, 1920), 5–9.

Booker T. Washington, "Industrial Education for the Negro," in *The Negro Problem: A Series of Articles by Representatives of American Negroes of Today* (New York: James Pott, 1903): 9–21, 23–25, 28–29.

Henry Vincent, *The Story of the Commonweal: Complete and Graphic Narrative of the Origin and Growth of the Movement* (Chicago: W. K. Conkey, 1894), 49–53.

Arthur C. Parker. "The Social Elements of the Indian Problem," *American Journal of Sociology* 22 (September 1916): 254–257.

Eugene V. Debs, "The Socialist Party's Appeal," in *The Independent* (New York: S. W. Benedict, 1908), 875–880.

Chapter 5

Photo: Courtesy of http://www.photolib.noaa.gov.

Herbert Hoover, "The Importance of the Preservation of Self-Help and of the Responsibilities of Individual Generosity as Opposed to Deteriorating Effects of Government Appropriations," in William S. Myers, ed., *The State Papers and Other Public Writings of Herbert Hoover*, vol. 1 (New York: Doubleday, Doran, 1934), 496–497, 499.

Dorothy Day, "Houses of Hospitality," *Commonweal*, April 15, 1938, 683–684.

Harry L. Hopkins, *Spending to Save: The Complete Story of Relief*, 112–118, 120–123. Copyright 1936 by W. W. Norton & Company, Inc. used by permission of W. W. Norton & Company, Inc.

Huey Long, "Redistribution of Wealth," January 14, 1935, 74th Congress, *Congressional Record* 79, pt. 1: 410–412.

Upton Sinclair, *Immediate Epic: The Final Statement of the Plan* (Los Angeles: End Poverty League, 1934), 1–2, 5–11.

Frances Perkins, *The Roosevelt I Knew* (New York: Viking Press, 1946), 278–285, 287, 289–295, 297–301.

Ernest Lundeen, "Workers' Unemployment, Old-Age, and Social Insurance Bill—History and Status of H.R. 2827," April 3, 1935, 74th Congress, *Congressional Record* 79, pt. 5: 4970–4971.

Chapter 6

Photo: courtesy of the Associated Press, http://photoarchive.ap.org.

Martin Luther King, Jr., "Where Do We Go from Here." Reprinted by arrangement with the Estate of Martin Luther King Jr., c/o Writers House as agent for the proprietor, New York, NY. Copyright 1956 Martin Luther King Jr., copyright renewed 1984 Coretta Scott King.

Malcolm X, "The Ballot or the Bullet," in George Breitman, ed., *Malcolm X Speaks: Selected Speeches and Statements*, 31–36, 38–40. Copyright 1965, 1989 by Betty Shabazz and Pathfinder Press. Reprinted by permission.

Sargent Shriver, "A Retrospective View: The Founders," in Edward Zigler and Jeanette Valentine, eds., *Project Head Start: A Legacy of the War on Poverty* (New York: Free Press, 1979), 49–61, 65–67.

Johnnie Tillmon, "Welfare Is a Women's Issue," *Liberation News Service*, no. 415, February 26, 1972.

"Cesar Chavez Talks in New York," *Catholic Worker* 34, no. 5 (June 1968): 1, 6. Copyright 2006 the Cesar E. Chavez Foundation, www.chavezfoundation.org.

Indians of All Nations, "Alcatraz Proclamation to the Great White Father and His People, 1969," Center for World Indigenous Studies, http://www.cwis.org.

Chapter 7

Photo: Courtesy of Rick Reinhard.

Physician Task Force on Hunger in America, *Hunger in America: The Growing Epidemic*, 175–180. Copyright 1985 by Physician Task Force on Hunger in America and reprinted by permission of Wesleyan University Press.

Doug A. Timmer, D. Stanley Eitzen, and Kathryn D. Talley, *Paths to Homelessness: Extreme Poverty and the Urban Housing Crisis*, 181–184, 187–188. Copyright 1994 by Westview Pres, Inc. Reprinted by permission of Westview Press, a member of Perseus Books, LLC.

Robert Pollin, "Living Wage, Live Action," *Nation* (November 23, 1998): 15, 17–20. Reprinted with permission from *The Nation*. For subscription information, call 1-800-333-8536. Portions of each week's *Nation* magazine can be accessed at http://www.thenation.com.

Tony Mazzocchi, Bruce J. Klipple, Kay McVay, Ralph Nader, and Thomas Geoghegan, "Labor Leaders and Allies Call for Repeal of Taft-Hartley Act," *Labor Standard* 4, no. 2 (Fall 2002): 25–26.

Brian McWilliams, "We Demand Fair Trade—Not Free Trade," *Labornet Newsline*, November 30, 1999, http://www.labornet.org/news/121599/06.html (accessed July 18, 2005).

William J. Wilson, *The Truly Disadvantaged: The Inner City, the Underclass, and Public Policy*, 150–155. Copyright 1987 by the University of Chicago Press.

Randall Robinson, "America's Debt to Blacks," *Nation* (March 13, 2000): 5–6. Reprinted with permission from *The Nation*. For subscription information, call 1-800-333-8536. Portions of each week's *Nation* magazine can be accessed at http://www.thenation.com.

George W. Bush, "President Bush Implements Key Elements of His Faith-Based Initiative," White House, December 12, 2002, http://www.whitehouse.gov/news/releases/2002/12/print/20021212-3.html (accessed July 26, 2005).

Michael Sherraden, "Building Assets to Fight Poverty," *Shelterforce* 110 (March–April 2000), http://www.nhi.org/online/issues/110/sherraden.html (accessed July 20, 2005). Reprinted by permission of *Shelterforce*. Copyright 2000 National Housing Institute.

Carrie Dann, "Petra Speech," Western Shoshone Defense Project, November 7, 2003, http://www.wsdp.org/whatsnew.htm#110703-petra (accessed July 28, 2005).

Index

About the Author

Scott Myers-Lipton, an Associate Professor of Sociology at San Jose State University, is the author of numerous scholarly articles on education, civic engagement, and racism. To expore solutions to poverty, Myers-Lipton has taken students over the past fifteen years to live at homeless shelters, the Navajo and Lakota nations, and to Kingston, Jamaica.